The Development of Sex Differences

STANFORD STUDIES IN PSYCHOLOGY, V

Editors

Robert R. Sears   Leon Festinger   Douglas H. Lawrence

The Development of
Sex Differences

EDITED BY ELEANOR E. MACCOBY

with contributions by

Roy G. D'Andrade
Sanford M. Dornbusch
David A. Hamburg
Lawrence Kohlberg

Donald T. Lunde
Eleanor E. Maccoby
Walter Mischel
Roberta M. Oetzel

Stanford University Press
Stanford, California

Stanford University Press
Stanford, California
© *1966 by the Board of Trustees of the*
Leland Stanford Junior University
Printed in the United States of America
ISBN 0–8047–0308–6
Original edition 1966
Last figure below indicates year of this printing:
79   78   77   76   75   74   73   72   71

Preface

This volume grew out of the discussions of a work group that met at Stanford University during 1962, 1963, and 1964 to discuss sex differences. The group was sponsored (and its moderate expenses underwritten) by the Committee on Socialization and Social Structure of the Social Science Research Council; the Committee's work was supported by NIH Grant M4160.

Roberta Oetzel was research assistant to the work group during a large portion of its life, and provided invaluable aid in locating reference materials. Irven DeVore and A. K. Romney met regularly with the group and contributed extensively to the discussions. A number of other persons met with the group occasionally, including Erik H. Erikson, Nevitt Sanford, Evelyn Hooker, Paul Mussen, Herbert Leiderman, Lucy Rau, Robert Greenburg, and Albert K. Cohen. Their contribution to the thinking that underlies the following chapters is gratefully acknowledged.

E.E.M.

Contents

DAVID A. HAMBURG AND DONALD T. LUNDE
Sex Hormones in the Development of Sex Differences in Human Behavior
page 1

ELEANOR E. MACCOBY
Sex Differences in Intellectual Functioning
page 25

WALTER MISCHEL
A Social-Learning View of Sex Differences in Behavior
page 56

LAWRENCE KOHLBERG
A Cognitive-Developmental Analysis of Children's Sex-Role Concepts and Attitudes
page 82

ROY G. D'ANDRADE
Sex Differences and Cultural Institutions
page 173

SANFORD M. DORNBUSCH
Afterword
page 204

ROBERTA M. OETZEL
Annotated Bibliography
page 223

Classified Summary of Research in Sex Differences
page 323

The Development of Sex Differences

Sex Hormones in the Development of Sex Differences in Human Behavior

DAVID A. HAMBURG
Stanford University

DONALD T. LUNDE
Stanford University

For a long time now, biologically oriented workers have assumed that sex hormones have something to do with the development of sex differences in the behavior of human beings. Most psychosocially oriented workers, however, have paid little if any attention to such a possibility. Even though there is at present little firm evidence that sex hormones do play an important role in the development of human behavioral sex differences, there are intriguing possibilities to be explored in this area. In this chapter we will summarize several recent lines of research which are, we believe, intrinsically interesting to the student of mammalian sex differences, and which suggest experimental approaches for similar studies of man. Some of these approaches are rather novel and might easily have been overlooked except for the fact that they have led to some rather surprising and potentially important findings in respect to infrahuman mammalian species. Recent investigations in a variety of disciplines suggest that complex interactions among genetic, hormonal, and environmental factors determine the development of sex differences in human behavior. New scientific techniques now being developed will permit us to analyze these interactions in future years.

This work was supported by N.I.H. Grant MH10976. We are very much indebted to Dr. Beatrix Hamburg for her helpful suggestions in the preparation of this paper.

THE PHENOMENON OF PUBERTY: SEX
HORMONES AND THE BRAIN

The fact that sex hormones enter the brain and measurably affect its activity is now quite well established. Some of the work in this area, with special reference to progesterone, has been described in a recent paper (Hamburg 1965). Another active line of inquiry centers on the factors that determine the timing of puberty. We wish to summarize these data, and in turn relate them to data on the psychological consequences of early and late maturation, particularly in respect to sex differences.

There is now a large body of data which indicates that the onset of puberty involves an interaction between the sex hormones and certain cells of the brain. We shall describe later how hypersecretion of the ovaries, testes, and, in certain cases, the adrenals can precipitate precocious puberty. However, in the normal course of events, the secretion of these glands in childhood is quite minimal, even though the glands themselves are capable of producing larger amounts of hormone (Donovan 1963).

The secretion of sex hormones is stimulated by gonadotrophins that originate in the anterior lobe of the pituitary gland; release of the gonadotrophins, in turn, is controlled by circulating sex hormones in the manner of a feedback system (Tepperman 1962). (Gonadotrophins are hormones that promote development and secretion in the ovaries and testes, and regulate the female menstrual cycle.) It is becoming increasingly clear that the pituitary gland is subject to the higher control of the brain via the hypothalamus. And recent evidence indicates that prior to puberty the hypothalamic centers are very sensitive to minute amounts of circulating sex hormones (Everett 1964). Donovan (1963) suggests that the sensitivity of certain CNS cells to gonadal steroids diminishes throughout childhood, ultimately permitting the release of gonadotrophin in amounts sufficient to induce puberty. In his view, the interval between birth and puberty for any species represents the time required for the nervous system–hypothalamic mechanism to mature and escape from the restraining influences of minute quantities of gonadal hormone.

Electrolytic destruction of the inhibitory gonadal feedback area of the hypothalamus will precipitate precocious puberty in rats (Donovan and van der Werff ten Bosch 1959). And certain environmental variables, such as handling, illumination, exposure to cold, and mechanical stimulation of the cervix, will influence the timing of puberty in rats and guinea pigs (Everett 1964). The possibility that environmental influences may have similar effects on human development is an intriguing one that has not yet been adequately explored. While it is clear that nutrition is an important factor in the growth rate of human beings, there is some evidence that adverse psychological conditions may impede growth even when nutrition is adequate (Tanner 1962).

Now that it has become apparent that the onset of puberty is triggered by the brain rather than by an autonomous system of endocrine glands, the role of environmental factors in promoting or delaying this phenomenon must certainly be considered. It is of interest that puberty, as defined by menarche or adolescent growth spurt, has been occurring at increasingly earlier ages over the past 100 years in many different countries; for example, the average age of menarche has decreased from 16–17 years in 1860 to 12–13 years in 1960 (Tanner 1962). While this finding is usually ascribed to better nutrition, it is not really known whether nutrition is the only factor, or even the major factor, involved in this striking shift.

The notion that time of onset of puberty might have specific psychological consequences has received attention in studies of late maturers vs. early maturers. Early-maturing boys appear to enjoy greater peer-group prestige than late-maturing boys. The same is not true for girls. Early-maturing girls were rated by observers as more submissive or socially indifferent than late-maturing girls; they also scored lower than late-maturing girls on peer-group ratings of popularity and prestige. This type of finding has been reported in several studies (for example, Eichorn 1963), and does tend to support the concept that the sexes respond in different ways to early onset of puberty.

In the most recent paper available at the time of this writing, Jones (1964) summarizes her years of research in this field as follows:

In general it has been shown that boys who are accelerated in physical development in adolescence seem to be advantaged in the peer culture. In adulthood, although physical differences no longer distinguish the extreme maturity groups, some psychological differences still exist. The early developers cling to their early success pattern, continue to be well socialized and to make a good impression. Late developers, carrying over a childhood pattern, are adventurous, rebellious, and assertive. They are also more flexible, suggesting some possibly salutary effects of what was interpreted as an adolescent social disadvantage.

A recent follow-up on late-maturing boys indicates that many of them responded to the challenge of adolescent difficulties by developing coping abilities that have continued to serve them well in adult life (Jones 1964). While this finding has little to do with the subject at hand, it is itself an interesting observation, and highlights the complexity of the long-term developmental process. Unfortunately, when systematic comparisons are made between direct observational ratings on the one hand, and psychological tests or interview measures on the other, important methodological problems emerge (Mussen and Jones 1963, Jones and Mussen 1963, Jones 1964). Nevertheless, there is good reason to suspect that in some environments major variations in the timing of puberty will turn out to have differential consequences for males and females. It is unfortunate that the pioneering studies in this field were made before it was possible to obtain accurate hormone measurements.

EXCRETION OF SEX HORMONES IN NORMAL CHILDREN

Only in recent years have biochemical methods for direct determination of hormones in the blood or urine been available. Consequently most of the data in the literature were obtained by bioassay. This method involves injecting urine or blood into a laboratory animal and measuring subsequent changes in some tissue known to respond to a given hormone. For example: the uterus, ovaries, and vagina of the mouse change in response to female hormones; the prostate of the mouse and the comb of the capon change in response to male hormones. Such methods measure the activity rather than the amount of hormones, and present formidable problems in standardization.

A consensus of the relevant findings in hormone measurement will be presented here. But one should bear in mind that these are generalizations, and that subtle variations probably still remain to be detected by more direct and accurate means. Tanner (1962) has reviewed some of the studies regarding gonadotrophin excretion in children. As might be expected, these hormones are not detectable in young children, but appear in detectable amounts a few years prior to puberty, increase rather rapidly during adolescence, and then reach a plateau in adulthood (fluctuating with the menstrual cycle in females).

One standard (nonbioassay) hormonal assay measures 17-ketosteroids in the urine (measured in milligrams per 24 hours and reflecting the concentration of male hormones). Although considered to reflect excretion of androgenic hormones, the 17-ketosteroids represent a mixture of hormone metabolites, a variable fraction of which is derived from adrenal and testicular androgens (Lipsett and Korenman 1964). The values reported by Talbot et al. (1943) for 17-ketosteroid excretion in children are typical of those found by many investigators. Values of .15 were found at age three, rising only to 1.4 at age nine. However, the values begin to increase fairly rapidly shortly thereafter, reaching a level of 8.1 mg. per 24 hours by age 17. The rise in 17-ketosteroids is found to occur early in early-maturing boys and late in late-maturing boys (Tanner 1962). Although there is no significant difference in the amount of 17-ketosteroids excreted by boys and girls from early childhood up to adolescence, adult men (ages 20–40) do secrete more 17-ketosteroids than adult women.

Dorfman and Shipley (1956) have reviewed 276 papers dealing primarily with the measurement of 17-ketosteroids in different populations and the results obtained when measurements were correlated with a wide variety of physical and psychological data. However, the fact that 17-ketosteroid determinations do not reflect any specific hormone or any specific hormonal activity makes these studies difficult to appraise.

Measurement of 17-ketosteroids (also called 17-oxosteroids) in blood has yielded results similar to those obtained by measurement in urine. In children three to five years of age, no 17-ketosteroids are found in the blood, but after the age of eight there is a gradual increase, with maximum levels reached between the ages of 20 and 40. Interestingly enough, there is a high level of 17-ketosteroids in the blood of the newborn, even higher than that found in the mother; but this is only a transient finding, and 17-ketosteroids are not detectable after the first week of life (Bongiovanni and Smith 1961). Unfortunately we do not know whether the high level of 17-ketosteroids in the neonate is found only in male infants, although it is a reasonable assumption that this is the case. It has been suggested in the past that these hormones may be secreted by the fetal adrenal gland or the placenta, but there is some recent evidence that the hormone-secreting cells in the fetal testis are a source of testosterone, and ultimately of 17-KS, in the urine (Harris 1964). Moreover, recent evidence makes it increasingly likely that these fetal androgens have some effect on the fetus's developing central nervous system. This possibility will be considered in some detail in a later section.

Bioassay determinations of androgenic hormones in urine indicate that negligible amounts of these substances are present until about eight–ten years of age, at which time there is a rather sharp increase for both sexes, with the absolute values for boys reaching levels about twice as great as those found for girls (Tanner 1962). There are at present no data on estrogen or progesterone levels in the blood of children. However, estrogenic activity has been measured in the urine of children by bioassay. Very low levels are found in both girls and boys until about eight or nine years of age. (Small amounts of estrogen are produced in the male by the testes and the adrenal glands.) At this time the excretion rate for girls increases, becoming particularly accelerated at about age 11. But the excretion of estrogens does not become cyclic until about 18 months prior to menarche, the time the female cyclic pattern normally establishes itself. Secondary sex characteristics begin to appear, and the growth spurt starts at about the time the pattern becomes cyclic (Nathanson, Towne, and Aub 1941). There is a very slight increase in estrogen excretion in boys during puberty, but it is not at all comparable to the increase in 17-ketosteroids that occurs in boys and girls at this time. The excretion of estrogens is not cyclic in males, nor is the excretion of 17-ketosteroids cyclic in females.

It is clear that direct determinations of hormones in the blood would be more desirable than measurement of urinary hormonal activity, which reflects the final disposition of hormonal metabolites after processing by the liver and clearance by the kidney. Blood-level measurements bring one a significant step closer to the activities of the endocrine glands and the actual substances that affect the various target organs. Very recently, methods have become available for such determinations. Thin-layer chromatography and gas-liquid chromatography show great promise in this area. Application of the latter method to measurement of testosterone in human blood is described in a recent paper by Brownie et al. (1964). In our own laboratory we are using a similar method to measure progesterone levels in blood. Another progesterone assay, using paper chromatography and a fluorescence reaction, has recently been described (Heap 1964).

The method of immunoassay is proving very useful for measuring gonadotrophins and other proteinaceous hormones with antigenic properties (Wolstenholme and Cameron 1962). At present, the best possibilities for specific and sensitive measurement of the gonadotrophins appear to lie in the further development of immunochemical methods. The increasing availability of new techniques for measuring sex hormones must surely stimulate interest in behavior-endocrine studies. For example: what correlations can be established between changes in the levels of various sex hormones and intensity of motivation for sexual experience during adolescence? Is (as clinical evidence suggests) sex motivation in females linked to androgens? Is there a sex-differential in some aspects of aggressive behavior around puberty, and can it be correlated with changes in androgen? Questions of this sort can now be investigated much more effectively than they have been in the past.

ENDOCRINE ABNORMALITIES IN CHILDREN

It is possible that a study of conditions that constitute exaggerations of the normal state of affairs might help us understand the more subtle influences of sex hormones on behavior in children. Three such conditions will be discussed here: (1) surgical removal of the sex glands; (2) congenital abnormalities in the function of certain endocrine glands; and (3) administration of sex-hormones to pregnant women and its subsequent effects on the offspring.

Male castration was practiced from ancient times until the late nineteenth century. Havelock Ellis (1928) noted that the earlier the operation is performed, the less marked are sexual desires in later life. Re moval of the ovaries, however, had no effect on female sex motivation, a finding which is in accord with current evidence that sex motivation in the female is related to androgenic hormones secreted by the adrenal glands, rather than to the female hormones secreted by the ovaries. The basis for this view lies in observations that adrenalectomy in women often produces a decrease in desire for sexual experience, whereas treatment with androgenic hormones may produce a striking increase in such desire, even in seriously ill and debilitated women (Filler and Drezner 1944, Foss 1951, Waxenberg et al. 1959). Discussing the effects of androgen administration on both sexes, Money (1961) points out several changes in behavior that are well supported by clinical observations: (1) increased sexual activity of hypogonadal men on androgen therapy; (2) decrease in sexual activity reported by such men during periods when treatment is discontinued; and (3) increased sexual desire in women on androgen therapy.

As a result of congenital abnormalities or tumors, a child's ovaries, testes, or adrenal glands may secrete either excessive or deficient amounts of sex hormones. A large collection of such case histories is presented in a volume by H. H. Young (1937). Unfortunately, the information on the behavior of these patients is rather anecdotal in nature; we can say only that their behavior may be quite aberrant, particularly in the realm of sexual behavior. Similarly, a high incidence of psychopathology, particularly with respect to psychosexual differentiation, is reported by Money (1963) in his review of 21 cases of Klinefelter's syndrome, a chromosomal anomaly that involves the presence of three (XXY) rather than two sex chromosomes. Although these subjects are male in appearance, they are characterized by infertility, poor virilization at puberty, and weak sex motivation. Money (1965a) suggests: "It is possible that the testicular deficit in these individuals is related to a discrepancy of some sort in neurosexual differentiation." (p. 70.)

Precocious sexual development may be associated with a primary disease of the hypothalamic region of the brain or of the sex glands or adrenals. Probably, in some of these cases, the hypothalamic sex centers of the brain matured early, causing premature secretion of the sex hormones and maturation of the reproductive organs. Again, the behavioral data are scanty, but it is reported that psychosexual development usually proceeds in accordance with chronological age in these cases (Seckel 1946). Fertilization by boys with precocious sexual development is said to be rare, but pregnancy among girls with this condition is fairly common. Eighty-four out of 310 females recorded as sexually precocious became pregnant before the age of 15, including 16 who were between 6 and 11 years of age at delivery (Reuben and Manning 1922, 1923). Whether this precocious behavior can be attributed to sexual aggressiveness or sexual naïveté is not noted in most of the cases, however.

Congenital adrenal hyperplasia (formerly called adrenogenital syndrome) results from a defect in the metabolism of the fetal adrenal glands. The glands so affected produce an excess of androgenic hormones, which virilizes the female child. Virilization may occur in utero, with the result that the newborn's clitoris is enlarged and resembles a penis, and the labial folds may be fused and resemble a scrotum. Such patients have all the normal internal female reproductive organs. However, on occasion these pseudohermaphrodites have been mistakenly reared as boys.

In the past pseudohermaphroditism was often thought to be associated with mental retardation, psychosis, and homosexuality. Although this does not appear to be the case, the children so affected do tend to show retarded psychosexual and emotional development. They are frequently shy and dependent, with feelings of inferiority about their physical appearance. Their intellectual ability usually corresponds to their age. If reared as girls, they are not likely to be homosexuals (Bleuler and Stoll 1962).

On the other hand, Money (1965) reports that "eroticism" in some of these patients tends to be more characteristic of the male in some respects: "Erotic arousal with a strong genitopelvic component [results] from the stimulation of visual and narrative perceptual material [and is] accompanied by erection of the clitoris, hypertrophied in this syndrome, and masturbation or the willingness for sexual intercourse with even a transitory partner. The imagery of the erotic thoughts and desires is all suitably feminine . . . ; the unfeminine aspect of the experience applies only to the *threshold* and the *frequency* of arousal, and to the amount of sexual *initative* that it might engender. The reaction has occurred in the treated as well as the untreated state of the syndrome, but is attenuated by treatment which consists of feminizing clitoral surgery and hormonal correction with cortisone. There is a possibility, therefore, of a residual androgenic effect, even after the high fetal and childhood levels are regulated to normal. The informative cases will be those whose excessive adrenal androgens were controlled from birth onward, but these patients are still too young to be valid informants." (p. 69–70, italics ours.)

Congenital adrenal hyperplasia may also occur in boys, producing precocious sexual development, but only a few such cases have been studied. Bleuler and Stoll (1962) report: "In spite of their pseudopubertas precox, intellectual development corresponds to their age, and emotional and psychosexual development is rather retarded. The physical strength and the premature physical masculinity form a strange contrast to the shy and rather childish mental attitude." (p. 651–52.) Again, the child's reaction to a gross physical abnormality probably plays an important part in his general attitude.

In addition to the results of defective endocrine-gland function, there may be abnormal effects produced by hormone injections which are now widely used in medicine for a variety of disorders. Experiments with infrahuman mammals have shown that hormones administered during pregnancy or early in infancy can have striking permanent effects on later behavior. The interesting question is, of course, whether similar effects are likely to be found in man. In light of present evidence, the most interesting possibility is that excessive amounts of androgen may act on the developing reproductive tract and brain of the fetus to produce masculinizing effects: Such effects might occur either because of excessive androgen synthesized by the fetus (as occurs in congenital adrenal hyperplasia), or because of excessive androgen transmitted from the mother through the placenta (as occurs when pregnant women take androgenic compounds).

Synthetic hormones with androgenic properties are sometimes given to pregnant women for treatment of threatened abortion. One study of 21 cases of female pseudohermaphrodism (enlarged clitoris and varying degrees of fusion of the labial folds) in newborns revealed that in 18 of these cases, the mother had taken hormones during pregnancy (Wilkins et al. 1958). In 15 of these cases, the drug taken was 17-ethinyl-testosterone, which is a synthetic steroid chemically similar to the male hormones. It would be of great interest to study these subjects in later years, to see whether the masculinizing hormones received during early development have had any permanent effects on behavior. To date, very little work in this area has been done on humans. Since many pregnant women who take these hormones do not give birth to masculinized babies, it is possible that some defect in metabolism is present in cases where it does occur. The timing of administration may be important, e.g., there may be a critical period for central-nervous-system effects (Goy, Bridson, Young 1964).

It is also interesting to note that even though the fetus may be strikingly affected, the mother does not usually show any signs of virilization when taking these hormones. Nonpregnant women, however, may experience deepening of the voice, hirsutism, and clitoral enlargement while taking these drugs. In accord with these findings, a recent study of Diamond and Young (1963) showed that significant male-like sexual behavior could be induced with testosterone in nonpregnant female guinea pigs, but not in pregnant ones. This effect in the nonpregnant animals could be blocked by administration of progesterone, a hormone that is secreted by the placenta in large amounts during pregnancy, giving rise to the suggestion that the mother may have a certain "protection" from masculinizing hormones during pregnancy that the fetus does not enjoy.

Another interesting clinical situation is the testicular feminizing syndrome (Wilkins 1965). In this syndrome, a genetic male (46 chromosomes, XY) begins early embryonic differentiation as a male. Thus the internal genitalia are generally masculine. However, during the final stage of differentiation, there is evidently a failure of androgen secretion by the fetal testis, and so the external genitalia develop along feminine lines. As adults, these persons have a female body structure as a result of the estrogen secreted by their feminizing testes. Money (1965b) reports that their psychosexual and gender role in childhood is feminine, and remains so in adult life; this is presumably because they are reared as females in keeping with the appearance of the external genitalia. He raises the question whether the failure of androgen secretion in late fetal life may somehow heighten the brain's capacity to comply with the demands of female sex assignment and rearing. In any event, this is another clinical situation in which the brain has abnormal sex-hormone exposure in utero, and in which behavioral observations are so far quite scarce. These children provide another scientific opportunity to search for possible behavioral consequences of early endocrine variation.

THE EFFECTS OF PROGESTERONE ON BRAIN AND BEHAVIOR

There is biochemical, neurophysiological, and behavioral evidence that one of the principal female sex hormones, progesterone, enters the brain and affects brain function (Hamburg 1965). When radioactive progesterone is injected into adult female rats (systemically), it may be detected in the brain during the first hour, and is selectively retained in the hypothalamus thereafter. Even a day later, a good deal of the injected progesterone (or some metabolic product of it) is selectively retained in the hypothalamus. Among the effects of progesterone on brain function are the following: (1) general anesthesia in the case of large doses (Merryman 1954); (2) sedation in the case of moderate doses (Hamburg 1965); (3) elevation of threshold for convulsive seizures (Woolley and Timiras 1962); (4) facilitation of various aspects of reproductive behavior (Young 1961).

In the human menstrual cycle, there is systematic fluctuation of progesterone levels over a functionally significant range (Zander 1961). There is suggestive evidence of concomitant fluctuation in some aspects of behavior (Benedek and Rubinstein 1942). In the course of human pregnancy, progesterone levels vary considerably more than they do during the menstrual cycle (Lloyd and Leathem 1964). It is plausible that some aspects of the behavior of pregnant women may be related to these exceptionally high progesterone levels. At the end of each menstrual cycle, and at the end of pregnancy, there is a sharp fall in progesterone levels (Zander 1961). It is now possible to investigate critically the possibility that this fall in progesterone level, accompanied by withdrawal of progesterone from the brain cells, might be related to the frequent behavioral disturbances of the premenstrual and postpartum periods. Because many women suffer mild, transient behavioral disturbances in the premenstrual and postpartum periods—but only some get into serious difficulty—the problem of differential susceptibility comes into focus. Susceptibility might well be influenced by such environmental factors as a woman's feelings about her own mother. Moreover, genetically determined differences in progesterone metabolism might also affect susceptibility. Such possibilities are currently under investigation in interdisciplinary behavior-endocrine-genetic research (Hamburg 1965).

MALE SEX HORMONES IN THE DEVELOPMENT OF BEHAVIOR IN INFRAHUMAN SPECIES

As a result of his experiments with guinea pigs and rats, Harris (1964) concludes that sex hormones have a double-action effect on the brain. During fetal or neonatal life hormones act in an inductive way on an undifferentiated brain (as they do on the undifferentiated genital tract) to organize certain circuits in male or female patterns. In the adult animal, the gonadal hormones act on the central nervous system in an excitatory or inhibitory way, thus affecting the neural regulation of gonadotrophic hormone secretion and the expression of overt patterns of sexual and sex-related behavior.

Harris and Levine (1962) have found that male rats who are castrated during the first 24 hours of life retain the basic female-type hypothalamic mechanism (common to both sexes during embryonic life) for regulating gonadotropic secretion in later life. If castration is delayed until the second 24 hours of life, only a few males retain the female mechanism; by the third day, all male rats have developed a male-type mechanism. The neural site of action of testosterone in this organizational process appears to be (at least partly) in the hypothalamus. In similar experiments with female rats, these investigators found that administration of testosterone to newborn female rats results in abolition of estrous behavior and in exaggerated male behavior patterns, particularly in the aggression sphere. Young, Goy, and Phoenix (1964), who have done similar pioneering work with guinea pigs, have more recently extended their work to a primate species, rhesus macaque. They have given testosterone to pregnant monkeys throughout the second quarter of gestation. Though it is difficult to maintain pregnancy under these conditions, they have succeeded in producing female pseudohermaphroditic offspring with genital alterations such as hypertrophy of the clitoris. Their work was based on the Wisconsin Primate Laboratories' finding that infant male monkeys are more aggressive than infant female monkeys. Accordingly, the masculinized females were, from the second month on, allowed unrestricted social interaction with two untreated females 20 minutes a day, five days a week, in a specially designed playroom. The results of observations of hundreds of such sessions have now been analyzed. Several social behavior patterns known to be sexually dimorphic and irrelevant to mating behavior appear to have been influenced in the masculine direction by prenatal administration of androgen. The social behavior of the untreated females did not differ importantly from that described for normal females, but the behavior of the treated females (androgen to mother in pregnancy) much more closely resembled Harlow's description of the behavior of male monkeys. The masculinized females threatened, initiated play, and engaged in rough-and-tumble play more frequently than the controls. Like normal males, these masculinized females also withdrew less often from the initiations, threats, and approaches of other subjects. They also showed a greater tendency toward mounting behavior than did the untreated females. How generalized is this masculinizing effect on behavior? So far, the behavior has held up under these conditions: (1) same-sex and mixed-sex infant play groups; (2) two environments—a small playroom and a large playroom (Goy 1965). How long does this male-like behavior last? Some animals have been studied well into the third year of life, and they continue to be quite high in social-threat behavior. The other aggressive characteristics appear to have diminished by the third year under the laboratory conditions in which they have been studied so far (Goy 1965).

If a similar relation between androgen and aggressive behavior exists in homo sapiens, how might it express itself? In view of the enormous dependence of the human species on learning processes, it seems quite unlikely that the early exposure of hypothalamic cells to androgen would establish fixed, complex patterns of aggressive behavior for a lifetime. It is much more likely that early exposure to androgen would affect humans in more subtle ways. Perhaps the influence of androgen during a critical period in brain development on the circuits destined later to mediate aggressive behavior would have CNS-differentiating effects that would facilitate ease of learning aggressive patterns and increase readiness to learn such patterns. For example, the hormone in a critical period might affect later sensitivity to certain stimulus patterns. Threshold of response to certain agonistic stimuli might be lowered, with the result that these stimuli might take on distinctly arousing properties. Or, certain patterns of action might become more rewarding as a result of the early hormone action on the central nervous system; e.g., the large-muscle movements so critical in agonistic encounters might be experienced as highly gratifying and therefore be frequently repeated. The possibilities for experimental analysis of this problem in higher primates are potentially quite important for understanding the development of aggressive behavior in man. Such an approach should take into consideration the interactions of genes, hormones, and learning processes.

Recent field studies of primate behavior (DeVore 1965) reveal several characteristics of ground-living old-world monkeys that are pertinent to the present discussion: (1) There is much evidence of rough-and-tumble play among males. Their frequent repetition of such play patterns amounts in fact to a kind of practice of aggressive behavior over several years, from infancy onward. In this way, the males develop the strength and skills necessary for the defense of the group. (2) There is marked sexual dimorphism in anatomy and behavior. The adult males defend the group and settle internal disputes; they are larger and stronger than the adult females. Taking the experimental and field observations together, it appears that the male's aggressive predisposition (presumably based on genetic factors mediated by hormonal effects on brain differentiation and muscle growth) is developed through social learning and ultimately put to adaptively significant use. These observations pertain rather generally to complex old-world monkeys and to great apes that spend much of their time on the ground, and may well have significance for the evolution of man.

These recent experiments demonstrating early hormonal effects on brain differentiation add an interesting element of complexity to the search for hormone-behavior correlations. The traditional approach centered on *contemporary* correlations, e.g., concomitant fluctuations in the level of a hormone and the performance of a particular kind of behavior. These recent studies call attention to the possibility of *developmental* correlations, in which the presence of a hormone in adequate amounts during an early critical period may have consequences throughout the life span, even when the hormone is no longer present (or is present in much smaller quantity).

FACTORS IN THE DEVELOPMENT OF GENDER ROLE

In the delivery rooms of many hospitals it is the custom to wrap the newborn baby in either a pink or a blue blanket, depending on the sex as determined by the appearance of the genitalia. From this moment on, the child's maleness or femaleness is constantly reinforced. It is difficult, then, to determine the extent to which the child's learning of his sex role may be influenced by underlying biological predispositions. An attempt to cast some light on this subject was made by Money, Hampson, and Hampson in their studies of persons whose original sex assignment was either incorrect or ambiguous because of the appearance of their external genitalia. Most of the persons studied were females with congenital adrenal hyperplasia, the condition described on pp. 8–9 of this chapter. On the basis of these studies (which involved extended clinical observations and psychological evaluations of pseudohermaphroditic patients), the hypothesis has been advanced that gender role is entirely the result of a learning process which is quite independent of chromosomal, gonadal, or hormonal sex (Money 1961, Hampson and Hampson 1961). In other words gender role is, for all practical purposes, determined entirely by environmental conditions during the first few years of life. In addition, the finding of "poor psychological adjustment" among patients who underwent a reassignment of sex after early childhood has led to the concept of a "critical period" for establishment of gender role between the ages of roughly 18 months and 3 years (Money, Hampson, and Hampson 1957, Hampson 1955, Money 1961).

Detailed psychological data are not available in these papers. It is therefore difficult to know what sort of criteria were applied in evaluating a given patient's gender role. Methods of study consisted of interviews in which attention was paid to general mannerisms, deportment and demeanor, play preferences and recreational interests, spontaneous topics of discussion, content of dreams and fantasies, reports on erotic practices, replies to direct and oblique inquiry, and responses to projective tests (Money and Hampson 1955, Hampson 1955). Classification of responses as either masculine or feminine was apparently determined on the basis of comprehensive clinical impressions. Detailed data are presented in one case of "unequivocal femininity" in a patient with gonadal agenesis (Hampson, Hampson, and Money 1955). Attention is paid to fantasies of going to a dance dressed in a long evening gown with a boyfriend, and getting married in a white satin dress to a handsome man. The patient also reported homosexual experiences and fantasies, however. It seems clear that in ordinary terms most of these patients do conform to their assigned sex role; i.e., a person with male hormones who has been raised as a girl will usually want to dress like a girl, engage in activities that are common to girls, and marry a man.

In a comprehensive review of their research, Hampson and Hampson (1961) emphasize that the appearance of the external genitals at birth usually determines the sex to which a baby is assigned and in which it is reared. It is remarkable that some children are reared in a sex contradicting their predominant external genital appearance. It is possible for such pseudohermaphrodites to establish a gender role entirely in agreement with assigned sex and rearing, despite the paradoxical appearance of their external genitalia. In this series, there were 25 individuals with a marked degree of contradiction between external genital appearance and assigned sex. Of the 16 older patients, all have lived at least to teen age with ambiguous or contradictory genital appearance. And all but two of the 25 individuals had been able to come to terms with their anomalous appearance, and establish a gender role consistent with their assigned sex and rearing. The authors have very little to say about how these individuals came to terms with this situation. They refer to "the enormity of the problem these people had to surmount in coming to terms psychologically with their paradoxical appearance." (p. 1412.) However, none of this group had ever had a psychotic illness.

The basic point made by these authors is that there is a very close relationship between the sex of assignment and rearing and the establishment of a masculine or feminine gender role. They see this relationship as overriding all others. Indeed, the Hampsons and Money believe that humans are psychosexually neutral at birth. This concept has recently been criticized in a major review by Diamond (1965). After considering a great variety of clinical and experimental evidence covering behavioral, endocrine, anatomic, and genetic factors, he reaches the following conclusion:

The evidence and arguments presented show that, primarily owing to prenatal genic and hormonal influences, human beings are definitely predisposed at birth to a male or female gender orientation. Sexual behavior of an individual, and thus gender role, are not neutral and without initial direction at birth. Nevertheless, sexual predisposition is only a potentiality setting limits to a pattern that is greatly modifiable by ontogenetic experiences. Life experiences most likely act to differentiate and direct a flexible sexual disposition and to mold the prenatal organization until an environmentally (socially and culturally) acceptable gender role is formulated and established. (p. 167.)

Beach (1965) reaches a similar conclusion:

... Without questioning the primary importance of individual experience and social learning in gender role development, the potential contribution of constitutional factors can be regarded as an unresolved issue. It is at least conceivable that there are sex differences in the functional characteristics of the male and female brain, that such differences are manifest at birth, and that they have some effect upon the acquisition of social behavior tendencies, including learning the gender role. (p. 565.)

Then, do sex hormones play any part in the development of gender role? They play an obvious role in influencing the differentiation of the internal and external genitalia, as well as promoting the development of secondary sex characteristics. Whether or not future investigators find more subtle effects may depend on the criteria used in defining gender role. What is the gender role of the woman who uses her hypertrophied clitoris as a penis in coitus? Or the woman who wears a dress on social occasions but is a professional wrestler and lifts weights for a hobby? Furthermore, the detection of hormonal effects will very likely require direct hormone measurement in a developmental research design, and consideration of the facility with which various patterns of behavior are learned—especially patterns that may have been basic components of gender roles throughout the evolution of human societies.

SEX DIFFERENCES IN THE BEHAVIOR OF INFANTS

In an earlier section, we described sex differences in the behavior of infant monkeys, and the influence of testosterone on the development of these differences. In addition to the male infant's greater proclivity for aggressive play (Harlow 1962) and for mounting behavior, two other differences deserve mention. In field studies of several species of old-world monkeys and great apes (DeVore 1965, Jay 1965), there are indications that young females show considerably greater interest in infants, and engage in more grooming behavior than do young males. These four kinds of early sex differences in behavior in several species of nonhuman primates raise the question whether any similar differences may be observed in human infants.

Several current studies are suggestive of the directions sex differences in the behavior of human infants may take. Bell and Costello (1964) have found that newborn females react more to the removal of a covering blanket than newborn males, and that females show lower thresholds to air-jet stimulation of the abdomen. Wolff (1965) has made similar observations, suggesting that females of two–three months are more responsive to skin exposure than males of the same age. Bell and Darling (1965) have found that human newborn males raise their heads higher than newborn females. Weller and Bell (1965) have found that newborn females are significantly higher in basal skin conductance than newborn males.

Thus we begin to see several sex differences in newborn human infants. Since the newborn period is one of considerable biological instability, it will be important to see whether such differences can be ascertained dependably from the second week of life onward. It is entirely possible that a variety of sex differences in the behavior of early infancy will be established during the next few years. If this turns out to be the case, it will be a matter of great interest to determine how these differences affect the infant's orientation to his environment, his readiness for different learning experiences, and his relationships with other people.

Whether such differences in infantile response patterns are mediated by hormonal effects on brain during fetal life remains for future research to clarify.

SEX DIFFERENCES IN SUSCEPTIBILITY TO DISEASES

It is a striking fact, well documented by medical statistics, that the human male is considerably more vulnerable than the female to a variety of diseases. More males than females die during each decade of life. This fact may stimulate inquiry into the mechanisms involved in such differential susceptibility. The fact that differential susceptibility exists draws attention to the mechanisms involved in sex differentiation in general; e.g., anatomical sexual dimorphism in mammals is primarily a function of a masculinizing hormone secreted by the fetal testis. Both sexes are exposed to female sex hormones in the uterus. The recent but already classic experiments of Jost have shown that there is a critical period during which the development of the internal reproductive structures takes place. The testes must secrete a masculinizing hormone (androgen) during this period if differentiation is to take a male course. Thus there is a sense in which the differentiation of a male genital tract (and, as we have already indicated, certain male circuits in the brain) is a more complex process than female differentiation. It is possible, but at present quite unproved, that this additional complexity may contribute to the vulnerability of the male.

Sexual reproduction is very important in evolution because it provides the genetic variability upon which natural selection operates. Sexual reproduction was made possible by the evolution of specific sex-determining chromosomes. The female has two large X chromosomes (genetic constitution XX); the male has only one X chromosome and one male-determining Y chromosome that is very much smaller than the X (genetic constitution XY). The X chromosome carries many genes in addition to those directly responsible for sex determination. Genes of the X chromosome have been shown to have an important bearing on susceptibility to a number of noninfectious human diseases (Childs 1965) including the following: (1) vitamin-D-resistant rickets; (2) nephrogenic diabetes insipidus; (3) glucose-6-phosphate dehydrogenase deficiency; (4) immunoglobulin deficiency; (5) clotting disorders; (6) color vision defects; (7) hypoperathyroidism. Moreover, Washburn, Medearis, and Childs (1965), by searching medical literature (particularly the Johns Hopkins Hospital case records covering the period from

1930 to 1963) have found sex differences in susceptibility to infections. Their analysis is consistent with the expectations of a genetic hypothesis that concerns a gene locus on the X chromosomes of human beings, which is involved in synthesis of immunoglobulins. In general, one might expect greater resistance to infectious diseases in that sex for which hetero-zygosity is possible, i.e., female—and this is the empirical result. Once again, males are more susceptible. More direct evidence for the hypoth-esis must come from comparative studies of the immune mechanism in the two sexes.

The disparity in size between the X and Y chromosomes means that females (XX) have a double dose (2 alleles) of many genes for which the male has only a single dose (1 allele). Since alleles frequently in-volve different variations on a basic theme at a given locus, situations are well known in genetics in which one allele compensates for the po-tentially dangerous effects of the other. It is quite plausible, though not yet established, that such situations may exist in respect to the X chro-mosome; if so, the female's second allele would protect her against the potentially dangerous effects of the other allele. The male would have no such protection. Problems of this sort have not yet been investigated with respect to behavior and its disorders, but they are quite pertinent to problems of mental retardation and psychosis. In principle, there is no reason why such processes, on a more subtle basis, might not enter into the development of normal behavior.

Washburn, Medearis, and Childs's work on susceptibility to diseases highlights a significant biological sex difference that manifests itself in various functional systems. Does the brain escape these effects? Will similar behavioral sex differences in susceptibility to disorder be estab-lished in future research? There is another way in which sex differences in susceptibility to illness may lead to sex differences in behavior. This concerns psychological reactions to recurrent or chronic illness. Such reactions would vary greatly with environmental conditions; e.g., in groups that strongly value male strength and self-sufficiency, early sus-ceptibility to illness may have quite unpleasant implications for young boys. In any event, this area of differential susceptibility to disease is now experiencing a resurgence of interest, based substantially on the newer prospects for analyzing the mechanisms involved in such sus-ceptibility. The possibility of including behavioral variables in such studies deserves serious consideration.

CONCLUSION

In this paper, we have reviewed several lines of recent inquiry into the role of sex hormones in the development of sex differences in human behavior. While there is little conclusive evidence on the nature, extent, and mechanisms of sex-hormone effects on the development of behavior in man, there is considerable recent evidence that suggests promising new approaches. Some areas that appear particularly promising are: (1) neuroendocrine processes governing the timing of puberty, and psychological reactions to variations in timing; (2) studies of sex hormones by biochemical methods throughout childhood and adolescence in relation to behavioral variables; (3) the study of endocrine abnormalities in children, particularly those involving early exposure of the female brain to high quantities of male sex hormone; (4) sex differences in behavior after puberty, particularly those relating to the function of female sex hormones in the menstrual cycle and pregnancy; (5) developmental studies on nonhuman primates, especially those analyzing interactions of male sex hormone and social environment in the formation of aggressive and mating behavior: (6) sex differences in behavior of human infants, with an examination of developmental as well as contemporary behavior-hormone correlations; (7) sex differences in susceptibility to brain diseases and to severe behavior disorders.

In all of the processes just mentioned there are complex interactions between genetic, endocrinological, and environmental variables. Future clarification of these interactions appears to depend on the successful integration of concepts and techniques from both the behavioral and the biological sciences.

REFERENCES

Beach, F. (1965) Retrospect and prospect. In F. Beach (ed.), *Sex and behavior*. New York: Wiley.

Bell, R., and N. Costello. (1964) Three tests for sex differences in tactile sensitivity in the newborn. *Biologia Neonatorum, 7,* 335–47.

———, and J. Darling. (In press) The prone head reaction in the human newborn: relationship with sex and tactile sensitivity. *Child Develpm., 36,* 943–49.

Benedek, T., and B. Rubinstein. (1942) The sexual cycle in women. National Research Council, Washington, D.C.

Bleuler, M., and W. A. Stoll. (1962) Psychological manifestations of hyper-

and hypoactivity of the adrenal cortex. In H. W. Deane (ed.), *Handbuch der exper. pharm.*, Vol. 1, *The adrenocortical hormones*. Berlin: Springer-Verlag.

Bongiovanni, A. M., and J. D. Smith. (1961) The androgens. In C. H. Gray and A. L. Bacharach (eds.), *Hormones in blood*. New York: Academic Press.

Brownie, A. C. (1964) Determination of testosterone in human peripheral blood using gas-liquid chromatography with electron capture detection. *J. clin. Endocrin., 24*, 1091–1102.

Childs, B. (1965) Genetic origin of some sex differences among human beings. *Pediatrics, 35*, 798–812.

DeVore, I. (ed.). (1965) *Primate behavior*. New York: Holt, Rinehart & Winston.

Diamond, M. (1965) A critical evaluation of the ontogeny of human sexual behavior. *Quart. Rev. Biol., 40*, 147–75.

——, and W. C. Young. (1963) Differential responsiveness of pregnant and nonpregnant guinea pigs to the masculinizing action of testosterone propionate. *Endocrin., 72*, 429–38.

Donovan, B. T. (1963) The timing of puberty. In *The scientific basis of med. ann. reviews*. London: Athlone Press.

——, and J. J. van der Werff ten Bosch. (1959) The hypothalamus and sexual maturation in the rat. *J. Physiol.* (London), *147*, 78–92.

Dorfman, R. I., and R. A. Shipley. (1956) *Androgens*. New York: Wiley.

Eichorn, Dorothy J. (1963) Biological correlates of behavior. In *Child psychology, N.S.S.E., Yearbook No. 63, Part I*. Chicago: Univ. of Chicago Press.

Ellis, H. (1928) *Studies in the psychology of sex*, Vol. 3. Philadelphia: F. A. Davis.

Everett, J. W. (1964) Central neural control of reproductive functions of the adrenohypophysis. *Physiol. Reviews, 44*, 373–431.

Filler, W., and N. Drezner. (1944) The results of surgical castration in women under forty. *Am. J. Obst. Gyn., 47*, 122–24.

Foss, G. L. (1951) The influence of androgens on sexuality in women. *Lancet, 1*, 667–69.

Goy, R. (1965) Unpublished paper presented at Conference on Sex Research, University of California, Berkeley.

——, W. Bridson, and W. Young. (1964) Period of maximal susceptibility of the prenatal female guinea pig to masculinizing actions of testosterone propionate. *J. comp. and physiol. Psychol., 57*, 166–74.

Hamburg, David A. (In press) Effects of progesterone on behavior. In Rachmiel Levine (ed.), *Endocrines and the nervous system*. Baltimore: Williams and Wilkins.

Hampson, Joan G. (1955) Hermaphroditic appearance, rearing, and eroticism in hyperadrenocorticism. *Bull. Johns Hopkins Hosp., 96*, 265–73.

Hampson, J. L., and Joan G. Hampson. (1961) The ontogenesis of sexual behavior in man. In W. C. Young (ed.), *Sex and internal secretions*, Vol. II. Baltimore: Williams and Wilkins.

———, Joan G. Hampson, and J. Money. (1955) The syndrome of gonadal agenesis (ovarian agenesis) and male chromosomal pattern in girls and women: Psychologic studies. *Bull. Johns Hopkins Hosp., 97,* 207–26.

Harlow, H. (1962) The heterosexual affectional system in monkeys. *Amer. Psychologist, 17,* 1–9.

Harris, G. (1964) Sex hormones, brain development, and brain function. *Endocrin., 75,* 627–48.

———, and S. Levine. (1962) Sexual differentiation of the brain and its experimental control. *J. Physiol., 163,* 42P–43P.

Heap, R. B. (1964) A fluorescence assay of progesterone. *J. Endocrin., 30,* 293–305.

Jay, P. (1965) Field Studies. In A. Schrier, H. Harlow, and F. Stollnitz (eds.), *Behavior of nonhuman primates, modern research trends.* New York: Academic Press.

Jones, Mary C. (1964) Psychological Correlates of Somatic Development. Presidential Address, Division 7, Amer. Psychol. Assoc., Sept. 1964.

———, and P. H. Mussen. (1963) Self-conceptions, motivations, and interpersonal attitudes of early- and late-maturing girls. In R. E. Grinder (ed.), *Studies in adolescence.* New York: Macmillan.

Lipsett, M. D., and S. G. Korenman. Androgen metabolism. *J.A.M.A., 190,* 757–62.

Lloyd, C. W., and J. H. Leathem. (1964) Fertilization, implantation and pregnancy. In C. W. Lloyd (ed.), *Human reproduction and sexual behavior.* Philadelphia: Lea and Febiger.

Merryman, W. (1954) Progesterone anesthesia in human subjects. *J. clin. endocrin., 14,* 1,567–69.

Money, J. (1961) Sex hormones and other variables in human eroticism. In W. C. Young (ed.), *Sex and internal secretions*, Vol. II. Baltimore: Williams and Wilkins.

———. (1963) Cytogenetic and psychosexual incongruities with a note on space-form blindness. *Am. J. Psych., 119,* 820–27.

———. (1965a) Influence of hormones on sexual behavior. *Ann. Rev. of Med., 16,* 67–82.

———. (1965b) Psychosexual differentiation. In J. Money (ed.), *Sex research, new developments.* New York: Holt, Rinehart & Winston.

———, and Joan G. Hampson. (1955) Idiopathic sexual precocity in the male: management report of a case. *Psycho. Med., 17,* 1–15.

———, Joan G. Hampson, and J. L. Hampson. (1957) Imprinting and the establishment of gender role. *A.M.A., Arch. Neur. and Psych., 77,* 333–36.

Mussen, P. H., and Mary C. Jones. (1963) The behavior-inferred motivations of late- and early-maturing boys. In R. E. Grinder (ed.), *Studies in adolescence.* New York: Macmillan.

Nathanson, I. T., L. E. Towne, and J. C. Aub. (1941) Normal excretion of sex hormones in childhood. *Endocrin., 28,* 851–65.

Reuben, M. S., and G. R. Manning. (1922, 1923) Precocious puberty. *Arch. Pediat., 39,* 769–85; *40,* 27-44.

Seckel, H. P. G. (1946) Precocious sexual development in children. *Med. Clinics of N. Amer.,* Jan., 183–209.

Talbot, N. B., et al. (1943) Excretion of 17-ketosteroids by normal and by abnormal children. *Amer. J. of Dis. in Child., 65,* 364–75.

Tanner, J. M. (1962) *Growth at adolescence* (2d ed.). Oxford: Blackwell Scientific Publications.

Tepperman, J. (1962) *Metabolic and endocrine physiology.* Chicago: Year Book Med. Publishers.

Washburn, T., D. Medearis, and B. Childs. (1965) Sex differences in susceptibility to infections. *Pediatrics, 35,* 57–64.

Waxenberg, S. E., et al. (1959) The role of hormones in human behavior: changes in female sexuality after adrenalectomy. *J. clin. Endocrin., 19,* 193–202.

Weller, G., and R. Bell. (In press) Basal skin conductance and neonatal state. *Child Develpm.*

Wilkins, L., et al. (1958) Masculinization of the female fetus associated with administration of oral and intramuscular progestins during gestation: non-adrenal female pseudohermaphrodism. *J. clin. Endocrin., 18,* 559–85.

Wilkins, L. (1965) *The diagnosis and treatment of endocrine disorders in childhood and adolescence* (3d ed.). Springfield, Ill.: Charles Thomas.

Wolff, P. (1965) Unpublished paper presented at the Tavistock Conference on Determinants of Infant Behavior, London, September 1965.

Wolstenholme, G. E. W., and M. P. Cameron (eds.). (1962) *Immunoassay of hormones. CIBA Found. Coll. of Endocrin.,* Vol. 14. Boston: Little, Brown.

Woolley, Dorothy E., and Paola S. Timiras. (1962) The gonad-brain relationship: effects of female sex hormones on electroshock convulsions in the rat. *Endocrin., 70,* 196–209.

Young, H. H. (1937) *Genital abnormalities, hermaphroditism and related adrenal diseases.* Baltimore: Williams and Wilkins.

Young, W. C. (1961) The hormones and mating behavior. In W. C. Young (ed.), *Sex and internal secretions,* Vol. II. Baltimore: Williams and Wilkins.

Young, W. C., R. Goy, and C. Phoenix. (1964) Hormones and sexual behavior. *Science, 143,* 212–18.

Zander, J. (1961) The chemical estimation of progesterone and its metabolites in body fluids and target organs. In A. Barnes (ed.), *Progesterone.* Augusta, Michigan: Brook Lodge Press.

Sex Differences in Intellectual Functioning

ELEANOR E. MACCOBY
Stanford University

This chapter will present and evaluate several possible explanations of the differences found between the performances of boys and girls on a variety of intellectual tasks. As a preliminary step the findings concerning sex differences in average proficiency on these tasks will be briefly summarized. Then any sex differences in the way intellectual performance correlates with other variables (such as personality factors and socialization experiences) will be discussed. And finally, these findings will be considered in the light of known or inferred differences in situations or demands impinging upon the two sexes, to see whether these might influence the nature of intellectual development.

SEX DIFFERENCES IN AVERAGE PERFORMANCE

Several detailed reviews of the differences between the sexes in average performance on tests of abilities are available in the literature (Anastasi 1958, Terman and Tyler 1954), and the results of the studies included in these reviews as well as those appearing more recently are summarized in the bibliography at the end of this volume. The relevant studies will not be completely referenced here. The primary conclusions to be drawn from them are:

(1) *General intelligence.* Most widely used tests of general intelligence have been standardized to minimize or eliminate sex differences. Whether differences are found on any particular test will depend on the balance of the items—whether there are more items of a kind on which one sex normally excels. There is a tendency for girls to test somewhat

higher on tests of general intelligence during the preschool years, boys during the high school years. There is a possibility that the latter finding is in part a function of differential school dropout rates; more boys drop out, leaving a more highly selected group of boys in high school. But some longitudinal studies in which the same children have been tested repeatedly through their growth cycle show greater gains for boys than girls. Sontag et al. (1958) and Ebert and Simmons (1943) both report this finding; Bayley (1956, 1957) does not. The changes in tested intelligence that occur during late adolescence and adulthood appear to favor men somewhat; that is, women decline somewhat more, or gain somewhat less, depending on the test used (Terman and Oden 1947, Bradway and Thompson 1962, Bayley and Oden 1955, Haan 1963).

(2) *Verbal ability.* Through the preschool years and in the early school years, girls exceed boys in most aspects of verbal performance. They say their first word sooner, articulate more clearly and at an earlier age, use longer sentences, and are more fluent. By the beginning of school, however, there are no longer any consistent differences in vocabulary. Girls learn to read sooner, and there are more boys than girls who require special training in remedial reading programs; but by approximately the age of ten, a number of studies show that boys have caught up in their reading skills. Throughout the school years, girls do better on tests of grammar, spelling, and word fluency.

(3) *Number ability.* Girls learn to count at an earlier age. Through the school years, there are no consistent sex differences in skill at arithmetical computation. During grade school years, some studies show boys beginning to forge ahead on tests of "arithmetical reasoning," although a number of studies reveal no sex differences on this dimension at this time. Fairly consistently, however, boys excel at arithmetical reasoning in high school, and the differences are substantially in favor of men among college students and adults. In a longitudinal sample, Haan finds men accelerating more than women in arithmetical ability during early adulthood.

(4) *Spatial ability.* While very young boys and girls do not differ on spatial tasks such as form boards and block design, by the early school years boys consistently do better on spatial tasks, and this difference continues through the high school and college years.

(5) *Analytic ability.* This term has several meanings. It is used to refer to the ability to respond to one aspect of a stimulus situation with-

out being greatly influenced by the background or field in which it is presented. In this sense, it is equivalent to what Witkin calls "field independence." On measures of this trait, such as the Embedded Figures Test and the Rod and Frame Test, boys of school age score consistently and substantially higher than girls (Witkin et al. 1954). Sigel et al. (1963), however, did not find sex differences on an embedded-figures test among a sample of five-year-olds, nor did Maccoby et al. (1965) among four-year-olds.

A related meaning of "analytic ability" is concerned with modes of grouping diverse arrays of objects or pictures. People who group "analytically"—put objects together on the basis of some selected element they have in common (e.g., all the persons who have a hand raised)— have been shown to be less influenced by background conditions in recognition tests, and hence are analytic in the Witkin sense as well. Boys more commonly use analytic groupings than do girls. How early this difference emerges is still an open question. Sigel did not find sex differences in grouping behavior among four- and five-year-olds. Kagan et al. (1963) did find clear sex differences among children in the second to fourth grade.

(6) *"Creativity."* There are relatively few studies comparing the sexes on aspects of creativity, and the outcome depends on the definition of the term. If the emphasis is on the ability to break set or restructure a problem, there is a tendency for boys and men to be superior, particularly if the problem involves a large perceptual component. Breaking set is involved in the tasks used to measure "analytic ability," discussed above, and in some of the tests that have a high loading on the space factor.

If creativity is thought of in terms of divergent, as distinct from convergent, thinking (see Guilford 1956), the evidence appears to favor girls somewhat, although the findings are not consistent. A task requiring children to think of ways in which toys could be improved showed that in the first two grades of school, each sex was superior when dealing with toys appropriate to its own sex, but by the third grade, boys were superior on both feminine and masculine toys. On the other hand, girls and women do better on a battery of divergent tasks measuring the variety of ideas produced for the solution of verbally presented problems (Klausmeier and Wiersma 1964, Trembly 1964).

(7) *Achievement.* Girls get better grades than boys throughout the

school years, even in subjects in which boys score higher on standard achievement tests. In adulthood, after graduation from school, men achieve substantially more than women in almost any aspect of intellectual activity where achievements can be compared—books and articles written, artistic productivity, and scientific achievements. A follow-up study of gifted children showed that while gifted boys tended to realize their potential in their occupations and creative output, gifted girls did not.

How large are the group differences summarized above? It is difficult to find a satisfactory answer to this question, for some studies report that a difference between the sexes is statistically significant, without giving the actual magnitude of the mean scores that are being compared. Even when mean scores are given, there is a problem of the meaning of the units on the scale—whether they are equal throughout the scale. With these reservations in mind, existing information does suggest that sex differences in spatial ability and in some aspects of analytic ability are substantial from the early school years on, and that sex differences in mathematical reasoning by high school age are also substantial, while differences in verbal ability are less marked. But on all measures reported, there is considerable overlap between the distribution of scores of the two sexes.

CORRELATIONS BETWEEN INTELLECTUAL PERFORMANCE AND PERSONALITY CHARACTERISTICS

So far, we have been summarizing the known differences between the sexes in their average performance on a variety of tasks. But this, of course, does not provide a complete account of sex differences. Even on tests where the distribution of scores is the same for the two sexes (in mean and standard deviation), the array of scores will often correlate differently with other variables for boys and girls (Sigel 1964). We will now examine what is known concerning the linkages between performance on intellectual tasks and other characteristics, especially personality characteristics, to see whether the nature of these linkages is different for the two sexes.

Impulse Control

For the present, we will use the term "impulse" to designate high levels of undirected activity and the inability to delay or inhibit behavior that is incompatible with goal-directed activity. We assume that the ability to persist at a task involves inhibition of competing response tendencies, hence we include both "distractability" and low task persistence as indicating lack of impulse control.

Sigel et al. (1963) report a study of children four to five years old, in which observational measures were taken of (1) emotional control, (2) cautiousness, and (3) attentiveness. In addition, each child was given a grouping test, in which he had to select from an array of pictures the one that was most like a standard. Some children adopted a "descriptive part-whole" grouping style (called analytic responses by Kagan et al. 1963). The sexes did not differ on Sigel's three measures of impulsiveness. But for boys, the frequency of analytic grouping was positively correlated with emotional control, cautiousness, and attentiveness, while for girls these correlations were negative. That is, the girl who used this grouping style was impulsive, the boy controlled.

A similar result was obtained by Kagan et al. (1964) working with the Fels longitudinal sample. He reports a correlation of .45 between "emotional control" and the use of analytic concepts in a grouping test for boys, while the corresponding correlation for girls is −.20.

In a study by Sutton-Smith et al. (1964) it was found that adopting a winning strategy in a game of tick-tack-toe (previously found to correlate with I.Q.) was characteristic of girls who were aggressive, dominant, and hyperactive, while the boys who adopted a winning strategy at this game were not especially active and showed a preference for "conceptual recreations."

Murphy (1962) reports that, for boys, a measure of "coping" is correlated with "the ability to balance gratification and frustration" (which we may take to be a measure of impulse control); for girls, these two variables are not correlated. Among girls, on the other hand, coping is positively correlated with speed or tempo of behavior, a factor that does not relate to coping among boys.

Kagan and Moss, in their longitudinal study (1962) done at the Fels Institute, report that measures of hyperkinesis (high levels of undirected activity) during childhood correlate negatively with adult intellectual interests for men, while the correlation is slightly positive for women. It appears, then, from these varied studies, that impulsiveness is a negative factor for at least some aspects of intellectual development in boys, but for girls it is a less negative—and perhaps even a positive—factor.

Fearfulness and Anxiety

The Kagan and Moss study also dealt with the relationship between fearfulness and intellectual development. Boys who were timid and cautious in early childhood had higher I.Q.'s and developed greater intellectual interests in adulthood; for girls, the correlations between fearfulness and measures of intellectual performance were zero or negative. For example, timidity, measured during the 10–14-year age period, correlated −.63 with the degree of intellectual interests the girl displayed in adulthood, while the comparable figure for boys was .26. Bayley and Schaefer (1964) working with a different longitudinal sample, find timidity and reserve to be negative factors for both sexes, but especially so for boys during middle childhood and adolescence. The correlations they report between I.Q. and absence of shyness in earlier childhood, however, are more positive for girls than for boys, and hence more consistent with the Kagan and Moss findings. It may be that the relationship between timidity and intellectual performance is highly age-specific, and more so for boys than for girls.

Correlations between measures of anxiety and measures of aptitude or achievement are substantially negative for girls and women, while the correlations are either low negative, zero, or positive for boys and men. The evidence fairly consistently points to this difference in the role anxiety plays for the two sexes (Davidson and Sarason 1961, Iscoe and Carden 1961, Russell and Sarason 1965, Walter et al. 1964), although there is one set of contrary findings (French 1961).

Aggression and Competitiveness

In one study (Maccoby and Rau 1962), aggressiveness, as measured by a peer-nomination technique in classrooms of fifth-grade children, was negatively related (slightly but significantly, $r = -.27$) to a measure of total intelligence (PMA) for boys, and unrelated to this measure for girls. And in the same study, anxiety over aggression was positively related to intelligence for boys ($r = .39$), unrelated for girls. In the Fels sample (Moss and Kagan 1962) nonphysical aggression was positively related to I.Q. among girls, unrelated among boys. E. K. Beller (1962) found, in a sample of five- and six-year-old children, a strong negative relationship between aggressiveness and performance on an embedded-figures test for boys, while these variables were uncorrelated for girls. As previously noted, Sutton-Smith's finding on a winning game strategy yielded positive correlations with aggressiveness for girls, but not for boys. Thus aggressiveness appears to be more of an inhibitor, or less of a facilitator, for intellectual development among boys than among girls.

In the Fels sample, competitiveness was found to correlate with I.Q., and with progressive increases in I.Q., for both sexes, but the correlations are higher for girls than boys (Sontag et al. 1958, Moss and Kagan 1962).

Level of Aspiration and Achievement Motivation

The evidence is not clear whether boys or girls have a higher correlation between ability (as measured by I.Q. tests) and achievement. Phillips et al. (1960), working with seventh-grade children, found the correlation to be higher for boys. Coleman (1961) reports that among high school students, boys named as "best scholar" had higher I.Q. scores than girls so named, despite the fact that the girls had higher average I. Q. scores in the population studied. He suggests that girls of this age are caught up in a "double bind." They wish to conform to their parents' and teachers' expectations of good academic performance, but fear that high academic achievement will make them unpopular with boys. As a result of these dual pressures, Coleman suggests, the brightest girls do creditably in school but less than their best. On the other hand, the brightest boys feel free to excel in scholarship and do so in fact.

Terman and Oden's follow-up study of gifted children (1947) disclosed that, for girls, there was no relationship between the level of occupational achievement and I.Q. as measured during the school years, while for boys this correlation was substantial. There is evidence that girls who are underachievers in high school usually begin to be so at about the onset of puberty (Shaw and McCuen 1960), while for boys underachievement in high school usually has an earlier onset. This contrast is a further indication that the achievement drop-off among girls as they reach maturity is linked to the adult female sex role.

While additional studies contrasting age levels are needed to confirm the point, it appears that the social pressures to do well or poorly in school may have a reverse time sequence for the two sexes. As noted above, the pressures on bright girls not to do as well as they can tend to be augmented in adolescence, so that correlations between ability and achievement ought to be higher during the early school years. By contrast, peer-group pressures on boys in the early school years are often (though not always) in the direction of achievement in sports and other nonacademic pursuits; and boys of this age are frequently engaged in efforts to achieve autonomy, especially in relation to their mothers, with the result that they are less willing than girls to accede to the demands of their predominantly female teachers. In adolescence, however, especially for middle-class boys, the pressures for college entrance and professional preparation begin to be felt, with the result that the more intelligent boys begin to buckle down at this time. Even in high school, however, the boys' more autonomous approach to their school work is indicated in the greater selectivity of their efforts: boys are likely to do well in subjects that interest them and poorly in subjects that bore them, while girls tend to perform uniformly in all their school subjects (Coleman 1961).

One factor that may operate to produce a higher correlation between aptitude and performance for boys throughout the school years is that boys appear to evaluate their own abilities and performance more realistically than girls. Crandall et al. (1962) asked children how well they expected to do on a new task they were about to undertake. Among boys, the brighter the boy, the better he expected to do on the new task ($r = .62$). Among girls, the brighter the girl the *less* well she expected to do on a new task ($r = -.41$). Furthermore, when the children were asked whether they believed that their score on a task was mostly a function of their own efforts, or a matter of chance or luck, the brighter boys more often believed that success was an outcome of their own efforts. Among the girls, there was no relationship between I.Q. and belief in self-responsibility versus chance. P. S. Sears (1963) similarly found a positive correlation between a measure of intelligence and boys' self-appraisal of their own abilities, while these variables were essentially uncorrelated for girls.

There is some evidence that girls appear to be more afraid of failure, and more disorganized by it, than boys. Harmatz (1962), working with college students, found that when women were working on a fairly difficult task and were told that they were not doing well on it, both their level of aspiration and their performance declined, as compared with a control group of women who did not receive this negative feedback. This is consistent with McClelland's (1953) finding that among women the level of achievement motivation (as reflected in TAT stories) is not affected by an "arousal" treatment involving academic competition, while among men it is increased. Moriarty (1961) observed the task orientation and coping behavior of a group of preschool children while they were taking individually administered intelligence tests. She found that while girls initially approached the task in a more organized way, as the tasks became harder and failures were encountered, the girls became less integrated in their performance and more desirous of leaving the field than did boys.

Murphy (1962) makes a similar observation concerning the behavior of children of nursery school age during an intelligence test: "Confronted with difficulty, a larger number of boys became more active in expressing autonomy, while girls tended to become more passive." (p. 210.) Crandall and Rabson (1960), working with children ranging in age from three to nine years, found that when children were offered the choice of returning either to tasks at which they had previously failed or to tasks at which they had previously succeeded, girls more often chose to repeat their earlier successes, while boys tended to prefer working further on tasks they had not mastered previously. The evidence is not entirely consistent, however. Yonge (1964), working with college men and women, found that when given insoluble problems presented as an I.Q. test, women attempted more problems but made more errors. The increased error rate may indicate some disorganization of behavior under failure, and this would be consistent with earlier findings; but the increase in number of problems attempted does not reflect the usual pattern of decreased level of aspiration with failure among women. Perhaps the Yonge findings are a function of a highly selected sample. In any case, the bulk of the findings seem to indicate that boys are more likely to rise to an intellectual challenge, girls to retreat from one. What may be a physiological indicator of this phenomenon was noted by Leiderman and Shapiro (1963) in their study of autonomic responses during group problem solving with an ambiguous task. While being rewarded for initiations of a solution, the Galvanic Skin Potential of female subjects decreased, that of male subjects increased.

Sex-typing

"Masculinity" and "femininity" have been measured in a number of ways. Some of the standard measures have a single scale running from masculine to feminine. Others (Brim 1958, Oetzel 1961) measure masculinity and femininity independently, so that it is possible for an individual to obtain a high score on both measures if he possesses traits commonly labeled as characteristic of the two different sexes. Using the latter kind of measure, Oetzel found that, among fifth-grade boys, total PMA scores were positively correlated with femininity and slightly negatively correlated with masculinity; in other words, the brighter boys were considerably more feminine and slightly less masculine than their less intelligent peers. Among girls, however, total PMA scores were slightly positively correlated with both masculinity and femininity. This means that the high I.Q. girl is likely to be dominant and striving (characteristics labeled "masculine"), but she may also act more "grown-up" and be more anxious to do things for other people than her less intelligent peers (behaviors normally classified as "feminine").

Oetzel's study investigated sex-typing among groups of eleven-year-old children with uneven profiles of abilities, and she found that the children who were more skillful at spatial tasks than verbal or numerical tasks tended to be low in masculinity if they were boys, high in masculinity if they were girls. This trend was confirmed (significantly for boys) in a study with the Fels longitudinal sample (Maccoby et al. 1963). The low masculinity of boys who tested high on spatial ability is especially notable in view of the fact that boys normally score higher on space tests than girls do.

The Fels longitudinal study (Moss) reports that a young child's interest in the games and activities characteristic of the opposite sex is positively correlated with I.Q.; that is, the brighter girls are more likely to enjoy baseball and other boys' games, while the brighter boys will more often engage in feminine activities.

Both Barron (1957) and MacKinnon (1962) report that men who are outstanding in originality or creativity score more toward the feminine end of an M-F scale than do their less creative counterparts. This difference, they say, reflects a greater breadth of interests among creative men; for example, such men have aesthetic interests, which are usually included as feminine indicators on an M-F scale because women are, on the average, more likely than men to have strong aesthetic interests.

Bieri (1960) studied sex-typing in relation to performance on an embedded-figures test. He found that men who obtained high scores on this test (and hence would be labeled "analytical") revealed identification with their mothers rather than their fathers on the semantic differential. Analytical female subjects, by contrast, were characterized by a high level of identification with their fathers. This latter finding is consistent with the observations of Plank and Plank (1954), who studied the autobiographies of a group of outstanding women mathematicians, and found that there was evidence in all of them of a strong attachment to, and identification with, their fathers rather than their mothers.

The studies cited so far indicate that analytic thinking, creativity, and high general intelligence are associated with cross-sex-typing, in that the men and boys who score high are more feminine, and the women and girls more masculine, than their low-scoring same-sex counterparts. There are a few exceptions in the literature to this generalization. Milton (1957) correlated scores on the Terman-Miles M-F scale with scores on problems requiring restructuring and breaking set, and found that the more masculine subjects of both sexes did best on these problems. In a study of young boys, Anastasiow (1963) administered a toy-preference test of sex-typing, and found a curvilinear relation between masculine sex-typing and ease of learning first-grade-level reading and arithmetic, with the high-masculine group doing best on school tasks, the high-feminine next best, and the intermediate group least well. So the evidence for boys is somewhat equivocal (the differences perhaps being a function of how sex-typing is measured), although the weight of evidence does support an association between femininity and intellectual performance. For girls and women, the evidence consistently points to masculinity as a correlate of intellectuality.

It is important to note, however, that this cross-sex typing does not imply that intellectual individuals are sexually uninterested in, or unattractive to, the opposite sex. It merely means that they share more of the interests and activities normally characteristic of the opposite sex.

Dependency, Passivity, and Independence

For both sexes, there is a tendency for the more passive-dependent children to perform poorly on a variety of intellectual tasks, and for independent children to excel. However, for some kinds of tasks, the relationships are stronger for boys than for girls, and for others the reverse is true. In the Fels longitudinal study, observational measures of dependency were taken, and were then related to I.Q. (Moss and Kagan, 1962). For boys, the correlations ranged from zero to slightly positive. For girls, they were negative; that is, the less dependent girls were the brighter ones.

Also using the Fels sample, Sontag et al. (1958) studied the personality factors associated with progressive increases in I.Q., and found that independence was a factor for both sexes, but that the relationship was considerably stronger for boys. Bieri, studying the correlation of performance on the Embedded Figures Test with "acceptance of authority," found that subjects who refuse to accept authority do considerably better on the EFT; this was true for subjects of both sexes, but the relationship was even greater for the male subjects. Nakamura (1958) gave his subjects a set of problems requiring restructuring for their solution. He also gave the subjects a perceptual test in which they could either rely upon their own judgments or go along with the rigged consensus of a group of observers. The subjects who did best on the restructuring problems were those who resisted the conformity pressures in the perceptual situation, and, again, the correlation was higher for male subjects.

Witkin (1962) summarizes the work done by himself and others relating analytic perceptual style (field independence) to a variety of indicators on the dependence-independence dimension. The evidence he cites is impressive in showing that both global (field dependent) perceivers and those who have difficulty breaking set in problem solving are dependent in their interpersonal relations, suggestible, conforming, and likely to rely on others for guidance and support. Most of Witkin's work has been done with boys alone, so we do not have evidence from this source concerning sex differences that may exist in the magnitude of the relationship between an analytic cognitive style and an independent orientation toward others.

PARENT-CHILD RELATIONSHIPS AND INTELLECTUAL FUNCTIONING

There are relatively few studies that relate the child-training behavior or attitudes of parents to the intellectual characteristics of their children. There are several reports of such relationships based on the Fels longitudinal sample (Crandall et al. 1964, Moss and Kagan 1958, Sutton-Smith et al. 1964), and one based on the Berkeley Growth Study (Bayley and Schaeffer 1964). These studies agree in reporting quite substantial sex differences in the kinds of parental behavior that relate to a child's intellectual proficiency, although there are discrepancies in the precise nature of the predictors for each sex. The samples are small, and findings seem to depend upon the age of the child when the parental measures and child measures are taken.

Crandall et al. (1964) studied mothers and fathers separately, measuring their behavior and attitudes toward both sons and daughters. Parent behavior was found to relate significantly to the child's academic success only for parent-daughter pairs. Mothers who were less nurturant toward their daughters (during the preschool years) had the more academically successful daughters. Supportive behavior by the father (more praise, less blame) in relation to the daughter's academic performance was associated with high performance on the daughter's part, while direct pressure from the father toward his daughter for better school achievement was related to poor performance, specifically in reading. Parental behavior, as measured in this study, was not related to academic success among boys.

Moss and Kagan (1958) found that maternal acceleration attempts during the preschool years had a temporary effect upon boys—correlating positively with I.Q. at age three—but that this relationship had disappeared by age six. No such relationship at either age level was found for girls. These writers do report, however, that maternal protection and warmth during the early years of life are related to high I.Q. in later years for boys. For girls, by contrast, the crucial factor in the development of I.Q. appears to be relative freedom from maternal restriction—freedom to wander and explore.

Sutton-Smith et al. (1964), working with the Fels children on one aspect of intellectual performance (adopting a winning strategy in tick-tack-toe) found that maternal acceleration attempts were slightly negatively associated with the performances of both sexes, but that punitiveness (as reflected in severity of penalties) was positively correlated for girls and uncorrelated for boys.

Bayley and Schaeffer (1964) report data on 26 boys and 27 girls from the Berkeley Growth Study. This study was primarily designed to provide longitudinal data on mental and motor development, and information on maternal behavior during the child's early years was obtained only during the testing sessions with the child. A major finding of this study is that maternal behavior as observed during these sessions predicts a number of later-developing characteristics for boys, but few for girls. This finding stands in contrast to the Crandall report that parental behavior is correlated with the school performance of girls but not boys. It should be noted that the Crandall measures were concurrent, and the Bayley and Schaeffer measures predictive over a considerable span of years. But other studies with the Fels sample, which involved predicting the child's later intellectual characteristics from early maternal practices, revealed as strong relationships for girls as boys, albeit different relationships. It remains to be seen, then, whether the effects of early socialization are more lasting for one sex than another. The studies based on the two different longitudinal samples are consistent, however, in this respect: the Berkeley study also shows that the absence of maternal intrusiveness is a more important factor in the intellectual development of girls than boys, while warmth and close attentiveness to the child during the early years are positive factors only for boys.

Bayley and Schaeffer present an intriguing hypothesis concerning sex differences in intellectual development. They suggest that the intellectual performance of boys is more responsive to environmental events, while that of girls has a larger component of genetic control. They note that in their sample the correlation between the child's I.Q. and the parents' estimated I.Q.'s is higher for girls. And, as previously noted, they find more lasting relationships between early maternal behavior and the child's later I.Q. scores for boys than for girls. They reanalyze the data from the early Skodak–Skeels study of adopted children, and show that while the correlation between the I.Q.'s of adopted children and the estimated I.Q's of their natural parents is significant for girls, it is not for boys.

This hypothesis is new, and remains to be checked against other bodies of data. Moss and Kagan (1958) find that while the correlations between parent and child I.Q. develop earlier in girls (Honzik, 1957, also finds this to be true), the boys catch up with the girls by age six. Furthermore, as we have seen, data from the Fels sample do show fairly lasting relationships between early maternal behaviors and the later intellectual development of girls. Existing data, then, do not permit us either to support the hypothesis or to reject it unequivocally, and the issue must remain open for further evidence.

POSSIBLE CAUSAL FACTORS OF SEX DIFFERENCES
IN INTELLECTUAL ABILITIES

The research summarized so far has shown that (1) there are a number of aspects of intellectual performance on which the sexes differ consistently in the average scores obtained, and that (2) whether or not there is a difference in average performance on a given task, there are some substantial sex differences in the intercorrelations between intellectual performance and other characteristics of the individual or his environment. We turn now to an examination of several possible explanations for these differences.

Developmental Timetable

Physiologically, girls mature faster than boys. And because certain aspects of intellectual development cannot occur until the relevant physical structures are complete, we might expect girls to develop some abilities earlier than boys. For example, at birth the cortical structures relevant to speech are not fully formed. Insofar as speech must wait until they are, we might expect girls to talk sooner than boys. The physiological timetable, of course, determines not only the individual's rate of development in early life but also the age at which he reaches his optimum level, the duration of his stay at this level, and the time of onset and the rate of the aging process. The fact that females mature faster during the first part of the life cycle does not necessarily imply that they begin to age sooner, although they may, despite their greater average longevity.

The sex differences found in general intelligence during the early part of the life span, insofar as these differences may be determined from tests standardized to minimize them, do seem to parallel the physiological trends. That is, girls get off to a faster start in language and in some other aspects of cognitive performance. Moreover, parent-child resemblances in intelligence set in earlier for girls than boys. The sexes are very similar during the early and middle school years, and then boys begin to forge ahead in some ability areas during the high school years. But Bayley (1956) has shown that the rate of intellectual growth is unrelated to the rate of physical growth if one scores both in terms of the per cent of mature growth attained. Hence it does not appear that there is any single developmental timetable controlling both physical and mental growth.

As noted earlier, the evidence concerning sex-related I.Q. changes during adulthood is neither extensive nor entirely consistent, though there is some indication that a gradual decline in some aspects of intellectual functioning sets in earlier among women. There is no evidence whether these changes parallel other aspects of aging. In any case, even if some of these differences could be accounted for in terms of different developmental timetables, it is doubtful whether some of the major differences we have noted could be so explained. It is difficult to see, for example, why maturational factors should produce greater differences between the sexes in spatial than verbal performance. Nor why a fast-developing organism should show different kinds of relationships between intellectual functions and personality traits than a slow-developing organism. We must therefore turn to different explanatory concepts.

Direct Effects of Sex-typed Interests

Perhaps the explanation for the differences we have noted is very simple: members of each sex are encouraged in, and become interested in and proficient at, the kinds of tasks that are most relevant to the roles they fill currently or are expected to fill in the future. According to this view, boys in high school forge ahead in math because they and their parents and teachers know they may become engineers or scientists; on the other hand, girls know that they are unlikely to need math in the occupations they will take up when they leave school. And adult women, most of whom become housewives or work at jobs that do not make many intellectual demands, decline in measures of "total intelligence" because such tests call upon skills that are not being used by adult women as extensively as they are used by adult men. As far as women's lack of creativity and intellectual productivity is concerned, we could argue that women are busy managing households and rearing children, and that these activities usually preclude any serious commitment to other creative endeavors. Undoubtedly, matters of opportunity and life setting play a very large role in the relative accomplishments of the two sexes. That this is not the whole story, however, is suggested by a study of Radcliffe Ph.D.'s (1956), in which it was found that the women Ph.D.'s who had taken academic posts had published substantially less than their male counterparts, and that this was just as true of unmarried academic women as it was of married ones. Thus women who are as well off as men (or perhaps better off) with respect to alternative demands on their time are nevertheless less productive. It is difficult to attribute this fact to anything about the professional roles they currently occupy. If their behavior is role-determined, it must be determined by sex roles established or anticipated earlier in life.

Some of the major sex differences we have noted—some appearing at a fairly early age—do not appear to have any direct relevance to adult sex roles, actual or anticipated. Does a girl of nine do poorly on an embedded-figures test because she thinks that this kind of skill is not going to be important for her later on in life, and well on a spelling test because she thinks this kind of skill is going to be important? It is doubtful whether either children or adults see those ability areas where we have detected the greatest sex differences as sex-role specific. This is not to say that sex-typing is irrelevant to intellectual development. But it is doubtful whether the sex differences in spatial ability, analytic style, and breaking set can be understood in terms of their greater direct relevance to the role requirements of one sex or the other.

Opportunities to Learn

Do the sexes differ in their opportunities to learn the skills and content of the ability areas where stable sex differences have been found? It has been widely assumed that girls' early verbal superiority might be due to their spending more time with adults, particularly with their mothers. From research on birth order and experimental studies of the effects of verbal interaction with adults in language acquisition, it may be safely inferred that the amount of a child's contact with adults does influence his language development. Preschool girls are kept at home with their mothers, the argument goes, while boys are allowed to go out to play with age-mates. As a result, girls have more opportunity to develop language skills. But when children enter school, and boys are exposed to intensive stimulation from the teacher, they catch up. A weakness of this argument is that it does not explain why boys catch up in vocabulary and reading comprehension, but not in fluency, spelling, and grammar. And furthermore, we lack direct evidence that preschool girls are kept at home more. Although it fits our stereotypes of the two sexes to think of girls as more protected, we must consider the possibility that girls may actually be given more freedom than boys. Because girls mature faster, perhaps parents can trust them sooner than boys to play away from home with little adult supervision. We simply lack information on this point.

Similarly, it has been suggested that boys acquire greater spatial and perceptual-analytic ability because they have more opportunity to explore their environment at an early age—more opportunity to manipulate objects. Again, we have no evidence that this is so. It is true that if one watches nursery school children at play, one is more likely to find boys building with blocks and girls placing doll furniture in a doll house or pretending to cook with beaters and bowls; but it is difficult to see why one of these kinds of object manipulation should lead to greater spatial ability than the other. We know little about what kinds of learning experiences are involved when a child dissects stimuli (as the analytical, field-independent child does) instead of responding to them globally, but it is difficult to see why sheer quantity of stimulus exposure should make a difference beyond a certain point. That is, it is reasonable to suppose that a child who is subjected to severe stimulus deprivation may find it difficult to make fine perceptual discriminations, and hence might perceive more globally. But normally reared children of both sexes have considerable opportunity to move about in space and explore a variety of objects. We suspect that exposure to a variety of stimuli is a necessary but not sufficient condition for the development of an analytic cognitive style, and that children of both sexes, if they grow up in a normal environment, will have enough stimulus contact to permit, if not ensure, this development.

"Identification" and Modeling

It has been thought that girls may be more verbal and boys more quantitative because children tend to model themselves primarily upon the same-sex parent (Carlsmith 1964). Since mothers are typically more verbal and fathers typically more skilled at quantitative tasks, the argument goes, modeling the same-sex parent will produce differential patterns of abilities in boys and girls.

There are a number of difficulties with this explanation of the typical sex differences in ability profiles. Not all aspects of intellectual functioning are susceptible to modeling. Vocabulary and verbal fluency are aspects of a parent's intellectual equipment that a child can copy. Normally, his spelling is not. Yet girls maintain superiority throughout the school years in spelling and fluency, though not in vocabulary. Much of a parent's quantitative reasoning is done covertly, so that it is not accessible for copying, and very little spatial thinking is communicated from parent to child. Yet it is in spatial performance that we find the most consistent sex differences.

Sex differences in verbal ability occur at a very early age, long before the child is able to identify which parent is the same sex as himself, and long before he begins to copy same-sex models differentially (see Kohlberg's chapter in this volume). Sex differences in verbal ability decline during the age period when the rise of identification and differential modeling ought to increase them. And consistent sex differences in quantitative ability do not appear until adolescence, long after the time when boys and girls have begun to prefer same-sex models. For these reasons we do not believe that the identification hypothesis provides an adequate explanation of the sex differences in ability profiles noted at the beginning of this chapter.

Sex-typed Personality Traits as Mediating Processes

Numerous studies have shown that girls are more conforming, more suggestible, and more dependent upon the opinion of others than boys. And as mentioned earlier in this chapter, a number of studies have demonstrated that these very personality traits are associated with (1) field dependency (global perceiving), and (2) lack of ability to break set or restructure in problem solving. Witkin et al. (1962) have suggested that herein lies the explanation of sex differences in field independence and analytic style—that girls are more field-dependent and less analytical because of their greater conformity and dependency.

Why should there be any relationship between the cluster of personality dispositions that we may call the dependency cluster and individuals' characteristic modes of dealing with a stimulus array? Two possible reasons suggest themselves. First, an individual who is dependent and conforming is oriented toward stimuli emanating from other people; perhaps he finds it difficult to ignore these stimuli in favor of internal thought processes. Analytic thinking appears to require more internal "processing"; Kagan et al. (1963) have shown it to be associated with longer reaction times than global responding. Dependent children have been shown to be more distractible (Rau 1963); their internal processing is interrupted, perhaps because of their greater orientation toward external interpersonal cues. This orientation probably helps them in certain kinds of intellectual performance; they should do better in recognizing names and faces, for example. But tasks calling for sequential thought may be hindered by a heavy reliance on external, interpersonal cues.

A second and related reason why one might expect to find a connection between the independence-dependence personality dimension and the mode of dealing with a stimulus array in problem solving has to do with activity. The dependent-conforming person is passive, waiting to be acted upon by the environment. The independent person takes the initiative. Intellectual tasks differ in how much activity they require, so that the passive person is more at a disadvantage on some tasks than others. Vocabulary tests, for example, depend upon previously established associations, and therefore involve less trial and error than tasks that require restructuring or finding the answer to a previously unsolved problem.

We are postulating, then, that dependency interferes with certain aspects of intellectual functioning. But there are other aspects of intellectual performance that dependency may facilitate—achievement, for example. Sears (1963) has found that, among girls, projective measures of "need affiliation" are positively related to academic achievement; in other words, achievement efforts can be motivated by a desire for social approval, and in the Sears work this proved to be true to a greater degree for girls than boys.

On the basis of the above considerations, we find it plausible to believe that some of the sex differences outlined in the first section of the chapter may be traced to boys' greater independence and activity, girls' greater conformity and passive-dependency. We do not know whether these personality differences between the sexes are in any degree innate, or whether they are entirely a product of the social learning involved in the acquisition of sex roles; but we do suggest that the existence of the differences may have a bearing upon the intellectual development of the two sexes.

A second theory concerning the origins of sex differences in intellectual functioning may be derived from MacKinnon. We noted earlier that high I.Q., and more particularly creativity and originality, appear to be associated with cross-sex-typing in both sexes. MacKinnon has suggested that this may be due to the absence of repression. He argues that a man can only achieve a high degree of "masculinity" (as our culture defines it) by repressing the feminine character elements that all men possess. And presumably the converse would be true of women: ultra-femininity is only achieved through the repression of masculine tendencies. Repression, MacKinnon argues, has a generalized impact upon thought processes, interfering with the accessibility of the individual's own previous experiences. An individual who is using repression as a defense mechanism cannot be, to use MacKinnon's term, "fluent in scanning thoughts." MacKinnon has evidence that creativity is in fact associated with the absence of repression (as indicated through person-ality-assessment tests), and Barron reports that originality is associated with "responsiveness to impulse and emotion." Witkin reports that his field-independent people are less likely to use repression as a defense mechanism than his field-dependent people. If MacKinnon is right, this should mean that field-independent men are somewhat more feminine than field-dependent men. There is some evidence from Bieri's study that this is indeed the case.

If MacKinnon's hypothesis is to be used to explain sex differences in intellectual performance, we would have to assume that women typically repress more than men, since they are more "field-dependent" and less adept at breaking set than men. It is difficult to see why a girl should have to repress her masculine tendencies more strongly than a boy does his feminine tendencies; on the contrary, social pressure is much strong-er against a boy who is a sissy than against a girl who is a tomboy. Furthermore, women are freer to express feelings (with the exception of hostility) than men in our society. Hence it is difficult to characterize women as generally subject to repression. Furthermore, while it is true that they are more field-dependent, women are not any less "fluent in scanning thoughts," if we take their performance on divergent thinking and verbal-fluency tests as an indicator. Some aspects of women's intel-lectual performance, then, could be attributed to repression if there were evidence of greater repression in women, but others could not.

There appears to be some contradiction between the prediction that we could make on the basis of MacKinnon's repression theory and the prediction from Witkin's theory about dependency. To be creative, Mac-Kinnon says, a man must be able to accept and express the feminine as-pects of his character. Surely, one element of this femininity would be passive-dependency. Yet, passive-dependency, we have argued earlier, interferes with analytic thinking and some aspects of creativity. It would appear that the correlation between intellectual performance and cross-sex-typing ought to be stronger for women than for men, since among women masculinity implies both independence and absence of repression—two positive factors in intellectual performance. For men, however, femininity implies absence of repression (a positive factor) and passive-dependency (a negative factor). As we noted earlier, the evidence for cross-sex-typing as a correlate of intellectual abilities is stronger for women than for men.

So far, we have been discussing two mediating factors—repression and passive-dependency—which presumably affect both sexes in the same way. We noted earlier, however, that there were several traits, such as impulsiveness, aggression, and hyperkinesis, which appeared to be positive correlates for girls and negative ones for boys. Kagen, Moss, and Sigel (1963) first called attention to these differences, saying, "It is possible that analytic and nonanalytic responses are the product of different causal agents in boys and girls. Specifically, motoric impulsivity may be one of the primary antecedents of nonanalytic, undifferentiated conceptual products for boys, but of less relevance for girls' conceptual responses." (p. 111.)

How can a mediating process facilitate or inhibit intellectual growth for one sex and not the other? We do not think it necessary to suppose that different psychological principles govern the intellectual development of the two sexes; therefore we would like to explore two alternative possibilities to explain these opposite-direction effects. The first is that we have not been measuring comparable processes in the two sexes, and that when we specify the variables more exactly, same-direction correlations will emerge. For example, when we measure total activity level, we might get opposite correlations for the two sexes between activity level and measures of intellectual performance, because a high total activity level may have a different "meaning" for the two sexes, in the sense that it forms part of a different constellation of attributes. There is some indication from a recent study on activity level (Maccoby et al. 1965) that this is the case. But if we measure a selected aspect of activity, such as the ability to inhibit motor movement or the amount of intersituational variation in activity, we can and do obtain correlations with intellectual performance that are similar for both sexes. It is also possible that scores on total aggression will not relate clearly to intellectual performance, while scores that reflect whether the aggression is directed and instrumental would do so. If these distinctions were made in the measurement of aggression, the sex differences in the way aggression correlates with cognitive performance might well disappear.

The second possible explanation of these opposite-direction correlations involves an assumption of curvilinearity. Let us assume that there is a single personality dimension, running from passive and inhibited at one end of the scale to bold, impulsive, and hyperactive at the other. A tentative hypothesis might be that there is a curvilinear relationship between this dimension and intellectual performance, so that both the very inhibited and the very bold will perform less well, while those who occupy the intermediate positions on the inhibited-impulsiveness dimension will perform optimally. We suggest further that boys and girls, on the average, occupy different positions on the dimension we have described. There is reason to believe that boys are more aggressive, more active, and less passive than girls. Whether the differences are innate or the outcome of social learning is not so important here. The important point is that these temperamental differences do exist. The situation that we hypothesize may be graphed as follows:

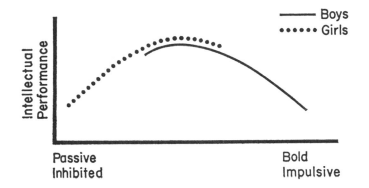

If the hypothesis holds, it would follow that for optimum intellectual performance, most girls need to become less passive and inhibited, while most boys need to become less impulsive. However, for those girls who do happen to be highly impulsive (as much so as the average boy, or even more so), impulsiveness should be a negative factor, as timidity should be for those boys at the passive end of the scale.

A parallel analysis may be made of anxiety as it affects intellectual performance in the two sexes. There is substantial evidence (beginning with the theoretical formulation of the problem by Taylor and Spence, 1952) that the relation of anxiety to performance is curvilinear. Either very high or very low levels of anxiety interfere with performance on a variety of tasks; intermediate levels facilitate performance. If women and girls have a high base level of anxiety, then increases in anxiety above their base level will frequently carry them past the optimum point of the curve, and result in inhibition or disorganization of performance. If boys and men have a low base level of anxiety, increases in anxiety will more often either improve performance, or move them through the middle portions of the curve where changes in performance would not be found.

In evaluating this hypothesis, we must first ask whether the two sexes do in fact differ in their base level of anxiety. As may be seen from the summary in the Oetzel bibliography, there is very strong evidence for greater anxiety in girls when anxiety is measured with paper-and-pencil tests like the CMAS or TASC. However, the tendency for girls to score higher in anxiety on these tests has been attributed to their greater willingness to admit to such feelings, and is not conclusive evidence that any more basic difference exists. The answer to the question will no doubt depend upon how anxiety is defined. In two studies that measure physiological reactions to stress (Sontag 1947, Berry and Martin 1957), females were found to have greater autonomic reactivity. Jersild and Holmes (1935) presented standardized fear situations in a laboratory situation to children of nursery school age, and obtained higher average "fear" scores for girls than boys. Some unpublished work by Kagan done with infants during the first year of life shows that when girls are set down on the floor in a strange room, they cling to the mother's leg longer before crawling away to explore objects; also they are more upset when placed behind a barrier so that the mother is visible but inaccessible. Harlow's finding that monkeys go to the mother for contact comfort when presented with fear stimuli gives us some basis for inferring that the behavior of the infants in Kagan's study was motivated by timidity—i.e., that the girls are more frightened than the boys by the strange situation in which they have been placed. With these various pieces of evidence in mind, we believe it to be a reasonable hypothesis that girls do have a higher base anxiety level than boys, so that increments from this base level might be expected to have a different effect for the two sexes.

We have so far discussed two "personality" dimensions that might bear a curvilinear relation to intellectual performance: anxiety, and a dimension running from inhibited-passive to bold-impulsive. Neither of these dimensions is precisely defined; if we wish to test the validity of the formulation, we must specify more exactly the behavioral dispositions that distinguish the sexes and bear the hypothesized curvilinear relation to intellectual performance. We must note, for example, that although the sexes do differ on such aspects of "impulsivity" as frequency of temper tantrums, aggression, and activity, they do not consistently differ on the "reflectivity-impulsivity" dimension (Kagan et al. 1964), so that this aspect of impulsivity would not be relevant to the explanation of sex differences offered here. Further differentiation will also be needed on the "intellectual performance" dimension. It is quite possible, for example, that "analytic style" and performance on spatial tests are related to impulsiveness or anxiety in the manner described, while certain aspects of verbal ability are not.

GENETIC VERSUS ENVIRONMENTAL CONTRIBUTIONS

In the preceding section, we have discussed sex differences in personality traits as possible mediators of differences in intellectual performance. Assuming that the evidence is sufficient to convince the reader that there is indeed a substantial probability that such attributes as fearfulness, impulsiveness, independence, etc. do have a bearing on intellectual functioning, then it may be valuable to consider briefly the origins of the sex differences in these personality traits, with a view to discovering if the intellectual characteristics of either sex are likely to change as cultural conditions change. To what extent are boys more active or more aggressive because they are trained to adopt these socially defined sex-appropriate characteristics, and to what extent are they more active because of a substratum of biological determination with which environmental inputs must interact? Mischel, in this volume, has taken a social-learning point of view, arguing that the known socialization inputs to the two sexes are sufficiently different in the appropriate ways to produce known sex differences in dependency and aggression (and by implication in other personality traits as well). Hamburg, on the other hand, has presented evidence that in primates sex-specific hormones govern not only specifically sexual behavior, but also various kinds of social behavior. Male-hormone treatment administered to a pregnant animal increases the incidence among the female offspring of rough-and-tumble play, and decreases the tendency to withdraw from the initiations, threats, and approaches of others. An interesting point emerging from Hamburg's report is that sex differences in social behavior may be related to endocrine influences even though there is no detectable sex difference in hormone concentrations at the time the behavior is observed. This point is important because of the fact that present methods of measurement do not reveal any differences between young boys and girls in the concentration of male or female hormones present in their bodies, even though their social behavior might suggest the presence of such a difference. This might be taken to mean that the differences in social behavior could not be a product of differential hormonal factors in the two sexes. Hamburg points to the possibility that hormonal "sensitization" during the prenatal period may contribute to the arousal of sex-appropriate behavior later in the life cycle, when the specific hormone concentrations are no longer present.

D'Andrade, analyzing the cross-cultural evidence in his chapter, notes that certain temperamental differences seem to be cross-culturally universal, and are found even in societies where most of the usual environmental pressures toward sex-typing are absent (e.g., the Kibbutzim in Israel). He also suggests that certain differential behavior in the two sexes is directly conditioned by such physical differences as size, strength, and biological role in the bearing and suckling of children; these differences are then generalized to similar activities and become institutionalized in occupational roles and other cultural prescriptions, in preparation for which anticipatory sex-typing occurs in childhood.

Let us assume, then, that the sex-typed attributes of personality and temperament which we have found to be related to intellectual functioning are the product of the interweaving of differential social demands with certain biological determinants that help to produce or augment differential cultural demands upon the two sexes. The biological underpinnings of the social demands for sex-typed behavior set modal tendencies for cultural demands, and set limits to the range of variation of these demands from one cultural setting to another. Still, within these limits considerable variation does occur, between families, between cultures, and in the nature of the behavior that a social group stereotypes as "feminine" or "masculine." Is there any evidence that such variations are associated with the nature or quality of intellectual performance in the two sexes?

In an attempt to measure cultural influences outside the home, Minuchin (1964) compared the performances of boys and girls in "modern" and "traditional" schools. In this study, an effort was made to control for social class and intellectual ability of the children, in order to isolate the effects of the two school atmospheres. In the traditional school, behavior was more sex-typed during play sessions than in the modern school. And in intellectual tasks, there were greater sex differences in problem solving and coding tasks in the traditional schools than in the modern ones. These findings would be consistent with the hypothesis that strong social demands for sex-typed behavior, such as aggression in boys and conformity-passivity in girls, play a role in producing some of the sex differences we have seen in intellectual performance. The proof of this point, however, would rest on experimental attempts to change the nature of intellectual performance through changes in the social expectations for sex-typed behavior. Only one attempt of this kind has been reported. Carey (1955) attempted to improve problem-solving behavior by changing "attitudes" toward such behavior. Group discussions directed toward improving the subjects' self-confidence in problem-solving tasks were held; these discussions emphasized the fact that it was socially acceptable to excel at problem solving. The discussion sessions improved the performance of college women but not of college men, suggesting that beliefs that skill in problem solving was not appropriate behavior had been an impediment to the normal performance of women but not of men. More such experimental evidence is needed to provide information on the difficulties and possible effects of influencing culturally prescribed behavior. It would be valuable, too, to have information on the extent of sex differences in intellectual performance in societies with high sex-role differentiation, and to compare these findings with similar findings for societies in which sex-role differentiation is minimized.

The findings on socialization practices within families, as they relate to intellectual development in the two sexes, point first of all to the fact that the environmental factors embodied in parent-child interaction do indeed make a difference in the child's intellectual performance. But more importantly, these findings indicate that the same environmental input affects the two sexes differently, and that different factors are associated with optimal performance for boys and girls. The brighter girls tend to be the ones who have not been tied closely to their mother's apron strings, but have been allowed and encouraged to fend for themselves. The brighter boys, on the other hand, have had high maternal warmth and protection in early childhood. We find, then, that environmental effects are not merely something added to, or superimposed upon, whatever innate temperamental differences there are that affect intellectual functioning. Rather, there is a complex interaction. The two sexes would appear to have somewhat different intellectual strengths and weaknesses, and hence different influences serve to counteract the weaknesses and augment the strengths.

REFERENCES

Anastasi, Anne. (1958) *Differential psychology* (3d ed.). New York: Macmillan.

Anastasiow, N. (1963) The relationship of sex role patterns of first-grade boys to success in school. Unpublished doctoral dissertation, Stanford University.

Barron, F. (1957) Originality in relation to personality and intellect. *J. Pers.*, *25*, 730–42.

Bayley, Nancy. (1956) Individual patterns of development. *Child Develpm.*, *27*, 45–74.

———. (1957) Data on the growth of intelligence between 16 and 21 years as measured by the Wechsler-Bellevue Scale. *J. genet. Psychol.*, *90*, 3–15.

———, and Melita H. Oden. (1955) The maintenance of intellectual ability in gifted adults. *J. Geront.*, *10*, 91–107.

———, and E. S. Schaefer. (1964) Correlations of maternal and child behaviors with the development of mental abilities: data from the Berkeley Growth Study. *Soc. Res. Child Develpm. Monogr.*, *29*, No. 6, 3–79.

Beller, E. K. (1962) A study of dependency and aggression in early childhood. Progress Report, Project M-849, Child Development Center, New York, N.Y.

Berry, J. L., and B. Martin. (1957) GSR reactivity as a function of anxiety, instructions and sex. *J. abnorm. soc Psychol.*, *54*, 9–12.

Bieri, J. (1960) Parental identification, acceptance of authority, and within-sex differences in cognitive behavior. *J. aborm. soc. Psychol.*, *60*, 76–79.

Bradway, Katherine P., and Clare W. Thompson. (1962) Intelligence at adulthood: a 25-year follow-up. *J. educ. Psychol.*, *53*, 1–14.

Brim, O. G. (1958) Family structure and sex role learning by children: a further analysis of Helen Kock's data. *Sociometry*, *21*, 1–16.

Carey, Gloria L. (1955) Reduction of sex differences in problem solving by improvement of attitude through group discussion. Unpublished doctoral dissertation, Stanford University.

Carlsmith, Lynn. (1964) Effect of early father absence on scholastic aptitude. *Harvard educ. Rev.*, *34*, 3–21.

Coleman, J. S. (1961) *The adolescent society*. Glencoe, Ill.: The Free Press.

Crandall, V. J., Rachel Dewey, W. Katkovsky, and Anne Preston. (1964) Parents' attitudes and behaviors and grade school children's academic achievements. *J. genet. Psychol.*, *104*, 53–66.

———, W. Katkovsky and Anne Preston. (1962) Motivational and ability determinants of young children's intellectual achievement behaviors. *Child Develpm.*, *33*, 643–61.

———, and A. Rabson. (1960) Children's repetition choices in an intellectual achievement situation, following success and failure. *J. genet. Psychol.*, *97*, 161–68.

Davidson, K. S., and S. B. Sarason. (1961) Test anxiety and classroom observations. *Child Develpm.*, *32*, 199–210.

Ebert, Elizabeth, and Katherine Simmons. (1943) The Brush Foundation study of child growth and development. I: Psychometric tests. *Soc. Res. Child Develpm. Monogr., 8,* No. 2.

French, J. W. (1961) A study of emotional states aroused during examinations. College Entrance Examination Board, Research and Development Reports. March 1961, R.B., 61–66.

Guilford, J. P. (1956) The structure of intellect. *Psychol. Bull., 53,* 267–93.

Haan, Norma (1963) Proposed model of ego functioning: coping and defense mechanisms in relationship to I.Q. change. *Psychol. Monogr., 77,* No. 571.

Harmatz, M. G. (1962) Effects of anxiety, motivating instructions, success and failure reports, and sex of subject upon level of aspiration and performance. Unpublished master's thesis, University of Washington.

Honzig, Marjorie P. (1957) Developmental studies of parent-child resemblance in intelligence. *Child Develpm., 28* (2), 215–27.

Iscoe, I., and Joyce A. Carden. (1961) Field dependence, manifest anxiety, and sociometric status in children. *J. consult. Psychol., 25,* 184.

Jersild, A. T., and F. B. Holmes. (1935) Children's fears. *Child Develpm. Monogr.,* No. 20, 1–356.

Kagan, J., and H. A. Moss. (1962) *Birth to maturity.* New York: John Wiley & Sons.

————, H. A. Moss, and I. E. Sigel. (1963) The psychological significance of styles of conceptualization. In J. C. Wright and J. Kagan (eds.), Basic cognitive processes in children. *Soc. Res. Child Develpm. Monogr., 28,* No. 2.

————, Bernice L. Rosman, Deborah Day, Albert J. and W. Phillips. (1964) Information processing in the child: significance of analytic and reflective attitudes. *Psych. Monogr., 78,* No. 1.

Klausmeier, H. J., and W. Wiersma. (1964) Relationship of sex, grade level, and locale to performance of high I.Q. students on divergent thinking tests. *J. educ. Psychol., 55,* 114–19.

Leiderman, P. H., and D. Shapiro. (1963) A physiological and behavioral approach to the study of group interaction. *Psychosom. Med., 25,* 146–57.

Maccoby, Eleanor E. Woman's intellect. (1963) In S. M. Farber and R. L. Wilson (eds.), *The potential of woman.* New York: McGraw-Hill.

————, Edith M. Dowley, J. W. and R. Degerman. (1965) Activity level and intellectual functioning in normal preschool children. *Child Develpm., 36,* 761–70.

————, J. W. Hagen, L. W. Sontag, and J. Kagan. (1963) Unpublished report, Laboratory of Human Development, Stanford University.

————, and Lucy Rau. (1962) Differential cognitive abilities. Final report, Cooperative research project No. 1040, Owen House, Stanford University.

MacKinnon, D. W. (1962) The nature and nurture of creative talent. *Amer. Psychologist, 17,* 484–95.

McClelland, D., J. W. Atkinson, R. A. Clark, and E. L. Lowell. (1953) *The achievement motive*. New York: Appleton-Century-Crofts.

Milton, G. A. (1957) The effects of sex-role identification upon problem-solving skill. *J. abnorm. soc. Psychol.*, *55*, 208–12.

Minuchin, Patricia. (1964) Sex role concepts and sex typing in childhood as a function of school and home environments. Paper presented at American Orthopsychiatric Association, Chicago.

Moriarty, A. E. (1961) Coping patterns of preschool children in response to intelligence test demands. *Genet. Psychol. Monogr.*, *64*, 3–127.

Moss, H. A., and J. Kagan. (1958) Maternal influences on early I.Q. scores. *Psychol. Rep.*, *4*, 655–61.

———, and J. Kagan. (1962) Unpublished manuscript.

Murphy, Lois B. (1962) *The widening world of childhood*. New York: Basic Books.

Nakamura, C. Y. (1958) Conformity and problem solving. *J. abnorm. soc. Psychol.*, *56*, 315–20.

Oetzel, Roberta (1961) The relationship between sex role acceptance and cognitive abilities. Unpublished master's thesis, Stanford University.

Phillips, B. N., E. Hindsman, and C. McGuire. (1960) Factors associated with anxiety and their relation to the school achievement of adolescents. *Psychol. Rep.*, *7*, 365–72.

Plank, Emma H., and R. Plank. (1954) Emotional components in arithmetic learning as seen through autobiographies. In R. S. Eissler et al. (eds.), *The psychoanalytic study of the child*, Vol. IX. New York: International Universities Press.

Radcliffe committee on graduate education for women. (1956) *Graduate education for women*. Cambridge: Harvard University Press.

Rau, Lucy. (1963) Interpersonal correlates of perceptual-cognitive functions. Paper presented at Society for Research in Child Development, San Francisco.

Russell, D. G., and E. G. Sarason. (1965) Test anxiety, sex, and experimental conditions in relation to anagram solution. *J. Pers. soc. Psychol.*, *1*, 493–96.

Sears, Pauline S. (1963) The effect of classroom conditions on the strength of achievement motive and work output on elementary school children. Final report, Cooperative research project No. 873, Stanford University.

Shaw, M. C., and J. T. McCuen. (1960) The onset of academic under-achievement in bright children. *J. educ. Psychol.*, *51*, 103–8.

Sigel, I. (1964) Sex differences in cognitive functioning re-examined: a functional point of view. Paper presented at Society for Research in Child Development, Berkeley, California.

———, P. Jarman, and H. Hanesian. (1963) Styles of categorization and their perceptual, intellectual, and personality correlates in young children. Unpublished paper, Merrill-Palmer Institute.

Sontag, L. W. (1947) Physiological factors and personality in children. *Child Develpm., 18,* 185–89.

——, C. T. Baker, and Virginia A. Nelson. (1958) Mental growth and personality development: a longitudinal study. *Soc. Res. Child Develpm. Monogr., 23,* No. 68.

Sutton-Smith, B., V. J. Crandall, and J. M. Roberts. (1964) Achievement and strategic competence. Paper presented at the Eastern Psychological Association, April 1964.

Taylor, Janet A., and K. W. Spence. (1952) The relationship of anxiety level to performance in serial learning. *J. exp. Psychol., 44,* 61–64.

Terman, L. M., and Melita H. Oden. (1947) *The gifted child grows up.* Stanford: Stanford Univer. Press.

Terman, L. M., and Leona E. Tyler. (1954) Psychological sex differences. In L. Carmichael (ed.), *Manual of child psychology* (2d ed.) New York: John Wiley & Sons.

Trembly, D. (1964) Age and sex differences in creative thinking potential. Paper presented at the American Psychological Association's annual convention.

Walter, D., Lorraine S. Denzler, and E. G. Sarason. (1964) Anxiety and the intellectual performance of high school students. *Child Develpm., 35,* 917–26.

Witkin, H. A., R. B. Dyk, H. F. Faterson, D. R. Goodenough, and S. A. Karp. (1962) *Psychological differentiation.* New York: John Wiley & Sons.

——, Helen B. Lewis, M. Herzman, Karen Machover, Pearl B. Meissner, and S. Wapner. (1954) *Personality through perception.* New York: Harper.

Yonge, G. D. (1964) Sex differences in cognitive functioning as a result of experimentally induced frustration. *J. exp. Educ., 32,* 275–80.

A Social-Learning View of Sex Differences in Behavior

WALTER MISCHEL

Stanford University

This chapter presents a social-learning interpretation of the development of sex-typed behaviors. The first section reviews some basic social-learning principles and their relevance for an understanding of sex differences in social behavior. The second section examines some of the major findings on sex differences, and demonstrates that these findings are consistent with expectations from the present formulation.

THE SEX-TYPING PROCESS

Sex-typed Behaviors

In social-learning theory, *sex-typed behaviors* may be defined as behaviors that typically elicit different rewards for one sex than for the other. In other words, sex-typed behaviors have consequences that vary according to the sex of the performer. Because of these differential consequences sex-typed behaviors tend to have different values and to occur with different frequencies for the two sexes. The consequences that follow sex-typed behavior do not necessarily have to be administered by others; they may also be self-administered.

According to social-learning theory, the acquisition and performance of sex-typed behaviors can be described by the same learning principles used to analyze any other aspect of an individual's behavior.* In addi-

This review of the literature, and many of the author's studies cited in it, was supported in part by Research Grant MH6830 from the United States Public Health Service, National Institutes of Health.

* The learning principles discussed in this chapter are elaborated more fully by Rotter (1954) and Bandura and Walters (1963).

tion to discrimination, generalization, and observational learning, these principles include the patterning of reward, nonreward, and punishment under specific contingencies, and the principles of direct and vicarious conditioning.

Sex-typing is the process by which the individual *acquires* sex-typed behavior patterns: first he learns to *discriminate* between sex-typed behavior patterns, then to *generalize* from these specific learning experiences to new situations, and finally to *perform* sex-typed behavior. In addition, the sex-typing process includes direct and vicarious conditioning of a multitude of stimuli that acquire differential value and elicit different emotional and attitudinal responses from the sexes. Statements about "appropriate" sex-typing involve inferences about the extent to which the individual performs behaviors that are considered to be typical of his own sex, and the degree to which these behaviors have acquired value for him.

Acquisition of Sex-typed Behavior

Observational learning from live and symbolic models (i.e., films, television, and books) is the first step in the acquisition of sex-typed behavior. Most of the research on the development of sex differences has been guided by such Freudian-derived concepts as "identification," "incorporation," "internalization," and "introjection." The use and misuse of these terms has been discussed extensively in the literature (e.g., Rotter 1954, Sanford 1955, Hill 1960, Bandura and Walters 1963); and several pleas have been made to abolish them altogether (e.g., Hill 1960). It has been pointed out (Bandura and Walters 1963) that observational learning is generally labeled "imitation" in experimental psychology and "identification" in personality theories. Despite the fact that numerous distinctions have been proposed, the two terms really describe the same behavioral phenomena: both "imitation" and "identification" refer to the tendency for a person to reproduce the actions, attitudes, and emotional responses exhibited by real-life or symbolic models. It is of considerable theoretical importance that observational learning can take place without direct reinforcement to the observer. A wide range of direct and indirect imitative responses may be elicited, or inhibited, both in the presence and in the absence of a model.

A number of recent studies (e.g., Bandura and Walters 1963) describe in detail some of the conditions that tend to facilitate observational learning. A nurturant relationship between the observer and the model seems to facilitate imitation (e.g., see Bandura and Huston 1961), but is not a necessary condition for its occurrence. There is considerable evidence for an association between a social agent's power and willingness to reward, and his effectiveness as a model (e.g., P. S. Sears 1953, Payne and Mussen 1956, Mussen and Distler 1959, Mussen 1961, Mussen and Rutherford 1963, Mischel and Grusec 1966). Moreover, children imitate in varying degrees the behaviors of more than one model, even when one model is decidely more powerful and rewarding than the others (Bandura, Ross, and Ross 1963a); therefore the behavior produced by this kind of imitation has considerable novelty, and is not merely a faithful copy of the behavior of a single model. The degree to which children adopt a model's behavior is affected by the consequences, observed or inferred, of the model's behavior. Thus children who observed a model displaying aggressive behavior successfully were more likely later to act aggressively themselves than those who observed a model displaying aggressive behavior that led to negative consequences (Bandura, Ross, and Ross 1963b).

When boys and girls are exposed to male and female adults who vary drastically in their power or control over resources, they tend to imitate the behaviors of the more powerful adult (Bandura, Ross, and Ross 1963a). In such a situation, if the male adult has greater control over resources than the female, both boys and girls imitate his behavior to a greater degree. Likewise, if the female adult has greater power over rewards than the male, her behavior tends to be imitated more frequently by both boys and girls. This experiment demonstrates that cross-sex imitation occurs, and is facilitated when the opposite-sex model has greater power than the same-sex model. It becomes clear why cultures —all of which vary in the degree to which one sex or the other controls valuable resources—produce differential degrees of cross-sex behavior. When females have markedly less access to powerful rewards than males, they may emulate male behavior to the degree that such cross-sex behavior is tolerated. Moreover, cross-sex behavior is increased by exposure to the opposite-sex behavior of older children as well as adults. This is reflected in the greater incidence of cross-sex behavior in children who have older opposite-sex siblings (Brim 1958).

A recent study (Mischel and Grusec 1966) shows that children acquire components of observed behavior even when the child is the object of the behaviors and experiences direct aversive consequences as a result of them. The authors found that children acquired, rehearsed, and transmitted components of punitive behaviors that had been directed at them by social agents. These behaviors included imposing aversive delay periods on the child and verbally criticizing his behavior. Moreover, the extent to which children subsequently rehearsed these behaviors and transmitted them to another person was affected by the power and willingness to reward shown by the social agent who initially performed them.

The degree to which the observer attends to the model determines in part the extent and accuracy of his observational or imitative learning, and his attention is in turn presumably affected by such variables as his previous reinforcement history with similar models. The extent to which the child is exposed to same-sex models may vary considerably, but in most cultures, and certainly in ours, exposure to models of both sexes is sufficient for the child to acquire many responses from the repertoires of both sexes.

The child learns many behaviors through contiguity, with no direct reinforcement. Factors that increase the degree to which the observer attends to the model's behaviors are likely to increase the extent and accuracy of learning. Characteristics of the model, such as his power and willingness to reward, and probably the observer's own motivational state, are likely to increase the observer's attentiveness. The manner in which the model's behavior is presented, with respect to the frequency, rate, and clarity of presentation, critically affects the extent to which the modeled behaviors are acquired. Through observational learning boys and girls typically acquire many of the behaviors of both sexes. Men know how to apply face powder, and women know how to place cigars in their mouths, although through differential practice they may differ in the skill with which they execute such behaviors, particularly when the behaviors involve complex motor skills.

Performance and Response Consequences

The consequences that occur when a child first attempts to perform sex-typed behaviors are critical determinants of their subsequent performance. In addition to the effects of direct reinforcement for specific behaviors, the child learns to make generalizations about sex differences in response-consequences for complex patterns of behavior, both from his own experiences and from his observations of live and symbolic models. These experiences include observational learning of the labeling of behaviors with respect to their appropriateness or inappropriateness for the sexes.

Thus, although boys and girls learn the behaviors of both sexes, they differ in the degree to which they perform and value these behaviors. The present definition of "sex-typed behavior" stresses the difference in outcome as a function of the performer's sex. Boys and girls discover that the consequences for performing such behaviors are affected by their sex, and therefore soon perform them with different frequency. These reinforcement consequences are both direct and inferred, and most sex-typed behaviors need not be performed by the child in order for him to learn that they have differential consequences for the sexes.

The fact that children rapidly learn differences in parental expectancies concerning sex-appropriate behavior is illustrated in a study by Fauls and Smith (1956). Five-year-olds of both sexes were exposed to a series of paired pictures depicting a sex-appropriate and a sex-inappropriate activity. Both their personal preferences and their beliefs about the activity that mother and father would prefer for boys and girls were elicited (e.g., "Which does mother want the boy to do?"). Boys chose "masculine" activities more often than girls did, and children of both sexes indicated that the parents preferred the activities appropriate to the child's sex more often than the sex-inappropriate activities.

Anticipated and Inferred Response Consequences

Reinforcement is an important determinant of response selection in performance. However, response acquisition or learning is regulated by sensory and cognitive processes that may be facilitated by reinforcement but are not dependent upon it (Bandura and Walters 1963). Such learning includes concept formation and a semantic repertoire. Children learn the physical and social similarities and differences between the sexes, and rapidly identify their own sex. In addition to learning the anatomical and socially correlated distinctions between the sexes, they also gradually acquire information, in varying degrees, about the kinds of behavior that are socially approved for the two sexes. This learning can affect the child's sex-typed activities by providing information about probable outcomes for responses before they are actually performed. Thus it should be clear that performance is often determined by inferred response consequences rather than by direct "trial and error" learning. With humans, information transmitted through verbal or other symbols can dramatically reduce the number of trials needed for errorless performance. Instructions on how to reach the nearest exit in a fire are more effective than trial-and-error gropings in the dark. Likewise, a man does not have to be arrested for wearing dresses in public to learn about the consequences for such behavior.

Conditioning, Cognitive Mediation, and Values

Differences in the attitudes and emotional responses of the sexes to specific stimuli arise from differences in their conditioning histories; and again conditioning can be both direct and indirect. It has been repeatedly demonstrated that a stimulus, once conditioned by contiguity with an unconditioned stimulus (e.g., food or pain-producing shock), can serve as the basis for further higher-order conditioning (Mower 1960). Through such higher-order conditioning, words and other symbols can become powerful conditioned stimuli with the capacity to elicit autonomic responses. These words or symbols in turn affect the value of other previously neutral stimuli if they become associated with them (Staats and Staats 1957, 1958). For example, when verbal stimuli with negative connotations, like "ugly" or "bitter," are associated with other labels, such as the names of persons or nations, these latter words soon acquire unpleasant connotations. In contrast, when the same names are paired with positively conditioned words like "sweet" and "pretty," they become rated as pleasant. Extrapolating to sex differences, it is apparent that numerous activities, goals, interests, and the like acquire differential value for the sexes by being differentially associated with positive or negative outcomes and labels. Labels like "sissy," "pansy," "tough," or "sweet" acquire differential value for the sexes, and their application can easily affect the value of other previously neutral labels.

First-order and higher-order conditioning can also occur vicariously when a person receives no direct positive or aversive stimulation, but merely observes contiguity between a stimulus and an emotional response exhibited by another person (Berger 1962). For example, adults who repeatedly observed the sounding of a buzzer paired with feigned fear responses displayed by the experimenter's confederate developed conditioned psychogalvanic responses to the sound of the buzzer alone (Bandura and Rosenthal 1966). Furthermore, when conditioned stimuli become firmly established, their eliciting power transfers or generalizes not only to physically similar stimuli (Grant and Shiller 1953) but also to semantically related stimuli (Lacey and Smith 1954); these generalizations often involve complex cognitive networks. Thus direct and indirect first-order and higher-order conditioning significantly affects the emotional responses of the sexes in a multitude of different and complex ways.

It is often mistakenly assumed that social-learning theories deny the existence of mediating cognitive processes. Men and women, as well as boys and girls, do think. They experience wishes, fears, and hopes; they even dream. The present social-learning view does not deny such intrapsychic activities. The critical point of difference between this position and others (e.g., see Kohlberg's chapter in this volume) is in the referents selected for the analysis of behavior. In the present formulation, discriminable antecedent events, rather than inferred intrapsychic activities, are used to predict and analyze behavior. Thus, although the existence of mediating processes is acknowledged, they are not attributed the causal powers usually assigned to them in "cognitive" and "dynamic" theories. Instead, behavior is predicted on the basis of an analysis of the relevant social-learning history and the specific stimulus situations and contingencies in which the predicted behavior occurs. Social-learning theory does not consider a person "empty" or "passive": it simply views an individual's social behavior as under the control of internal and external stimuli whose effects are lawfully determined by his previous learning history.

Kohlberg rightly states that boys and girls label themselves as male and female, and that these judgments of sex identity, once firmly established, tend to be irreversible. However, the abundant individual differences found within each sex, and the fact that the behaviors of the sexes overlap to a great degree, suggest that there are many ways to be a boy or girl—and even more ways to be a man or woman. Sex differences in behavior are not, for the most part, universal entities. The fact that most sex differences in behavior are determined by the specific responses of a particular culture to such behavior is illustrated by the failure to replicate in Holland (Houwink 1950) more than a few of the M-F items that differentiated the sexes in the United States (Terman and Miles 1936).

In the cognitive-developmental view proposed by Kohlberg (p. 89, this volume), "once the boy has stably categorized himself as male, he then values positively those objects and acts consistent with his gender identity." According to the present view, the child's behaviors and values are determined not by his gender role, but by his social-learning history. Moreover, there is little current evidence that cognitive changes in opinions, beliefs, or values produce behavior changes (Festinger 1964). On the contrary, there is considerable evidence (e.g., Festinger 1957, Brehm and Cohen 1962) that cognitive and value changes occur as a result of particular behavioral performances. That is, values and cognitions are realigned to make them consistent with behavior, and may even be used to justify behavior. An individual who eats grasshoppers and can find no external justification for his behavior feels they must be delicious.

Self-reinforcement and Interactions between Observational Learning and Direct Training

Although sex differences in self-reward patterns have received little systematic attention, it seems likely that some of the major differences in the behaviors of the sexes reflect differences in the kinds and levels of standards adopted for self-reward in different performance areas. There are probably very great sex differences in the performance levels used to evaluate achievements in areas as diverse as arithmetic, baseball, and child care. Some recent research (e.g., Kanfer and Marston 1963, Bandura and Kupers 1964, Mischel and Liebert 1966) illustrates how phenomena such as the "internalization of standards," in which the organism is clearly "active," can be explained by social-learning principles. To document this, and to show the interaction between observational and direct-training experiences, one of these studies (Mischel and Liebert 1966) is described in some detail below.

Humans evaluate their own performance and frequently set standards that determine in part the conditions under which they reward or punish themselves. Failure to meet self-imposed performance standards often results in self-denial or even harsher self-punishment, whereas attainment of self-imposed standards more typically leads to liberal self-reward and a variety of self-congratulatory responses. Research on infrahumans may find it easy to neglect this phenomenon, but it is apparent that, for humans, self-administered reinforcements constitute strong incentives both for learning and for the maintenance of behavior patterns. Undoubtedly the sexes differ in the kinds of standards they set for themselves in many performance areas.

In life situations reward standards are usually transmitted by individuals who exhibit their own self-reward criteria and also reinforce the observer's adherence to particular criteria. The modeled and directly reinforced behaviors do not have to be congruent and the criteria used by social agents for administering rewards to themselves may be (and often are) different from the criteria they impose on others. Consider, for example, the father who points out the virtues of self-denial and hard work to his child while simultaneously and persistently indulging himself. Frequent reference is made to the importance of "consistency" in child-rearing practices; consistency in this case usually means consistency in training techniques rather than consistency between the model's training procedures and his own behavior. The study to be described investigated the effects of discrepancies in the stringency of the self-reward criteria used by an adult and the standards he imposed on a child (Mischel and Liebert 1966).

Children participated with a female adult model in a task that seemingly required skill but on which scores were experimentally controlled. A plentiful supply of tokens that could be exchanged for rewards was available to both the model and the subject. In one experimental group the model rewarded herself only for high performances but guided the subject to reward himself for lower achievements; in a second group the model rewarded herself for low performances but encouraged the subject to reward himself only for high achievements; in the third group the model rewarded herself only for high performances and guided the child to reward himself only for equally high achievements. After exposure to these experimental procedures, measures were obtained of the self-reward patterns that the children displayed in the model's absence.

It was reasoned that the reward criteria adopted by subjects would reflect both the criteria the model had used for herself and the criteria she had imposed on the subjects. If the observed and imposed criteria were consistent, they should be adopted readily. Therefore, greatest stringency would be shown by those children who were held to a stringent standard and also observed a model who was stringent with herself. These children would be more likely to use higher standards for reward than either the children who received the same stringent direct training but observed a lenient model or those who were permitted leniency themselves. Moreover, if the observed and imposed criteria were discrepant, the less stringent alternative should be adopted. When the criterion leading to more reward was the one that the subjects were directly trained to adopt, they would have little conflict about rewarding themselves generously in the model's absence, and would maintain the lenient criterion on which they were trained. In contrast, those who were trained to be stringent but observed a more lenient model would reward themselves more liberally when there were no external constraints. In the model's absence their behavior would reflect conflict about adopting the lower criteria yielding more frequent reward used by their model and the more stringent standards that had been imposed on them. Therefore it was anticipated that subjects would adopt lenient criteria more frequently when they had been permitted greater leniency themselves than when they observed it in another. All these hypotheses were strongly supported by the data. Moreover, in a post-test in which the children demonstrated the game to another younger child, they consistently imposed on him the same standards that they had adopted for themselves.

The results of this experiment showed how patterns of self-reinforcement may be affected jointly by the criteria displayed by social models and the standards directly imposed on the observer, with the resultant behavior determined by a predictable interaction of both processes. Perhaps most interesting is the fact that children who were trained to adopt stringent criteria by a model who set similarly stringent standards for herself adopted and transmitted more stringent reward criteria than those who received the identical direct training from a model who exhibited greater leniency in her own self-reward. Many seeming paradoxes in the relationships between child-training practices and the child's subsequent behavior may reflect insufficient attention to the discrepancies between the behaviors the child observes and the behaviors he is directly trained or guided to perform. A mother who tries to train her daughter to be "feminine" while she herself behaves in a "masculine" fashion might very well rear a child whose scores show conflict on masculinity-femininity scales.

Response Selection and Specific Contingencies

In any given situation a number of previously learned response alternatives are available to the individual. Each response in an array or repertoire of responses can be thought of as having a particular probability for occurring or being elicited in that stimulus situation. Each response or response pattern has a consequence associated with it, both on the basis of previous outcomes with the same or related responses in similar situations, and the inferred consequences in the present situation. Each response consequence likewise has a particular reward value or incentive value associated with it. The response pattern that occurs is the one with the greatest probability of leading to the most valued outcome available in that situation.

Both psychoanalytic theories and trait theories (e.g., Guilford 1959) assume that individuals have response dispositions or traits that are fairly stable and general, that exist in the person and are manifested relatively early in life. These traits are viewed as main determinants of behavior and are thought to depend very little on specific situational contingencies between particular responses and their outcomes. Much of the research on sex differences has been guided by such trait formulations, with a search for the general dimensions, or traits, on which the sexes differ. Probably the main dimensions used most frequently in studies of sex differences are aggression and dependency.

Social-learning theory makes no assumptions about the generality or consistency of behavior patterns across stimulus situations. The extent to which similar response patterns are manifested in a variety of situations is viewed as a function of the degree of learned stimulus generalization for that response pattern and the specific contingencies in the situation rather than as a function of relatively situation-free underlying traits. The fact that individuals discriminate between contingencies, even in behaviors often used as referents for stable traits, has been demonstrated often. For example, Mischel and Staub (1965) investigated delay of reward behavior by measuring children's choices of immediate, less valuable rewards as opposed to delayed but more valuable rewards. As a first step, children obtained either positive information (success), negative information (failure), or no information at all for their performance on a series of tasks. Thereafter the children made real choices between immediately available, less valuable noncontingent rewards and more valuable contingent rewards. The contingencies for attainment of the more valuable rewards were successful performances on tasks similar and dissimilar to the tasks the children had already performed. A main effect was due to the specific contingencies, with children clearly discriminating between them and choosing more valuable rewards more frequently when the contingency for their attainment involved less risk. Children who had failed on related earlier tasks chose rewards contingent on successful performance on similar tasks less frequently than those who had succeeded. The behavior of children who had obtained no information about their initial performance was determined by their generalized expectancies for success on such tasks, presumably based on previous outcomes in similar situations.

Although these findings are not surprising, they point to the importance of considering specific contingencies for the accurate prediction of behavior. There is no reason to expect behaviors such as aggression and dependency to be stable across situations unless the situations and contingencies are similar. The degree to which individuals discriminate between situations in their performance of behavior is also documented in a study of highly aggressive boys (Bandura 1960). Parents who punished aggression in the home (but simultaneously exhibited aggressive behavior themselves, and encouraged it in their sons' peer relationships) produced boys who were nonaggressive at home but markedly aggressive at school.

The Specificity of Sex-typed Behavior

In view of the foregoing, it is understandable that intercorrelations between different measures of sex-typing often do not achieve statistical significance or replication when retested (e.g., Borstelman 1961). When we consider the probable differences in outcome to an American adolescent boy for sewing a dress during school recess and sewing a tent patch during a boy scout expedition, we can understand the degree to which specific consequences of sex-typed behaviors are determined by the situation in which they are performed. The object at which behavior is directed and numerous other details of the situation may determine the consequences of the behavior. For example, males are expected to show physical aggression toward some males under some circumstances but rarely toward old men, senators, or their grandfathers. Moreover, boys and girls may respond differently to their own behavior for the same aggressive or dependent act in the absence of external reinforcing agents and self-administer different consequences for the same response.

We can document this argument with examples from dependency research. Although Beller (1955) found correlations ranging from .48 to .83 in teacher ratings of five dependency components in nursery school (and similarly high correlations for components of "independence"), there is a possibility of a "halo" effect in the teachers' ratings. Mann (1959), rating 41 nursery school children on six kinds of dependency behavior, found only one of fifteen intercorrelations among components significant. Likewise, Heathers (1953), observing nursery school children, found that frequencies of "affection-seeking" and "approval-seeking" were unrelated. R. Sears (1963) found only very modest intercorrelations between five observational ratings of dependency for preschool girls and no support for consistency in boys.

Factor analyses also reveal multiple factors for what appear to be similar behaviors. Thus Gewirtz (1956) did a factor analysis of nine observational measures of attention-seeking, and found that even this one dependency component may be at least two-dimensional. One factor seemed to involve direct, active verbal attempts to maintain the attention of the adult; the other involved nonverbal passive actions. It should be noted that the interrelationships between measures of dependence and independence are also unclear (Hartup 1963).

Of course, traits can only be inferred from behavorial measurements, which themselves contain "errors of measurement," but even psychometricians are granting that trait fluctuations reflect more than imperfections in the measuring instruments (Loevinger 1957). The unimpressive intercorrelations frequently obtained between different measures used as referents for either "dependency" or "aggression" re-emphasize both the importance of specificity in the analysis of sex-typed behaviors and the need for focusing upon specific contingencies in specific situations when analyzing the antecedents of sex-typed behaviors. Indeed, the utility of describing behavior with molar trait units (e.g., dependency) is increasingly questioned (e.g., Brim 1960, Hartup 1963).

Consider the sex differences in the intercorrelations between measures that are subcategories of a broader class of sex-typed behaviors (e.g., various dependency measures such as "touching and holding," or "positive attention"). If a child has been rewarded persistently for "positive attention-seeking," but "touching and being near" has either been unrewarded or has led to negative consequences, a positive correlation between the two measures will not be obtained. For any class of sex-typed behaviors there may be systematic differences in the extent to which subcategories of that behavior tend to have correlated or uncorrelated outcomes for the two sexes. The child learns about these outcomes both through his own experiences and through observational learning in specific situations, and then generalizes and discriminates on the basis of these experiences. For example, certain forms of dependency may be sanctioned more frequently for females than for males; and the sexes may differ in the amount and kind of discriminations and generalizations they learn in particular behavior areas. To the extent that this occurs, sex differences are to be expected in the degree to which subcategory measures are intercorrelated. Some support for sex differences in the generality of particular patterns of sex-typed behaviors comes in the form of more (and stronger) intercorrelations for girls than boys on five observation measures of dependency (R. Sears 1963), whereas the reverse holds for aggression, with more intercorrelations among aggression variables for boys than for girls (Lansky et al. 1961, R. Sears 1961).

The development of such discriminations and generalizations is based on more than direct initial outcomes and physical similarity between stimuli. The labeling used by parents and other live and symbolic models is of major importance in developing discriminations and generalizations. For either sex the "appropriateness" of certain sex-linked behaviors changes both with the situation and the age level. For example, different forms of "dependency" may be labeled as broadly acceptable (leading to positive or at least nonaversive outcomes) in many situations for the female but not the male. To the degree that this occurs, higher intercorrelations between dependency measures in different situations should be found for females.

Likewise, there may be systematic sex differences in the kinds of behaviors that are reinforced uniformly and over a long period of time. For example, a variety of dependent behaviors may be sanctioned for both sexes when they are very young; later, however, dependency in boys becomes increasingly unacceptable, although similar dependent behaviors in girls may be condoned. Such age-correlated differences in outcomes would produce sex differences in the temporal stability of particular sex-typed behavior patterns. A longitudinal study by Kagan and Moss (1962) suggests that this indeed occurs. In this study childhood dependency and passivity were related to adult dependency and passivity for women, but not for men, and conversely, "the developmental consistency for aggression was noticeably greater for males" (p. 95).

Inferences from Test Behavior

Research on sex differences has relied heavily on self-report measures. From a social-learning viewpoint, the determinants of such self-reports may be different from those affecting behavior in more natural situations, and it is hazardous to extrapolate from behaviors reported on a questionnaire to behaviors in a nontest situation. Statements about differences in sex-appropriate behaviors are probably correlated, but very imperfectly, with the actual sex-determined response consequences to the performer of such behavior in a specific situation. For example, although hunting would undoubtedly be considered a "masculine" activity on most questionnaires about sex differences, and more males than females would list it as a preferred activity, the response consequences for a properly attired lady riding gracefully to hounds are not necessarily less positive than for her gentleman companion.

The admission of particular responses in a testing situation may have different value and may lead to different consequences because of the individual's sex. For example, self-reports about test anxiety are apt to be less acceptable for school-age boys than for school-age girls. Sex stereotypes suggest that admitting anxiety, especially about school matters, is not considered "manly" for boys. This is congruent with the finding by Sarason et al. (1960) that boys have consistently lower scores on self-report anxiety measures. This does not necessarily indicate that self-reports about high test anxiety are considered sex-appropriate for girls. It may be that although boys are not supposed to report anxiety about schoolwork, girls may either do so, or not do so, with neither response leading to negative consequences. Therefore the finding that boys report less anxiety than girls should not be taken as evidence that boys "have" less anxiety than girls: the data merely show that girls report more anxiety than boys.

Sex differences may exist on self-reports when none exist in nontest behavior and vice versa. For example, on a self-report measure involving hypothetical choices between immediate but smaller rewards and delayed but larger rewards, girls show significantly greater willingness to wait for larger rewards. However, in situations in which the child has to make real choices between one or the other, no sex differences are found (Mischel 1966). The above findings show that sex differences in self-report or self-description and in overt behavior do not necessarily correspond with each other. Boys may be less willing than girls to report "unmanly" feelings, and girls may be less willing to report "impulsiveness," but such self-reports need not be correlated with sex differences in nontest behavior.

A more complicated manifestation of the same phenomenon may be involved in a recent study (Crandall, Katkovsky, and Preston 1962). Expectancy statements about intellectual ability were found to be highly positively correlated with measures of intelligence for boys but negatively for girls. As Crandall et al. suggest, boys and girls may be differentially rewarded for stating intellectual-achievement expectations and standards. Boys may be rewarded for stating expectations and standards that are accurate (e.g., they are taught to "face the facts"), whereas girls may be criticized for stating high, albeit realistic, expectations (they are taught that "boasting" is unfeminine).

As another illustration, consider the finding that women tend to be more "persuasible" than men (e.g., Hovland et al. 1959). These differences may in part reflect the fact that most of the tasks or topics used have different value for the sexes. Studies that compare behavior change in the two sexes in response to influence must take two considerations into account: sex differences in the reward value of the behavior that is being influenced, and sex differences in the reward value of the consequences to the person for changing that behavior. Changes in statements about expectancies for academic success following manipulated success-and-failure experiences provide a further example. First, the specific academic performance areas involved may have different values for the sexes (e.g., mechanical engineering, home economics). Second, the act of changing such verbal expectancy statements may have different reward values for the sexes. Probably the acknowledgment of generalized or pervasive failure has more of a negative outcome for males than for females. Therefore female college students are more likely than males to lower their expectancy statement following failure, particularly in public situations, although there are no sex differences following success (Mischel 1958).

The manner in which sex differences in reward values may produce sex differences in the amount of behavior change is illustrated by the work of McClelland and his colleagues (1953). Achievement motivation was increased for males, but not for females, following a test reported to measure intelligence under conditions designed to stimulate achievement needs. However, when the intervening experience involved a challenge to social rather than intellectual acceptability, achievement scores increased significantly in females but not in males.

The specificity of sex-typed responses illustrated in the preceding section indicates that sex-typed responses are affected by the situation in which they are made and by such variables as the sex of the person eliciting the response (E), with interaction effects between sex of E and sex of S. Such interactions have been reported in studies of dependency and imitation (e.g., Rosenblith 1959, Gewirtz 1958). However, a well-controlled study (Borstelmann 1961) investigating the interaction between the sex of S and the sex of E in preschool children's sex-typed preferences (Brown 1956) and two other choice procedures found no significant effects. In Borstelmann's study children merely indicated choice preferences with respect to interesting objects and activities. There is no reason to expect behavior to be affected by E's sex unless S has learned that the particular behavior will lead to different consequences as a function of the observer's sex. For example, achievement needs inferred from TAT themes are positively related to choice preferences for delayed larger, as opposed to immediate smaller, rewards for adolescent boys tested by male E's, and negatively related for adolescent girls tested by female E's (Metzner and Mischel 1962). With opposite-sex pairs the relationships between the two variables are negligible. These relationships, which have been replicated, may merely reflect the fact that adolescent girls who have learned to wait for rewards and to anticipate the consequences of their own behavior are less likely to expect positive consequences for telling achievement-oriented stories to women, whereas young men who delay immediate gratification have learned that achievement-oriented stories are appropriate and expected when the stories are elicited by male experimenters. Many reported sex differences in correlational patterns may reflect mediation by such situational variables. The interrelationships between subject, experimenter, and situational variables have recently become the focus of much research (e.g., Sarason and Minard 1963).

DIFFERENCES BETWEEN THE SEXES

In our culture the two sex-typed behavior patterns that have received most research attention are aggression and dependency. Most of the differences between the sexes in the frequency of behaviors reported and reviewed in the literature (see the bibliography in this volume) can be interpreted as reflecting sex differences in the direct and inferred response consequences and reward values of these behaviors. Some of the main reported differences for aggression and dependency will be reviewed briefly.

Aggression

Sex differences in aggression have been noted in children of three years; indeed, aggression has become one of the main defining variables in delineations of masculine and feminine behavior (R. Sears 1965). Fairly consistently, boys show greater physical aggression and more "negativistic" behavior (e.g., negative attention-getting, antisocial aggression, physical aggression). There are fewer sex differences found for verbal aggression; occasionally girls are more verbally aggressive than boys. Girls tend to show greater "prosocial" aggression, e.g., stating of rules with threats of punishment for breaking them.

The above findings seem consistent with reported sex differences in direct training with respect to aggression. For example, Sears, Maccoby, and Levin (1957) found that parents made the greatest distinctions in the rearing of boys and girls in the area of aggression. A significantly larger proportion of boys were permitted to express aggression toward their parents; boys were also allowed to show more aggression to other children, and were more frequently encouraged to fight back if another child started a fight. The finding that girls obtained somewhat more praise for "good" behavior, and were somewhat more often subjected to withdrawal of love for "bad" behavior, suggests a possible antecedent for the development of greater "prosocial" aggression (e.g., strong verbalizations about the goodness or badness of behavior, punishment and threats for bad behavior, and approval for verbal righteousness). The above relationships, although not strong, are consistent with the view that physical or antisocial aggression is less sanctioned for girls than boys in our culture, and indeed that physical aggression is expected and rewarded for boys more than it is for girls. In contrast, "prosocial" aggression, which is tolerated in girls, is probably more readily labeled "sissy stuff" and is unlikely to be rewarded either by peers or by parents when displayed by boys.

Recent laboratory studies by Bandura (1965) on preschool children's imitation of aggressive models show that sex differences in aggression can be a function of different response consequences for aggressive behavior. In several studies Bandura and his colleagues found that after exposure to aggressive models, boys tended to perform more imitative physical aggression than girls (Bandura and Walters 1963). In a later study (Bandura 1965) boys and girls again observed an aggressive model (on film) who was either rewarded, punished, or left without consequences. As predicted, post-exposure tests revealed that response consequences to the model had produced differential amounts of imitative behavior, with children in the model-punished condition performing significantly fewer imitative aggressive responses than the children in the other two groups. The next phase of the experiment is of greatest interest for the present discussion. Children in all three treatment conditions were then offered attractive reinforcements (pretty sticker pictures and additional juice treats) for aggressive behavior. The introduction of these positive incentives for performance of aggressive behaviors practically wiped out the previous disparity between the performances of the sexes. The author further suggests that the inhibitory effects of differing reinforcement histories for aggression were clearly reflected in the finding that during the reward phase of the experiment boys were more easily disinhibited than girls.

These results indicate that although boys and girls may be similar in their knowledge of aggressive responses, they differ in their performance of such responses because of the sex-determined response-consequences they have previously obtained and observed for such behavior. It is, of course, also quite likely that males and females learn to attend differentially to male and female models, and there is some evidence that persons attend more closely to behaviors displayed by members of their own sex (Maccoby et al. 1958). Likewise, the sexes may have different degrees of exposure to male and female models, and may therefore differ even in the repertoires of behaviors they acquire. For example, it would not be surprising if males are more exposed to male models displaying a wide variety of aggressive skills and behaviors (e.g., TV wrestlers), and that they consequently acquire (as well as practice) a more elaborate (or at least different) repertoire of such behaviors.

Dependency

No strong sex differences in dependency are observed at early ages (e.g., nursery school), with the possible exception of greater male incidence of "negative attention" (R. Sears 1965), which, in any case, is related to aggression measures. But even at the early ages there is some trend toward greater dependency on the part of girls. At older ages (high school and college) girls are consistently higher on dependency measures (see Classified Summary, p. 327). These findings seem consistent with the widely assumed greater permissiveness toward female dependency in our culture.

The greater incidence of dependent behavior for girls, and the greater incidence of aggressive behavior for boys, seems directly explicable in social-learning terms. Dependent behaviors are less rewarded for males, and physically aggressive behaviors are less rewarded for females, in our culture; consequently there are mean differences between the sexes in the frequency of such behaviors after the first few years of life. Unfortunately, present evidence that the sexes are indeed treated differentially by their parents with respect to the above behaviors is far from firm, and much more detailed investigations are needed of the differential reward patterns and modeling procedures used by mothers, fathers, and other models. The current empirical evidence is equivocal, although consistent with a social-learning view. For example, recent studies (e.g., Carlson 1963) report that parental "attitudes" differ toward boys and girls. Certainly this seems reasonable if one recalls that even the arrival of newborns in our culture is heralded with different color schemes and decor in the nursery. Similarly, Droppleman and Schaefer (1961) obtained separate ratings of fathers and mothers made by seventh-grade boys and girls on a number of rearing variables. Girls, more often than boys, reported that both parents were affectionate, and, less often than boys, reported that parents were rejecting, hostile, and ignoring. Girls also reported more than boys did that they had received affection as children. Both sexes said that mother gave more affection than the father. Likewise, Kagan and Moss (1962) found differences in the temporal stability of maternal variables for boys and girls. As Kagan and Moss suggest: "It is possible that girls and boys receive different patterns of maternal treatment during the childhood years, and a more rigorous, microscopic examination of the mother-child interaction might reveal the details of these differences." (p. 209.)

As these examples suggest, most field studies investigating antecedents of dependency have tended to focus on generalized parental variables as antecedent socialization conditions. Such generalized variables as affection, child-centeredness, indulgence, and acceptance have been used with relatively less attention to specific aspects of dependency training. Thus several field studies reported positive relations between parental demonstrativeness and warmth, and the dependency of children. For example, Sears, Maccoby, and Levin (1957) found that mothers who were affectionately demonstrative responded positively to their children's dependent behavior, and also described their children as high in dependency. Moreover, a correlational analysis of field data from families of aggressive and inhibited children indicated that parents who were affectionate, warm, and rewarded dependency, and had spent a great deal of time caring for their sons, had children who tended to show a high degree of dependency behavior (Bandura 1960).

Definitive demonstrations from field studies that dependent behaviors are more frequently permitted and rewarded for girls, and that the opposite is true for physically aggressive behaviors, are difficult to obtain. One would expect more "microscopic" inspection to reveal such differences. Such microscopic scrutiny would have to focus on the sex-linked response differences in paternal and maternal as well as other adult and peer models at different phases in the socialization process. It would have to be highly specific with respect to situational variables, and would have to examine differences in the situations in which behavior patterns lead to different outcomes for males and females as well as any more general stable differences in the treatment of the sexes. Moreover, such an examination would have to explore differences in the ways in which similar behaviors are differentially evaluated and labeled because of the performer's sex.

Differences in External Correlates

It has been reasoned (e.g., Sears 1963, Kagan and Moss 1962) that the same phenotypic behavior—for example, dependency—may have different "psychological meaning" when displayed by the two sexes. If there are systematic sex differences in the response consequences of a behavior pattern, the antecedents and correlates of that pattern should be different for the two sexes. For example, consider extensive dependency in a seven-year-old boy and girl. For the girl, dependency is more likely to have been consistently permitted and rewarded, whereas extensive dependency in the boy may mean that he is not adequately performing new and more age-appropriate responses. Dependent boys and girls may even get opposite consequences from parents and peers for highly similar behaviors. For girls the dependent behavior may lead to an acceptable and even prized outcome; for boys, it may mean a failure to learn new adequate age-appropriate responses. In the one, the behavior may be correlated with indices of parental warmth and satisfaction, adjustment, and numerous signs of age-appropriate behaviors; in the other, the opposite correlates may be found.

Thus R. Sears (1963) reports that for preschool girls, dependency is correlated with indices of maternal permissiveness for dependency (and sex). In girls, "dependency seems to be acceptable or even desired, and mothers who encourage intimacy achieve their aims." (p. 60.) For boys, in contrast, various forms of dependent behaviors (none of which are significantly intercorrelated) seem to be associated with "coldness in the mother, slackness of standards, and a rejection of intimacy by the father." (p. 60.) For example, "positive attention-seeking" appears to be associated with the mother's satisfaction with her daughter. Referring to dependency antecedents in boys, Sears indicates "an inhibited and ineffectual mother—and to some extent father, too—who provides little freedom for the boy, and little incentive for maturing." (R. Sears 1963, p. 62.) It is possible that dependency is directly reinforced in girls, whereas dependency in little boys may indicate a failure to acquire independent behavior and would thus be correlated with other indices of poor adjustment.

It seems very likely that in our culture girls receive more reward for dependency than boys. In laboratory studies it has been demonstrated that a permissive attitude toward dependency, and reward for dependency, increases children's dependency behavior. For example, in a study by Heathers (1953) children aged six to twelve were blindfolded and asked to walk an unstable and narrow plank eight inches above the floor. Children who accepted help from the experimenter at the starting point tended to have parents who encouraged their children to depend on others rather than themselves. It is also of interest that prior reward for dependency facilitated children's learning (on a verbal-conditioning and paired-associate learning task) when correct responses were reinforced by verbal approval (Cairns 1962). Cairns' data, and Ferguson's (1961), suggest that high-dependent children learn more rapidly than low-dependent children when rewarded by approval. To the extent that females are indeed more dependent than males, approval and other social reinforcements should lead to more rapid learning for them. The investigation of sex differences in the effectiveness of particular classes of reinforcements may be a promising area, although overlap in degree of dependency (and in the value of other reinforcements) between the sexes is likely to minimize sex differences in reinforcement effectiveness.

It is also plausible that the results of studies reporting greater female "conformity" and greater female concern with social approval may reflect a stronger history of dependency reinforcement for these women.

This chapter outlined some basic concepts of social-learning theory, and then used these concepts to explain how sex-typed behaviors are acquired. The importance of situational variables in the performance of sex-typed behaviors was stressed, and the usefulness of traits as units of study was questioned. The paper focused on sex differences in aggressive and dependent behaviors, and interpreted some of the differences between the sexes and some of the correlational patterns reported within each sex. Disparities between the individual's self-reports and his overt behavior were noted and interpreted.

Among the many questions requiring further empirical investigation are the conditions under which modeling effects are heightened, possible sex differences in the effectiveness of particular modeling procedures, and the investigation of sex differences in the effectiveness of different classes and patterns of rewards and punishments. The interactions between sex of subject and sex of experimenter or model, particularly in life-like social contexts, also require further investigation. The current literature documents numerous sex differences in the frequency of different behaviors, in self-reports, and in correlational patterns. The development of a detailed topography of specific sex differences would be of interest to researchers committed to exploring substantive differences in the behavior of the sexes. At present most researchers acknowledge the existence of major sex differences, but for experimental purposes attempt to "control out" such differences in order to demonstrate other main effects. Although one researcher's independent variable is often another's "error term," it is clear that sex is a variable which should not be ignored in research.

REFERENCES

Bandura, A. (1960) Relationship of family patterns to child behavior disorders. Progress Report, U.S.P.H. Research Grant M1734, Stanford University.

——. (1965) Influence of model's reinforcement contingencies on the acquisition of imitative responses. *J. Pers. soc. Psychol.*, 1, 589–95.

——, and Aletha C. Huston. (1960) Identification as a process of incidental learning. *J. abnorm. soc. Psychol.*, 24, 1–8.

————, and Carol J. Kupers. (1964) The transmission of self-reinforcement through modeling. *J. abnorm. soc. Psychol.*, *69*, 1–9.

————, and T. L. Rosenthal. (1966) Vicarious classical conditioning as a function of arousal level. *J. Pers. soc. Psychol.*, *3*, 54–62.

————, Dorothea Ross, and Sheila A. Ross. (1963a) A comparative test of the status envy, social power, and secondary reinforcement theories of identificatory learning. *J. abnorm. soc. Psychol.*, *67*, 527–34.

————, Dorothea Ross, and Sheila A. Ross. (1963b) Vicarious reinforcement and imitative learning. *J. abnorm. soc. Psychol.*, *67*, 601–7.

————, and R. H. Walters. (1963) *Social learning and personality development*. New York: Holt, Rinehart & Winston.

Beller, E. K. (1955) Dependency and independence in young children. *J. genet. Psychol.*, *87*, 23–25.

Berger, S. M. (1962) Conditioning through vicarious instigation. *Psychol. Rev.*, *69*, 450–66.

Borstelmann, L. J. (1961) Sex of experimenter and sex-typed behavior of young children. *Child Develpm.*, *32*, 519–24.

Brehm, J. W., and A. R. Cohen. (1962) *Explorations in cognitive dissonance*. New York: John Wiley.

Brim, O. G. (1958) Family structure and sex role learning by children: a further analysis of Helen Koch's data. *Sociometry*, *21*, 1–15.

————. (1960) Personality development as role learning. In I. Iscoe and H. Stevenson (eds.), *Personality development in children*. Austin: University of Texas Press.

Brown, D. G. (1956) Sex role preference in young children. *Psychol. Monogr.*, *70*, No. 14 (Whole No. 421).

Cairns, R. B. (1962) Antecedents of social reinforcer effectiveness. Unpublished manuscript, Indiana University.

Carlson, R. (1963) Identification and personality structure in preadolescents. *J. abnorm. soc. Psychol.*, *67*, 566–73.

Crandall, V. J., Anne Preston, and Alice Rabson. (1962) Motivational and ability determinants of young children's intellectual achievement behaviors. *Child Develpm.*, *33*, 643–62.

Droppleman, L. F., and E. S. Schaefer. (1961) Boys' and girls' reports of maternal and paternal behavior. Paper read at Amer. Psychol. Assoc., August 31, 1961, New York City.

Fauls, Lydia B., and W. D. Smith. (1956) Sex-role learning of five-year-olds. *J. genet. Psychol.*, *89*, 105–17.

Ferguson, P. E. (1961) The influence of isolation, anxiety, and dependency on reinforcer effectiveness. Unpublished master's thesis, University of Toronto.

Festinger, L. (1957) *A theory of cognitive dissonance*. Stanford: Stanford University Press.

————. (1964) Behavioral support for opinion change. *Public Opinion Quart.*, *28*, 404–17.

Gewirtz, J. L. (1956) A factor analysis of some attention-seeking behaviors in young children. *Child Develpm., 27,* 17–36.

———, and D. M. Baer. (1958) The effect of brief social deprivation on behaviors for a social reinforcer. *J. abnorm. soc. Psychol., 56,* 49–56.

Grant, D. A., and J. J. Schiller. (1953) Generalization of the conditioned galvanic skin response to visual stimuli. *J. exp. Psychol., 46,* 309–13.

Guilford, J. P. (1959) *Personality.* New York: McGraw-Hill.

Hartup, W. W. (1963) Dependence and independence. In H. W. Stevenson et al. (eds.), *Child psychology,* 62nd Yearbook of the National Society for the Study of Education. Chicago: University of Chicago Press.

Heathers, G. (1953) Emotional dependence and independence in a physical threat situation. *Child Develpm., 24,* 169–79.

Hill, W. F. (1960) Learning theory and the acquisition of values. *Psychol. Rev., 67,* 317–31.

Houwink, R. H. (1950) The attitude-interest analysis test of Terman and Miles and a specimen revision for the Netherlands. (In Dutch.) *Ned. Tijdschr. Psychol., 5,* 242–62.

Hovland, C. I., and I. L. Janis (eds.). (1959) *Personality and persuasibility.* New Haven: Yale University Press.

Kagan, J., and H. A. Moss. (1962) *Birth to maturity: A study in psychological development.* New York: John Wiley.

Kanfer, F. H., and A. R. Marston. (1963) Conditioning of self-reinforcing responses: an analogue to self-confidence training. *Psychol. Rept., 13,* 63–70.

Lacey, J. I., and R. L. Smith. (1954) Conditioning and generalization of unconscious anxiety. *Science, 120,* 1045–52.

Lansky, L. M., V. J. Crandall, J. Kagan, and C. T. Baker. (1961) Sex differences in aggression and its correlates in middle-class adolescents. *Child Develpm., 32,* 45–58.

Loevinger, Jane. (1957) Objective tests as instruments of psychological theory. *Psychol. Rep. Monogr.* No. 9, Southern University Press.

Maccoby, Eleanor E., W. C. Wilson, and R. V. Burton. (1958) Differential movie-viewing behavior of male and female viewers. *J. Pers., 26,* 259–67.

Mann, N. (1959) Dependency in relation to maternal attitudes. Unpublished master's thesis, State University of Iowa.

McClelland, D. C., J. W. Atkinson, R. A. Clark, and E. L. Lowell. (1953) *The achievement motive.* New York: Appleton-Century-Crofts.

Metzner, R., and W. Mischel. (1962) Achievement motivation, sex of subject, and delay behavior. Unpublished manuscript, Stanford University.

Mischel, W. (1958) Sex differences in the generalization of expectancies. Unpublished manuscript, Harvard University.

———. (in press) Research and theory on delay of gratification. In B. A. Maher (ed.), *Progress in experimental personality research,* Vol. 3. New York: Academic Press.

———, and Joan Grusec. (1966) Determinants of the rehearsal and transmission of neutral and aversive behaviors. *J. Pers. soc. Psychol.*, *3*, 197–205.

——, and R. M. Liebert. (1966) Effects of discrepancies between observed and imposed reward criteria on their acquisition and transmission. *J. Pers. soc. Psychol.*, *3*, 45–53.

——, and E. Staub. (1965) The effects of expectancy on working and waiting for larger rewards. *J. Pers. soc. Psychol.*, *2*, 625–33.

Mowrer, O. H. (1960) *Learning theory and behavior*. New York: John Wiley.

Mussen, P. H. (1961) Some antecedents and consequents of masculine sex-typing in adolescent boys. *Psychol. Monogr.*, *75*, No. 2 (Whole No. 506).

——, and L. Distler. (1959) Masculinity, identification, and father-son relationships. *J. abnorm. soc. Psychol.*, *59*, 350–56.

——, and E. Rutherford. (1961) Effects of aggressive cartoons on children's aggressive play. *J. abnorm. soc. Psychol.*, *62*, 461–64.

Payne, D. E., and P. H. Mussen. (1956) Parent-child relations and father identification among adolescent boys. *J. abnorm. soc. Psychol.*, *52*, 358–62.

Rosenblith, Judy F. (1959) Learning by imitation in kindergarten children. *Child Develpm.*, *30*, 69–80.

Rotter, J. B. (1954) *Social learning and clinical psychology*. Englewood Cliffs, N.J.: Prentice-Hall.

Sanford, N. (1955) The dynamics of identification. *Psychol. Rev.*, *62*, 106–18.

Sarason, I. G., and J. Minard. (1963) Interrelationships among subject, experimenter, and situational variables. *J. abnorm. soc. Psychol.*, *67*, 87–91.

Sarason, S. B., K. S. Davidson, F. F. Lighthall, R. R. Waite, and B. K. Ruebush. (1960) *Anxiety in elementary school children*. New York: John Wiley.

Sears, Pauline S. (1953) Child-rearing factors relating to playing sex-typed roles. *Amer. Psychologist*, *8*, 431 (abstract).

Sears, R. R. (1961) Relation of early socialization experiences to aggression in middle childhood. *J. abnorm. soc. Psychol.*, *63*, 466–92.

——. (1963) Dependency motivation. In M. R. Jones (ed.), *Nebraska symposium on motivation*. Lincoln: University of Nebraska Press.

——. (1965) Development of gender role. In F. Beach (ed.), *Sex and behavior*. New York: John Wiley.

——, Eleanor E. Maccoby, and H. Levin. (1957) *Patterns of child rearing*. New York: Harper.

Staats, A. W., and Carolyn K. Staats. (1958) Attitudes established by classical conditioning. *J. abnorm. soc. Psychol.*, *57*, 37–40.

Staats, Carolyn K., and A. W. Staats. (1957) Meaning established by classical conditioning. *J. exp. Psychol.*, *54*, 74–80.

Terman, L. M., and Catherine C. Miles. (1936) *Sex and personality: studies in masculinity and feminity*. New York: McGraw-Hill.

A Cognitive-Developmental Analysis of Children's Sex-Role Concepts and Attitudes

LAWRENCE KOHLBERG
University of Chicago

Even if one does not accept the Freudian saga of the libido, one can hardly question the psychoanalytic assumption that sexuality constitutes the most significant area of interaction between biological givens and cultural values in human emotional life. If biological instincts are important in any area of man's social life, they are certainly most important in the sexual domain. Therefore it is in this area that we will most likely discover the nature of the interaction between biological and cultural patternings.

Oddly enough, our approach to the problems of sexual development starts directly with neither biology nor culture, but with cognition. In this chapter we shall elaborate and document a theory which assumes that basic sexual attitudes are not patterned directly by either biological instincts or arbitrary cultural norms, but by the child's cognitive organization of his social world along sex-role dimensions. Recent research evidence suggests that there are important "natural" components involved in the patterning of children's sex-role attitudes, since many aspects of sex-role attitudes appear to be universal across cultures and family structures, and to originate relatively early in the child's development. This patterning of sex-role attitudes is essentially "cognitive" in that it is rooted in the child's concepts of physical things—the bodies of himself and of others—concepts which he relates in turn to a social order that makes functional use of sex categories in quite culturally universal ways. It is not the child's biological instincts, but rather his cognitive organization of social-role concepts around universal physical dimensions, which accounts for the existence of universals in sex-role attitudes.

Our theory, then, is cognitive in that it stresses the active nature of the child's thought as he organizes his role perceptions and role learnings around his basic conceptions of his body and his world. We shall stress (as does Mischel in this volume) the importance of the observational learning of social roles, i.e., learning that results from observation of the behavior of others rather than learning that results from reinforcement of one's own responses. We shall point out that this learning is cognitive in the sense that it is selective and internally organized by relational schemata rather than directly reflecting associations of events in the outer world. In regard to sex-role, these schemata that bind events together include concepts of the body, the physical and social world, and general categories of relationship (causality, substantiality, quantity, time, space, logical identity, and inclusion).

While we are talking about cognitive organization, and universals common to all children in sexual cognitions, we must take into account the fact that basic modes of cognitive organization change with age. As Piaget and his followers have documented in depth and detail, the child's basic cognitive organization of the physical world undergoes radical transformations with age development. So, too, do the child's conceptions of his social world. We shall review research findings which suggest that not only do young children's sex-role attitudes have universal aspects, but also that these attitudes change radically with age development. These age changes do not seem to be the result of age-graded sex-role socialization, but rather to be "natural" changes resulting from general trends of cognitive-social development. There is little reason to accept Freud's (1905) and Gesell and Ilg's (1943) view that these age changes are directly related to the maturation of the body or of body instincts. Instead, we shall review evidence suggesting that these trends are the result of general experience-linked changes in modes of cognition. Sex-role concepts and attitudes change with age in universal ways because of universal age changes in basic modes of cognitive organization. Increasing evidence from studies in the Piaget tradition suggests culturally universal developmental shifts in conceptualizations of physical objects. Because children's sex-role concepts are essentially defined in universal physical, or body, terms, these concepts, too, undergo universal developmental changes. As an example, recent research indicates that children develop a conception of themselves as having an unchangeable sexual identity at the same age and through the same processes that they develop conceptions of the invariable identity of physical objects.

Our cognitive point of view, then, will lead us to a developmental focus upon attitudes common to children of a given age. Research findings on common attitudes have, for the most part, emerged as incidental results of studies dealing with individual differences and their sociocultural determinants. It appears to us that the most intelligent way to approach theory and research in this area would be to focus equally upon commonalities and upon individual differences, starting with the clear commonalities and moving on to the more ambiguous data on individual differences when these data can be interpreted against a clear background of attitudes common to boys and girls of given ages.

In the present chapter we shall adopt this developmental strategy by first surveying research on common attitudes and age trends, and then considering findings on individual differences. We shall emphasize a number of findings which suggest that developmental-level concepts are useful not only for understanding age trends, but also for understanding much individual variability within age groups. The greatest individual variations in children's sex-role attitudes (within a given culture) are those related to age and to intellectual and social maturity. In addition many research findings seem to indicate that parent attitudes differentially stimulate or retard the development of many basic sex-role attitudes, rather than teaching them directly through reinforcement or identification.

We have stressed the ways in which our approach to psychosexuality is both cognitive and developmental. As for the central issue of biological versus cultural patterning, our approach here is "interactional" in a rather special sense. There are few psychologists today who do not accept "interaction" in the sense of recognizing both biological-genetic factors and cultural-environmental factors as significant nonadditive quantitative forces in sexual development. Even extreme instinct theorists, like Freud or Lorenz, recognize that there are environmental influences upon sexual attitudes, and even extreme social-learning or cultural theorists acknowledge genetic differences in body characteristics and in temperament. Accordingly, discussions of the quantitative contributions of biological and cultural factors to individual variation in sexual attitudes have little conceptual significance. The critical theoretical issue here is the conception of the basic source of patterning in sexual attitudes, not the quantitative contribution of the factors that may influence or deflect this pattern in individual cases.

The basic claim of theories of sexual instinct like Freud's libido theory is that the basic patterning of sexual attitudes is instinctual and "natural" in its origins, but that the expressions of these patterns are eventually channeled, distorted, or influenced by cultural forces. In contrast, social-learning theories of sex-role development, such as Walter Mischel's in this volume, see the patterning of sexual attitudes as a reflection of the patterning, or sex-typing, of the culture. Cultural socializing agents sex-type their own and the child's behavior, and the child's resultant "acquisition and performance of sex-typed behaviors can be described by the same learning principles used to analyze any other aspect of an individual's behavior" (Mischel, this volume, p. 56). At its extreme, as elaborated by Bandura and Walters (1963), the social-learning view holds that a "normal" heterosexual patterning of sexuality is the result of a learned conformity to cultural role patterns through punishment, reward, and observational learning, while abnormal patternings of sexuality are a result of behavior learned from deviant models or of the failure to learn the normal pattern because of ineffectual teaching or lack of reinforcement by socializing agents.

In contrast to either of these views, we see the child's social and sexual attitudes neither as direct reflections of cultural patterns nor as direct reflections of innate structures. Both research results and clinical observation indicate that much of the young child's thinking about sex roles is radically different from the adult's. His physical concepts of anatomical differences, birth, sexual relations, etc., are quite different, as are his concepts of the social attributes and values of males and females. Following Piaget's argument concerning physical concepts, we shall contend that these differences are due not to ignorance or inadequate teaching patterns, but to qualitative differences between the structure of the child's thought and the adult's. The child's sex-role concepts are the result of the child's active structuring of his own experience; they are not passive products of social training. Although certain basic "normal" adult sexual concepts and attitudes typically emerge from these childish attitudes, these adult attitudes are to be viewed as developmental restructuring of earlier attitudes rather than as the products of direct learning of an arbitrary cultural reality. At any given point, the child uses his experiences of his body and his social environment to form basic sex-role concepts and values, but at any given point environmental experiences also stimulate restructuring of these concepts and values.

It appears to us that this interactional point of view best fits the clinical data on sexual psychopathology and its relationship to early experience. Ever since Freud's (1905) classic statement, it has been recognized that sexual abnormalities are incomprehensible if one assumes that there is a single innate or "normal" pattern of sexuality. As David Hamburg's chapter in this volume indicates, there is clear evidence that hormonal and genetic factors influence the level of sexual arousal, but there is no clear evidence that these factors determine the patterning of sexuality, i.e., its aims and objects. Money and Hampson (Hampson and Hampson 1961) find that hermaphrodites who are chromosomally and hormonally of one sex lead normal sex lives patterned in terms of the opposite sex if they have been reared as a member of that sex.

At first, this and other evidence seems to support the social-learning assumption that basic sexual attitudes are directly patterned by cultural expectations and reinforcement. However, it is extremely difficult to account for recurrent forms of adult sexual psychopathology in terms of the general mechanisms of social reinforcement or modeling, since abnormal sex-role behaviors are obviously highly resistant to both cultural expectations and social reinforcement. It was this double-edged problem of sexual psychopathology that led Freud to postulate that there are innate "abnormal" or deviant instinctual sexual patterns which unfold in early childhood, and which can be fixated through childhood experience. On the one hand, therefore, it is clear that human sexual behavior is not the product of a strict and fixed instinct, or there would be no sexual psychopathology. On the other hand, it is just as clear that sexual behavior is not simply culturally patterned, or there would be no recurrent and resistant forms of sexual psychopathology in cultures and families that strongly disapprove of them.

Freud's notions of definite and instinctively patterned sexual stages have not stood up well in the face of direct psychological observations of children, although such observations clearly suggest infantile sexual interests, concerns, and pleasures in various body zones. However, in modified forms the notion that an experience at a critical period in the unfolding of instinctive patterns can affect subsequent attitudes and behaviors has received considerable support from animal and clinical research. In ground-nesting birds, early exposure to a moving object leads to imprinting, not only of following responses but of later sexual ones. Money, Hampson, and Hampson (1957) report critical-period phenomena which suggest that there is something like sexual imprinting in humans. They suggest that the development of normal adult sexual behavior is contingent on having been socially assigned to a given sex before the age of three or four. Hermaphrodites assigned at birth to one sex because of external genital characteristics have sometimes been reassigned later to the other sex, so that their social sex identity will be more consistent with their internal sex characteristics. Money and Hampson report that if this is done before age three–four, the child's later sexual adjustment is normal. If it is done after this age, real maladjustment seems to result.* Money and Hampson use the term imprinting to describe this critical-age-period phenomenon in sex-role attitudes, since it is obviously not the result of the usual social reinforcement mechanisms, which are in principle reversible. The critical-period phenomena described by Money and Hampson are, however, obviously not genuine imprinting phenomena. As observed in birds, imprinting takes place at a very early period through exposure to a definite object. In contrast, the "imprinting" described by Money and Hampson occurs throughout the first three or four years, and is not the result of exposure to a definite object. Instead it is the fixation of an "abstract" self-concept or identity. Rearing a person as a member of one sex rather than the other does not mean that there will be a difference in exposure to parents or other love objects; there will be, however, a difference in labeling of the self. Such labeling is perhaps irreversible because basic cognitive categorizations are irreversible. After a certain point, social reinforcement cannot readily reverse or change basic categorizations of constancies in the child's physical world, though such reinforcement can readily change categorizations at earlier cognitive stages before constancies are stabilized (Smedslund 1961). In a similar way the child aged two to four is very uncertain of the constancy of his sexual identity, and the label "boy" is for him as arbitrary as the label "Johnny." Once his sexual identity has been cognitively stabilized in the Money and Hampson "critical period," it must become extremely difficult to change it by social sex-role reassignment.

---

* Owing to the fact that their sample is small and their data largely retrospective and based on pediatric report, self-report, etc., Money and Hampson's conclusions are only tentative. A critical review of Money and Hampson's findings is presented by Diamond (1965).

In general, then, our theory accepts the notion that there are important linkages between childhood experiences and adult psychopathology. It does so without postulating either biologically based critical periods or biologically patterned childhood sexual instincts. Instead, these linkages are explained in terms of the cognitive distortions characteristic of childhood sexual concepts, distortions which may become "fixated" by certain interpersonal experiences that stabilize distorted conceptions of body interactions and body feelings.

Our stress upon the cognitive basis of sex-role attitudes and their development does not mean that we are shifting our attention away from the motivational and emotional aspects of sex-role attitudes. We shall argue, however, that motivational aspects of sex-role development are best understood in terms of a theory of the self and of identification that rests on general competence, effectance (White 1959), and self-regard motives, rather than upon infantile sexual drives or attachment and dependency motivations unique to the early parent-child relationship. The child's sexual identity is maintained by a motivated adaptation to physical-social reality and by the need to preserve a stable and positive self-image. We shall argue that motives to love and identify with parental models in the critical childhood years derive primarily from the child's adaptation to this reality and from his self-maintaining motives, rather than from fixed instincts or primary drives. Accordingly, sexual identifications with parents are primarily derivatives of the child's basic sexual identity and his self-maintaining motives—not the reverse, which is what psychoanalysis and social-learning theories have held. Our chapter, then, will start with fundamental concepts and findings on the development of the child's basic sex-role concepts and sex-role identity, and will move on to a consideration of how this identity determines the development of parent-identifications.

SEX-ROLE IDENTITY AS A PRODUCT OF COGNITIVE GROWTH

The Money and Hampson data suggest to us the following points: (1) Gender identity, i.e., cognitive self-categorization as "boy" or "girl," is the critical and basic organizer of sex-role attitudes. (2) This "gender identity" results from a basic, simple cognitive judgment made early in development. Once made, this categorization is relatively irreversible and is maintained by basic physical-reality judgments, regardless of the vicissitudes of social reinforcements, parent identifications, etc. Claiming that a simple gender self-categorization organizes sex-role attitudes, we can postulate the following: (3) Basic self-categorizations determine basic valuings. Once the boy has stably categorized himself as male, he then values positively those objects and acts consistent with his gender identity. This assumption that there are tendencies toward cognitive consistency which lead to the formation of values consistent with self-conceptual cognitive judgments has been elaborated and documented by "clinical" self-theorists (Rogers, Lecky, Kelly) and by "experimental" cognitive-balance theorists (Festinger, Osgood and Tannenbaum, Newcomb, Rosenberg).

Our view of the importance of gender identity in psychosexual development is not shared by many social-learning theorists, including Walter Mischel (see the preceding chapter). In Mischel's view, sex-typed behavior and attitudes are acquired through social rewards that follow sex-appropriate responses made by the child or by a relevant model. The social-learning syllogism is: "I want rewards, I am rewarded for doing boy things, therefore I want to be a boy." In contrast, a cognitive theory assumes this sequence: "I am a boy, therefore I want to do boy things, therefore the opportunity to do boy things (and to gain approval for doing them) is rewarding."

The Money and Hampson "critical period" data suggest that by age five children have a stable gender identity which determines the value —rather than being primarily instrumental in the achievement—of many social rewards. This suggestion is supported by several experimental studies relating the child's sex-typing to social-reward factors. In one such study, DeLucia (1961) presented kindergarten children with a series of paired pictures of masculine and feminine toys, and asked them which toy a pictured same-sex child would like to play with. Responses of sex-typed preference were moderately stable, with a test-retest reliability of .76 obtained using the same form, and a reliability of .66 obtained using alternate forms. The children were then divided into experimental groups, and given social reinforcement for sex-appropriate responses on a parallel set of pictures. One group received reward ("That's a good one"), one group received punishment ("Oh, no, that's not a good one") as well as reward, and one group received no reinforcement at all. The original sex-typing test was then readministered to the subjects. Among boys, no general effect of reinforcement was found. Neither reward nor punishment by a female experimenter led to any change in sex-typing in boys. Reward by a male experimenter led to slight decline in boys' masculine response, while punishment combined with reward led to a slight increase in sex-typed response. Girls (ever the more adaptive and conforming sex) showed a slight increase in sex-appropriate response under reinforcement regardless of the type of reinforcement or the sex of its agent. None of these reinforcement effects quite achieved the conventional level of statistical significance.

The DeLucia study, then, suggests that responses indicating "I want to be masculine (or feminine)" are fairly stable in kindergarten children, and quite independent of the child's desire for social reward and approval in the immediate situation. Another experimental study, that of Epstein and Leverant (1963), suggests that not only do masculinity-femininity values maintain themselves without immediate situational reinforcement, but that these values actually determine the value of some situational rewards for children of kindergarten age. In this study, boys aged five to seven were divided into high- and low-masculine groups according to their scores on the It Scale (Brown 1956), a picture test of sex-typing very similar to the one used by DeLucia. Both groups were then verbally conditioned by approval from two E's, one male and one female. The high-masculine-scoring boys showed more effective learning when reinforced by a male E rather than a female E. In contrast, low-masculine-scoring boys showed no differences in learning that could be attributed to differences in the sex of the reinforcing E. This study is only one of many indicating the power of sex-role classifications and values in determining the effectiveness of social reinforcement (Stevenson 1965).

The experimental studies just reviewed indicate that some concept of "sex-role identity" is necessary, even in the interpretation of social-learning experiments on behavior change due to reinforcement. It is hard to change sex-typing behavior experimentally by social reinforcement; it is easy to change the influence of social reinforcement by changing its relationship to the child's basic sex-role categorizations. Most social-learning analyses have recognized the need for some concept of "sex-role identity," but have usually defined such a concept as a product rather than a cause of social sex-role learning. One example is provided by Kagan (1964, p. 144):

A sex-role identity represents the degree to which an individual regards himself as masculine or feminine. The degree of match or mismatch between the sex-role standards of the culture and an individual's assessment of his own overt and covert attributes provides him with a partial answer to the question, "How masculine (or feminine) am I?"

Kagan's conception of sex-role identity assumes that the child first develops some general tendency toward masculinity through temperament, reinforcement, and parent identifications, and then becomes concerned about assessing himself in relation to cultural sex-role standards. This notion of self-conceptual identity as a product rather than an instigator of sex-role attitudes is also found in psychoanalytic identity theory. This theory holds that an identity is formed as a result of an ego-organization of prior parent identifications that takes place in adolescence (Erikson 1950).

This usage of the notion of sex-role identity arises from the clinical study of adolescent or adult sex-role "identity crises." It is apparent that a particular individual's performance of certain responses in a sex-typed fashion may be a matter of indifference to the individual and to the culture. At certain points in development, and under certain circumstances, however, these responses may become critically important to the individual because he associates them with his inner doubts about his actual or desired sex role. In considering such sex-role-identity concerns, however, a number of distinctions must be made. In the first place, concerns and uncertainties about masculinity-femininity are not simply or directly related to the actual degree of discrepancy between an individual's behavior and cultural standards of masculinity and femininity. Clinical studies indicate that an "objectively" or behaviorally masculine male may have doubts about his masculinity in an adolescent "identity crisis," while an objectively "effeminate" male may go through life without any concern about his sex-role identity. The fact that self-concept concerns about masculine-feminine identity have little to do with cultural standards of masculinity-femininity is also indicated by studies using M–F tests. These studies indicate that there is little relationship between self-rated masculinity-femininity and conformity of tested attitudes to cultural sex-typing (M–F test scores). They also indicate that there is little relationship between masculinity-femininity and self-reported, rated, or tested maladjustment, anxiety, or neuroticism (Terman and Miles 1936, Gray 1957, Webb 1963, Sutton-Smith and Rosenberg 1960).

In the second place, self-conceptual or measured masculinity-femininity must not be confused with identification with homosexual or heterosexual roles, or with an active as opposed to a passive erotic role. While mean differences in masculinity-femininity are found between groups of self-identified homosexuals and controls, many self-identified homosexuals produce normal or above-normal scores on M–F tests (Terman and Miles 1936). In general only "passive" male homosexuals (or "active" female homosexuals) make fewer appropriately sex-typed responses than controls. Interview studies indicate that some male homosexuals view themselves as masculine and as taking the masculine homosexual role, some view themselves as feminine and as taking the feminine homosexual role, and others view themselves as masculine and consider masculinity to have nothing to do with homosexuality or a particular homosexual role (Hooker 1965). The test and interview literature on overt homosexuality and masculinity-femininity suggests that masculinity-femininity attitudes among homosexuals are primarily determined by homosexual subcultural role definitions, rather than that homosexual roles are primarily defined by stable traits or attitudes of masculinity-femininity.

In the third place, self-assessments concerning masculinity-femininity and homosexuality-heterosexuality must be distinguished from basic self-categorizations of biological gender identity. A firm gender identity as "male" is possible even though the individual neither thinks himself, nor is, "masculine" by cultural standards. An individual is categorized as belonging to the male gender on the basis of a single unchangeable physical characteristic; he is judged as more or less masculine in terms of a large set of cultural stereotypes and standards. When we meet a male at a party, we categorize him as male regardless of the masculinity or femininity of his behavior and appearance, and so does he himself. We take this fact of "gender identity" for granted in adults because almost all nonpsychotic adults (including homosexuals) know their own gender identity. The great majority of male homosexuals do not desire a female gender identity (Hooker 1965). (Presumably if homosexuals did not accept their own gender identity, they would not feel antipathetic toward the opposite sex.)

Gender identity is perhaps the most stable of all social identities.

If an American adult is asked what social class he belongs to, he is very often "objectively" incorrect; and if he is asked whether he is a Jew or a German or a Catholic or a Californian, he may be uncertain and engage in a long discussion of the criteria for being placed in these categories. The only category of social identity that is as basic and clear as gender is age, but age, unlike gender, continually changes. As we know, children lie to themselves and others in order to appear older, and middle-aged women lie to themselves and others in order to appear younger.

Even though the psychology of adult personality may take gender identity for granted, the genesis of this identity is still of great interest for developmental psychology. We have pointed out that adult gender identity is a basic cognitive reality judgment, and not a derivative of social rewards, parent identifications, or sexual identifications. At the same time, however, this gender identity had to develop. As we shall now attempt to demonstrate, the reality judgment "I really am and always will be a boy [or girl]" is the result of a cognitive development which is quite independent of variations in social sex-role training, and which is central to the development of other aspects of sex-role attitudes.

Obviously, this process begins with the child's hearing and learning the verbal labels "boy" and "girl." The child's verbal learning of his own gender label occurs quite early, usually sometime late in the second year of life. Gesell et al. (1940) report that two-thirds to three-fourths of 3-year-olds answered correctly the question "Are you a little girl or a little boy?" while the majority of 2½-year-olds did not answer it correctly. At this early age, however, correct self-labeling does not imply correct self-classification in a general physical category. The label "boy" may be a name just like the name "Johnny." The child may recognize that there are other boys in the world, just as there may be other Johnnies, but this recognition need not imply a basic criterion for determining who is a boy any more than it does for determining who is a Johnny; nor does it necessarily imply that everyone in the world is either a boy or a girl, or a Johnny or a non-Johnny. In the second year, the child learns that "boy" is a name which may be applied to others, and he may even experience a vague pleasurable "identification" in such common labeling. But this extension of the label does not imply the ability to make categorizations. A 2½-year-old boy, Tommy, observed by the writer, would go around the family circle saying, "I'm boy," "Daddy boy," "Mommy boy," "Joey [brother] boy." After correction he eliminated his mother from the list, but did not label people outside the family correctly.

In the third year of life then, the child seems to know his own sex label, and to generalize it unsystematically to others on the basis of a loose cluster of physical characteristics. Rabban (1950) reports that about two-thirds of a group of 60 middle-class and working-class children aged 30 to 41 months (with an average age of three years) were able to reply correctly to the questions "Which doll looks most like you?" and "Is it [the doll] a boy or a girl?" Such generalization of a correct self-label to a doll did not, however, imply generally correct discrimination of the sex of the doll. Rabban reports that only about half of his 3-year-old group was able to label correctly six dolls (father, mother, two boys, two girls) as "boy" or "girl." By age four almost all of Rabban's children labeled themselves and the dolls correctly. By four, children tend to label gender by some general physical criteria, primarily clothing and hair-style (Conn and Kanner 1947, Kohlberg 1966, Katcher 1955).

The findings discussed so far merely suggest that children learn gender self-labeling early (age two–three), and in the next two years learn to label others correctly according to conventional cues. Obviously there is more to the development of a stable gender identity than this. Investigations of this "more" have started from two points of view: the psychoanalytic and the cognitive-developmental. Both recognize that the young child's use of gender concepts is confused, and that correct and stable gender identification depends upon the child's ability to classify a physical object, the body. Both agree that the development of a stable gender identification is an important psychosexual developmental task, but disagree about how this development takes place: the psychoanalytic view stresses the interaction between the child's wishes and the adult's provision or denial of anatomical information in this development (Freud 1908), whereas the cognitive-developmental view holds that the child's difficulties in establishing gender definition closely parallel his difficulties in establishing stable definitions of physical concepts in general, and that the former are resolved as the latter are (Kohlberg 1966). While both theories point to a number of important developments in gender-identity concepts, the central focus of both is upon the constancy of gender identity. The child's gender identity can provide a stable organizer of the child's psychosexual attitudes only when he is categorically certain of its unchangeability.

The fact that the young child is not certain of the constancy of gender identity before the age of five–six has been demonstrated by Kohlberg (1966a). In the course of this study, children of four to eight were asked whether a pictured girl could be a boy if she wanted to, or if she played boy games, or if she wore a boy's haircut or clothes. Most four-year-olds said that she could be a boy if she wanted to, or if she wore the appropriate haircut or clothes. By age six–seven, most children were quite certain that a girl could not be a boy regardless of changes in appearance or behavior. These findings correspond to more anecdotal observations. The following comments were made by Jimmy, just turning four, to his 4½-year-old friend Johnny:

Johnny: I'm going to be an airplane builder when I grow up.

Jimmy: When I grow up, I'll be a Mommy.

Johnny: No, you can't be a Mommy. You have to be a Daddy.

Jimmy: No, I'm going to be a Mommy.

Johnny: No, you're not a girl, you can't be a Mommy.

Jimmy: Yes, I can.

Among other difficulties, it would seem that Jimmy does not recognize that the category "male" applies to both boys and fathers, and that while age changes occur, gender changes do not. As another example, Philip (aged 3 years, 10 months) told his mother, "When you grow up to be a Daddy, you can have a bicycle, too [like his father]."

Rabban (1950) found that the majority of his 3-year-olds did not correctly use generalized sex labels, and did not reply correctly to the question "When you grow up, would you like to be a mamma or a daddy?" In contrast, 97 per cent of his 5-year-olds replied correctly. In light of findings discussed later, it is likely that the change in responses to questions of desired future identity primarily reflects cognitive stabilization of sex-role categories rather than changes in role preference.

From the cognitive-developmental point of view, the stabilization of gender-identity concepts is only one aspect of the general stabilization of constancies of physical objects that takes place between the years three and seven. The development of such conceptual constancies has been discussed by Piaget in terms of the conservation of physical-object properties under apparent changes. Piaget and his followers (Piaget 1947, Wallach 1963) have demonstrated that children below the age of six–seven do not view physical objects as retaining an invariable mass, number, weight, length, etc. when the perceptual configuration in which the objects appear varies. While Piaget has only considered and studied conceptual constancies involving conservation of an object's quantity along some dimension, it appears that qualitative constancies of category or generic identity develop in the same period and in parallel fashion (Kohlberg 1966a). Thus a majority of 4-year-old children said that a pictured cat could be a dog if it wanted to, or if its whiskers were cut off. By age six–seven, most children were firm in asserting that a cat would not change its identity in spite of apparent perceptual changes. Similar results have been found by DeVries (1966), using a live cat that is covered by a dog mask within the child's view.

The results of Kohlberg and DeVries's developmental studies of constancy of species and gender identity can be questioned from two points of view. One is the common-sense point of view, which would question purely verbal evidence that young children do not believe in constancy of identity. The other is the psychoanalytic view, which sees the young child's unrealistic thoughts about sexual constancy as largely a product of his wishes and fears. In contrast, the Piaget view assumes, first, that there is a parallelism or correspondence between the cognitive-verbal and affective aspects of the development of reality orientations, and, second, that cognitive-structural changes, rather than affective changes, are the primary sources of development in reality orientations.

In Piaget's view, the infant is from the start motivationally oriented toward contacting, maintaining, and mastering objects rather than toward pure tension discharge. The child's gradual increase in reality orientation, his increased awareness of the constancy of the existence and identity of external objects, is the result of increased cognitive differentiation of the self and the world rather than the result of basic qualitative changes in motivational processes. Like Piaget, Freud also stressed the importance of the child's spontaneous processes in determining his basic reactions to the "reality," and viewed infantile and adult thought processes as structurally or qualitatively different from one another (primary and secondary processes). However, Freud stresses motivational changes as basic to the development of different modes of thought. Infantile thought has the structure of fantasy; it is governed by the pleasure principle and the desire for immediate gratification. Mature thought is governed by the reality principle, by the delay of gratification, and by stable attachments to external objects. In more mundane terms, psychoanalysis holds that the young child's unrealistic thoughts about sexual identity are the result of his wishes and fears. Where emotional preoccupations are strong, fantasy thought predominates over secondary-process thought.

An example suggesting this psychoanalytic interpretation of gender identity is a spontaneous response made by Jimmy, a boy just turned five: "I can be a girl, you know. I can. I can wear a wig and have my throat so I can talk like a girl." It would seem plausible to attribute the immature logic of this statement to the fact that the boy's wishes and conflicts in this area were strong enough to override his interests in being realistic or correct. On another occasion, however, the writer (experimenter) had the following conversation with Jimmy:

Experimenter: Do airplanes get small when they fly away in the sky?

Jimmy: Yes, they get real tiny.

Experimenter: Do they really get small, or do they just look small?

Jimmy: They really get small.

Experimenter: What happens to the people inside?

Jimmy: They shrink.

Experimenter: How can they shrink and get small?

Jimmy: They cut their heads off.

These statements might also be taken as motivationally determined, rather than as a reflection of Jimmy's general level of thinking. Obviously, in the second conversation, Jimmy doesn't care about being correct, and ends up making a "fantasy" response. Sometimes Jimmy may care too much (sex-role), sometimes too little (airplane query), but if his general level of thinking is the same, it is hard to maintain that this level is a product of affective rather than cognitive-structural factors.

In order to compare the cognitive-structural and the affective interpretations of gender-identity beliefs in young children, the Kohlberg (1966a) study asked the correlational question: "To what extent is level of development of belief in constancy consistent from physical and emotionally neutral types of constancies to social and emotionally charged constancies?"

In addition to the gender-identity task, children aged four–six were given three other conservation tasks: constancy of the species identity of the cat, conservation of mass of a piece of clay under various shape changes, and conservation of length of a piece of gum. The age norms for the gender-identity and species-identity tasks were found to be similar, with constancy on both slightly preceding constancy on conservation of quantitative dimensions of the classical Piaget type. Not only was the age development of the various constancy tasks parallel, but the gender-identity task was found to correlate quite highly ($r = .52$ to $.73$) with the other tasks among children of a given age. Even with mental age partialed out, correlations of gender identity with the other conservation tasks were substantial ($r = .36$ to $.64$). This evidence of consistency clearly indicates the importance of general cognitive-structural features in the child's beliefs about gender identity.

In addition to affective factors, psychoanalytic theory holds that the adult's withholding of anatomical information plays an important role in the child's uncertainties about the constancy of gender identity. In fact, however, the Kohlberg (1966a) study suggests that young children revealing early exposure to parental anatomical "enlightenment" were no more advanced in sex-role constancy than children who did not reveal such enlightenment. The children of four–seven who indicated anatomical awareness in explaining "how you could tell boys from girls when they had clothes on" and "when they had clothes off" were not more advanced in sex-role constancy than were those who did not indicate such anatomical awareness (Kohlberg 1966a). In general, even the enlightened younger child does not use genital differences as the basic criterion for sex-classification. The writer has recorded questions from enlightened children in their third and fourth year who wanted to know whether they would still be boys if they did not have a penis. These questions indicate that awareness of genital differences does not directly lead to their use as the primary criterion of gender categorization or of gender constancy.

The major implication of the Kohlberg study is that the process of forming a constant gender identity is not a unique process determined by instinctual wishes and identifications, but a part of the general process of conceptual growth. As soon as we wish to consider what such a gender identity means to the child, however, we must consider the issues raised by psychoanalytic theory concerning the universal meanings of gender differences, meanings believed to derive from genital concepts and values.

Unfortunately, psychoanalytic theory has tended to treat the connotative and symbolic meanings of genital differences as somehow unique. Actually there is a great deal of evidence that culturally universal connotative or metaphoric meanings exist for various objects; see, for example, the cross-cultural common metaphoric or connotative meanings of objects found on the Osgood semantic differential (Kumata and Schramm 1956, Triandis and Osgood 1958). The existence of common symbolic meanings for objects does not, therefore, depend upon the unique features of sexual instincts and repression, nor does it depend upon innate archetypes; common symbolic meanings exist because of the general dispositions of humans to concrete symbolic thought (Werner and Kaplan 1964). As an example, wisdom universally connotes light (and light, wisdom) because abstract concepts of knowing are related to concrete concepts of seeing. The equation of the two concepts is understandable in terms of the universal aspects of the concept of knowing, a concept that develops through experience and does not imply any innate archetype of knowledge or of light.

It is hardly surprising, then, that there are a number of cross-culturally common connotative meanings of the concepts "man" and "woman" (Kumata and Schramm 1956, Triandis and Osgood 1958). In general, males are connotatively perceived to be more active, powerful, and aggressive than women in all countries so far studied. A careful interpretation of Margaret Mead's (1961) evidence of cultural diversity in sex roles is not inconsistent with these objective findings, as is suggested by Roy D'Andrade's chapter in this volume.

Not only are there a number of apparent universals in the connotations of gender role, but these universals are found very early (by age five–six) among American children. Fathers are perceived as more powerful, punitive, aggressive, fearless, instrumentally competent, and less nurturant than females (Emmerich 1959a, 1959b, 1960, Kagan 1956, Kagan and Lemkin 1960, Kagan, Hoskin, and Watson 1961, Smith 1966). Thus power and prestige appear as one major attribute of children's sex-role stereotypes, aggression and exposure to danger as another major attribute, and nurturance and child care as a third. Associated with recognition of child care as a feminine function is the general differentiation of maternal, inside-the-home functions from paternal, outside-the-home functions (Lindskoog 1964).

The child's connotations of sex differences do not seem to be the result of direct learning of the actual sex roles of his parents or siblings.

In spite of the known variability in parental role behavior in the American society, there is a remarkable consensus among young children in their conceptions of differences between mother and father roles as revealed by the studies of parent stereotypes previously cited. With regard to the dimensions cited, there is little difference in role conceptions between middle-class and lower-class children, or between children from the predominant white culture and those from a more "matriarchal" Negro subculture (C. Smith 1966). Research also suggests that these simple and general stereotypes develop just as quickly and clearly in children who do not have parent models as in those who do. The C. Smith (1966) study involved a comparison of the stereotypes of father-absent and father-present boys at two ages (five and seven) and at two levels of intelligence. Father-absent boys were not significantly different from controls in differentiating father and mother roles on nurturance, power, aggression, and competence (though they were significantly less likely to choose the father as the primary physical disciplinarian than the father-present boys). While studies of maternal absence have not been carried out, studies of sex-role stereotypes of working and non-working mothers point in a similar direction. Girls with working mothers appear to have the same primarily domestic definition of adult feminine-maternal roles as do girls with nonworking mothers (Hartley 1959–60, 1964).

The studies just mentioned suggest that the child's development of sex-role stereotypes is not the product of the direct perception of differences in the behavior of his own parents. The few studies correlating children's parent stereotypes with the parents' report of their own role behavior suggest similar conclusions. Children's doll-play perceptions of punitiveness and nurturance by mother and father were found to be uncorrelated with parental reports of child-rearing behavior in these areas (Emmerich 1959a).

If it seems unlikely that a young child's sex-role stereotypes are a direct reflection of parental behavior, it also seems unlikely that they are the product of direct learning or of communication of the sex-role stereotypes and norms held by his parents or by the adult culture. Although children are undoubtedly influenced by the parent-role stereotypes held by parents and peers, it does not seem plausible that young children's stereotypes are learned directly from adults. This implausibility arises from the findings of the studies cited showing more clear-cut stereotyping of parent and sex roles in young children (five to eight) than in older children or adults (Emmerich 1961, 1964, Bennett and Cohen 1959, Jenkins and Russell 1958). These findings do not suggest that the development of these stereotypes is an orderly learning of adult norms.

If children do not learn basic sex-differentiating parent-role stereotypes through direct transmission of cultural role definitions, then how do they learn them? Many stereotypes seem to arise from perceived sex differences in bodily structure and capacities. Genital differences are only one of a number of body differences having diffuse connotations for masculinity-femininity stereotypes. The stereotype of masculine aggressiveness has a body-image basis because it is linked to the child's belief that males are physically more powerful and more invulnerable than females. By age five–six, all children seem to express this belief. Almost every one of twenty-four first-grade children said that boys fight more than girls. When asked "Why don't girls fight like boys?" the most frequent response was "because girls get hurt easier than boys" (Kohlberg, unpublished data).

Stereotypes of masculine aggression derive not only from body concepts, but also from highly visible differences in extra-familial roles. By age four–five, almost all of a group of sixteen American children showed awareness of the fact that only males play the extra-familial roles (policeman, soldier, fireman, robber, etc.) involving violence and danger (Kohlberg, unpublished data). This cross-culturally universal male specialization in roles of violence far outweighs subtle family differences in minor expressions of verbal and physical hostility in determining the child's basic sex-role stereotypes.

Similarly, perceived body and gross sex differences determine basic sex-role stereotypes on the power dimension. Children appear to become clearly aware of adult sex differences in size and strength at around age four–five (Horowitz 1943, Kohlberg, unpublished data), and attach great significance to them. Size and strength are particularly significant for two reasons. First, because the general concreteness of young children's thought leads them to define social and behavioral attributes in concrete body terms. Social power is thought to result from physical power (strength, aggressive capacities, etc.), which in turn derives from physical size. Second, the first basic social differentiation made by children is that of age-size (babies, boys and girls, grown-ups), a differentiation that precedes gender differentiation. Concepts of age (time) are more difficult for the child than size concepts, and are assimilated to the latter. Thus size becomes a basic indicator for all the important age-status differences, e.g., differences in strength, in knowledge or smartness, in social power, and in self-control. Since sex-role differentiation usually follows age-role differentiation and is also size-linked, it tends to take on connotations of age differentiation.* It appears likely, then, that children's stereotypes of masculine dominance or social power develop largely out of this body-stereotyping of size-age and competence. Children agree earliest and most completely that fathers are bigger and stronger than mothers, next that they are smarter than mothers, and next that they have more social power or are the boss in the family (Kagan and Lemkin 1960, C. Smith 1966). While children under five do not seem to differentiate parent roles by social power, children of six or older consistently attribute more social power to the father (Emmerich 1959b, 1961, Kagan and Lemkin 1960, C. Smith 1966).

As with aggression, gender stereotyping of social power derives from highly visible differences in extra-familial roles as well as from connotations arising from body differences. As D'Andrade's chapter indicates, all societies preferentially assign high-power extra-familial roles to males. By age six–seven, almost all of a small sample of American children were aware that high-power roles (President, policeman, general) were so assigned (Kohlberg, unpublished data).†

* In our earlier discussion of the young child's lack of constant gender-identity concepts, we quoted four-year-old Philip's comment to his mother that "When you grow up to be a Daddy, you can have a bicycle, too [like Daddy]." On another occasion, Philip climbed up on a chair so as to be higher than his seated parents and said, "Look I'm higher than a grown-up, I'm older than a grown-up now." These comments taken together are quite typical illustrations of the young child's fusion of the age, sex, and size dimension of status.

† In addition, the general assignment of the work role to the father leads children of six and older to attribute superior social power and prestige to him. A majority of boys and girls aged six name the father as "the one who is best in the family," and advance as the most common reason that "he works and makes the money" (Kohlberg 1966a). Children of four and five are much less likely to name the father as the best, or to mention earning money as a reason for his status. The younger children do not understand that money is received in exchange for work (they think money comes from the bank or store), and think of the mother as the economic provider since she actually buys the food, etc. This growth in comprehension in the years five–six, together with a growing awareness that males are assigned the significant extra-familial roles, are probably the major causes of the previously mentioned increase in attribution of social power to the father in those years.

In the light of the existence of other universal gender stereotypes, partly based on nongenital body imagery, the psychoanalytic notions of genital symbolism become both more plausible and less uniquely significant components of the child's gender-role concepts. While we can argue that the psychoanalytic assumption of organized infantile sexual or genital drives or instincts is not correct, we cannot argue that the psychoanalytic stress upon children's genital concepts is unjustified. A wide range of observational studies clearly indicate that the genitals are a source of quite intense interest, pleasurable stimulation, and concern to preschool children. Taken together with the fact that the basic adult definition of gender identity centers upon genital differences, this necessarily implies that children's gender-role conceptions will focus heavily upon genital differences.

The significance of the genitals for children's conceptions of gender roles is somewhat complicated by a fact stressed by Freud, the fact that the young child has a good deal of difficulty in learning that there are generalized genital differences between the sexes, and does not complete this learning until the early school years. This seems indicated by the studies of Conn (1940) and of Conn and Kanner (1947), who were able to elicit knowledge of genital differences in a doll-play interview from only 50 per cent of children aged four–six, from 72 per cent of children aged seven–eight, and from 86 per cent of children aged eleven–twelve. The children in these studies, however, were largely lower-class, and interviews with their parents indicated that many of the children had not been told about basic anatomical differences. Another study by Butler (1952), however, suggests a similar degree of ignorance among children of four–five from progressive academic homes. Although 15 of the 17 children had been informed by their parents of anatomical differences, Butler was only able to elicit awareness of genital differences from five of these 15 children.

These results are fairly consistent with another study by Katcher (1955) using a quite different technique. Katcher asked children to put together correctly and identify the gender of several cut-out figures that were separated into head, trunk, and below-the-trunk sections. The figures to be assembled were a clothed boy, girl, man, and woman, and an unclothed boy, girl, man, and woman. Few errors were made by children over three in assembling and identifying the sex of the clothed figures. In contrast, children aged three to six made many more errors in identifying the gender of the genital section, and in matching it with the gender of the hair and trunk sections of the unclothed figure. Some error in genital assignment was made by 88 per cent of the threes, by 69 per cent of the fours, and by 31 per cent of the sixes. Taken together with the other studies, the Katcher study suggests that children do not form clear general concepts of genital differences until age five–seven, even when they are extensively enlightened by parents.

The fact that children are still confused about genital differences at an age (four–five) when they clearly stereotype sex-roles in terms of size, strength, aggression, and power strongly suggests that genital concepts do not form the direct basis for these other connotations of gender differences. The research does suggest a confused early awareness of genital differences that fuses with other sex-typed physical attributes in early stereotyping, but which is neither causally nor developmentally essential to the formation of these stereotypes. The traditional psychoanalytic approach to the problem assumes that the genital and sexual imagery of adults and adolescents develops in early childhood. It is more plausible, however, to assume that the genitals acquire added significance and centrality, first when the child realizes that they are the central basis of gender categorization (at around age six–seven), then when the child develops a definite conception of sexual intercourse (at a slightly older age), and finally when the child experiences actual sexual drives in adolescence.

Some research findings bearing on the role of genital symbolism in the imagery of adults and adolescents have been obtained from the Franck test. Sex differences in imagery on this test may be interpreted as the result of differences in genital aspects of body imagery. The test is a figure completion test designed to stimulate the production of genital symbolism. Consistent sex differences were found in eight countries: the males made more angular closed designs; the females more open rounded designs (Franck [no date], McElroy 1954, Jakoda 1956). The fact that these geometrical tendencies are related to body image is suggested by the fact that males spontaneously draw angular shapes, but prefer rounded shapes when asked to judge completed forms. If the non-body aspects of masculinity (e.g., clothes or games) were signified by angular tendencies, most likely these would be preferred by males as well as produced by them.

While the distinction between preference and spontaneous completion ("self-projection") suggests that body imagery may be involved in the Franck test, it is not at all clear that the symbolism involved is actually genital symbolism. The female figure is more rounded in a non-genital fashion, the male figure is more angular. Characteristically masculine objects like a gun or a knife or a truck are often angular, characteristically feminine household objects like dolls, dishes, and cooking utensils are often rounded. A preliminary pilot study of the preference reactions of young children to the Franck designs suggests that sex-appropriate preferences are found at age four and do not increase in subsequent years (Katz 1959). In light of the fact that both Freudian theory and empirical research suggest confusion about anatomical differences at this age (with Freudian theory postuating phallic preference for both sexes), it is not clear that these differences in imagery preference are specifically symbolic of the genitals. It seems more plausible to view basic masculine-feminine imagery as representing the concrete body-centered and object-centered thought of the child, with genital awareness only one of the many elements of that thought. It is probably just as correct to postulate that the psychological meaning of genital differences is determined by (or symbolizes) masculine-feminine stereotypes of power, aggression, angularity, etc., as it is to postulate that the meaning of these masculine-feminine stereotypes is determined by (or symbolizes) genital imagery.

These connotative meanings of genital differences become especially significant when one considers the problem of psychosexual identity in relation to the Freudian theory of feminine "penis envy." The Freudian theory assumes the existence of early and universal tendencies to attribute superior power and status to the male role. As D'Andrade's chapter suggests, these tendencies are found in all cultures. Although the extent to which power and status are sex-typed differs widely among cultures, whatever sex-typing does exist favors the male. Our review of early gender stereotypes indicates that by age five–six, children award greater power, strength, and competence (and consequently more status) to the male.* At early ages (three–four), the father is not awarded more prestige than the mother, but by ages five–six he is (Kohlberg

---

* This does not mean that the masculine role is considered superior on all value dimensions. Young children award a number of superior values to females, including nurturance, moral "niceness," and attractiveness, but basic power-prestige values are primarily awarded to the male. For various reasons, it seems that masculine forms of prestige are more concrete, and are recognized earlier than feminine forms of prestige.

1966a). As we shall document in the next section (in Figures 3 and 4), girls between the ages of five and eight do not show an increase in preference for same-sex objects and activities, whereas boys do.

These findings might be used to support a psychoanalytic interpretation of growing awareness of genital differences. Up until age four–five, the child is confused about anatomical sex differences. As he becomes more aware of these differences, he might attribute superior prestige to the male. According to Freud's (1908) theory, the child's difficulty in learning the basic anatomical differences between the sexes arises primarily from his tendency to attribute superior value to the male genitalia. This leads children of both sexes to deny anatomical sex differences. The girl's positive evaluation of the penis leads her to believe that she will either possess this organ in the future, or has possessed it in the past. The boy's positive evaluation of the penis leads him to attribute it to others whom he values or identifies with, such as his mother. These factors, combined with the concrete and artificialistic nature of the child's thought, are believed to lead the child to think that the girl's lack of a penis is the result of a willed human action, a castration. In the boy this notion is supposed to intensify the "castration anxiety" caused by fear of retaliation for his Oedipal wishes. In the girl this notion is supposed to arouse castration shame and resentment of her mother for creating her without a penis.

In addition to suggesting that various age-developmental processes are necessary for the acquisition of correct anatomical discrimination, the studies of Conn (1940) and Conn and Kanner (1947) suggest the presence of some of the components of children's sexual concepts postulated by Freud. While Conn and Kanner did not feel that their subjects experienced any shock or trauma when they became aware of the existence of genital differences, these writers do report that a sizeable number of their children aged six to nine (1) believed that both boys and girls "had the same" but that the girl's was smaller, or (2) believed that the girl's had been longer or would be longer at some time, or (3) expressed the notion that the genital characteristics of the opposite sex were "funny" or "wrong" or that "everyone should have the same," or (4) believed that the girl's had been "cut off." In other words, the data suggest that young children have considerable difficulty accepting as natural the genital differences between the sexes.

While the tendencies to "deny" the anatomical differentiation just mentioned are consistent with Freudian theory, they are equally compatible with a cognitive-developmental theory, which does not assume the existence of either a infantile phallic sexuality or a central Oedipal complex with attendant castration concerns. On purely cognitive grounds, the child would be expected to be uncertain about anatomical constancy. This uncertainty would be expected to cause him some concern about the integrity and constancy of his own body. It seems likely that some combination of fascination and threat is experienced when there is an awareness of the existence of a body which is like the self's but which is also basically different from it. Instead of interpreting these feelings of fascination and threat (which are also present in the attitudes of men, women and chimpanzees toward the maimed and deformed) as stemming from specific castration concerns, it seems more plausible to view them as an expression of the child's general uncertainty about anatomical constancy. In addition, the child might well find it difficult to accept basic anatomical differences between himself and those to whom he is attached (or with whom he is identified), such as his mother or sister. Theories of cognitive dissonance lead us to expect that the child will value that which is like himself, and to see himself as being like that which he values. It also seems likely on purely cognitive grounds (de Saussure 1933) that both sexes would take the male anatomy as more basic in defining some sexually undifferentiated human-body schema, i.e., that the female body would be conceived as the negative of the masculine, rather than as a positive entity.

In general, our stress upon cognitive factors seems justified by the age regularity and general cognitive consistency of the development of both concepts of gender identity and concepts of genital differences. If purely affective factors were involved, one would expect a large number of noncognitive individual differences in children's awareness of gender constancy and anatomical differences, factors not apparent in the research findings on normal children.

In summary, then, we have reported evidence of the development of basic and universal conceptions of gender role in children between the ages of three and seven. First, there is the development of constant gender categories, second, the development of awareness of genital differences, and third, the development of diffuse masculine-feminine stereotypes based largely on the connotations of nongenital body imagery. In the next section, we shall attempt to explain how these developing concepts are actually translated into sex-typed preferences and values (sometimes called "sex-role identification").

THE DEVELOPMENT OF MASCULINE-FEMININE VALUES

In the previous section we have attempted to show that the child's basic concepts of his sex-role are his own, and that they are the result of his active interpretation of a social order which makes use of sex categories in culturally universal ways. If these sex-role concepts and identities are the child's own, so, too, are the values and behaviors these concepts generate. Our belief that these concepts will generate masculine-feminine values rests on the assumption that the child engages in "spontaneous" evaluations of his own worth and the worth of others, and that he has "natural" tendencies to ascribe worth to himself, to seek worth, to compare his own worth with that of others, and to evaluate others'.

This approach to the development of sex-typed values differs radically from both the social-learning and psychoanalytic approaches to this problem. These last two approaches, which have dominated research on masculinity-feminity development for a generation, have treated masculinity-femininity attitudes and measures as reflecting "sex-role internalization," or sex-role "identification," which, in turn, has been thought to result from identification with socializing agents, or from reinforcement by socializing agents for sex-typed behavior. Whereas we assume that the child constructs his own sex-role values within a sex-typed social order, these approaches assume that sex-role values are acquired by the internalization of external cultural values, a process that is accomplished through a set of general mechanisms of conformity-learning (Sears, Rau, and Alpert 1965, Miller and Swanson 1960, Mussen and Rutherford 1963, Kagan 1964, Burton and Whiting 1961, Lynn 1959).

Before elaborating our own view, we shall briefly cite the research findings that have led us to question the role-internalization approach to masculine-feminine values. In this approach, scores on masculinity-femininity tests are used to measure the degree of learning, or internalization, of parental or cultural sex-role standards. The tests that have been interpreted in this fashion include the following:

1. The Terman-Miles M-F Test (Terman and Miles 1936). A multiple-choice pencil-and-paper test for adolescents and adults with subtests for interests, emotional attitudes, free association, and information.

2. The Gough Test (Gough 1952). A dichotomous-choice pencil-and-

paper test for adolescents and adults composed of attitude and interest items.

3. The Franck Test (Franck and Rosen 1949). A test of symbolic geometrical-figure completions or figure preferences.

4. The Rosenberg and Sutton-Smith Play and Games Test. A pencil-and-paper test of preferred games (Rosenberg and Sutton-Smith 1959).

5. The It Scale for Children (Brown 1956). A "projective" test for children aged 3 to 12. The child is given a selection of pictured toys and activities, and then asked to choose those which "It," an ambiguously sexed stick figure, would prefer.

6. The Toy Preference Test. A set of pictured toys which the child is asked to select in order of preference. Various forms have been developed by Rabban (1959), DeLucia (1963), and Sears, Rau, and Alpert (1965).

7. The Pictures Test. A similar test for children using pictures of masculine and feminine activities (Sears, Rau, and Alpert 1965).

All of these tests (except the Franck) have been developed and validated according to the same purely empirical rationale, that of statistical sex differences. Items are scored as masculine or feminine on the basis of the fact that there are significant differences in the frequency of choices of the item by males and by females. The use of these tests as measures of sex-role internalization or identification seems to involve the following set of assumptions:[*]

1. These tests should measure a general learning of sex-role norms. Items in each test should correlate positively with one another, and tests should correlate positively with one another. In fact, correlations between sex-typing items and between tests are extremely low among adolescents and adults, though they are somewhat higher among young children.

2. The tests should measure an attitude that is not easily "fakeable." In fact, masculinity-femininity test responses are readily faked.

3. The tests should relate to other measures of socialization, norm internalization, or social adjustment. In fact, no general correlations are found between these tests and measures of morality or social adjustment.

4. Age development on these measures should be in the direction of

---

[*] Documentation of research evidence concerning these assumptions is presented in detail elsewhere (Kohlberg, in press). Some of this evidence is also referred to in later sections of this paper.

increased masculinity-femininity or increased conformity to cultural prescriptions. In fact, at some ages masculinity responses in males, and femininity responses in females, increase; at others they decrease.

5. The tests should measure a developmentally stable or irreversible attitude. In fact, it is difficult to predict an individual's masculinity-femininity score on the basis of a test given earlier in his development.

6. Scores on masculinity-femininity tests should be related to parental expectations in this area. Studies do not indicate such a relationship.

7. Scores on these tests should be related to the masculinity or femininity of parental models. Studies do not indicate such a relationship.

8. Scores on these tests should be related to the presence in the home of a same-sex parent model. Studies do not indicate such a relationship.

It seems unlikely, therefore, that such masculinity-femininity tests can be used as measures of sex-role internalization. It may, of course, be possible in the future to develop a test that could measure some theoretical conception of sex-role identification. Such a possibility, however, will not solve the problem of explaining the development of the empirically observed sex-role attitudes encompassed by the current masculinity-femininity tests. On this problem, we feel that the cognitive-developmental approach casts some light.

In considering this problem, it should be made clear that masculinity-femininity attitude tests need not represent all the important behavioral sex differences to be found in a culture. In the main, these tests reflect conscious sex-typed interests and values that are easily verbalized. The tests do not clearly represent either innate sex differences of a temperamental sort, or highly specific situational behaviors subject to culturally sex-typed reinforcement (the sort of behavior considered in Mischel's chapter). It is not surprising, then, that the results on these tests should fit a cognitive self-conceptual interpretation.

Our analysis of the results will focus upon age-developmental trends in masculine-feminine values; in other words, we shall consider those individual differences in sex-typed attitudes that are also related to age differences. Since the most obvious, regular, and basic trends in childhood psychological development are trends of cognitive-conceptual growth, it is plausible to interpret age trends in sex-role values as being largely determined by cognitive developments in sexual concepts such as those discussed in the last section. In one case, we saw that the responses to the value question "Do you want to be a Daddy [or Mommy]?" changed dramatically as the children grew older and became aware of the constancy and generality of gender categories. Typically, measures of social values or preferences are relatively "projective," i.e., there is greater individual variation, or less consensus, in the responses to questions having to do with social values than to those concerning the cognitive nature of the social objects involved or those involving the choice of a (morally) right action in particular situations. In large part, however, individual differences in values, in conceptions of the ideal, are reflected by parallel although smaller individual differences in conceptions of the real (Kohlberg 1966b). This is particularly true for individual differences in values that show age-developmental regularities.

Our approach, then, assumes that the cognitive learning of sex-role concepts leads to the development of new values and attitudes, and that neither socializing pressures nor direct motive teaching is a necessary part of this process. We shall postulate the following five mechanisms by which the development of sex-role concepts leads directly to the development of masculine-feminine values: (1) The tendency to schematize interests and respond to new interests that are consistent with old ones. (2) The tendency to make value judgments consistent with a self-conceptual identity. (3) The tendency for prestige, competence, or goodness values to be closely and intrinsically associated with sex-role stereotypes, e.g., the association of masculinity with values of strength and power. (4) The tendency to view basic conformity to one's own role as moral, as part of conformity to a general socio-moral order. (5) The tendency to imitate or model persons who are valued because of prestige and competence, and who are perceived as like the self.

All of these mechanisms by which concepts are assumed to generate values rest on the assumption that the child is a valuing and value-seeking organism. Thinking about value development has long been dominated by the notion that the child's judgments of himself and others are internalizations of parental-cultural judgments. In fact, everyday observation indicates that children possessed of language are constantly making spontaneous judgments of good and bad about other people and objects, and spontaneous judgments (mostly of good) about themselves and their actions. The assumption that children seek to ascribe judgments of "good" to themselves simply because judgments of good have been associated with love and reward hardly does justice to the variety of spontaneous seekings of worth to be found in young children. Judgments of value by others, and associated rewards, are influential factors in determining the child's valuing, but they are not their sole or basic origin. Any parent who has attempted to change the peculiar high value a young child has set on some object or activity that has nothing to do with reducing primary drives or winning social approval will be convinced of this.

In seeking the basis of children's spontaneous valuing tendencies, we must turn first to children's interests, since these are observable long before the child makes verbal value judgments. The observations of Piaget (1952) have been particularly useful in documenting the extent of the young infant's interests in objects and events that have no plausible relationship to primary drives. White's (1959) review of the experimental literature clearly indicates that the infant has a tendency to explore, to learn, to act upon, and to master external objects and stimuli; he groups these tendencies under the common heading of "effectance" or "competence" tendencies, rather than treating each tendency as a distinct primary need or drive. Piaget (1952), who treats these tendencies under the rubric "assimilation," is able to define the interest value of objects and events in terms of the extent to which a particular object or event does, or does not, fit into the infant's existing behavioral organization or schemata.

Our first mechanism, the tendency to respond to new activities and interests that are consistent with old ones, is an expression of this notion of Piaget's. It implies both the tendency to autonomous expansion and generalization of interests to new activities and objects, and the tendency for these new interests to have a relationship of match, or consistency, to old interests and schemata. By the age of two, there are a number of quite clear sex differences in behavior and interests, including differences in the interest value of toys (Vance and McCall 1934, Benjamin 1932), in activity rate, in aggressiveness (Haltwick 1937), and fearfulness (Jersild 1943). Probably some of these differences have an innate basis, while others result from parents' exposing boys to one type of toys and playmates, and girls to another. These early sex differences are specific interest differences; they are not a reflection of general masculinity-femininity values, or an expression of a desire to maintain a masculine or feminine self-concept. These interests tend to become generalized, however, as they assimilate new objects or activities that are consistent with them.

Schemata and interests are not yet concepts and values. As we have seen, the child by the age of three has a concept of self and a concept of gender that he relates to himself. By age three–four, the child also tends to make judgments of good and bad about things, and to maintain that whatever he makes, does, or owns is as good or better than those things other children do, make, or own (Greenberg 1932). At this age, then, the child has a naive or egocentric tendency to value anything associated with or like himself. Accordingly, the child tends to value positively objects and activities that represent his gender identity because his gender identity is part of himself. This mechanism is so obvious that it is recognized by children themselves. A boy aged four expressed a preference for a male babysitter. When his parents asked him why he liked boys better, his seven-year-old brother intervened to say, "because he's a boy himself, of course." As the child becomes older, the tendency to equate the self with good is tempered by increased tendencies toward objective and consistent valuings, and by increased tendencies toward objective and consistent conceptualizations of the self. There is a general age-developmental trend toward differentiation of the concept of the actual self and the concept of the ideal or good self. At all ages, however, there is a tendency toward cognitive balance, or consistency, between the self-concept and judgments of values (Brown 1961). This balance is maintained by two tendencies. The first tendency, to equate the self with the good, causes the child to engage in activities or to acquire objects judged to be good. The second tendency causes the child to judge as good activities and objects that are part of the self, similar to the self, associated with the self, or enhance the activities of the self.

If there were not ample evidence for the first tendency, knowledge of an individual's self-concept would be useless in predicting behavior. In our discussion in the previous section, we documented this tendency by citing experimental studies which indicate that by the age of five children's responses to sex-typed reinforcements are already determined by sex-typed values. Young children's sex-typed value statements predict the social reinforcers they seek or the learnings they engage in.

With regard to the tendency toward positive valuation of those things that are consistent with, or like, the self, we expressed the view that young children were especially egocentric or self-projective in their value judgments. It is, of course, also true that young children's value statements are more likely to be influenced by external suggestion and reinforcement (as opposed to prior value judgments and self-conceptions) than are those of older children or adults (Kohlberg 1966b). At the same time, however, this apparent conformity is more likely to be strictly specific and behavioral, and does not involve a shift of basic values in the direction of the values held by the external reinforcing agent. This double quality of the young child's evaluative tendencies has been termed "egocentrism" by Piaget (1947). Following Piaget, studies by Lerner (1937) and others indicate that the young child usually does not make a distinction between the value he places upon objects and the value that others place upon objects; that is, he does not recognize that the value of an object differs for different people. This makes him particularly "suggestible" in his specific valuings, because the fact that others value an activity or object may make it valuable per se. At the same time, however, the child is likely to assume that these others who lead him to value particular objects have the same bases for valuing that he does; hence he assimilates the "objective" social values of others to his own egocentric value perspective. Therefore, unlike an adult, the child is much more likely to "impose" his self-based values upon the world because he assumes that they form the basis of the valuings of others.

In the sex-role area, this tendency toward egocentric evaluation leads children of both sexes to think that their own sex is best in some absolute sense. In reply to the question "Is it better to be a boy or a girl?" Minuchin (1964) found that 85 per cent of a group of ten-year-olds said their own sex was better. Kohlberg (unpublished data) has found similar results for a small sample of children of five to seven. Hartley, Hardesty, and Gorfein (1962) obtained similar results when they asked children of eight to eleven what sex baby they would prefer to have, and what sex child an unspecified adult husband or wife would prefer. S. Smith (1939) also reports preferential valuing of the same-sex in children of nine to fourteen. In part, this same-sex valuing reflects the encouragement of sex-appropriate behavior by socializing agents. However, this encouragement is not interpreted by young children as representing the relativistic social norm "It is good to act in conformity with one's own sex," but rather as representing the egocentric absolute value "My sex is better than the other sex."

The tendency for the young to make egocentric valuings in the sex-role area has been documented in Kohlberg's (1962) study of children's reasons for believing that a neutral "It" figure would prefer the various sex-typed objects and activities pictured in Brown's (1956) It Scale for children. Almost half of these reasons were egocentric projections of the child's own personal evaluation. When asked why the It figure would like a particular toy, the child would reply, "because I have a toy like it at home." The other half of the reasons given were sex-role relevant rather than personal, but they were made in terms of the absolute value of the object rather than in terms of the object's sex-appropriateness. Examples were: "dresses are better than pants," or "Mommies are better than Daddies."

In contrast, 6–7-year-old children made objective or role-appropriate choices. Instead of projecting their own preferences, the older children tried to anticipate the It figure's choices based on sex category. For example: "If It's a boy he wouldn't want to play with dolls, would he? He is a boy, isn't he?" The choice is defined by a role-appropriate preference rather than by the imagined absolute value of the toy or by the respondent's own preference.

The 4–5-year-olds' positive evaluation of the same-sex or of the sex-typed, then, seems to reflect an egocentric or absolutistic evaluation of whatever is like the self. At this egocentric level, however, the boy values the masculine as it is identified with himself; he does not value the masculine as an absolute stereotype, standard, or category. Accordingly, sex-typed preference at age four–five on the It Scale and on similar tests is at about the 65–75 per cent level. Such partial, rather than categorical, sex-typed preference would be expected for the egocentric extension of a self-image. In contrast the responses of children six–seven tend to be more consistent, with boys making 100 per cent masculine choices on the It Scale, and girls making either 100 per cent masculine or 100 per cent feminine choices depending upon their classification of the sex of the It figure.

In part, the categorical and objective choices made by older children on the It Scale reflect a developing moral-conformity mechanism that we shall discuss shortly. These choices also reflect a curvilinear developmental trend toward maintaining all the criteria involved in gender categorization. We stressed the egocentric evaluation of the like-self in the young child's sex-typed preference. At the core of this general self-projective evaluation is the child's need to maintain his gender identity. Until the child, at around age seven, establishes an abstract, constant definition of gender based on anatomy, his gender self-categorization is related to every possible sex-typed attribute. As an example, Peter, just turning six, made the following comments while his father was carrying his mother's purse along with the groceries: "Why are you carrying the purse, Dad, are you a lady or something? You must be a lady, men don't carry purses." With a child younger than Peter, we find that gender-identity classifications are not systematically contingent on consideration of all the attributes associated with the category. With an older child, when an essential or categorical gender identity is clearly differentiated from accidental or stereotypical indicators of masculinity, a more discriminating and less compulsive use of sex-typing is involved in judgments of gender identity. It was noted earlier that middle-class parents are less sex-typed in their preferences for their school-age children than the children themselves (Schedler 1965). In part, this is because adults tend to perceive the differences between arbitrary and essential gender-identity criteria more clearly than children do.

The two mechanisms that we have discussed so far are mechanisms by which existing self-conceptions are "projected" into positive evaluations of activities and roles. In addition, social stereotypes tend to have value connotations that exist quite apart from the child's previous association of these stereotypes with actual rewards. In the preceding section, we attempted to demonstrate that children form sex-role stereotypes simply on the basis of body-image factors and gross differences in social-role assignment. The stereotyping of masculinity as powerful and competent implies a positive evaluative component to the stereotype. (The semantic differential studies show a positive correlation between the basic power and evaluation dimensions of connotative meaning.) This power value motivates a child to enact or conform to the stereotype, regardless of the rewards associated with the role.

Experimental studies by Bandura, Ross, and Ross (1963) demonstrate that young children learn to imitate or play the role of an individual perceived to possess power or resources, without receiving any direct or indirect reward for such role-playing. In other words, the mere recognition of a role as powerful or competent leads to the desire to play this role. Some social-learning theorists have explained that the child tends to imitate or enact power roles because he receives vicarious reinforcement. In other words, if the child imitates a role model he will get what the role model gets. However, one experimental study by Bandura, Ross, and Ross (1963) suggests that it is possession rather than consumption of resources that leads to modeling. The study showed that an adult E said to own an assortment of candies and goodies was more imitated than an adult E whom the child observed eating the goodies. Apparently imitation was caused by an appeal to the primary competence value of power and control, not by an appeal to vicarious drive reduction.

We may best document this third mechanism of value (power-prestige stereotyping), and its interaction with the second mechanism (positive evaluation of the like-self), by considering the age trends in boys' and girls' masculine-feminine preferences. Typical age trends for sex-typed preferences for activities and toys are presented in Figure 1 (boys) and Figure 2 (girls). These trends were obtained from: a "pictures test" of sex-appropriate activities developed by Sears, Rau, and Alpert (1965) on which age trends were gathered by Kohlberg (in press); a measure of toy preference developed by Rabban (1950); another measure developed by DeLucia (1963); and Brown's It Scale (1950) on which age norms were gathered by Brown (1957), by Hartup and Zook (1960), and by Kohlberg (in press).

Figure 1 indicates that boys' preferential sex-typing of activities, toys, and objects is quite well established (over 65 per cent of choices are sex-appropriate) by age three–four, and that it increases with age thereafter, probably reaching some sort of ceiling at about age six–seven. The test results on the early establishment of such sex-typed preferences are supported by observational studies as well (Vance and McCall 1934, Benjamin 1932).

As Figure 2 indicates, the age trends for sex-typed preferences of girls are less clear-cut. Figure 2 indicates that girls, too, have a well-established pattern of sex-typing at age three–four; however, there is a subsequent age increase on some measures and an age decline on others.

The sharp age decline by girls on the It Scale is largely due to the fact that the "neutral sex" figure about whose preferences the child is asked actually is masculine in appearance. With increased age, girls become less self-projective and more oriented to this reality aspect of the test (Kohlberg 1962, Brown 1962, Lansky and McKay 1963). While the dramatic age decline in the It Scale is largely artifactual, the measures summarized in Figure 2 all indicate that there is no clear age increase in girls' sex-typed preference after age four, as there is for boys'.

The findings for age trends in preference for same-sex peers are roughly similar to those for sex-typed preferences in activities and objects. Age trends for peer preference are presented in Figures 3 and 4.

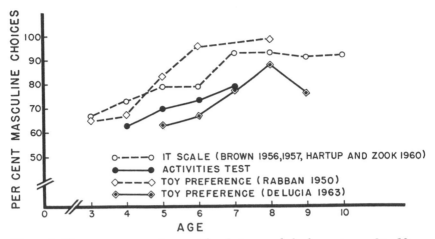

Figure 1. Mean percentage of masculine choices made by boys at ages 3 to 10 on four tests of sex-typed preferences.

(Unless otherwise indicated, data are from Kohlberg and Zigler 1966)

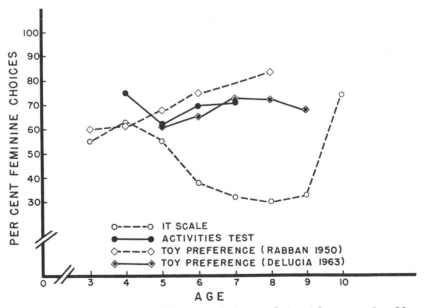

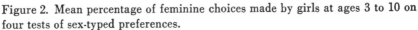

Figure 2. Mean percentage of feminine choices made by girls at ages 3 to 10 on four tests of sex-typed preferences.

(Unless otherwise indicated, data are from Kohlberg and Zigler 1966)

Figure 3. Mean percentage of same-sex peer choices made by boys at ages 3 to 7.
(Unless otherwise indicated, data are from Kohlberg and Zigler 1966)

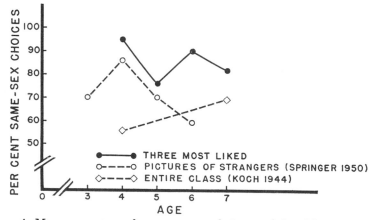

Figure 4. Mean percentage of same-sex peer choices made by girls at ages 3 to 7.
(Unless otherwise indicated, data are from Kohlberg and Zigler 1966)

Figure 3 indicates that boys show clear same-sex preferences at age
three–four, and that these preferences remain stable or increase slightly
with age.* Figure 4 suggests that girls' same-sex preferences for peers
are established early but may decline with age. In this respect, the findings for girls' same-sex peer preferences parallel the findings for same-
sex preferences for objects and activities.

* The relatively low same-sex scores in the Koch (1944) study, especially for the four-
year-olds, is probably specifically due to the paired comparison method used. When Koch
(1944) actually observed frequency of friendship contacts in preschool interaction
among some of the same subjects, she found about 80 to 90 per cent of such contacts
were same-sex.

Figures 1–4 indicate that sex-typed preferences are established early. The data on parent identification discussed in the next section indicate that boys are still mother-oriented at age four, when sex-typed preferences for objects, activities, and playmates are already clearly established. Accordingly, these preferences cannot be explained by same-sex parent identification. Nor can these age trends be interpreted in terms of cummulative discrimination learning of reinforced culturally defined sex-appropriate responses. Boys' same-sex preferences increase regularly with age in a fashion consistent with this notion, but girls' do not.

It seems quite reasonable to attribute the same-sex preferences of both boys and girls aged three–five to the child's tendency toward self-projective and identity-maintaining evaluations. These same-sex preferences are too generalized to be simply extensions of innate or early acquired sex differences in specific interests and temperament. As already discussed, the reasons given by children of this age for their choices were concerned, not with their specific interests, but with judgments of their own value (Kohlberg 1962). The children's statements that their own sex is better, and their marked preference for same-sex peers, can only be explained on this basis.

In contrast, it appears to us that the responses received from children aged five to eight can only be explained by the fact that during this age period both sexes award greater value or prestige to the male role. In our discussion of masculine-feminine stereotypes in the preceding section, we noticed an age-developmental increase (years four to six) in the award of power and competence to the adult male role. We attributed this increase to a growing awareness of the occupational order and to a growing understanding of economic functions and powers. In addition to the age-related increase in attribution of power and competence to the masculine role, we noted an age-related decline in egocentric self-projective modes of valuing in favor of evaluations in terms of place in a social order. For girls, the decline of the egocentric mode of conceiving the "like-self" as best coincides with a growing awareness of the superior prestige of the male adult role. As with measures of sex-typed preference of activities and playmates, girls make fewer judgments than boys that their own sex is better (Hartley, Hardesty, and Gorfein 1962, Minuchin 1964), and girls' preferential evaluations of their own sex decrease with age (S. Smith 1939). This interpretation is supported by the close parallel between age trends in girls' same-sex preferences and age trends in same-race preferences of children of mildly disadvantaged racial groups.

Thus Springer (1950) found a decline at ages five and six in Hawaiian Orientals' preference for other Orientals (as opposed to Caucasians) similar to the decline in girls' preferences for girls.

Although sex-role value stereotypes may affect girls' sex-typed preferences, they do not make girls want to give up their own gender identity. Girls continue to prefer feminine objects and activities at all ages, and their own preferences seem to be even more feminine than their more objective and stereotyped judgments of value. Girls score higher on feminine preference when asked "which do you like" than when asked "which do girls like" (Hartup and Zook 1960). Furthermore, girls have the option of playing a feminine role in a man's world, whereas boys do not have the option of playing a masculine role in the woman's world. In other words the girl can have "opposite sex" interests, and yet maintain her same-sex values more readily than the boy.

More basically, however, adult female stereotypes are positive enough to make femininity attractive to young girls, even though adult females are perceived as less powerful and competent than males. While the stereotype of adult femininity is inferior in power and competence to the male, it is still superior to that of a child of either sex. The mother or teacher is thought to be both more competent and more feminine in appearance, dress, and manner than the young girl. Therefore stereotypes of femininity do appeal to the young girl's desire for competence and power. It should also be noted that stereotypes of femininity rate higher than stereotypes of masculinity in a number of important areas of value or prestige. The fact that the male role is associated with aggression and the female role with nurturance and dependence relations suggests that females are stereotyped as "nicer" than males. Since aggression is a major component of "badness," it is not surprising that almost all girls and most boys of six–seven say boys do more bad things than girls (Kohlberg, unpublished data). Mothers are said to be "nicer" than fathers by a majority of both boys and girls of four–seven (Kagan and Lemkin 1960). "Niceness" is a very important value to school-age American girls, connoting nonaggression, interpersonal conformity, restraint, and nurturance or helpfulness. Another obvious stereotypical distinction between males and females, partly associated with "niceness" stereotypes, has to do with the superior attractiveness of females in the areas of physical beauty, concern with the aesthetic-ornamental in non-body areas, and interpersonal and sexual charm.

In considering these distinctively feminine values, we have noted that these values, like masculine power-achievement values, appeal to basic competence motivation. A boy's desire for power and instrumental competence promotes his desires to be masculine, but his identity-maintaining desire to play masculine roles crystallizes competence motivation into a striving for power and achievement values. In the case of girls, feminine roles award an ample, if somewhat lesser, scope for power and competence motivation, but much of this motivation is channeled into values that are not competence or achievement values in the usual sense. However, the pursuit of attractiveness, goodness, and social approval is ultimately based on the same needs for control of the environment, for self-esteem, and for successful achievement as are the more obvious masculine competence values.

Our discussion of feminine moral-niceness values leads us to consider our fourth basic mechanism, the tendency to perceive conformity to a role pattern as morally right and deviance from it as morally wrong. Since Durkheim, social psychology has accepted and experimentally documented the basic notion that socially shared expectations exert a normative force upon the individual, even in the absence of direct reinforcement or rewards for conformity to these expectations. While middle-class American adults invoke few overt or direct sanctions against children who do not conform to sex-role stereotypes, they do use sanctions to promote conformity to the moral norms of honesty, obedience, industry and control of aggression. Nevertheless children often seem to view same-sex behavior as morally required, and to express punitive sentiments to children who deviate from sex-typed behavior. It seems likely that this tendency is largely the result of the child's conceptions of a socio-moral order in which each person has his place and duties, and in which deviation should be punished. Piaget (1947), in his study of the child's moral judgment, has stressed the tendency of the young child to view any deviation from the social order as bad or wrong, even if such a deviation would not be considered bad by adults. The child does not distinguish between conventional social expectations and moral laws and duties. Furthermore, Piaget's work suggests that nonmoral physical regularities or laws are thought of in terms of socio-moral law, obligation, and purpose. The physical constancies underlying the child's concepts of gender identity tend to be identified with divine or moral law, and the need to adapt to the physical realities of one's identity are viewed as moral obligations.

As an example, children of five–seven frequently say that a girl can't be a boy because "God made her a girl and she has to stay a girl, that's what God meant her to be" (Kohlberg 1966a).

The moralization of sex-role stereotypes, along with the moralization of all sorts of stereotypes, appears to increase in the years five to eight (Kohlberg 1964). This is particularly true for girls of five–seven who often give reasons for not stealing or murdering such as, "It's too rough, it's too noisy to shoot guns, it's not nice" (Kohlberg, unpublished data). At later ages, moral principles (such as equality and social utility) tend to be distinguished from conventional stereotypes, so that conventional sex-role stereotypes tend to lose their moral quality. This is another reason why parents' sex-typing is less rigid than that of their children (Schedler 1965).

The curvilinear age development of moralistic sex-role stereotypes is probably quite similar to the more thoroughly studied development of moralistic racial stereotypes. Research on "authoritarian personality" (Adorno et al. 1950) has found that strong racial prejudices and stereotypes are associated with strong masculine-feminine stereotyping. These tendencies are in turn correlated with diffuse moralism of an age-developmentally immature variety (Kohlberg 1964).

The fact that moralistic attitudes aid in translating sex-role stereotypes into evaluative forces does not mean that the formation of sex-typed values are expressions of a general process of identification and superego formation, as psychoanalytic and social-learning theorists have sometimes suggested. Among children aged four–seven, no correlations have been found between sex-typed preferences on masculinity-femininity tests and measures of resistance to temptation, of guilt, or of development of moral judgment (Sears, Rau, and Alpert 1965, Heinicke 1953, Krebs 1965). It should also be noted that the stereotyping of the feminine role in terms of moral conformity and niceness values does not engender a stronger conscience in girls. Where sex differences are found in measures of resistance to temptation, or in measures of guilt under conditions of apparent nonsurveillance, the differences are in the direction of a stronger conscience in boys (Kohlberg 1963). The moralization of sex-role differences, then, is not part of a general identification-internalization process through which sex-roles are reputedly learned, but is only one of several mechanisms through which developing sex-role concepts influence attitudes.

SEX-ROLE DEVELOPMENT AND PARENT IDENTIFICATION

At the beginning of the previous section, we summarized briefly our reasons for rejecting the hypothesis that masculinity-femininity scores represent a global identification with one's sex-role resulting from identification with a same-sex family model. At the same time we listed identification or modeling as the fifth mechanism by which developing sex-role concepts are translated into masculinity-femininity values and attitudes. This way of looking at identification differs enough from both the psychoanalytic and the social-learning views of identification to warrant fairly detailed elaboration and application to the research findings. Our examination of research findings will center mainly on trends for boys. This is because the focus of our analysis is upon age-developmental shifts in parent identifications. Theory postulates, and research finds, clear shifts for boys but not for girls. Accordingly, the interpretation of developmental mechanisms of identifications in girls is much more complex and ambiguous, and will be fully treated elsewhere (Kohlberg, in press).

Our conception of the identification concept rests somewhere midway between the social-learning treatment of identification as a situational modeling or imitation, and the psychoanalytic treatment of identification as a sudden, totalistic, and permanent incorporation of parental images. It is clear that almost all of the child's social learning has a major imitative component; indeed, social learning is by definition mainly imitation. Analysis of most social or imitative learning does not require the use of arcane concepts of identification, as Bandura indicates (Bandura 1962, Bandura and Walters 1963). The fact that children copy the responses of persons considered competent, good, or powerful does not require conceptions of identification. In general, the child copies others' acts because the very fact that someone else performs these acts makes them appear more interesting, right, socially acceptable, or likely to lead to reward than acts he has not seen performed by others. Most imitative social learning can be adequately viewed in these terms, and efforts to link such learning to identification concepts can lead only to confusion.

Nonetheless, case studies of personality development frequently point to more totalistic types of imitation having the following characteristics (Sears 1957, Bronfenbrenner 1960, Emmerich 1959a, Kagan 1958,

Slater 1961): (1) General traits, attitudes, and values are imitated rather than specific acts. (2) These imitated traits form a unitary cluster or package representing the child's conception of the total personality of the individual model. (3) The modeled behavior is maintained independently of the social rewards or of the rational value associated with the behavior.

The identification notion, then, implies that imitative behavior is derived from a general conception of the real or ideal self molded on the child's conception of a particular person, i.e., that imitation arises from a perceived conceptual similarity between the self and the model rather than from a conception of the situationally or socially appropriate, and accordingly is resistant to situational reward. The identification concept also implies that this generalized and intrinsic tendency to imitate another's behavior rests upon the existence of a strong emotional attitude or tie to the other, i.e., upon a relationship of love for, or of control by, the model.

The cognitive-developmental approach, like the psychoanalytic, recognizes the organizing role of the self, or ego, in social development, and hence recognizes the need for such a concept of identification in explaining the effects of love, hate, and fear upon social development. However, we find it impossible to believe that such basic and near-universal personality functions as morality or masculinity-femininity are the primary or direct products of parent identification (Kohlberg 1963, 1964). There are too many developmental and cultural forces that tend to produce "normal" morality or normal sex-role attitudes for us to see these attitudes as contingent on special unique relationships to parental models. While idiosyncratic or pathological features of personality may be direct products of certain identification processes, normal developmental functions are not.

Our second disagreement with psychoanalytic identification theory is with the assumption that identifications are fixed and early established structures. While certain imitatively learned expressive traits may be established early, motivated attitudes of identification shift with development (Karon 1953). Although adequate longitudinal studies of identification have not yet been carried out, the available evidence indicates that attitude (as opposed to expressive-trait) measures of relative identification with the father or mother change markedly with development. Kohlberg (1966a) assessed stability over a one-year period using doll-play tests of relative imitation and of relative attachment to the father and mother. The tests themselves had a good short-term retest stability even when alternate forms were employed (correlations between alternate forms administered with a two-week interval were .92 for father-imitation and .58 for father-attachment). Over the one-year interval, however, the longitudinal stability of the tests was low. (Retest correlations for father-imitation were −.23 for boys and .35 for girls; for father-attachment, .11 for boys and .42 for girls.) These findings suggest that parent-identification attitudes are age-specific reactions to developmental tasks, reactions that are not predictable from early acquisitions of traits like those of one parent or the other.

This notion of parent identifications as phases in adaptation to developmental role tasks implies a cognitive and more or less conscious structuring of identification attitudes.* It is apparent that any elaborated identification (as distinct from an imitative behavior) involves a comparison of the self-concept and the concept of the other, and also involves some concept of a process by which a person comes to occupy a role or becomes like another person. As cognitive development leads to basic changes in these concepts, there are changes in the content and process of identification with the parent.

In addition to stressing the development of the conceptual aspects of identification tendencies, we will also stress the role of general effectance, or competence motivation, in identification attitudes. (Psychoanalytic theory postulates either libidinal conservation or ego defense as motivation for identification.) While the clinical literature (e.g., Bettelheim) suggests dramatic cases of identification based on ego-survival motives, the survival aspects of competence or ego motives seem only distantly related to the identification that functions in the development of a normal personality.

Our analysis starts with an assumption shared by both psychoanalytic and social-learning theorists, the assumption that a fairly close relationship exists between sex-role attitudes and attitudes of identification with the same-sex parent. The empirical studies (especially of boys) consis-

---

* In fact, most research measures of perceived or desired similarity between the self and the parent are clearly measures of conscious tendencies, though these measures facilitate verbalization of this abstract tendency by asking what the parent is or does, and what the self is or does in particular contexts. Such "conscious" or attitude-identification measures seem appropriate in light of the difficulty of specifying the meaning of an unconscious perception of the self as being like the parent.

tently show a cluster of correlations linking together masculine preference, imitation of the same-sex parent, and affectional attitudes shown
toward the same-sex parent. Low to moderate correlations have been
found fairly consistently between measures of boys' masculine preference and measures of their tendency to imitate their fathers or to perceive themselves as similar to them (Hartup 1962, Kohlberg, in press,
Payne and Mussen 1956, Gray 1959, Karon 1953, Sopchak 1952). Similar correlations are also reported between masculine preference and
both the boy's affectional dependency upon the father and his tendency
to perceive the father as affectionate (Mussen 1961, Mussen and Distler
1959, Kohlberg, in press).

It is in the interpretation of these correlations that the cognitive-
developmental theory departs most concretely from other theories of
identification. Both psychoanalytic (Freud 1924, Bronfenbrenner
1960) and social-learning theories (Burton and Whiting 1961, Brim
1958, Kagan 1964, Lynn 1959, Sears, Rau, and Alpert 1965) view such
correlations as indicating that identification with the same-sex parent
is the prerequisite for, or cause of, appropriate sex-typed attitudes, dis-
agreeing only in their assumptions about the motives or conditions favoring identification with the same-sex parent. In contrast (see Figure 5)
the cognitive-developmental theory reverses the interpretation of the
causal direction of these correlations, seeing them as primarily resulting
from the tendency for boys high on masculine sex-typing to identify
with the father rather than for a high father-identification to cause high
masculine sex-typing.

We quoted earlier the study of Epstein and Leverant (1963) which
indicated that boys high on sex-typed preference learned better under
reinforcement by a male E than a female E, while boys low on sex-typed
preference learned equally well from either. At its simplest level, an
attitude of identification implies a generalized tendency to imitate or be
taught by a particular person or class of persons. In this sense, it is obvious that a boy who desires to engage in masculine activities will prefer
a male teacher or model to a female. The seven-year-old boy who explained that his younger brother wanted a male babysitter because "he
was a boy himself," went on to say that he (the seven-year-old) wanted
a male babysitter because "a girl can't teach me anything."

Only the assumption that identification derives from prior drives and
rewards could obscure the fact that the boy's preference for male models

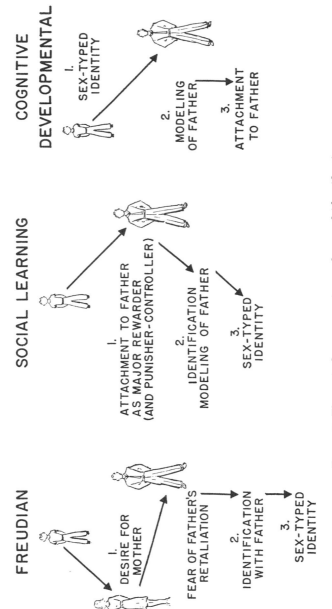

Figure 5. Theoretical sequences in psychosexual identification.

arises from previously formed masculine interests and values. We cited earlier Bandura's (1963) studies indicating that modeling occurs in the absence of direct external rewards, and in the absence of a prior nurturant relationship with the model (although these latter factors may increase imitation). We noted that the possession of certain resources by the model was one factor in such imitation. Even more basic, however, is the fact that modeling takes place regardless of the power or status of the model as long as the model's activities are interesting or colorful. Whether the model punches a Bobo doll ("a chance to reduce aggression drives"), or whether he engages in a "drive-neutral" act such as marching around the room with odd gestures crying "March, march," the children imitate him. Piaget (1952) and others have carefully documented the fact that infants of eight months or more regularly imitate interesting activities of other people in the absence of any history of reinforcement for such imitation. These imitations are neither the result of a conditioned association between imitation and reward, nor the result of an "imitative instinct," but are more a product of the child's tendencies to master or demonstrate a causal control of interesting environmental events. To reproduce an event by imitation is a form of mastery much as is the reproduction of an event by causal manipulation. Although physical events may be imitated, it is the activities of people that are primarily imitated because people are like the infant himself. Imitation develops from circular reaction (Piaget 1947). In other words, the infant first imitates only those adult sounds that are already in his repertoire; he does not imitate new sounds. Gradually circular imitation develops into imitation of new acts of the model. In our view, then, imitation or modeling is a primary and "natural" (though not instinctive) social tendency that does not require a physical drive-reducing or care-taking relationship but does require a relationship of similarity. The two-year-old boy exhausts himself tagging behind his older brother attempting to imitate every activity. This imitation is not based on a past history of affection and care. The two-year-old is likely to imitate his brother more than his mother because his brother performs more grossly interesting and comprehensible activities. When he is in need or distress, however, the two-year-old quickly turns to his mother, not to his model.

We have stressed that for the boy with masculine interests and values the activities of a male model are more interesting and hence more modeled. Our discussion of infant and peer imitation also suggests that

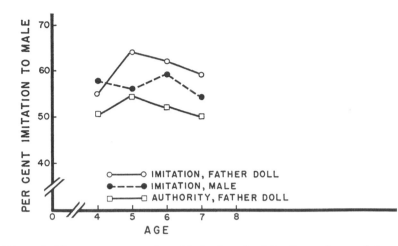

Figure 6. Mean percentage of total imitation of adults directed toward the male by boys at ages 4 to 7.

(Data from Kohlberg and Zigler 1966)

a boy's perception of similarity between himself and his father ("both male") should lead to modeling. This tendency for perceived similarity to lead to modeling and then to further perception of similarity has been experimentally documented as a general tendency in adults by Stotland and his coworkers (Stotland, Zander, and Nakoulen 1961). (The tendency has already been implied by our discussion of the tendency to value the like-self.) The existence of imitative tendencies based on primary effectance motivation and on similarity suggests that boys will have some tendency to imitate their fathers regardless of the actual reward, power, or affectional structure of their family, and that this tendency will develop after, and as a result of, the formation of a basic gender identity and masculine values.

The first fact that we shall place in evidence for the congnitive-developmental identification theory has already been documented in previous sections: the fact that both boys and girls have acquired an appropriate sex identity and relatively generalized sex-typed preferences and stereotypes at an age (four) at which it has been generally believed that both sexes still identify primarily with the mother.

In considering the age trends in boy's father-identification, one should consider separately the imitation and the dependency-attachment components of identification, although the two are found to be empirically correlated. Figure 6 presents age-developmental trends on a measure of imitation of the father doll as opposed to the mother doll, and on a measure of acceptance of authoritative suggestion from the father doll as opposed to the mother doll (Kohlberg 1966a, Kohlberg and Zigler 1966), and a measure of imitation of a male E as opposed to a female E. The doll-play test was adapted from Hartup (1962), who reports means similar to those found by Kohlberg for four- and five-year-olds. The test consisted of a number of items in which the father doll was shown engaging in one non-sex-typed behavior, the mother doll in another. The boy was then asked which behavior a boy doll would perform. The authority items were similar in form, but involving conflicting suggestions by the mother and father dolls.

Clear preferential imitation of the father on these tests is present by age four–five. (Figures 1 and 3 indicated that boys express a clear— over 65 per cent—preference for masculine activities and playmates by age four.) The experimental imitation measure is based on the number of designs copied from a male E divided by the total number of designs copied in two sessions of free design made by the child and an adult; one session with a male E, one with a female E. Here too, insofar as preferential imitation is established (over 55 per cent choice), it is present by age four. These experimental results are consistent with the findings of Rosenblith (1959, 1961), Bandura (1962) and Hartup (1958) that boys of four and five imitate male E's more than they imitate female E's.

The age-trend data, then, suggest that preferential imitation of fathers or adult male figures is established early, but neither as early nor as clearly as sex-typed preferences for activities and peers. The fact that the trends toward preferential imitation of strange males appear as early, or earlier than, preferential imitation of the father suggests that a general sex-typing factor, rather than a specific "father-identification" factor, is determining these trends. The tendency for "father-identification" to lag behind sex-typed preference becomes more clear-cut when we consider the age trends on measures of preferential affiliation or dependency presented in Figure 7.

The measures presented in Figure 7 are roughly parallel to the imitation measures in Figure 6. The doll-test measure (Kohlberg, in press) is based on items used by Ammons and Ammons (1943), who report similar means for children aged four and five. (A sample item: "Now the boy [doll] has to go to bed. Who does he want to go up with him to say goodnight, the father or the mother?") The other curves in Figure

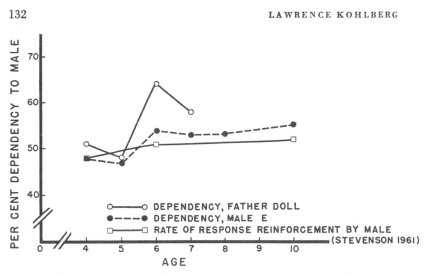

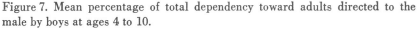

Figure 7. Mean percentage of total dependency toward adults directed to the male by boys at ages 4 to 10.
(Unless otherwise indicated, data are from Kohlberg and Zigler 1966)

7 represent relative desirability of social reinforcements dispensed by adult male (as opposed to female) experimenters. In the Kohlberg (in press) study children spent two sessions making sticker designs, one with a male E, one with a female E. The verbal comments initiated by the child were given scores of one to three based on the extent to which they seemed to require a nurturant response from the experimenter. The curve in Figure 7 represents the percentage of the child's total verbal dependency in the two situations that were initiated in the session with the male E. The curve from the Stevenson (1961) study, which represents the mean number of responses made while playing "drop the marble in the hole" with encouragement from a male E, is expressed as a percentage of the total number of responses in the sessions with the male and with the female E. (This curve has been derived from the Stevenson data in order to be comparable in form to the Kohlberg [in press] data.)

The trends of Figure 7, at least those from the Kohlberg study, clearly suggest that the age-developmental shift toward affiliation with father figures or adult males does not lead to clear preference for the male until about age six. The trends in Figure 6, presented in conjunction with those from Figures 1 and 3, do not support the view that affectional identification is primarily a causal antecedent of masculine preference. Were this the case, young boys would not show masculine sex-typing until they had formed a primary identification with the father. Instead these trends suggest the cognitive-developmental theoretical sequence diagramed in Figure 5. When we compare the dependency trends of Figure 7 with the imitation trends of Figure 6, it appears that the group trend for father preference in imitation precedes the trend for father preference in dependency by about one year. A comparison of Figure 6 with Figure 1 suggests, however, that preferential father-imitation comes somewhat later than general sex-typed preferences. While we do not have firm evidence that this group-trend sequence actually constitutes a general sequence in the development of individual children, there is some evidence that is consistent with this hypothesis. If the sequence held for individual development, we would expect that all boys who preferentially imitated the male would also show sex-typed preference for activities and objects (It Scale). In fact, only two of the 35 boys who preferentially imitated (55 per cent) the father doll failed to be same-sex-typed (55 per cent) on the It Scale. Similarly, the sequence notion leads us to expect that all boys who show preferential dependency for the male adult would also show preferential imitation of him (and would also be same-sex-typed on the It Scale). In fact, only one of the 26 boys who showed father dependency failed to show father-imitation and same-sex preference (Kohlberg, in press). A similar Guttman-scale pattern was found on the experimental dependency measure.

We have already considered the rather straightforward and obvious theoretical reasons which have led us to propose that formation of a gender identity and sex-typed preferences precedes preferential same-sex parent modeling for the boy. The reasoning behind our proposal that imitation precedes preferential father-attachment is part of a more general theory of attachment elaborated in detail elsewhere (Kohlberg, in press).

We have seen that imitation or modeling does not depend upon a prior relationship of nurturance or dependency. If modeling tendencies develop, however, a degree of emotional dependency or attachment almost inevitably follows. The desire to model eventually leads to the desire to be near the model, and to obtain his approval, i.e., to obtain assurance that the self's behavior is like the model's or conforms to his standards. The following sequence, (1) desire to be a role-occupant, (2) desire to imitate a prestigious role-occupant, and (3) emotional attachment to the model, can be observed in the formation of attachments by adolescents to friends or teachers. Given our assumption that the young school-age child has a sex-role identity and sex-role values, this sequence should be just as valid for the formation of attachments at earlier ages.

Although children do imitate those with whom they have no dependency relationship (e.g., siblings), a long-term modeling relationship tends to become one of affectional dependency. This occurs as soon as the child recognizes the need for a continuing relationship with his model, and as soon as he seeks assurance that the activity he has imitated is really shared or that it has really been done correctly. In early imitation, the child seems to feel that he possesses the desired attribute or activity as soon as he has completed the act of imitation. Somewhat later, imitation is accompanied by attention-seeking "look at me" behavior. The child wants the person he has imitated to watch his imitative act, so that the roles of admirer and copier are reversed. Although often not recognized as such, much attention-seeking is a naive form of sharing, an expression of the child's need to assure himself that the activity he finds so interesting and worthy of imitation is also felt by others to be interesting and worthy. Further development of the modeling process leads the child from attention-seeking to approval-seeking. "Look at me do it" becomes "Did I do it right?" The child, even though he can perform the act himself, still admires the adult as a generally superior performer and looks to him for approval. This desire for recognition and approval leads to the need for a continuing relationship with the model. The child wants to be like the model in general, and needs a stable relationship to attain this goal. Finally, when he has a close relationship with his model, he derives a vicarious sense of success or worth from those activities of the model that he cannot perform. At this point, then, modeling tends to become part of a unique relationship of identification or "satellization" (Ausubel 1957)—a relationship in which modeling, the desire for proximity, compliance, and dependence, and the enjoyment of vicarious esteem are all united.

We have stressed the mediating role that modeling tendencies based on a sense of similarity play in the development of the boy's affectional identification with the father. It is also clear that perceived similarity itself leads directly to affiliative or affectional tendencies. In the previous section we stressed the fact that gender similarity tends to lead to affiliation, i.e., that a boy likes other boys because other boys are like him. This general principle of homophily has been amply documented in the studies of adolescent and adult friendship formation. These studies stress both the tendency to value positively the like-self, and the role that similarity plays in facilitating empathy and sharing in affiliative relationships. That liking as well as imitating same-sex persons is part of the child's general sex-typed preference attitudes is suggested by the fact that preference for same-sex peers appears at the same early age as sex-typed activities and role preferences.

The findings just mentioned, however, indicate a time delay in the affiliative projection of the boy's sex-typed identity: his preference for same-sex peers is established before his preference for same-sex parent figures. The cognitive-developmental theory suggests two reasons for this discrepancy. The first is that the boy's classification of adult males in the common category "we males" is a more cognitively advanced achievement, and therefore comes later than his classification of other boys in that category. It is not until about age five–six, when the child begins to sort objects predominantly on the basis of similar attributes, that he forms groupings which include same-sex figures of diverse ages (Kohlberg 1966a, in press). The second consideration is that the boy's affectional tie to his mother is deep, and it takes some time before the boy's self-conceptual or sex-role identity considerations can lead him to subordinate it to the development of a tie to the father.

An illustration of the way in which the boy's dependency feelings interact with a narrow concrete use of gender labels is provided by a 3½-year-old boy, Joey. Joey was quite anti-girl, partly as a result of autonomous developmental tendencies, partly as a result of brainwashing by an older brother. When the younger boy was asked "Do you want any girls at your birthday party?" he answered "No, I hate girls, girls are icky." His mother then asked "Don't you like any girls?" The boy answered "No." His mother went on, "But I'm a girl." The boy replied, "I like you, but you're a big lady. I like big ladies. I like my teacher, too."

Conceptual development enters into the boy's father-identification, not only in the widening of the boy-male category, but in the increased tendency to base feelings of identification on relationships of similarity rather than on relationships of proximity and association. The young boy tends to feel his mother is most like him because feelings of social closeness and identification at young ages are based more on association than upon judgments of similarity. As conceptual relations between persons become based on attributes of similarity and class membership, so do definitions of social ties.

The close interrelationship between the development of categorical concepts and definitions of social bonds in terms of similarity, and the development of father identification in boys is suggested by one portion of the Kohlberg (in press) study. As part of this study, animal pictures were shown to the child in sets composed of four animals of the same species, two of which were of the same color. The child was then asked "Which animals like each other?" and "Which animals do the same [specified] activity?" Over 70 per cent of the responses of children of five and over named the same-colored animals for both these sets of questions, whereas four-year-olds did not choose the same-color animals beyond the level of chance (33 per cent). This rapid age increase in similarity choices parallels a similar age increase in object sorting by similarity (rather than by associative ties), and parallels as well the four-to-six age increase in father choices by boys. This age parallelism is not merely accidental: among boys of a given chronological or mental age, those who score high on the use of similarity in the animal test also tended to score high on the doll test of father-identification. The correlation between the two measures was .45 with mental age controlled. (Similar correlations were found between the animal test and the measure of same-sex peer preference.)

In summary, then, the boy prefers and imitates masculine roles and models, first, because he feels they are "like self," and, second, because he awards superior prestige, power, and competence to them. These tendencies lead him to develop preferential imitation and approval-seeking from the father, but only after a delay period. This delay period occurs because cognitive growth is required before the father can be categorized in terms of "we males," and before the father's occupational and familial role is perceived as more prestigeful than the mother's in terms of economic, occupational, and instrumental functions. During this early period (age four–eight) the boy's identification with the father tends to be assimilated to general stereotypes of the masculine role having little to do with the father's individual role and personality. To summarize our discussion of the various factors present in father-identification during the years four to eight, we report the following bedtime conversation of a five-year-old boy who had recently shown a marked shift of orientation from his mother to his academician father:

Oh, Daddy, how old will I be when I *can go hunting* with you? We'll go in the woods, you with your gun, me with my bow and arrow. Daddy, wouldn't it be neat if *we could lasso* a wild horse? Do you think we could do it? Do you think I could ride a horse backward if someone's leading me like you?

These comments suggest the following points: (1) Here dependency and attachment accompany and follow imitation of masculine activities. (2) The basic motive is competence. "Daddy, do you think *I could, that we would* do this." (3) The emphasis in imitation is on *we categorization.* (4) The content equated with *we activities* has little to do with the father's actual interests and abilities, and much to do with the concrete masculine sex-role stereotypes of children.

Our analysis of father-attachment as resulting from perceived similarity and from the desire for normative guidance is a logical extension of principles advocated by such cognitive social psychologists as Sherif and Schachter in their discussions of social affiliation and group formation. These principles have usually been ignored in discussions of parent-attachments and identification because of the tendency to analyze these attachments in terms of the early mother-child tie. Most theories of the formation of parental attachments derive these attachments from drives or instincts present in early infancy. However, these theories find it difficult to account for the formation of later basic attachments. Theories of primary social instincts, such as Bowlby's, have generally ignored the later-arising attachment to the father because this attachment cannot be explained in terms of the early imprinting of the infant's crying, following, holding, smiling, or other "instinctive" responses. Secondary-drive learning theories recognize the formation of later attachments to, or identifications with, the father, but have also encountered considerable difficulty in explaining them.

Secondary-drive theories propose that identification tendencies derive from anaclitic or dependency motives (Sears 1957, Sears, Maccoby, and Levin 1957, Mowrer 1950), which in turn derive from the association of parental caretakers with primary-drive reduction. The principle of stimulus generalization leads to the expectation that responses like the parent's would have some of the reinforcing value of the parent's own response. The substitute value of imitative responses would be expected to be highest under conditions of nurturance withdrawal by, or temporary absence of, the parent (Sears, Maccoby, and Levin 1957).

Such a theory has no ready basis for explaining the boy's shift of identification to the father. While maternal nurturance decreases, and the father's interaction with the child may increase, with age, the father does not become the primary caretaker or the primary expresser of love-nurturance in middle childhood. The withdrawal of the mother's nurturance should lead to more rather than less mother-identification in both boys and girls. And although both boys and girls are affected by the shift in care-taking, only boys exhibit a clear preferential identification with the father.

Although cultural sex-typing should differentially reward the boy for modeling the father rather than the mother, cultural sex-typing cannot by itself account for preferential father-identification within the anaclitic identification theory. Rewarded imitation of the father's behavior does not imply a shift to favoring the father as an object of dependency or affection. A shift in identification must imply a shift in the rewarding or affectional object, not in the typing of the behavior for which reward or affection is given.

It is apparent, then, that an anaclitic theory must account for father-identification, not in terms of the creation of a new identification, but in terms of a shift or displacement of existing mother-identification attitudes to the father. This has been the solution advanced by Mowrer (1950) and by Parsons and Bales (1955), who assume that early mother-identifications are undifferentiated or non-sex-typed, and that the process of cognitive discrimination of sex-role leads the boy to shift the sex-role-relevant aspects of this identification to the father. According to Mowrer (1950, pp. 607–8):

The first identification infants make with mother figures is undifferentiated. ... It is only at a later stage, presumably, that the child becomes aware of the partition of mankind into two sexes; and it is then that the father, who has played a somewhat subsidiary role up to this point, normally comes forward as the boy's special mentor, guide, and model in matters which will help the boy achieve full adult status in his society, not only as a human being, but also in the unique status of a man.

The additions to the notion of anaclitic identification suggested by Parsons and Mowrer attribute the boy's shift to the father to the age-linked cognitive development of sex-role categories and to the boy's consequent awareness of the need for a model who will help him achieve male status, essentially the same view that we are advancing here.

Partly because anaclitic theory cannot plausibly account for basic identifications with nonmaternal figures such as siblings or the father, a second school of social-learning theory stresses social power, authority, or status as the critical factor in post-infancy identifications. In one formulation, social power is defined in terms of control of desired resources, a control that is envied by the child. In this formulation, modeling takes place because the child receives vicarious reinforcement from the model's role performance (Whiting 1960, Burton and Whiting 1961, Kagan 1964, Bandura 1962). In another formulation, the adult's power over the child leads to identification because the child gains a sense of control over his fate through such identification ("identification with the aggressor"), or because the child needs to assume the attitudes of the adult in order to anticipate their impact on his destiny (Brim 1958, Mussen 1961).

The power theories of identification and the cognitive-developmental theory coincide in assuming competence-motivated identification or modeling without a prior base of physical or emotional dependency, and in assuming that identification is cognitively mediated by conceptions of the status and role of the model in the family or in society, rather than simply determined by the behavioral responses of the model as these impinge on the child. However, the cognitive-developmental theory differs from the power theory in the following respects: it does not restrict the appeal of a paternal model to power factors but includes any factor of interesting or competent activity; it focuses on the importance of cognitive similarity as males; it derives paternal power factors from the child's sex-stereotyping rather than from the father's actual power; and, finally, it assumes that an emotional-affectional attachment must accompany modeling before the latter leads to "identification."

It is because of these divergences that the cognitive-developmental theory is able to account for regular age shifts in the boy's identification with the father, something the power theories cannot do. The power theories of identification cannot account for these age shifts in terms of family-structure variables as such because the family's power structure does not change regularly according to the age of the child. As we have seen, however, cognitive development may lead to both age-developmental shifts in perceived power and competence, and to an increased awareness of the gender-similarity determinants of identification.

The most explicit effort to relate age shifts in identification to concepts of social power has been made by Whiting (1960). The Whiting analysis essentially focuses upon the Oedipal relationship and associated sleeping arrangements, and hence raises the same issues as the Freudian theory. Freud, of course, assumed that the girl's shift of attachment to the father was the result of a maturing heterosexual libido. However, his effort to account for the boy's identification with the father in terms of heterosexual libido is much less straightforward. According to Freud, the early pregenital attachment to the mother as a caretaker is accompanied by an anaclitic identification with her. The sexualized and possessive components of the boy's attachment to the mother, which develop during the years three to five, must be resolved by a giving up of the mother. If this renunciation is achieved through identification with the lost love object (anaclitic identification), it leads the boy to a feminine and homosexual identification. This renunciation cannot be achieved by status-envy identification, because the boy's desire to be like the father, and to possess his marital and other prerogatives, can only increase his possessive tie to the mother and his desire to displace the father. Accordingly, the boy's father-identification is believed by Freud to be based on a third factor, his fear of castration by his father.

Empirically, the Freudian theory assumes an age-developmental increase in fear of the father (caused by an increase in Oedipal heterosexual attachment to the mother) followed by a decrease in fear, a decrease in heterosexuality, and a parallel rise in father-identification and in moral processes in general. At present no research data exist that are directly relevant to these postulated developmental trends. One recent important study does report that young children of both sexes have an "unconscious" preference for pictures of opposite-sex peers and adults (as measured by relative pupil dilation) in spite of their conscious verbal preference for pictures of same-sex persons (Bernick 1965).

This study supports the Freudian notion of the early appearance of heterosexual interest (by age five, the age of the youngest subjects in the Bernick study). At the same time, however, the Bernick study did not support the Freudian notion of a "latency period" of declining heterosexual interest in middle childhood. A similar level of heterosexual interest was found at each age from five to sixteen. The Freudian theory of identification would lead to the expectation that the development of verbal same-sex values in middle childhood should represent a same-sex identification leading to repression of heterosexual interest or drive. The fact that the same-sex orientation in (verbal) values characterizing middle childhood is not paralleled by a decline in heterosexual interest in the pupil-dilation measure suggests that same-sex identifications are neither produced by, nor produce, a repression of heterosexual interest as such.

There is, then, at present little evidence for Freud's hypothesis that father-identification is the result of sexual threat or that it leads to a repression of heterosexual drives. There is, indeed, considerable observational and clinical evidence for the existence of a constellation of attitudes in young children that are partially compatible with Freud's notion of the Oedipus complex; e.g., fear of, and rivalry with, the same-sex parent (Kohlberg, in press). There is, however, little or no evidence that such fears of the father either precede or cause a positive father-identification. The Freudian "identification with the aggressor" conception of father-identification suggests that paternal punitiveness and sexual restrictiveness should correlate with father-identification measures in boys. But it is not these factors, but rather measures of paternal warmth, that seem to be positively correlated with boys' father-identifications (Kohlberg 1963).

One implication of the Freudian theory of identification, however, does receive some support from the research findings. This is Freud's hypothesis that morality is a product of the boy's father-identification. Several studies indicate that internalized moral judgments and increased behavioral control characterize development in the same years (four to seven) in which the boy's father-identification is increasing (Kohlberg 1963, 1964). A number of studies also indicate correlations between measures of father-identification (and its father-attitude antecedents) and measures of acceptance of the conventional moral code (Kohlberg 1963). In contrast to findings in other areas of personality development, the morality findings reviewed by Kohlberg (1963, p. 309) suggest that "the father seems to be more important, or at least as important, as the mother in the moral development of the child." This "appears to be due to the natural tendencies for the father to be perceived as an authority figure."

While the Freudian emphasis on the association of father-attitudes with morality receives some support from the research findings, the findings are not really consistent with Freud's theory that sexual identity and the superego are joint products of father-identification (Kohlberg 1963, 1964). In the first place, the observed correlations have not been between father-identification and impulse repression resistance to temptation) or intrapunitive guilt, but rather between father-identification and the development and acceptance of a conventional moral code. In the second place, normal morality may develop under conditions of low father-identification. In the third place, while both masculinity-femininity and morality measures show some correlation with measures of father-identification, they are not correlated with one another and hence do not represent a unitary product of father-identification (see pp. 122–23).

The findings on morality seem more consistent with the cognitive-developmental view of father-identification. According to this latter view, sex-typing, father-identification, and acceptance of the parental moral code are more or less successive stages in development. While sex-typing facilitates identification with the father, it does not in itself facilitate acceptance of the moral code. As we discussed earlier, moral niceness tends to be stereotyped as a feminine specialty, and as a result there is a certain conflict between masculine sex-typing and morality, between being a "real boy" and "being good." In contrast, father-conceptions and father-identifications acquire greater moral dimensions during the childhood years (Kohlberg, in press). There is first a developmental assimilation of adult-male and father concepts in the years four to six, and then a differentiation of these concepts in subsequent years. Accompanying this differentiation of masculine- and father-role concepts is a differentiation of the child's concept of the father role from his concept of his own father as a person distinct from other persons in the role (Kohlberg, in press). Moral identification in the childhood years means being like one's own father by being a good boy and conforming to one's father's expectations, not being like one's father by assuming behavior appropriate to the father role. Moral identification relates, then, to personal rather than positional identification with the father (Slater 1961). While measures of perceived or behavioral similarity to the father as a person correlate with measures of moral conformity, measures of identification with masculine or adult roles do not (evidence reviewed in Kohlberg 1963).

Accordingly, it would appear that in the boy's personality development, father-identification functions more to facilitate the development and acceptance of a moral code than to determine masculinity-femininity as such. In other words, there is a tendency for father-identification to lead to the development of social values, thereby facilitating adjustment, rather than a tendency for father-identification to facilitate adjustment by causing a strong sex-role identification. While consistent correlations between masculine sex-typing and measures of adjustment have not been found for adolescent or adult males (Terman and Miles

1936, Gray 1957, Webb 1963, Sutton-Smith and Rosenberg 1960), consistent correlations have been reported between measures of adolescent and adult males' identification with the father and high adjustment, high peer reputation, and low neuroticism (Osgood, Luce, and Tannenbaum 1957, Mussen 1961, Payne and Mussen 1956, Sopchak 1952, Gray 1959, Helper 1955).

In summary, then, there is little reason to support the Freudian view that father-identification is the result of an anxiety-based defensive inhibition of sexual or other impulses. While father-identification does relate to moral attitudes and adjustment, these relationships seem more interpretable as linked aspects in the development of positive identifications with normative social roles, than as aspects of either "superego-formation" or "sex-role identification." In de-emphasizing the role that father-identification plays in producing sex-role identification, however, we do not wish to deny the role of the boy's actual relationship to his father in consolidating or facilitating development of masculine values. We shall consider this role in our final section.

There is not space in the present chapter to consider the applications of our theory to the complex research findings on parent-identifications in girls. (Such an attempt will be made in Kohlberg, in press.) This task involves a detailed analysis of the major sex differences in sex-typed identification processes, and is complicated by the fact that there is no evidence of a clear age-linked shift in a girl's parent identifications. All theories have assumed that the girl identifies primarily with the mother throughout childhood, and available research data seem to support this assumption. These data (which parallel those for the boys presented in Figures 6 and 7) are presented in Figures 8 and 9.

Figures 8 and 9 indicate a clear preferential orientation to the mother at age four, a preference that declines in the years four to seven but never yields to a preferential identification with the father. These trends are consistent with the findings on sex-typed preferences discussed in the previous section, findings indicating that there is an increased orientation to the prestigious male role in these years. A variety of evidence discussed elsewhere (Kohlberg, in press) suggests that this developmental increase in father-identification consolidates, rather than weakens, the girl's feminine values or identification. For both sexes, identification with the expectations of the complementary role partner may facilitate identification with one's own role (Colley 1959, Johnson 1963, G. H. Mead 1932). The tendency for identification with one's own sex

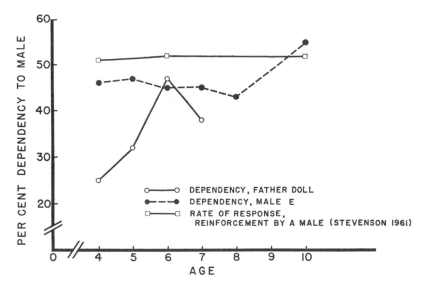

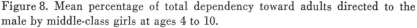

Figure 8. Mean percentage of total dependency toward adults directed to the male by middle-class girls at ages 4 to 10.

(Unless otherwise indicated, data are from Kohlberg and Zigler 1966)

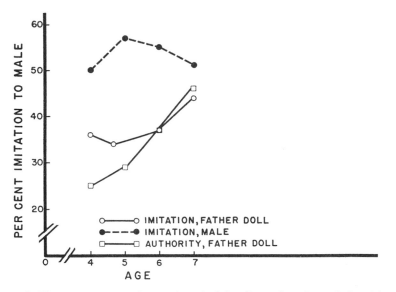

Figure 9. Mean percentage of imitation of adults directed to the male by girls at ages 4 to 7.

(Data from Kohlberg and Zigler 1966)

role to strengthen, and be strengthened by, identification with the opposite-sex partner is much stronger in girls than in boys. Freud's description of feminine heterosexual love as narcissistic-identificatory rather than anaclitic implies this statement, but there are also a multitude of "non-Freudian" reasons why this is so (see Kohlberg, in press).

THE IMPACT OF INTELLECTUAL DEVELOPMENT ON SEX-ROLE ATTITUDES

Our discussion of the development of sex-typing and parent identification has so far stressed "natural" (though not directly maturational) trends of age development rather than individual differences within an age group. This stress is consistent with "stage" theories, like those of Freud (1905), Gesell and Ilg (1943), Erikson (1950), and Piaget (1947), which view the child's personality as a reflection of age-typical motives and world-views rather than as a reflection of stable, individual personality traits. While stage theories focus primarily upon age-typical behavior, they are not at a loss to explain individual differences among children of a given age. Primarily, these behavior differences are viewed as reflecting individual differences in level or rate of development.

When one starts to talk about levels of development, one must take into consideration the fact there are two ways to measure development—intellectually and physiologically. Physiological-development measures can claim to represent a general-rate-of-development variable, since they correlate reasonably well with one another, and are reasonably stable or predictive over time (Tanner 1961). Psychometric measures of mental age have an even better claim to representing such a general-rate variable, since they correlate very well with one another, and are equally stable or predictive over time after the age of five (Jones 1954). The two measures or conceptions of developmental rate are conceptually and empirically distinct from each other, however. Beyond infancy, very small or zero correlations have been found between physical-growth measures and mental age, when chronological age and social class are held constant (Bayley 1940, Paterson 1930).

Insofar as classical psychoanalytic theory projects a general timetable for the development of sex-role attitudes in normal populations, one would expect this timetable to be closely connected to the process of physiological maturation. While the maturation of libidinal tendencies is hardly measurable in early childhood, it seems plausible to relate such maturation to the physiological and skeletal growth measures that predict the onset of puberty. Freud (1905, p. 583) assumes such a parallelism, even believing that the onset of the latency period is partly physiological, though he adds in a footnote that "the complete synchronization of anatomical preparation and psychical development is naturally not necessary."

While the findings on the onset of puberty are not clear-cut, it is not surprising to find that age of onset of puberty has a considerable impact upon heterosexual concerns. Early-maturing adolescent boys appear to engage in heterosexual activity earlier, to marry earlier, and to engage in more heterosexual activity, though the same is not true for girls (Kinsey et al. 1948, 1953). Early-maturing boys have been found to be somewhat higher on paper-and-pencil measures of masculinity than late-maturing boys of equivalent age and I.Q.; early-maturing girls have been found to be more feminine on these measures in one study (Terman and Miles 1936), though not in another (Mussen 1961).

It is, of course, possible that these correlations do not represent the direct impact of puberty upon sex-role attitudes: early-maturing boys may engage earlier in heterosexual activities because of greater opportunity. Not only are early-maturing boys seen as more mature by girls, but they also enjoy favored status in their same-sex peer group. Much higher correlations have been reported between early pubescence and peer-group status and participation than between early pubescence and sexual attitudes per se (Eichorn 1963). A review of case studies of "abnormally" precocious puberty (Dennis 1946, Money 1961), clearly suggests that puberty has a direct bearing on the arousal of heterosexual drives and fantasies (at least for boys). These observations allow us to compare normal children in the late "phallic" period (ages four to eight) with prematurely pubescent children of the same chronological age. The differences in intensity and clarity of sexual behavior are fairly striking. A quite large proportion of the precocious boys were reported to have definite heterosexual interests, imagery, and dreams, and to engage in masturbation or dreams leading to orgasm. In one case report (Le Marquand 1932), a boy who had attained puberty before his fourth year was reported to have made obvious and distressing sexual advances to adult women with whom he was left alone.

The studies of abnormally precocious puberty have a double bearing upon the psychoanalytic view of infantile libidinal stages. Observations of preschool children clearly indicate the existence of general tendencies to seek or enjoy stimulation of the skin and the Freudian "erogenous" zones, tendencies that are difficult to distinguish from desires to rub and cling to blankets, etc. However, these tendencies to skin stimulation do not seem to be accompanied by the intense drive characteristics or the relatively clear heterosexual imagery found in pubescent preschool children. It is only these precocious children who clearly express the heterosexual drives assumed by Freud to be characteristic of all children of this age. At the same time, however, these sexually advanced children are no more advanced than normal young "latency period" boys in general personality development. Thus the findings suggest that there is a qualitative difference between postpubescent and prepubescent sexuality due to physiological maturation, but they do not suggest that this difference is part of a continuous set of maturationally determined psychosexual personality stages. Unfortunately no studies of the relations between physiological maturity and age-linked sex-role attitudes in prepuberal children have been carried out. Such studies should shed considerable light on the Freudian theory of prepuberal maturational stages of psychosexuality.

In contrast to the Freudian theory of sexual stages linked to physical maturation, we have presented a theory of age trends in sex-role attitudes linked to cognitive development. Our analysis has been based on the Piagetian conception of cognitive growth as a process in which basic changes, or qualitative differences, in modes of thinking lead to transformed perceptions of the self and the social world. In our second section we traced out a few important age trends in the cognitive development of sex-role concepts (several others are discussed in Kohlberg, in press) and in the third and fourth sections we related these cognitive trends to parallel age trends in sex-role values or attitudes. Our logic implies that individual children of a given age who are relatively mature in the clearly cognitive aspects of sex concepts should also be relatively mature in sex-role attitudes. Indeed, moderate correlations between individual "cognitive" and "noncognitive" sex-role tasks are found, e.g., the correlation between a measure of gender constancy and the It Scale among children four to six was .54 (Kohlberg, in press). It will be recalled, however, that gender constancy formed part of a correlational cluster of Piaget "stage of conservation" or "stage of concrete operations" items. While distinguishable by factor analysis from other intellectual items, these Piaget stage tests are highly related to standard psychometric measures of mental age (r = .55 to .75 in varying age groups). As we have already stressed, all age-developmental cognitive tasks are heavily correlated with one another in children, and these correlations can be largely accounted for by a general mental maturity factor. Hence it is useful to consider the impact of cognitive development upon sex-role attitudes in terms of studies employing a general mental age or I.Q. measure.

A fairly large number of studies report low to moderate correlations between I.Q. and measures of masculinity-femininity (reviewed in Kohlberg and Zigler 1966). The study most systematically designed to investigate these relations from a developmental point of view was carried out by Kohlberg and Zigler. Kohlberg and Zigler compared the sex-role attitudes of bright (mean I.Q. = 132) and average (mean I.Q. = 104) middle-class children at each age level from four to ten. The children were retested at the end of one year to compare cross-sectional with longitudinal trends. Since physiological maturity and intellectual maturity are independent of each other in children of a given age, a comparison of children of the same chronological age but of different mental ages should indicate the impact of cognitive maturity, as opposed to physiological or instinctual maturity, upon sex-role development. (Since differences between bright and average children of the same chronological age cannot be easily explained as the result of age-grading of socialization pressures, peer culture, or school-grade placement, the comparison also allows some estimate of the impact of cognitive maturity, as opposed to age-graded socialization, upon the development of sex-role attitudes.)

The basic hypothesis of the Kohlberg-Zigler study was the Piaget-Werner hypothesis of parallelism in cognitive and social-affective development. This hypothesis states that emotion and motivation have a cognitive-structural aspect, and that parallel trends of structural development are to be found in both the "purely cognitive" and the affective domain. While an extensive research literature indicates that the best single behaviorally devised predictor or correlate of children's social behavior in various areas is the "nonsocial" trait of intelligence, no previous study has been devoted to examining systematically the import of these correlations for the hypothesis of developmental parallelism (Kohlberg and Zigler 1966).

The Kohlberg and Zigler study involved comparison of bright and average children on the seven measures of sex-role attitudes for which age-developmental trends were presented in Figures 1 through 9. Statistically significant I.Q. differences were found on the following six of the seven measures:

1. The It Scale for children—a projective test of sex-typing developed by Brown (1956).

2. The Pictures Test—another picture test of sex-typed preference developed by Sears and his coworkers (Borstelmann 1961, Sears, Rau, and Alpert 1965).

3. Sex-typing of verbal dependency in an experimental situation with a male and female E.

4. Doll-play choices designed to indicate relative attachment to mother and father, adapted from Ammons and Ammons (1949).

5. Doll-play choices designed to express relative imitation of father versus mother, adapted from Hartup (1962).

6. A measure of sex-typing of sociometric preference for other children.

No significant I.Q. effect was found for the seventh measure, sex-typing of imitation of an adult experimenter, but this measure also failed to represent reliably the development of sex-typed attitudes in the sense that it did not significantly differentiate between age or sex groups. In every case (except in the case of girls' responses to the It Scale, in which an artifact was found), the I.Q. differences could be plausibly interpreted as indicating that bright children were more advanced in terms of the age trends found among the average children. In some cases, the greater advance of the bright children could be attributed to the fact that bright children learn cultural sex-typing labels and discriminations more rapidly, and that they have superior test-taking abilities that permit them to detect the "right answer" to quasi-projective tests. While this would indicate the role of cognitive learning in attitude-test responses, it does not directly suggest the impact of cognitive-stage transformations upon sex-role attitudes, nor does it suggest that cognitive changes have an impact upon "real" affective-behavioral attitudes, rather than verbal attitudes. Such a verbal-learning interpretation of the differences between the bright and average children is much less plausible for some of the other measures used in the Kohlberg and Zigler study. The most clear example, which is presented in Figure 10, measures the proportion-

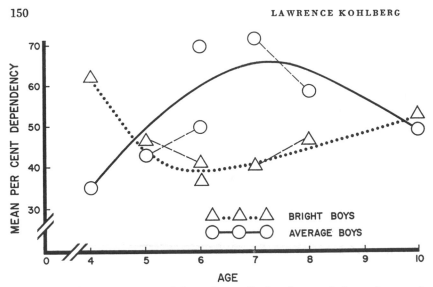

Figure 10. Mean percentage of dependency displayed toward the male experimenter by boys at six ages.

ate dependency shown by boys toward a male (as opposed to a female) examiner.*

Figure 10 indicates that the bright boys are preferentially oriented to the adult male at age four, at a time when the average boys are preferentially oriented to the adult female. As they grow older, the bright boys seem to shift to a preferential orientation to females, and then, from seven to ten, to shift once more to a neutral orientation. While the bright boys are becoming more female oriented (in the years four to six), the average boys are becoming more male oriented. From age six–seven, the average boys begin to become more female oriented, as the bright boys had done two years earlier. These trends suggest that the bright children precede the average children in a shifting developmental course, rather than simply learning the culturally correct response to a given task sooner. Such reversals, timed in terms of mental rather than chronological age, suggest that cognitive development involves conceptual re-

* Figure 10 (as well as the remaining figures in this section) presents both cross-sectional and short-term longitudinal trends. The means for bright or average children first tested at a given age are indicated separately from the means of children retested at that age. Dashed lines representing longitudinal trends connect the means of groups tested and then retested one year later. Since the cross-sectional and longitudinal trends in these figures are roughly consistent with one another, they are summarized by the smoothed trend lines for bright and average children.

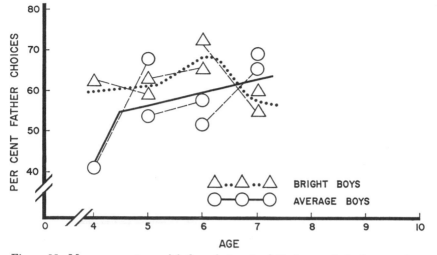

Figure 11. Mean percentage of father choices in doll play made by boys at four ages.

organizations of social attitudes, and that intellectual development initiates new social attitudes and developmental tasks, rather than simply facilitating learning or adaptation to tasks imposed by the social environment or by body maturation. Were the latter the case, the chronological age of developmental reversals should be the same for bright and average groups, with only the rate of acceleration in the new trend more advanced for the bright children.

This cognitive-developmental interpretation is strengthened by the results on the measures of preference for the father doll as opposed to the mother doll, results we discussed in the previous section. These results are presented in Figure 11, which combines the measures of imitation and attachment previously presented in Figures 7 and 9.

As in the verbal-dependency measure, the bright boys become male oriented before the average boys, but start to become more female oriented at around age six, the age when the average boys are still increasing in male orientation. Although developmental reversals are not found in this measure, it is difficult to interpret these trends as representing cumulative social-verbal learning of discrete elements. There is a radical increase in boys' orientation to the father doll in a narrow age period (four–five), which suggests either cognitive reorganization or age-specific socialization forces. Since the radical increase occurs earlier for bright than average subjects, the cognitive-reorganization interpretation appears to be the more plausible one.

Because there are less clear-cut developmental shifts in girls' sex-role attitudes than in boys', the findings for girls give less support to a cognitive-reorganization interpretation of I.Q. group differences. The findings for girls are, however, generally consistent with a developmental interpretation.

The age trends for girls on the measures of sex-typed experimental dependency and doll-parent orientation are presented in Figures 12 and 13. On both sets of measures the bright girls are slightly more male oriented at age four and remain so until age seven, when the average girls appear to "catch up" with them in this regard.

In general, then, the Kohlberg and Zigler findings suggest that I.Q. is an important correlate of individual differences in sex-role attitudes within age groups, and that I.Q. functions primarily as a rate-of-development variable, rather than as a fixed trait operating in the same direction at all ages. This developmental interpretation of correlations between general measures of intelligence and sex-role attitudes seems supported by other research comparisons between bright and average children of older ages, and between retarded and average subjects (Kohlberg and Zigler 1966).

Our discussion so far has been based on the oversimplified assumption that intelligence is an independent variable (rate of cognitive development) that influences sex-role attitudes. In contrast, Eleanor Maccoby's chapter in this volume reviews research results which suggest that sex-role attitudes represent a set of independent variables influencing cognitive functioning. Maccoby isolates some aspects of cognitive ability and cognitive style in which sex differences appear, and which seem to be influenced by sex-typed socialization practices and personality traits. She plausibly attributes sex differences in these abilities to personality variables of passivity-activity or control-impulsivity, with optimal cognitive functioning dependent upon a balanced distribution of these variables midway between "feminine" passivity-control and "masculine" activity-impulsivity. This suggests that children with high same-sex-typing will be intellectually handicapped, with the girls too passive, and the boys too active, for optimal cognitive functioning. A reconciliation of our analysis with that of Maccoby rests on two points. The first is that both innate sex differences and sex-typed socialization practices primarily affect *special* cognitive interests, abilities, and styles,

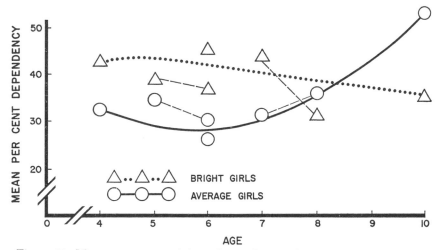

Figure 12. Mean percentage of dependency displayed toward the male experimenter by girls at six ages.

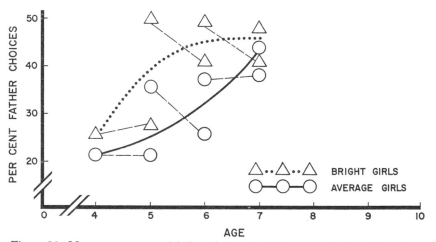

Figure 13. Mean percentage of father choices in doll play made by girls at four ages.

rather than *general* intelligence. The second is that general intelligence (I.Q.) predisposes *young children* toward high same-sex-typing on standard measures of sex-typed interests, while it predisposes *adolescents* toward low same-sex-typing on standard measures of sex-typed interests, a finding consistent with the cognitive-developmental interpretation.

With regard to the first point, it is clear that strong masculine interests in boys will lead to poor performances on cognitive tasks involving feminine interests, e.g., on tasks on which there are clear sex-differences in favor of girls. The reverse will be true for girls with strong feminine sex-typing. There do not appear to be any major sex differences in general intelligence, however, so it is not plausible to attribute to sex-typing a major causal role in the development of general intelligence.* The results interpretable in terms of Maccoby's hypothesis are results that appear for *special* cognitive abilities, with *general* intelligence controlled for or held constant.

As for the second point, studies of the correlations between general intelligence and same-sex-typing tests in young children (four to ten) report *positive* correlations between the two (Terman et al. 1925, Lefkowitz 1962, Kohlberg and Zigler 1966). Studies of adolescents and young adults tend to show low *negative* correlations between I.Q. and same-sex-typing (Terman and Miles 1936, Gough 1949). These seemingly contradictory correlations can be explained by the fact that age-development trends in childhood are toward same-sex-typing, while age-development trends in adolescence are toward a broadening of heterosexual interests to include interest in the activities of the opposite sex. Even later, college education, middle-class-work experiences, and parenthood widen sex-typed interests. Again, these trends appear earlier in bright than in average youths.

Negative correlations between general intelligence and same-sex-typed attitudes may also be due to two artifactual conditions. The first is that the American culture tends to regard boys with intellectual traits and interests as "feminine," and girls with these traits as "masculine." Psychologist or peer ratings of masculinity-femininity based on such stereotypes tend to show corresponding correlations with intelligence even though standardized tests of sex-typed attitudes do not. As an example, Kagan and Moss (1962) found a negative correlation between psychologists' ratings of early sex-typing and later intelligence. However, their ratings for boys were defined in terms of stereotypes in which gross motor activities were considered "masculine," and

---

* This in part may reflect the fact that constructors of general intelligence tests like the Stanford-Binet and the W.I.S.C. have eliminated sex-differentiating items. However, a survey of sex differences in tests not so constructed does not give the impression of any clear superiority of either sex on a majority of tests or across the developmental span.

more restrained and cognitive activities "feminine." Not surprisingly, the so-called "masculine" boys had lower I.Q.'s, and grew up to be mainly skilled manual workers, while the "feminine" boys grew up to be mainly professionals or intellectuals. The second artifact is that most masculinity-femininity tests force a choice between interests, so that an interest in something of interest to the opposite sex necessarily reduces the measure of sex-appropriate interests, and tends to cause breadth of interests to be reflected in a low score on sex-appropriateness of interests. Since there is some tendency for intelligence to be correlated with breadth of interest, this manner of constructing masculinity-femininity tests may generate some partly artifactual negative correlations between intelligence and same-sex attitudes.

If these two points are accepted, then, it would appear that Maccoby's analysis is valid for special cognitive traits, but that general intellectual maturity may be better looked on as a causal antecedent than a consequent of sex-role attitudes.

FAMILY AND CULTURAL DETERMINANTS OF CHILDREN'S SEX-ROLE ATTITUDES

Our discussion so far has stressed the view that the "natural" development of the child's body and role concepts determines the formation of his sex-role attitudes and identifications. This "natural" development is conceived to be the result of the relatively universal—as opposed to the individually varying—aspects of the child's experience. All children become aware of body differences, are exposed to basic gender labeling, and perceive certain salient differences in male and female roles inside and outside the family. In large part, individual differences in children's sex-role attitudes reflect variations in the development of these concepts, variations due to differences in age, general intelligence, and experiences stimulating development of sex-role concepts. As with most social attitudes, the greatest amount of variation in many measures of sex-role attitudes is related to age. Usually age variation in social attitudes has been viewed as a product of direct training, reinforcement, or socialization pressures exerted upon children at specific ages. While recognizing the existence of these forces, we still believe that age trends in sex-role development largely represent the general effects of cognitive experiences upon sex-role concepts and attitudes. We assume, then, that the social-environmental forces that influence the child's psychosexual development are the same forces that influence his cognitive development. As an example, it appears that lower-class father-absent children are lower on general tests of intellectual maturity than are lower-class children from father-present homes, and if such maturity is not controlled, then father-absent boys do appear to be much slower in the development of masculine preferences. If I.Q. is controlled, these differences are sharply reduced (C. Smith 1966). Thus it may be that a considerable part of the "retardation" in development of masculine identification in lower-class father-absent homes is due to the paucity of cognitive stimulation that tends to characterize these homes. As another example, the bulk of evidence (there is some limited evidence to the contrary) suggests that a higher socioeconomic status, because it facilitates the general development of social concepts, acts to stimulate age-development of sex-role attitudes (Kohlberg, in press).

The types of stimulation and experience stressed in our discussion so far have been "cognitive" in nature. It is apparent, however, that the emotional climate of the environment must play an important role in the stimulation or retardation of the development of sex-role attitudes. For obvious reasons, one would expect a family climate of warmth, expressiveness, security, integration of conflict, and high social participation to facilitate social development, and a family climate of coldness, hostility, anxiety, and conflict to retard it. The former climate allows for the exploration and integration of the new and the problematic, the latter does not. While such family-climate variables are not intrinsically cognitive, they seem to facilitate both intellectual and social-emotional age-developmental variables (Hunt 1961, Becker 1964, Kohlberg 1963, 1964). The notion of a family climate favoring or retarding development implies that the patterning of the child's sex-role attitudes comes from the cognitive organization of his total social world, and that the motives for development in these attitudes are essentially motives of competence, effectance, or self-esteem rather than motives of love, hate, and fear springing from or tied to the parents. This "developmental" interpretation of the influence of family environments differs radically from interpretations in which the child's sex-role attitudes are thought to be acquired through reinforcement learning or through identification, with the motive for development being essentially a seeking of social reinforcement from the parents. In this section, then, we shall make a brief review of the research findings on family correlates of children's sex-role attitudes in an effort to determine their application to these two interpretations. (A more adequate review is elaborated elsewhere [Kohlberg, in press].)

Some research findings suggesting the limitations of direct modeling and tuition notions of family influences on sex-role attitudes were touched upon earlier (see pp. 108–9), when we mentioned that measures of sex-typed preference were not found to be directly related either to measures of the parent's sex-typed preference (Terman and Miles 1936, Mussen and Rutherford 1963, Angrilli 1960) or to parental encouragement of appropriate sex-typing (Mussen and Rutherford 1963, Sears, Rau, and Alpert 1965). It seems apparent, then, that differences in children's sex-typing are not a direct reflection of gross parental teaching, modeling, and reinforcement of appropriate sex-typing.

The fact that parental expectations and reinforcements per se do not determine children's sex-typing has generally led researchers to believe that same-sex parent-identification determines sex-typing. The notion that identification with the same-sex parent is the central organizing principle in the formation of sex-typed attitudes also seems inconsistent with the research findings comparing the attitudes of boys from father-absent and father-present households. Most of these studies find little difference in masculinity-femininity attitudes (Barclay and Cusamana 1965, C. Smith 1966), with the remaining findings mixed; i.e., some indicate more masculine attitudes in father-absent boys (Lynn and Sawrey 1958, Terman and Miles 1936), and some indicate less masculine attitudes in father-absent boys (C. Smith 1966, Lynn and Sawrey 1958). Typically, these studies and subsequent reviews (e.g., Kagan 1964) have stressed the slight and ambiguous differences in the sex-role attitudes of these two groups of boys, and have failed to stress the overwhelmingly obvious findings of these studies: that there are little or no differences between the two groups on most measures. In almost any of the prevalent theories of parent-identification, the presence of the same-sex parent should be a necessary condition for the development of normal sex-role attitudes or identifications. Because of differences in individual parent relationships, father-present boys might be expected to vary greatly in sex-role identifications, but father-absent boys should be lacking all the critical components of sex-role attitudes.

In fact, the studies suggest that the father's absence retards development of masculine sex-typing rather than creating gross abnormalities or permanent deficits in the formation of a masculine identity. This conclusion is warranted, not only because the differences between the two groups on sex-typing measures are small or nonexistent, but because they seem to be age-specific. The Smith (1966) study found that masculinity scores on the It Scale were lower for father-absent lower-class Negro boys of five than for comparable father-present boys, but these differences had practically disappeared at age seven. The same age trends were found among father-absent and father-present boys, but the father-present boys seemed to develop faster in terms of these trends. The father-absent group also showed the same increase with age and with I.Q. in "identification" with a nonexistent stereotypical father (using measures taken from the literature including those described on p. 106), as the father-present group showed in "identification" with their actual fathers.

The studies so far discussed have all relied on verbal measures of sex-role attitudes. More long-range behavioral evidence suggesting that the presence of the father is not critical for the formation of a basic sex-role identification comes from a study by McCord, McCord, and Thurber (1962). These writers found no significant difference between matched father-absent and father-present lower-class boys aged 10 to 15 in ratings of femininity based on longitudinal case record evidence of playing with dolls, wearing feminine clothes, expressing the wish to be a girl, or engaging in overt homosexual behavior.*

The studies that have been most generally cited as supporting father-identification theories of masculinity-femininity are those that have demonstrated correlations between paternal warmth and masculine sex-typing in boys. Paternal warmth, both as perceived by the boy and as reported by the mother, has been found to correlate with both father-identification and masculinity of preferences (Mussen 1961, Mussen and Distler 1959, 1960, Mussen and Rutherford 1963, Payne and Mussen 1956, P. Sears 1953). Paternal warmth toward the child, particularly as perceived by the child or by the mother, is likely to be part of a global family predisposition to be warm or to present the appearance of warmth. The studies mentioned, however, have not found any consistent relationship

---

* A number of other studies indicate the existence of behavioral differences between father-absent and father-present boys, but caution must be used in attributing these differences to the role the father plays in the acquisition of appropriate sex-role identification (Kohlberg, in press).

between maternal nurturance and warmth and the boy's masculine- or father-identification, so that the results cannot be accounted for on these grounds.

It may be concluded, then, that a warm father-son relationship is conducive to the development of the boy's masculinity. How should these facts be interpreted? Most explanations of these facts in terms of identification assume that identification with the masculine role is the result of a covert imitation of the role behavior of the father based upon the unique emotional tie characterizing a relationship to a same-sex parent. However, the absence of correlation between the boy's sex-typing and that of his father, the low degree of correlation between measures of masculinity and measures of father-identification, and the small differences between father-present and father-absent boys cast doubt upon this interpretation. In particular, the McCord, McCord, and Thurber (1962) study suggests that a "bad" conflict-arousing father is worse for the boy's masculinity than no father at all. Both studies of father-absence and studies of father-warmth seem interpretable in this fashion. The father's warmth does not create the desire to be masculine (through the need to identify with a primary love object), it only facilitates it. The cold anxiety-arousing father curtails the boy's wish to explore the area of masculinity, whereas the warm father makes the boy feel more secure in this exploration.

Besides paternal warmth, the father-identification variable most generally considered to cause masculine attitudes in boys has been paternal power. Again, the findings seem to indicate that this variable plays a facilitating—rather than causal—role in the development of sex-role identification. Mussen and Distler (1959) found that kindergarten boys scoring high on same-sex preference on the It Scale, stereotyped or fantasied high power roles for the father in doll play, even though parent interviews did not indicate that the fathers of these boys actually occupied high power roles in the family (Mussen and Distler 1960). These findings suggest that boys strong in sex-typed values form clear stereotypes of masculine power and father-dominance, but that actual paternal power may not be a prerequisite for the development of masculine values. A recent study by Hetherington (1965), however, does indicate a clear relationship between paternal power and both sex-typed preference and father-identification. In this study, clear or extreme mother-dominant and father-dominant families were selected on the basis of power displayed by mother and fathers in experimentally observed discussions of disagreements about hypothetical problem situations involving child behavior. An equal number of children of each type of family were selected from each of three age groups (four–five, six–eight, nine–eleven). While both mother-dominant and father-dominant boys increased with age in same-sex-typing on the It Scale, the father-dominant boys were significantly higher than the mother-dominant boys at all ages. When the means on the It Scale for the two groups of boys are examined, however, it becomes apparent that this is not due to the fact that paternal power causes sex-typed values. The father-dominant boys in the Hetherington study have almost exactly the same It Scale scores as the unselected sample of boys studied by Brown (1957) (see Figure 1, p. 118). Indeed, Hetherington's father-dominant boys are not markedly higher on the It Scale than the father-absent boys studied by Smith (1966). Instead, it appears that strong mother-dominance, a "deviant" condition in the American culture, depresses or inhibits the development of boys' masculine sex-typing.

A similar interpretation seems to fit Hetherington's results on father-imitation. Hetherington asked one parent to select the (predetermined) prettiest pictures in a set while the child was watching, and then asked the child to select the prettiest. At a later occasion, the procedure was repeated with the other parent and with another set of pictures. The agreement of the child's choices with that of the parent constituted a measure of parent-imitation. While there were small age increases in father-imitation in both groups at all ages, the father-dominant boys imitated the father significantly more than the mother, and the mother-dominant boys imitated the mother more than the father. The mean per cent of total parent imitation directed toward the father by father-dominant boys was 56; the mean per cent of mother-dominant boys was 46. The degree of father-imitation demonstrated by Hetherington's father-dominant boys is comparable to the degree of father-doll and male-experimenter imitation shown by boys of comparable age in the Kohlberg (in press) study, while that of mother-dominant boys is considerably lower (see Figure 6). Again, it would appear that mother-dominance inhibits the development of preferential father-imitation in boys, rather than that father-dominance creates it.

In conjunction with findings on parent stereotypes discussed earlier, the Mussen and Rutherford and the Hetherington studies suggest that there are "natural" stereotypes of paternal power which facilitate the boy's competence-motivated identification with masculine and father-role attributes. If family reality is extremely or grossly discrepant from these stereotypes, the boy's masculine values do not develop strongly. Within the normal range of family variation, however, these power stereotypes operate to facilitate the formation of masculine values without direct correspondence or support from the realities of family structure.

The findings on maternal dominance seem consistent with other findings on maternal influences on boys' sex-typing. Maternal punitiveness (use of physical punishment) and severity or nonpermissiveness in matters of toilet training, politeness, sex play, etc. are negatively related to the boys' masculinity (Sears, Rau and Alpert 1965, Lefkowitz 1962, Mussen and Distler 1960). Such influences may be responsible for creating an atmosphere in which the masculine roles of the boy and his father are not perceived as having the usual power-competence components. It also seems plausible to view these correlations as indicating the more general developmentally inhibiting effects of a restrictive and anxiety-arousing atmosphere upon the boy's exploration of areas of masculinity. It will be recalled, however, that while maternal restrictiveness curtails boys' masculine preference, maternal warmth does not encourage it. Paternal warmth, however, does encourage masculine sex-typing. There are several possible interpretations of this finding, but the following, which we have stressed before, seems quite plausible: the father is "naturally" perceived as an authority figure, especially by the boy; therefore, active support by the father may be needed to make the boy feel unthreatened, whereas mere noninterference by the mother may be sufficient to avoid retarding the boy's masculine development.

The findings on girls' sex-typing are less consistent with the notion that a positive family climate leads to high same-sex identification. To explain these findings we must rely on the notion that feminine interests reflect a cautious and developmentally conservative stance for both girls and boys in the early school era (Kohlberg, in press). Feminine interests are thought to be conservative because they represent the home and the older tie to the mother rather than the outside world and the newer tie to the father, and because they represent the restrained, safe, and passive rather than the active, dangerous, and aggressive. Support for the notion that femininity reflects a conservative stance in both boys and girls comes from studies indicating that mother-identification (and femininity) is not positively correlated with measures of adjustment in girls, whereas father-identification is correlated with adjustment measures in boys (Osgood, Luce, and Tannenbaum 1957, Gray 1959, Sopchak 1952). If femininity is a conservative stance, the child, boy or girl, who is strongly controlled by the mother and discouraged from independent exploration might avoid the "masculine" area.

One major study (Sears, Rau, and Alpert 1965) reports findings on girls that are consistent with this point of view. They found that the same mother variables (use of physical punishment and ridicule, punishment for aggression to parents, high sex anxiety, severity of toilet training, and general nonpermissiveness) that seem to inhibit masculinity in the boy seem to promote femininity in the girl. Most obviously, these results suggest that socialization pressures toward inhibition and non-aggression produce "feminine" (i.e., passive nonaggressive) attitudes in both sexes. However, this latter interpretation may be oversimplified: boys receive on the average more severe physical punishment from mothers than girls do, and boys arouse more maternal sex anxiety than girls do; on these grounds one might expect boys to be more "feminine" than girls. In addition, the fact that maternal punitiveness for aggression does not actually lead to low aggression in boys makes it difficult to account for the "feminizing" effects of maternal punitiveness upon boys on these grounds. Some of these difficulties in interpreting the Sears, Rau, and Alpert findings may be avoided by assuming that maternal punitiveness inhibits development for both sexes, rather than directly causing fixed traits of passivity. The developmental interpretation also seems more able to account for the rather contradictory findings for girls at various ages and on various measures. While Hartup (1962) reports that his correlations between a paper-and-pencil test of maternal attitudes and preschool girls' doll-play imitation of the mother are consistent with the Sears, Rau, and Alpert findings, Mussen and Rutherford (1963) report somewhat contradictory correlations. They found that the child-rearing attitudes mentioned did not correlate with first-grade girls' femininity scores on the It Scale, which correlated instead with maternal warmth and self-esteem.

In light of the previously discussed bias factor in the It Scale, which makes it uncorrelated with other measures of femininity in school-age girls (Kohlberg 1962), there is some question about what these latter findings mean. However, it is possible that these findings reflect the fact that high feminine scores on the It Scale are age-decreasing at some ages (e.g., in the age range of the Sears subjects) but not at others (e.g., in the age range of the Mussen subjects). At the younger age (the Sears subjects), then, a girl's femininity might be responsive to developmentally inhibiting factors, whereas at the older age (the Mussen subjects), her femininity might be responsive to more developmentally facilitating family factors. Since the stability of the It Scale over this time period is extremely low for girls (r = .27, Kohlberg, in press), there is no reason to assume that similar family factors correlated with the test at different ages.

In addition to the notion that same-sex attitudes are more developmentally conservative in girls than in boys, two other postulates discussed earlier are useful in accounting for the fact that family correlates of sex-typing differ for the two sexes. The first postulate is that the power-competence of the male role is more important for the boys' masculine values than is the corresponding power-competence of the female role for girls' feminine values. This is suggested by the very different results obtained for boys and for girls in the Hetherington (1965) study of parent power. Dominance of the same-sex parent did not affect girls' sex-typing (It Scale) scores significantly, as it did boys'. The trend was for mother-dominant girls to be less feminine than father-dominant girls. Mother-dominant girls, however, did imitate their mothers more, and their fathers less, than father-dominant girls. Thus while there was a tendency for mother-dominant girls to preferentially imitate their mothers, this tendency to imitate the same-sex parent did not lead to greater identification with the culturally defined feminine role. Hetherington's study also suggests a second postulated sex difference in identification, a postulate documented in detail elsewhere (Kohlberg, in press). This is the assumption that the girl's sex-role identification is based more on identification with the complementary (father) role than is the boy's. While the boy defines his masculinity in terms of competitive achievement and acceptance in male groups (i.e., being "one of the boys"), the girl defines her femininity in terms of male acceptance and approval. Figures 2, 4, 8, and 9 indicate that while girls' sex-typed activities remained stable during the years four to eight, their orientation toward males increased; they became more dependent on males and imitated them more. This was also true for both mother-dominant and father-dominant girls in the Hetherington study. For both groups of girls, father-imitation went up with age and mother-imitation did not. However, the father-dominant girls showed a greater or more accelerated age increase in father-imitation than the mother-dominant girls. It has been found elsewhere (Kohlberg, in press, Sopchak 1952) that feminine sex-typing measures are positively, not negatively, correlated with measures of father-identification among girls of this age as well as among adolescents and adults. The only relationship that has been found between the sex-role attitudes of parents and their daughters is that the father's masculinity and his expectations for femininity in the girl are correlated with the girl's femininity (Terman and Merrill 1936, Mussen and Rutherford 1963).

In summary, then, the parent-child correlations for boys' sex-role attitudes seem to indicate that family climates can either facilitate or impede "natural" developmental trends. For girls, this interpretation is less satisfactory; but the complexity of the findings for girls, and the fact that they have not been replicated, makes it difficult for one to come up with an obvious alternative interpretation. Regardless of ultimate findings on parent-child sex-role correlates, the specificity of the correlations already established indicates that very generalized reinforcement and identification mechanisms do not in themselves provide an adequate explanation for the development of sex-role attitudes in children. These correlations become intelligible only when we interpret them in terms of the common or "natural" sex-role concepts, values, and identifications of children of a given age and sex. The development of these concepts and values, however, can be explained in terms of the basic cognitive-developmental trends and processes documented earlier in this chapter:

1. Gender identity or self-categorization as boy or girl is the basic organizer of sex-role attitudes.

2. This gender identity results from a basic physical reality judgment made relatively early in the child's development.

3. While this cognitive judgment is crystallizing into a conception of a constant, or categorical, gender identity during the years two to seven, the child's sex-role and body concepts may be influenced by certain environmental variables, with significant consequences for current and later sex-role attitudes.

4. Basic self-categorizations determine basic valuings. Masculine-

feminine values develop out of the need to value things that are consistent with or like the self.

5. Basic universal sex-role stereotypes develop early in young children. These stereotypes arise from the child's conceptions of body differences, conceptions that are supported by visible differences in the sex assignment of social roles.

6. These basic sex-role stereotypes, then, lead to the development of masculine-feminine values in children. Although in general these stereotypes award superior prestige-competence values to the male role, they also award a number of superior value attributes to the female role. As awareness of these prestige values and stereotypes develops in the years four to eight, there is a tendency for both sexes to attribute greater power and prestige to the male role. However, the greater relative prestige of the adult male role does not imply an absence or decline of absolute prestige, or positive value, of the female role, a prestige that is sufficient to channel the girls' competence strivings into feminine role values.

7. After masculine-feminine values are acquired, the child tends to identify with like-sex figures, in particular the like-sex parent. Desire to be masculine leads to the desire to imitate a masculine model, which leads to a deeper emotional attachment to the model.

8. While identification with a like-sex person, and the formation of sex-role values in general, may be facilitated and consolidated by appropriate parental behavior, this process seems to take place without the presence of a same-sex parent, and under a variety of child-rearing conditions. It would appear that the clearest influences of parental practices are negative, not positive; i.e., certain parent attitudes may create specific anxieties and conflicts inhibiting the development of appropriate sex-role attitudes, but it is not at all clear whether certain parent attitudes can create appropriate sex-role attitudes.

9. To a large extent, the foregoing trends follow a regular course of development, which is largely determined by cognitive (rather than physiological-chronological) maturity. These trends are the result of the child's cognitive-developmental organization of a social world in which sex roles are related to body concepts and to basic social functions in relatively universal ways.

10. On the motivational side, these developmental trends can be

interpreted as the product of general motives to structure, and adapt oneself to, physical-social reality, and to preserve a stable and positive self-image.

REFERENCES

Adorno, T. W., E. Frenkel-Brunswik, D. J. Levinson, and R. N. Sanford. (1950) *The authoritarian personality.* New York: Harper.

Ammons, R., and H. Ammons. (1949) Parent preference in young children's doll-play interviews. *J. abnorm. soc. Psychol., 44,* 490–505.

Angrilli, A. F. (1960) The psychosexual identification of preschool boys. *J. genet. Psychol., 97,* 329–40.

Ausubel, D. (1957) *Theory and problems of child development.* New York: Grune & Stratton.

Bandura, A. (1962) Social learning through imitation. In M. R. Jones (ed.), *Nebraska symposium on motivation.* Lincoln: University of Nebraska Press.

————, Dorothea Ross, and Sheila A. Ross. (1963) A test of the status envy, social power and secondary reinforcement theories of identificatory learning. *J. abnorm. soc. Psychol., 67,* 527–35.

————, and R. Walters (1963) *Social learning and personality development.* New York: Holt, Rinehart & Winston.

Barclay A., and D. Cusumana. (1965) Effects of father absence upon field-dependent behavior. Paper delivered at American Psychol. Assoc., September 1965.

Bayley, N. (1940) Factors influencing growth of intelligence in young children. In *Yearbook of the National Society for the Study of Education, 39.* Chicago: University of Chicago Press.

Becker, W. (1964) Effects of childrearing practices. In M. and L. Hoffman (eds.), *Review of child development research,* Vol. I. New York: Russell Sage.

Benjamin, H. (1932) Age and sex differences in the toy preferences of young children. *J. genet. Psychol., 41,* 101–29.

Bennett, E. M., and L. R. Cohen. (1959) Men and women: personality patterns and contrasts. *Genet. Psychol. Monogr., 60,* 101–53.

Bernick, N. (1965) The development of children's sexual attitudes as determined by the pupil-dilation response. Unpublished doctoral dissertation, University of Chicago.

Borstelmann, L. (1961) Sex of experimenter and sex-typed behavior of young children. *Child Develpm., 32,* 519–25.

Brim, O. (1958) Family structures and sex-role learning by children. *Sociometry, 21,* 1–16.

Bronfenbrenner, U. (1960) Freudian theories of identification and their derivatives. *Child Develpm., 31,* 15–40.

Brown, D. G. (1956) Sex-role preference in young children. *Psychol. Monogr.*, *70*, No. 14.

———. (1957) Masculinity-femininity development in children. *J. consult. Psychol.*, *27*, 197–205.

———. (1962) Sex-role preference in children: methodological problems. *Psychol. Rep.*, *11*, 477–78.

———, and A. Tolor. (1957) Human figure drawings as indicators of sexual identification and inversion. *Percept. mot. Skills*, *7*, 199–211.

Burton, J., and J. Whiting. (1961) The absent father and cross-sex identity. *Merrill-Palmer Quart.*, *7*, 85–97.

Butler, C. (1952) The influence of parents' emotional attitudes concerning sex on the sex education of their children. Unpublished master's thesis, Committee on Human Development, University of Chicago.

Campbell, E. H. (1939) The social-sex development of children. *Genet. Psychol. Monogr.*, *21*, No. 4.

Colley, T. (1959) The nature and origins of psychological sexual identity. *Psychol. Rev.*, *66*, 165–77.

Conn, J. H. (1940) Children's reactions to the discovery of genital differences. *Amer. J. Orthopsychiat.*, *10*, 747–55.

———. (1948) Children's awareness of the origins of babies. *J. Child Psychiat.*, *1*, 140–76.

———, and L. Kanner. (1947) Children's awareness of sex differences. *J. Child Psychiat.*, *1*, 3–57.

DeLucia, L. A. (1961) Some determinants of sex-role identification in young children. Unpublished master's thesis, Brown University.

———. (1963) The toy preference test: a measure of sex-role identification. *Child Develpm.*, *34*, 107–17.

Dennis, W. (1946) Adolescence. In L. Carmichael (ed.), *Manual of child psychology* (1st ed.). New York: Wiley.

de Saussure, R. (1933) Psychologie genetique et psychoanalyse. *Rev. Franc. Psychoanal.*, *6*, 365–403.

DeVries, Rheta. (1966) The development of constancy of object identity. Unpublished doctoral dissertation, University of Chicago.

Diamond, M. (1965) A critical evaluation of the ontogeny of human sexual behavior. *Quart. Rev. Biol.*, *40*, 147–73.

Eichorn, Dorothy. (1963) Biological correlates of behavior. In H. Stevenson (ed.), *Child psychology: sixty-second yearbook of the National Society for the Study of Education*. Chicago: University of Chicago Press.

Emmerich, W. (1959a) Parental identification in young children. *Genet. Psychol. Monogr.*, *60*, 257–308.

———. (1959b) Young children's discrimination of parent and child roles. *Child Develpm.*, *30*, 405–19.

———. (1961) Family role concepts of children ages six to ten. *Child Develpm.*, *32*, 609–24.

Epstein R., and S. Leverant. (1963) Verbal conditioning and sex-role identification in children. *Child Develpm.*, *34*, 99–106.

Erikson, E. (1950) *Childhood and society.* New York: Norton.

Fauls, L. B., and W. D. Smith. (1956) Sex-role learning of five-year-olds.
J. genet. Psychol., *89*, 105–17.

Franck, Kate. (1946) Preference for sex symbols and their personality correlates. *Genet. Psychol. Monogr.*, *33*, 73–123.

———. (n.d.) Franck drawing completion test: preliminary manual. Mel-
bourne, Australia Council for Educational Research.

———, and E. Rosen. (1949) A projective test of masculinity-femininity.
J. consult. Psychol., *13*, 247–56.

Freud, S. (1905) Three contributions to the theory of sex. In *The basic
writings of Sigmund Freud.* New York: Modern Library, 1938.

———. (1908) On the sexual theories of children. In *Collected papers,*
Vol. II. London: Hogarth Press, 1950.

———. (1924a) The infantile genital organization of the libido. *Collected
papers,* Vol. II. New York: International Psychoanalytic Press, 1924.

———. (1924b) The passing of the Oedipus complex. In *Collected papers,*
Vol. II. London: Hogarth Press, 1950.

Gesell, A., and Frances Ilg. (1943) *The infant and child in the culture of
today.* New York: Harpers.

———, et al. (1940) *The first five years of life: a guide to the study of the
preschool child.* New York: Harpers.

Gough, H. G. (1952) Identifying psychological femininity. *Educ. psychol.
Measmt.*, *12*, 427–39.

Gray, Susan. (1957) Masculinity-femininity in relation to anxiety and social acceptance. *Child Develpm.*, *28*, 203–14.

———. (1959) Perceived similarity to parents and adjustment. *Child
Develpm.*, *30*, 91–107.

———, and R. Klaus (1956) The assessment of parental identification.
Genet. Psychol. Monogr., *54*, 87–109.

Greenberg, P. (1932) Competition in children: an experimental study.
Amer. J. Psychol., *44*, 221–48.

Hampson, J., and Joan Hampson. (1961) The ontogenesis of sexual behavior in man. In W. C. Young (ed.), *Sex and internal secretions.* Baltimore: Williams & Wilkins.

———, and J. Money. (1955) Idiopathic sexual precocity. *Psychosom.
Med.*, *17*, 16–35.

Hartley, Ruth E. (1959–1960b) Children's concepts of male and female
roles. *Merrill-Palmer Quart.*, *6*, 153–54.

———. (1964) A developmental view of female sex-role definition and
identification. *Merrill-Palmer Quart.*, *10*, 3–17.

———, and F. Hardesty. (1962) Children's perception and expression of
sex preferences. *Child Develpm.*, *33*, 221–27.

————, and F. Hardesty. (1964) Children's perceptions of sex-roles in childhood. *J. genet. Psychol., 105,* 43–51.

Hartup, W. W. (1962) Some correlates of parental imitation in young children. *Child Develpm., 33,* 85–97.

————. (1958) Nurturance and nurturance withdrawal in relation to the dependency behavior in young children. *Child Develpm., 39,* 191–201.

————, and E. A. Zook. (1960) Sex-role preferences in three- and four-year-old children. *J. consult. Psychol., 24,* 420–26.

Hattwick, B. A. (1937) Sex-differences in behavior of nursery school children. *Child Develpm., 8,* 343–55.

Heinicke, C. M. (1953) Some antecedents and correlates of guilt and fear in young boys. Unpublished doctoral dissertation, Harvard University.

Helper, M. M. (1955) Learning theory and the self-concept. *J. abnorm. soc. Psychol., 51,* 184–94.

Hetherington, M. (1965) A developmental study of the effects of sex of the dominant parent on sex-role preference, identification and imitation in children. *J. Pers. and soc. Psychol., 2,* 143–53.

Hooker, Evelyn. (1965) Gender identity in male homosexuals. In J. Money (ed.), *Sex research.* New York: Holt, Rinehart & Winston.

Horowitz, Ruth. (1943) A pictorial method for study of self-identification in preschool children. *J. genet. Psychol., 62,* 135–48.

Hunt, J. McV. (1961) *Intelligence and experience.* New York: Ronald.

Isaacs, S. (1930) *Intellectual growth in young children.* London: Routledge, Kegan Paul.

Jahoda, G. (1956) Sex differences in preferences for shapes: a cross-cultural replication. *Brit. J. Psychol., 47,* 126–32.

Jenkins, J. J., and W. A. Russell. (1958) An atlas of semantic profiles for 360 words. *Amer. J. Psychol., 71,* 688–99.

Jersild, A. (1943) Studies of children's fears. In R. G. Barker, J. S. Kounin, and H. Wright (eds.), *Child behavior and development.* New York: McGraw-Hill.

Johnson, M. (1963) Sex-role learning in the nuclear family. *Child Develpm., 34,* 319–35.

Jones, H. (1954) The environment and mental development. In L. Carmichael (ed.), *Manual of child psychology.* New York: Wiley.

Kagan, J. (1956) The child's perception of the parent. *J. abnorm. soc. Psychol., 53,* 257–58.

————. (1964) The acquisition and significance of sex-typing and sex-role identity. In M. Hoffman, and L. Hoffman (eds.), *Review of child development research,* Vol. I. New York: Russell Sage.

————, Barbara Hosken, and Sara Watson. (1961) The child's symbolic conceptualization of the parents. *Child Develpm., 32,* 625–36.

————, and Judy Lemkin. (1960) The child's differential perception of parental attributes. *J. abnorm. soc. Psychol., 61,* 446–47.

————, and H. Moss. (1962) *Birth to maturity*. New York: Wiley.

Karon, H. (1953) A study of identification. Unpublished doctoral dissertation, Harvard University.

Katcher, A. (1955) The discrimination of sex differences by young children. *J. genet. Psychol.*, *87*, 131–43.

Katz, Phyllis. (1959) Responses of young children to the Franck test. Unpublished term paper, Yale University.

Kinsey, A. C., W. B. Pomeroy, and C. F. Martin. (1948) *Sexual behavior in the human male*. Philadelphia: Saunders.

————, W. B. Pomeroy, C. F. Martin, and P. H. Gebhard. (1953) *Sexual behavior in the human female*. Philadelphia: Saunders.

Koch, Helen. (1944) A study of some factors conditioning the social distance between the sexes. *J. soc. Psychol.*, *20*, 79–107.

Kohlberg, L. (1962) A note on the interaction of cognitive set, stimulus artifact, and sex-role attitudes in a projective measure of sex-role identity. Unpublished mimeographed paper, Center for Advanced Studies in Behavioral Sciences, Palo Alto, California.

————. (1963) Moral development and identification. In H. Stevenson (ed.), *Child psychology: sixty-second yearbook of the National Society for the Study of Education*. Chicago: University of Chicago Press.

————. (1964) The development of moral character and ideology. In M. and L. Hoffman (eds.), *Review of child development research*, Vol. I. New York: Russell Sage.

————. (1966a) *Stages in the development of children's conceptions of physical and social objects in the years four to eight*. Unpublished monograph, in preparation for publication as a book.

————. (1966b) Stage and Sequence: The developmental approach to moralization. In M. Hoffman (ed.), *Moral processes*. Chicago: Aldine Press.

————. (in press) *Psychosexual development in children*. New York: Holt, Rinehart & Winston.

————, and E. Zigler. (1966) The impact of cognitive maturity upon the development of sex-role attitudes in the years four to eight. *Genet. Psychol. Monogr.* (in press).

Krebs, R. The development of moral judgment in the years four to seven. Unpublished master's thesis, University of Chicago.

Kumata and Schramm. (1956) A pilot study of cross-cultural meaning. *Public Opinion Quart.*, *20*, 229–38.

Lansky, L. M., and G. McKay. (1963) Sex-role preferences of kindergarten boys and girls: some contradictory results. *Psychol. Rep.*, *13*, 415–21.

Lefkowitz, M. H. (1962) Some relationships between sex-role preference of children and other parent and child variables. *Psychol. Rep.*, *10*, 43–53.

LeMarquand, H. S. (1932) Suprarenal virilism. *Proc. roy. Soc. Med.*, *25*, 804–6.

Lerner, E. (1937) Perspectives in moral reasoning. *Amer. J. Sociol.*, *43*, 249–69.

Lindskoog, D. (1964) Children's differentiation of instrumental and expressive parent roles. Unpublished master's thesis, University of Chicago.

Lynn, D. G. (1959) A note on sex differences in the development of masculine and feminine identification. *Psychol. Rev., 66,* 126–35.

————, and W. L. Sawrey. (1958) The effects of father-absence on Norwegian boys and girls. *J. abnorm. soc. Psychol., 59,* 258–62.

McCord, W., Joan McCord, and Emily Thurber. (1962) Some effects of paternal absence on male children. *J. abnorm. soc. Psychol., 64,* 361–69.

McElroy, W. A. (1954) A sex difference in preference for shapes. *Brit. J. Psychol., 45,* 209–16.

Mead, G. H. (1932) *Mind, self, and society.* Chicago: University of Chicago Press.

Mead, Margaret. (1961) Sexual behavior. In W. C. Young (ed.), *Sex and internal secretions.* Baltimore: Williams & Wilkins.

Miller, D., and G. Swanson. (1960) *Inner conflict and defense.* New York: Holt.

Minuchin, Patricia. (1964) Children's sex-role concepts as a function of school and home environments. Paper presented at Amer. Orthopsychiat. Assoc., Chicago, March 1964.

Money, J. (1961) Sex hormones and other variables in human eroticism. In W. C. Young (ed.), *Sex and internal secretions.* Baltimore: Williams & Wilkins.

————, Joan Hampson, and J. Hampson. (1957) Imprinting and the establishment of gender role. *Arch. Neurol. Psychiat., 77,* 333–36.

Mowrer, O. H. (1950) Identification: a link between learning theory and psychotherapy. In *Learning theory and personality dynamics.* New York: Ronald.

Mussen, P. (1961) Some antecedents and consequents of masculine sex-typing in adolescent boys. *Psychol. Monogr., 75,* No. 2.

————, and L. Distler. (1959) Masculinity, identification, and father-son relationships. *J. abnorm. soc. Psychol., 59,* 350–56.

————, and L. Distler. (1960) Child-rearing antecedents of masculine identification in kindergarten boys. *Child Develpm., 31,* 89–100.

————, and E. Rutherford. (1963) Parent-child relations and parental personality in relation to young children's sex-role preferences. *Child Develpm., 34,* 589–607.

Osgood, C. (1960) The cross-cultural generality of visual-verbal synaesthetic tendencies. *Behav. Sciences, 5,* 146–69.

————, G. Luce, and P. Tannenbaum. (1957) *The measurement of meaning.* Urbana: University of Illinois Press.

Parsons, T., and R. Bales. (1955) *Family socialization and interaction process.* Glencoe, Ill.: Free Press.

Paterson, D. G. (1930) *Physique and intellect.* New York: Century.

Payne, D. E., and P. Mussen. (1956) Parent-child relations and father-identification among adolescent boys. *J. abnorm. soc. Psychol.*, *52*, 358–62.

Piaget, J. (1947) *The psychology of intelligence.* London: Routledge, Kegan Paul.

———. (1951) *Play, dreams, and imitation in childhood.* London: Routledge, Kegan Paul.

———. (1952) *The origins of intelligence.* New York: Int. Univ. Press.

Rabban, M. (1950) Sex-role identification in young children in two diverse social groups. *Genet. Psychol. Monogr.*, *42*, 81–158.

Rosenberg, B. G., and B. Sutton-Smith. (1959) The measurement of masculinity and femininity in children. *Child Develpm.*, *30*, 373–80.

———, and B. Sutton-Smith. (1960) A revised conception of masculine-feminine differences in play activities. *J. genet. Psychol.*, *96*, 165–70.

———, B. Sutton-Smith, and E. Morgan. (1961) The use of opposite sex scales as a measure of psychosexual deviancy. *J. consult. Psychol.*, *2*, 221–25.

Rosenblith, Judy F. (1959) Learning by imitation in kindergarten children. *Child Develpm.*, *30*, 69–78.

———. (1961) Imitative color choices in kindergarten children. *Child Develpm.*, *32*, 211–23.

Sears, Pauline (1953) Child rearing factors related to the playing of sex-typed roles. *Amer. Psychologist*, *8*, 431. (Abstract.)

Sears, R. R. (1957) Identification as a form of behavior development. In P. B. Harris (ed.), *The Concept of development.* Minneapolis: University of Minnesota Press.

———, Eleanor Maccoby, and H. Levin (1957) *Patterns of child rearing.* Evanston, Ill.: Row, Peterson.

———, Lucy Rau, and R. Alpert (1965) *Identification and child rearing.* Stanford: Stanford University Press.

Slater, P. (1961) Toward a dualistic theory of identification. *Merrill-Palmer Quart.*, *7*, 113–26.

Smedslund, J. (1961) The acquisition of conservation of substance and weight in children. III: Extinction of conservation of weight acquired normally and by means of empirical controls on a balance. *Scand. J. Psychol.*, *2*, 1–3.

Smith, C. (1966) The development of sex-role concepts and attitudes in father-absent boys. Unpublished master's thesis, University of Chicago.

Smith, S. (1939) Age and sex differences in children's opinions concerning sex differences. *J. genet. Psychol.*, *54*, 17–25.

Sopchak, A. L. (1952) Parental identification and tendencies toward disorders as measured by the MMPI. *J. abnorm. soc. Psychol.*, *47*, 159–65.

Springer, Doris V. (1950) Awareness of racial differences by preschool children in Hawaii. *Genet. Psychol. Monogr.*, *41*, 215–71.

Stephens, W. (1963) *The family in cross-cultural perspective.* New York: Holt, Rinehart & Winston.

Stevenson, H. W. (1961) Social reinforcement with children as a function of CA, sex of E and sex of S. *J. abnorm. soc. Psychol.*, *63*, 147–54.

———. (1965) Social reinforcement of children's behavior. In C. Spiker (ed.), *Advances in child development*, Vol. II. New York: Academic Press.

Stotland, E., A. Zander, and T. Natsoulas. (1961) Generalization of interpersonal similarity. *J. abnorm. soc. Psychol.*, *62*, 250–58.

Sutton-Smith, B., and B. G. Rosenberg. (1960) Manifest anxiety and game preferences in children. *Child Develpm.*, *31*, 307–11.

———, B. G. Rosenberg, and E. F. Morgan, Jr. (1963) Development of sex differences in play choices during preadolescence. *Child Develpm.*, *34*, 119–26.

Tanner, J. (1961) *Education and physical growth*. London: University of London Press.

Terman, L. M., and C. C. Miles. (1936) *Sex and personality studies in masculinity and femininity*. New York: McGraw-Hill.

———, and L. Tyler. (1954) Psychological sex differences. In L. Carmichael (ed.), *Manual of child psychology*. New York: Wiley.

Triandis, H. C., and C. E. Osgood. (1958) A comparative factorial analysis of semantic structures in monolingual Greek and American college students. *J. abnorm. soc. Psychol.*, *57*, 187–96.

Vance, T. F., and Louise T. McCall. (1934) Children's preferences among play materials as determined by the method of paired comparisons of pictures. *Child Develpm.*, *5*, 267–77.

Wallach, M. Children's thinking. (1963) In H. Stevenson (ed.), *Child psychology*. Chicago: University of Chicago Press.

Webb, A. P. (1963) Sex-role preferences and adjustment in early adolescents. *Child Develpm.*, *34*, 609–18.

Werner, H. (1948) *Comparative psychology of mental development*. Chicago: Wilcox & Follett.

———, and B. Kaplan. (1964) *Symbol formation*. New York: Wiley.

White, R. (1959) Motivation reconsidered: the concept of competence. *Psychol. Rev.*, *66*, 297–333.

———. (1963) Ego and reality in psychoanalytic theory. *Psychol. Issues*, Vol. III, No. 3. New York: International University Press.

Whiting, J. W. M. (1960) Resource mediation and learning by identification. In I. Iscoe and H. W. Stevenson (eds.), *Personality development in children*. Austin: University of Texas Press.

Winch, R. (1962) *Identification and its familial determinants*. Indianapolis: Bobbs-Merrill.

Sex Differences and Cultural Institutions

ROY G. D'ANDRADE
Stanford University

Psychology tends to consider sex differences as differences in personal characteristics. Anthropology, on the other hand, generally conceives of sex differences as social and cultural institutions. From this point of view sex differences are not simply characteristics of individuals; they are also culturally transmitted patterns of behavior determined in part by the functioning of society. Some of the ways in which sex differences have been culturally institutionalized will be reviewed in this chapter. Cross-cultural trends for male-female differences in the performance of daily activities, in the ascription of social statuses, in interpersonal behavior, in gender identity, and in fantasy productions will be presented. Also an attempt will be made to explain some of these empirically observed behavioral sex differences.

Anthropology, like astronomy, is a natural science in which experimentation is rarely possible. Unfortunately, under such conditions good descriptions are easier to construct than good explanations. At present there is even considerable disagreement within anthropology about what constitutes a proper or possible explanation of cultural phenomena. The four major types of explanation currently in use are: the *historical* (a particular custom exists because it was invented at some previous time, and then transmitted from generation to generation, or from society to society, to its present location in time and space); the *structural* (a particular custom exists as an expression of some more basic or underlying cultural or social condition, and can only be understood as a manifestation of this more basic condition); the *functional* (a particular custom exists because it maintains or integrates social life in some beneficial way); and the *reductionistic* (a particular custom exists because of the operation of some psychological or physiological mechanism). While all of these types of explanation carry some information and can be used predictively, in this review the primary emphasis will be on reductionistic explanations.

PHYSICAL DIFFERENCES

A comprehensive review of cross-cultural findings about physical sex differences will not be attempted here. However, some of these physical differences should be mentioned since they are basic to many of the explanations of behavioral sex differences. In all known human populations, males and females differ in primary sex characteristics and in many secondary characteristics as well. These secondary characteristics include, for the male, greater height, a higher muscle-to-fat ratio, a more massive skeleton, more body hair, etc. However, most of these differences in secondary sex characteristics are not absolute; they hold true only for a particular population. Furthermore, the average differences between the sexes vary from population to population. In height, for example, the mean difference between males and females is less than two inches for the Klamath, approximately six inches for the Nootka (both American Indian groups from the Northwest coast), and almost eight inches for the Shilluk (an African Negro group from the Eastern Sudan). As a result of the variance in population means, it is generally impossible to sex-type accurately on the basis of secondary sex characteristics alone unless population parameters are known. (Very probably this holds true not only for sex-linked physical characteristics, but also for behavioral characteristics as well.)

Secondary sex characteristics are not completely under genetic control, and can be affected by cultural and environmental factors. For example, cultural heightening of genetic secondary sex characteristics occurs frequently with regard to physical strength. The genetically determined greater size and more muscular body composition of the male results in a fairly large difference in physical strength between the sexes. This difference is often increased, however, by the tendency for males in most societies to perform those activities requiring rapid and extreme exertion. In Bali, where males do little heavy lifting work, preferring instead light, steady, many-handed labor, both males and females have slender somatypes. However, Balinese men who work as dock coolies under European supervision develop the heavy musculature more typical of males (Mead 1949).

Generally biological differences in primary and secondary sex characteristics are considered major factors in explaining universal cultural patterning of sex-typed roles. The family has been said to be "a biological phenomenon, . . . as rooted in organic and physiological structures as insect societies" (LaBarre 1954, p. 104). Thus LaBarre argues that the human mother-child relationship is based on the mutual gratifications involved in long-term breast feeding, and the husband-wife relationship on the permanent sexuality of the female. However, most anthropological explanations of regularities in sex differences are not based on biological differences alone, but on the complex interactions of biological differences with environmental and technological factors.

THE DIVISION OF LABOR

One well-documented finding about behavioral sex differences is that men and women not only tend to perform different activities in every culture, but that men tend to perform particular types of activities and women to perform others. This division of labor is especially sharp for subsistence and other economic activities. The following table, adapted from one of Murdock's early cross-cultural studies, presents the frequencies with which 224 societies have a sex-based division of labor with respect to activities dealing mainly with food production and collection (Murdock 1937).

The sex differences in Table 1 are quite strong for all activities except dairy operation, soil preparation, fowl tending, and shelter erection. Generally the male activities appear to involve behavior which is strenuous, cooperative, and which may require long periods of travel. The female activities, on the other hand, are more likely to involve the physically easier, more solitary, and less mobile activities. These differences appear to be more or less the direct result of physical male-female differences.

However, not all sex-specialized activities can be explained by physical differences. Most of the results in Table 2, which presents data on

TABLE 1

*Cross-Cultural Data from 224 Societies on Subsistence
Activities and Division of Labor by Sex*

Activity	Number of Societies in Which Activity is Performed by				
	Men always	Men usually	Either sex	Women usually	Women always
Pursuit of sea mammals	34	1	0	0	0
Hunting	166	13	0	0	0
Trapping small animals	128	13	4	1	2
Herding	38	8	4	0	5
Fishing	98	34	19	3	4
Clearing land for agriculture . . .	73	22	17	5	13
Dairy operations	17	4	3	1	13
Preparing and planting soil . . .	31	23	33	20	37
Erecting and dismantling shelter .	14	2	5	6	22
Tending fowl and small animals .	21	4	8	1	39
Tending and harvesting crops . .	10	15	35	39	44
Gathering shellfish	9	4	8	7	25
Making and tending fires	18	6	25	22	62
Bearing burdens	12	6	35	20	57
Preparing drinks and narcotics . .	20	1	13	8	57
Gathering fruits, berries, nuts . .	12	3	15	13	63
Gathering fuel	22	1	10	19	89
Preservation of meat and fish . . .	8	2	10	14	74
Gatherings herbs, roots, seeds . .	8	1	11	7	74
Cooking	5	1	9	28	158
Carrying water	7	0	5	7	119
Grinding grain	2	4	5	13	114

sex differences in the manufacture of objects, cannot be so explained. Weapon making, for example, is predominantly a male activity, even though it does not necessarily require more physical strength than the manufacture and repair of clothing. One possible explanation for the sex differences found in the manufacture of objects is that the objects being made are intended for use in activities that are directly related to physical differences. Thus weapon making is anticipatory to activities that do involve physically strenuous and mobile behavior. Murdock (1949) states:

It is unnecessary to invoke innate psychological differences to account for the division of labor by sex; the indisputable differences in reproductive functions suffice to lay out the broad lines of cleavage. New tasks as they arise are assigned to one sphere of activities or the other in accordance with convenience and precedent. Habituation to different occupations in adulthood and early sex typing in childhood may well explain the observable differences in sex temperament instead of *vice versa.* (p. 7.)

TABLE 2

*Cross-Cultural Data on the Manufacture of Objects and
Division of Labor by Sex*

Activity	Number of Societies in Which Activity is Performed by				
	Men always	Men usually	Either sex	Women usually	Women always
Metalworking	78	0	0	0	0
Weapon making	121	1	0	0	0
Boat building	91	4	4	0	1
Manufacture of musical instruments	45	2	0	0	1
Work in wood and bark	113	9	5	1	1
Work in stone	68	3	2	0	2
Work in bone, horn, shell	67	4	3	0	3
Manufacture of ceremonial objects	37	1	13	0	1
House building	86	32	25	3	14
Net making	44	6	4	2	11
Manufacture of ornaments	24	3	40	6	18
Manufacture of leather products .	29	3	9	3	32
Hide preparation	31	2	4	4	49
Manufacture of nontextile fabrics .	14	0	9	2	32
Manufacture of thread and cordage	23	2	11	10	73
Basket making	25	3	10	6	82
Mat making	16	2	6	4	61
Weaving	19	2	2	6	67
Pottery making	13	2	6	8	77
Manufacture and repair of clothing	12	3	8	9	95

The thesis here, to be considered in more detail below, is that the division of labor by sex comes about as a result of generalization from activities directly related to physical sex differences to activities only indirectly related to these differences; that is, from behaviors which are differentially reinforced as a result of physical differences to behaviors which are anticipatory or similar to such directly conditioned activities. Perhaps the complexity and strength of the factors that bring about and maintain the division of labor by sex can be illustrated by the following excerpt from M. E. Spiro's (1956) study of an Israeli Kibbutz.

The social structure of the Kibbutz is responsible for a problem of . . . serious proportions—"the problem of the woman. . . ." With the exception of politics, nothing occupies so much attention in the Kibbutz. . . . It is no exaggeration to say that if Kiryat Yedidim should ever disintegrate, the "problem of the woman" will be one of the main contributing factors.

In a society in which the equality of the sexes is a fundamental premise, and in which the emancipation of women is a major goal, the fact that there is a "problem of the woman" requires analysis. . . . The Youth Movement from which many Kibbutz values are derived was strongly femininist in orientation. The woman in bourgeois society, it is believed, was subjected to the male and tied to her home and family. This "biological tragedy of woman" forced her into menial roles, such as house cleaning, cooking, and other domestic duties, and prevented her from taking her place beside the man in the fields, the workshop, the laboratory, and the lecture hall.

In the new society all this was to be changed. The woman would be relieved of her domestic burdens by means of the various institutions of collective living, and she could then take her place as man's equal in all the activities of life. The communal dining room would free her from the burden of cooking; the communal nurseries, from the responsibilities of raising children; the small rooms, from the job of cleaning.

In a formal sense, the Kibbutz has been successful in this task. . . . In spite of "emancipation" which they have experienced in the Kibbutz, there is considerable sentiment among the women . . . that they would prefer not to have been "emancipated." Almost every couple who has left the Kibbutz has done so because of the unhappiness of the woman. . . . At a town meeting devoted to the "problem of the woman," one of the most respected women in Kiryat Yedidim—the wife of a leader of the Kibbutz movement—publicly proclaimed that the Kibbutz women had not achieved what they had originally hoped for; as for herself, after thirty years in Kiryat Yedidim she could pronounce her life a disappointment.

One source of the woman's poor morale is that many women are dissatisfied with their economic roles. . . . When the vattikim [original settlers] first settled on the land, there was no sexual division of labor. Women, like men, worked in the fields and drove tractors; men, like women, worked in the kitchen and in the laundry. Men and women, it was assumed, were equal and could perform their jobs equally well. It was soon discovered, however, that men and women were not equal. For obvious biological reasons, women could not undertake many of the physical tasks of which men were capable; tractor driving, harvesting, and other heavy labor proved too difficult for them. Moreover, women were compelled at times to take temporary leave from that physical labor of which they were capable. A pregnant woman, for example, could not work too long, even in the vegetable garden, and a nursing mother had to work near the Infants House in order to be able to feed her child. Hence, as the Kibbutz grew older and the birth rate increased, more and more women were forced to leave the "productive" branches of the economy and enter its "service" branches. But as they left the "productive" branches, it was necessary that their places be filled, and they were filled by men. The result was that the women found themselves in the same jobs from which they were supposed to have been emancipated—*cooking, cleaning, laundering, teaching, caring for children,* etc.

. . . What has been substituted for the traditional routine of housekeeping . . . is more housekeeping—and a restricted and narrow kind of housekeeping at that. Instead of cooking and sewing and baking and cleaning and laundering and caring for children, the woman in Kiryat Yedidim cooks *or* sews *or* launders *or* takes care of children for eight hours a day. . . . This new housekeeping is more boring and less rewarding than the traditional type. It is small wonder, then, given this combination of low prestige, difficult working conditions, and monotony, that the chavera [female member of the Kibbutz] has found little happiness in her economic activities. (pp. 221–30.)

The outcome of this attempt to alter radically the sexual basis of the division of labor appears to have been a tragedy. Margaret Mead (1949, p. 77) has pointed out that "envy of the male role can come as much from an undervaluation of the role of wife and mother as from an over-valuation of the public aspects of achievement that have been reserved for men." Apparently a cultural undervaluation of women cannot be corrected by abolishing the female role.

It is of interest that the Kibbutz had to alter the organization of the family in order to free women to perform previously male activities, especially in light of the anthropologist's argument that the formation of the family depends not only on biological differences and sexual alliance, but on the division of labor as well. Washburn and DeVore (1961) state:

The origin of the human family presents three problems: (1) the evolution of a helpless, slow-growing human infant, (2) the loss of oestrus, and (3) the male's role as an economic provider. . . . The male's role as an economic provider had certainly appeared by the Middle Pleistocene, when men were killing large animals. Hunting large animals was probably based on cooper-ation, and the band must have shared in the eating.

It cannot be proved, of course, that incest prohibitions and exogamous matings arose in the Middle Pleistocene, but it can be shown that the condi-tions which made such regulation advantageous arose at that time. All data suggest that the killing of large animals is a task for adult men and that, once hunting became important to the group, children had to depend on adults for many years. Both by increasing the importance of the male as provider, and by making control of a hunting area essential, large scale hunting activity created conditions that favored exogamous mating. The offspring of *Australopithecus* may have been just as independent as those of a chimpanzee, but the children of Ternifine or Peking man depended on the hunting of adult males, and their survival depended upon the relations between the young and the hunters. It is impossible to date the beginning of the human family or of the incest tabu, but the conditions that made these in-stitutions advantageous in the evolution of the species are concomitant with the hunting of large animals. (pp. 97–100.)

SEX DISTINCTIONS IN SOCIAL STRUCTURE

The speculative historical sequence proposed by Washburn and DeVore contains a series of causal links that relate physical sex differences, subsistence activities, and forms of social organization. While the hypothesis about the origins of the family is not directly testable, the more general notion that forms of social organization are are related to sex differences in subsistence activities can be partially investigated by an examination of the cross-cultural data.

First, with respect to the variety of forms of social organization found cross-culturally, it should be pointed out that the distinction of gender is basic to understanding many of these forms. That is, the distinction of gender is used not only as a basis for assigning activities, as in the division of labor, but also as a basis for transmitting rights and duties in the proper allocation of social statuses. Thus in the marital rules of residence, in the permitted forms of multiple marriage, in the criteria for membership in descent groups, and in kinship terminology, gender is used to decide who will live where, who can marry whom, who will belong to which group, and so on.

Furthermore, there tends to be a general cross-cultural bias concerning the use of gender as social criteria. The majority of societies organize their social institutions around males rather than females. For example, certain types of rules of residence group together spatially a core of kin-related males, while other rules of residence group together a core of kin-related females. In Murdock's World Ethnographic Sample of 565 societies, 376 societies are labeled as predominantly patrilocal (i.e., sons after marriage reside with or near their parental family), while only 84 are rated predominantly matrilocal (i.e., daughters after marriage tend to live with or near their parental family). With respect to descent groups, the ratio is roughly four to one in favor of membership being transmitted patrilineally through a line of males rather than matrilineally through females. For forms of multiple marriage the sex ratio is even more biased. Of the 431 societies that permit polygamous marriage, 427 permit men to have more than one wife, but only four permit women to have more than one husband.

Returning to the relation between subsistence activities and forms of social organization, it is possible, using only the categories of residence and descent group, to construct a simple typology of nine types of social organization that will account for over 95 percent of the societies in Murdock's World Ethnographic Sample (see Table 3). These nine types of social organization are:

1. No descent group—neolocal residence.
2. No descent group—biolocal residence.
3. No descent group—patrilocal residence.
4. No descent group—matrilocal residence.
5. Matrilineal descent group—matrilocal residence.
6. Matrilineal descent group—avunculocal residence.
7. Matrilineal descent group—patrilocal residence.
8. Patrilineal descent group—patrilocal residence.
9. Both matrilineal and patrilineal descent group—patrilocal residence.

Both the dominant form of subsistence activity and the degree of sex difference in the division of labor appear to affect which of these nine types of social organization will occur. Table 4 presents these data taken from a subsample of Murdock's World Ethnographic Sample (1957).

The results indicate that there is a complete network of relationships between division of labor by sex, subsistence activities, and types of social organization. Generally those subsistence activities which require predominantly male effort and which involve the use of economic capital, such as *animal husbandry* and *agriculture with cattle,* are likely to be both patrilineal and patrilocal. There are a large number of neolocal societies without descent groups that have *agriculture with cattle*

TABLE 3

Cross-Cultural Data on the Association between Rules of Residence and Descent Group for 428 Societies

| Rules of Residence | Descent Group | | | | |
	Patri-lineal	Matri-lineal	Mat. & Pat.	None	Total
Patrilocal	**177**	**9**	**17**	**78**	281
Matrilocal	0	**32**	2	**30**	64
Avunculocal	0	**15**	1	1	17
Bilocal	3	1	1	**33**	38
Neolocal	1	1	0	**26**	28
TOTAL	181	58	21	168	428

NOTE: Boldface indicates social organizations listed in typology presented above.

TABLE 4

Cross-Cultural Data on Sex Division of Labor (by Subsistence Activity) and Type of Social Organization (by Descent Group and Residence)

Sex Division of Labor	No Descent Group				Matrilineal			Patrilineal	Mat. & Pat.	Total
	Neo-local	Bi-local	Patri-local	Matri-local	Matri-local	Avuncu-local	Patri-local	Patri-local	Patri-local	
Agriculture with cattle										
Men do most	11	6	6	1	1	0	1	34	1	61
Both do	6	2	9	3	4	1	0	40	2	67
Women do most	0	0	0	1	0	0	1	12	2	16
TOTAL	17	8	15	5	5	1	2	86	5	144
Animal husbandry										
Men do most	0	0	2	0	0	0	1	14	0	17
Both do	1	0	2	0	0	1	0	10	1	15
Women do most	0	0	0	0	0	0	0	0	0	0
TOTAL	1	0	4	0	0	1	1	24	1	32
Agriculture without cattle										
Men do most	3	5	13	2	6	0	1	5	0	35
Both do	0	2	0	4	5	10	1	27	2	51
Women do most	2	4	9	4	5	2	1	14	2	43
TOTAL	5	11	22	10	16	12	3	46	4	129
Fishing										
Men do most	1	4	11	0	2	0	1	3	1	23
Both do	0	1	0	2	0	0	1	2	0	6
Women do most	0	0	1	0	0	0	0	0	0	1
TOTAL	1	5	12	2	2	0	2	5	1	30
Hunting and gathering										
Men do most	0	1	7	3	0	0	0	2	0	13
Both do	1	8	10	6	1	0	1	6	6	39
Women do most	0	0	0	0	0	0	0	0	0	0
TOTAL	1	9	17	9	1	0	1	8	6	52
TOTAL	25	33	70	26	24	14	9	169	17	387

Type of Social Organization

subsistence economies, but this is perhaps because most of these societies belong to the Western European tradition in which industrial manufacture rather than agriculture is actually the predominant form of economic activity.

In contrast to *agriculture with cattle* and *animal husbandry, agriculture without cattle,* which frequently involves both slash-and-burn techniques of farming and root crops rather than cereal grains, is more likely to depend on a greater proportion of female labor, and to occur with matrilineal descent groupings and matrilocal or avunculocal residence. Avunculocal residence, in which a man moves with his wife at marriage to live with his mother's brother or a classificatory equivalent, groups together a core of males who are matrilineally related. Such a rule of residence is thought to be a result of factors that operate to produce patrilocal residence acting on a previously matrilineal-matrilocal system (Murdock 1949). It is interesting that avunculocal residence most often occurs in societies that have a fairly balanced division of labor by sex. Aberle (1961), using Murdock's sample, found that avunculocal residence is also more likely to occur in societies with a hereditary aristocracy.

Hunting and gathering and *fishing* apparently only rarely create the kind of capital that is utilized in corporate descent groups; both sets of subsistence activities have few matrilineal or patrilineal groups, despite the fact that *fishing* and *hunting* are predominantly male activities with a high frequency of patrilocal residence.

The overall results suggest that both economic capital and sex bias in the use and control of this capital are important in forming corporate descent groups and in determining rules of residence. Although sex differences in who does the work appear to help determine which sex controls the economic capital, the evidence does not indicate that sex bias in the division of labor by itself can determine the type of residence or the formation of kinship groups.

INTERPERSONAL BEHAVIOR

Present interest in sex differences appears to emphasize the degree to which different kinds of interpersonal behaviors are innately sex-linked or are learned. Most anthropologists, having experienced the sense of discontinuity that comes from living in another culture, take the tremendous impact of learning on shaping sex-specific behaviors for granted.

As Mead concluded in her (1935) study of sex and temperament among three New Guinea tribes:

We have now considered in detail the approved personalities of each sex among three primitive peoples. We found the Arapesh—both men and women—displaying a personality that, out of our historically limited preoccupations, we would call maternal in its parental aspects, and feminine in its sexual aspects. We found men, as well as women, trained to be cooperative, unaggressive, responsive to the needs and demands of others. We found no idea that sex was a powerful driving force either for men or for women. In marked contrast to these attitudes, we found among the Mundugumor that both men and women developed as ruthless, aggressive, positively sexed individuals, with the maternal cherishing aspects of personality at a minimum. Both men and women approximated to a personality type that we in our culture would find only in an undisciplined and very violent male. Neither the Arapesh nor the Mundugumor profit by a contrast between the sexes: the Arapesh ideal is the mild, responsive man married to the mild, responsive woman; the Mundugumor ideal is the violent aggressive man married to the violent aggressive woman. In the third tribe, the Tchambuli, we found a genuine reversal of the sex-attitudes of our own culture, with the woman the dominant, impersonal, managing partner, the man the less responsible and the emotionally dependent person. These three situations suggest, then, a very definite conclusion. If those temperamental attitudes which we have traditionally regarded as feminine—such as passivity, responsiveness, and a willingness to cherish children—can so easily be set up as the masculine pattern in one tribe, and in another to be outlawed for the majority of men, we no longer have any basis for regarding such aspects of behavior as sex-linked.

We are forced to conclude that human nature is almost unbelievably malleable, responding accurately and contrastingly to contrasting cultural conditions. . . . Standardized personality differences between the sexes are of this order, cultural creations to which each generation, male or female, is trained to conform. There remains, however, the problem of the origin of these socially standardized differences. (pp. 190–91.)

How did these socially standardized differences in interpersonal behavior develop? Once we acknowledge the plasticity of human behavior, we must make some attempt to account for both the cross-cultural modal tendencies in behavior and the variation from these modes. For each of the kinds of interpersonal behavior discussed below, an estimate of the modal cross-cultural arrangement with respect to sex differences is presented, and then an attempt to find explanatory correlates of these behaviors is made.

SEXUAL BEHAVIOR

In an extensive survey of sexual behavior, Ford and Beach (1951) report a number of male-female differences that occur in most, if not all, of the 200 societies in their sample.

According to the rules of etiquette in our society the initiative in sexual advances should always be taken by the man. As in the sex act proper, the male is expected to assume the more active role. The majority of other societies for whom this information is available also believe that only men should take the initiative in seeking and arranging a sexual affair. (p. 110.)

Viewed in cross-cultural perspective, the practice of concealing the woman's genital region with some type of clothing is far more common than is covering the masculine sex organs. There are a number of societies in which the woman customarily covers her pubic region with some form of clothing, whereas the man does not conceal his genitals. Although there are a few societies in which both sexes are usually nude, there are no peoples who insist upon the man covering his genitals and at the same time permit the woman to expose her genital region. (p. 103.)

Sixty-one per cent of the 139 societies in our sample for whom evidence is available forbid a mated woman to engage in extra-mateship liaisons. In some societies the mated man is similarly restricted, although the great majority of these peoples are much more concerned with the behavior of the mated woman than with the mated man. (p. 123.)

The development of love magic has been particularly widespread in human societies. In nearly every society love potions or medicines, magical charms, or ritual acts are available for the man or woman who seeks the affection of a particular partner. . . . In cross-cultural perspective, generally speaking, love charms are much more often employed by men than by women. (pp. 108–9.)

In 49 (64 per cent) of the 76 societies other than our own for which information is available, homosexual activities of one sort or another are considered normal and acceptable for certain members of the community. The most common form of institutionalized homosexuality is that of the berdache or transvestite. The berdache is a male who dresses like a woman, performs woman's tasks, and adopts some aspects of the feminine role in sexual behavior with male partners. Less frequently a woman dresses like a man and seeks to adopt the male sex role. (p. 137.)

. . . It appears highly likely that human females are less likely than males to engage in homosexual relations. At any rate, in most other societies, as in our own, feminine homosexuality is accorded much less attention than is comparable behavior among males. In fact, specific information concerning homosexual women is available for only 17 of the peoples included in our sample. (p. 140.) . . . In all human societies for which there is adequate information males are more likely than females to stimulate their own sexual organs. (p. 248.) In our own and many other societies it is generally believed that the majority of women need more protracted stimulation than men if they are to experience sexual climax. ... Attitudes of people in other cultures toward this problem are of interest. But references to orgasm in the female in societies other than our own are relatively rare. This problem reflects a failure on the part of investigators to obtain such information, since no statements could be found which indicate that the women of any society fail to experience a sexual climax. (pp. 43–44.)

As far as actual sexual behavior is concerned, it develops somewhat more rapidly in certain societies than others. Some cultures fully approve of a variety of sexual practices among young boys and girls and between adolescents of both sexes. When there is any difference in treatment, the behavior of girls is more carefully controlled than is that of boys. (p. 204.)

In general, then, males appear to be more sexually active, females more sexually restricted. The evidence also suggests not only that sexual restrictions are more typically applied to females, but that females tend to be more inhibited by sexual restrictions than males (mutuality in sexual activity appears only in societies that are permissive rather than restrictive). The result of both these factors—greater sexual restrictiveness applied to women and greater ease of inhibiting female sexuality —would tend to create greater sex differences in the amount and kind of sexual activity in those societies that have more severe sex restrictions, with the males being much more active than the females and the females much less responsive than the males.

At present, two major social correlates of sexual restrictiveness have been found in cross-cultural research. One of these correlates, discussed by William Stephens (1963), involves the effect, of "civilization" and the "autocratic political state" on sexual activity. Stephens presents data taken from ethnographies and interviews with ethnographers which indicate that culturally permitted premarital and extramarital liaisons occur more frequently in noncivilized communities (24 out of 31 cases), and less frequently in civilized communities (2 out of 18 cases). Civilized communities, which are defined as communities belonging to "a society that embraces cities," are thought to have less sexual freedom because of their association with the autocratic state.

Why are civilized communities relatively strict about the regulation of sex and primitive societies rather liberal? ... I think the answer ultimately lies in the development of the state. Until 200 years ago, almost all civilized

communities were parts of kingdoms, that is, autocratic agrarian states. . . .
The development of the kingdom seems to bring with it certain basic changes
in the family. Among these are an elaboration of deference customs between
family members and a tightening of sex restrictions. When the kingdom, the
autocratic agrarian state, evolves into a democratic state, these family customs seem to gradually liberalize. (Stephens 1963, pp. 256–58.)

A second social correlate that has been found to be related to sexual
restrictiveness is the form of family organization. For example, of the
nine societies surveyed by Ford and Beach in which females but not
males are sexually restricted in childhood and adolescence, eight are
strongly polygynous. Of the 26 sexually permissive societies for which
information is available, only nine are strongly polygynous. Sexual restrictiveness, as measured by the Whiting and Child rating of the severity
of socialization of sexual behavior, has also been found to be significantly
related to polygyny (Whiting and Child 1953, Whiting 1961).

The reason for the relationship between polygyny and sexual restrictiveness (especially toward the female) is not obvious. Perhaps restrictiveness is needed because strong female sexuality on the part of adult
women poses too great a threat for the husband of many wives; strong
female sexuality may also pose a threat to the polygynously married
mother who must control the sexual behavior of her male children with
only diluted support from her husband. Or perhaps because both polygyny and autocratic states create or rely on unequal distributions of
authority and deference, mutuality in sexual behavior, which tends to
establish intimacy and equality, is discouraged.

AUTHORITY AND DEFERENCE

A second dimension of interpersonal behavior that has been investigated
cross-culturally with respect to sex differences involves authority and
respect relationships. Stephens, in a systematic study of authority and
deference between husband and wife, finds that in 21 of the 31 societies
in his sample there is clear evidence that the husband exercises "considerable" authority over his wife; in six societies the husbands are
"mildly" dominant over wives, and in five societies there is fairly equal
sharing of authority. In six other cases there appear to be separate spheres
of authority for husband and wife. In only four societies from this sample
does it appear that women may have more de facto authority in the family than males: the people of Modjokuta, Java, the Tchambuli of New

Guinea, the Jivarvo of South America, and the Berbers of North Africa. However, if power over groups larger than the family is considered, it is very likely all societies would be found to be male controlled (Stephens 1963).

In deference between husband and wife, Stephens finds a similar male bias. By deference, Stephens means the ritualistic acknowledgment of power, measured by the presence or absence of such behaviors as bowing or kneeling before another, having special speech etiquette, not joking, not contradicting, not being positionally higher than the other person, and so on. In only one society out of four is the wife not required to observe some of these customs with respect to her husband. Very rarely does the husband make any kind of deference to his wife—with the exception of the chivalrous males of Western European cultures, for whom this order is reversed.

Stephens finds the degree of deference between husband and wife to be strongly correlated with the degree of deference between father and son. Deference within the family, like sexual restrictiveness, correlates with an autocratic political state rather than a "tribal" political system.

One thing we see here is another patterning regularity, a parallel between family relationships and the larger social hierarchy. Autocratic societies, that is, autocratic agrarian societies—kingdoms—have autocratic families. As the king rules his subjects and the nobles subjugate and exploit the commoners, so does husband tend to lord it over wife, father rule over son, and ... Ego defer to grandfather, uncle, and elder brother. The family, in such societies, looks like a sort of kingdom in microcosm. As Ego defers to father and grandfather, so do the commoners defer to the nobles; and the deference customs are quite similar. Sometimes the *same* deference custom is given both to one's father and to the local lord. (Stephens 1963, p. 335.)

Another variable that appears to affect the distribution of authority and deference between the sexes is the degree to which men rather than women control and mediate property; and this in turn, it has been argued above, is affected by the division of labor and the cultural capacity to create capital. Support for this hypothesis is found in Gouldner and Peterson's correlation and factor-analytic study of cross-cultural data (Gouldner and Peterson 1962). The actual data were collected by Leo Simmons (1945), who scored 71 primarily nonliterate societies on 99 culture traits by means of a four-point scale of importance-unimportance. Fifty-nine of these traits were subjected to a factor analysis by

Gouldner and Peterson. The following tabulation presents the correlation coefficients for culture traits that are significantly related to patripotestal family authority and the subjection or inferiority of women.

	Subjection or Inferiority of Women	Patripotestal Family Authority
Patrilineal inheritance	.58	.65
Patrilineal succession	.51	.57
Patrilineal descent	.44	.66
Patrilocal residence	.25	.38
Herding	.21	.26
Matrilineal residence	—.24	—.23
Matrilineal descent	—.34	—.39
Matrilineal inheritance	—.41	—.63
Subjection or inferiority of women	—	.41

Generally we find that societies in which inheritance, succession, and descent-group membership are through males rather than females are more likely to concentrate power and respect in the hands of men. However, these structural variables do not always tell us which sex actually controls scarce resources and holds authority. Murdock presents the example of the Lovedu, one of the Bantu-speaking tribes of South Africa, as a culture which, despite its patrilineal, patrilocal, and polygynous structure, has granted a relatively high status to women (Murdock 1959). Among the Lovedu, polygynous women form strong coalitions against their husbands, forcing them to treat each wife with strict fairness. The Lovedu women's high status is partly the result of a matrilateral cross-cousin marriage system—a system in which a man marries his mother's brother's daughter or some woman from his mother's patrilineage. In such a system a woman holds an advantage in negotiating marriages; the Lovedu women, for example, have gained control of the bride prices, which involve considerable amounts of cattle.

It is interesting that the Tchambuli (the New Guinea tribe studied by Margaret Mead) also have a patrilineal system with matrilateral (mother's brother's daughter) cross-cousin marriage and female control of important property. Women appear to be the actual holders of power and to have the more practical and instrumental type of temperament.

Marriage conditions parallel those of the Lovedu; the application of the matrilateral cross-cousin marriage rule results in a polygynously married Tchambuli man having wives who are clan sisters and who typically form strong coalitions against him (Mead 1935).

Similar in many ways to the authority dimension of interpersonal behavior is the instrumental-expressive dimension of role behavior. Zeldich (1955) found consistent cross-cultural regularities among almost all societies having the husband-father role described as more instrumental, and the wife-mother role as more expressive. Whether this differentiation is based on factors external to the nuclear family or on the universal requirements of the family as a social system is not clear, although both kinds of factors may be involved.

AGGRESSION, CONFLICT, AND RESPONSIBILITY

A detailed and systematic cross-cultural study of sex differences in interpersonal behavior has been carried out by the Six Culture Socialization Project, directed by J. Whiting, I. Child, W. Lambert, and B. Whiting. (See B. Whiting, 1963, for ethnographic descriptions of these cultures.) In this study 24 children (aged three to ten) from each of the six cultures were observed by trained fieldworkers for 20 five-minute periods. Each child's behavior was then systematically recorded and coded. The initial results indicate that boys are more likely than girls to engage in physical aggression in all six cultures, while girls are more likely to act affectionately and responsibly. In five of the six cultures, girls are more likely to act sociably and succorantly; but in one cultural group, a Mixtecan Indian barrio in Oaxaca, Mexico, boys are significantly more sociable and succorant than girls (J. Whiting, personal communication).

Although the differences recorded above may be due to differential child-training practices rather than to innate sex-linked behavioral tendencies, the fact that the largest sex differences occur in the younger (three to six) rather than in the older (seven to ten) group gives less weight to the training hypothesis, which would predict the opposite result.

A second systematic investigation of the interpersonal behavior of children has been made by Melford Spiro in his study of children reared in an Israeli Kibbutz. These children were reared in peer groups primarily by female nurses in a culture in which sex differences are deliberately played down in accordance with the norms of Kibbutz ideology. Thus the effects on the child's behavior of different-sex socializers and cultural sex stereotypes are to some extent absent in this study. The children in the sample range in age from one to five years. Twenty-four boys and twenty-three girls were observed. In the area of interpersonal behavior, Spiro compares the frequencies of child-to-child interaction for the categories of integrative behavior, conflict behavior, and aggressive behavior by sex of initiator and sex of object. He summarizes his findings as follows:

In all (age) groups girls are more integrative (give aid, share, act affectionate, cooperate, etc.) than boys, and boys more disintegrative. In all groups boys engage in more acts of conflict (seizure of another child's possessions) than girls, and in all but one group the boys engage in more acts of aggression (disobedience, hitting, insulting, etc.) than the girls. Boys, moreover, are the recipients of the girls' excess integrations—boys are integrated more than the girls—but the girls are recipients of only part of the boys' excess disintegration. For though girls are the more frequent victims of conflict, boys are the more frequent victims of aggression.

Though more integrative than boys, girls also display more frequent symptoms of regression than boys. In all groups but one, for example, girls have a higher incidence of thumbsucking, and in the two groups for which there are data, girls exhibit more regressive play than do boys. (Spiro 1958, 247–48.)

For each observed sex difference, Spiro speculates on whether the difference is due to innate causes or to the child's attempt to model sex-linked adult behaviors. In many cases, both these factors seem to be present. However, it is Spiro's general conclusion that in this particular culture many of the sex differences observed are most reasonably accounted for by the innate sex-linked behavior hypothesis. Also, insofar as Spiro's categories of aggression and integration are similar to the Whitings' categories of physical aggression and responsibility, the sex differences in the Kibbutz study are in the same direction as in the six-culture study.

Even though some sex differences in interpersonal behavior may be biologically influenced, there is considerable evidence that the interpersonal behaviors of boys and girls are socialized quite differently. Barry, Bacon, and Child, in a cross-cultural survey based on ethnographic reports for 110 societies, found very consistent sex differences in the socialization of children age four or older. In general they found that boys are trained to be self-reliant and to achieve, while girls are trained to be nurturant, responsible, and obedient. Table 5 summarizes these findings.

TABLE 5

Cross-Cultural Ratings for Sex Differences on Five Variables of Childhood Socialization Pressure

(from Barry, Bacon, and Child 1957)

Variable	Number of Cultures with Ratable Information	Percentage of Cultures with Evidence of Sex Difference in Direction of		
		boys	neither	girls
Nurturance	33	0	18	82
Responsibility	84	11	28	61
Obedience	69	3	62	35
Achievement	31	87	10	3
Self-reliance	82	85	15	0

Concerning the validity of these findings, Barry et al. considered and discounted two possible sources of bias: the ethnographers and the raters. Ethnographers are trained, insofar as possible, not to translate their own cultural expectations to other cultures. And it is highly unlikely that the raters were the source of bias; if they had been, there would have been more of a tendency for the ambiguously recorded data to be interpreted in terms of the raters' own cultural conceptions of sex differences. However, the more ambiguous cases (in which only one of the two judges was able to make a rating) do not show an increase in sex differences. Therefore Barry et al. hypothesize that these sex differences are due to:

... Universal tendencies in the differentiation of the adult sex role. In the economic sphere, men are more frequently allotted tasks that involve leaving home and engaging in activities where a high level of skill yields important returns; hunting is a prime example. Emphasis on training in self-reliance and achievement for boys would function as preparation for such an economic role. Women, on the other hand, are more frequently allotted tasks at or near home that minister most immediately to the needs of others (such as cooking and water carrying); and in their pursuit a responsible carrying out of established routines is likely to be more important than the development of an especially high order of skill. Thus training in nurturance, responsibility, and less clearly, obedience, may contribute to preparation for this economic role. (Barry, Bacon, and Child 1957, p. 329.)

The argument presented here is similar to the one presented above in the discussion of the division of labor: that sex specialization occurs as a result of generalization from activities more directly conditioned by physical sex differences to activities anticipatory or similar to the directly conditioned activities. The strongest evidence for this hypothesis is the extent to which sex differences in socialization are associated with types of subsistence activities. Using Murdock's World Ethnographic Sample, Barry et al. tested the relationship between the extent of sex differences in socialization and other cultural variables such as residence rules, forms of marriage, and degree of political integration. Out of 40 comparisons, six significant associations were found. These were: (1) Grain rather than root crops grown. (2) Large or milk-producing animals rather than small animals kept. (3) Nomadic rather than sedentary residence. (4) Large animals hunted. (5) Fishing unimportant or absent. (6) Polygyny rather than monogamy.

Of these six variables, four deal directly with subsistence activities, and another, nomadism, is closely related to subsistence activities. Barry, Bacon, and Child conclude from these results that large sex differences will occur in "an economy that places a high premium on the superior strength and superior development of motor skills requiring strength, which characterize the male" (p. 330). The correlation between large sex differences in socialization and polygyny, however, is thought to be due to the effect of larger family units, which permit sharper sex differentiation than an isolated nuclear family in which the illness, death, or absence of one parent forces the other to take over some of the missing parent's activities. Romney, in a re-analysis of these data, suggests that the correlation between the types of subsistence activity that involve food accumulation and a child-training emphasis on compliance rather than assertion may be confounded with type of family organization. Thus, societies that rely primarily on food accumulation are also very likely to have father-absent families. If the sex of the socializing parent affects the way the child is socialized, the correlation between types of economy and child-rearing might then be the result of their relationship to type of family organization (Romney 1965).

IDENTITY

In the beginning of this review, it was emphasized that in all cultures biological sex differences are recognized as distinct social statuses for men and women. On the individual level these social statuses become psychological identities involving evaluative discriminations about one's own self and behavior. A male or female identity can be a product both of direct tuition (the child is taught to call and perceive himself as male or female) and of indirect tuition (the child is responded to or taught to behave in sex-specific ways, and so comes to respond to himself as others respond to him). Kohlberg's chapter in this volume discusses the hypothesis that children first learn their sex identities, and then attempt to acquire and master sex-appropriate activities.

Thus almost everyone in every society learns his sex status and the role behaviors appropriate to it (Linton 1942). Even the biological hermaphrodite can apparently learn one or the other of its possible sex statuses without great difficulty if one status is firmly assigned and not switched (Hampson 1965). Nevertheless, not everyone wishes to occupy only his or her actual sex status. Burton and Whiting (1961) distinguish three different kinds of status or identity:

We would like to define a person's position or positions in the status systems of this society as his identity. Furthermore, we would like to distinguish three kinds of identity: attributed, subjective, and optative. *Attributed identity* consists of the statuses assigned to a person by other members of his society. *Subjective identity* consists of the statuses a person sees himself as occupying. And finally, *optative identity* consists of those statuses a person wishes he could occupy.... It is our thesis that the aim of socialization in any society is to produce an adult whose attributed, subjective, and optative identities are isomorphic: "I see myself as others see me, and I am what I want to be." (p. 86.)

One of the ways in which a culture can institutionalize the potential discrepancy between assigned and optative identities is to permit certain persons to take on many of the role behaviors of the opposite sex, as, for example, in the institution of the berdache. Such transvestism often, but not always, involves homosexual behavior. Unlike transvestism, which is an open and overt expression of the wish to assume a feminine status, institutions such as the couvade and male initiation rites are thought to express a disguised and less conscious cross-sex optative identity. The couvade is a set of customs in which a husband participates ritually in the birth of his child by adopting some of the behavior and taboos of his wife, sometimes actually experiencing labor pains and postpartum fatigue.

Initiation ceremonies also appear to express an envy of the female role. For example, the initiation is often culturally perceived as a rebirth ritual in which men take a child and bring about his birth as a man by magical techniques stolen long ago from women. These techniques would lose their magical efficacy if women were ever to observe them. The need for the initiate to prove his manhood by bearing extreme fatigue and pain without complaint appears to indicate some uncertainty in sex identity.

What then are the cultural arrangements that might make men envy the opposite sex? Mead, in discussing societies known to her personally, observes:

What we find within these seven societies is that in [those societies] which have emphasized sucking [in nursing], the most complementary relationship of all bodily learning experience, there is the greatest symbolic preoccupation with the differentials between men and women, the greatest envy, over-compensation, ritual mimicry of the opposite sex, and so on. . . . When in addition male separateness from women has been developed into a strong institution, with a men's house and male initiation ceremonies, then the whole system becomes an endlessly reinforcing one, in which each generation of little boys grows up among women, identified with women, envying women, and then, to assert the endangered certainty of their manhood, isolate themselves from women. (Mead 1949, pp. 73–74.)

Working with cross-cultural data, Whiting and his associates have come to similar conclusions concerning the role of status envy and cross-sex identification in the functioning of initiation rites and in the couvade. Whiting distinguishes two sets of conditions: the first pertains to the persons who surround the infant and young child, those persons who presumably create the child's "primary" optative identity; the second pertains to the child's experiences in later childhood and adolescence, which create a "secondary," and sometimes conflicting, optative identity. The first set of conditions appears to involve mainly the presence versus the absence of the father in the household, with the expectation that "in the exclusive mother-infant case the mother should be seen as all powerful, all important, and insofar as she sometimes withholds resources, the person to be envied; and we predict the infant will covertly practice her role, and his optative identity will be female." (Burton and Whiting 1961, p. 88.)

In fact, this hypothesis has empirical support; societies that have exclusive mother-infant sleeping arrangements (in which the father sleeps in either a different hut or different bed while the mother and infant sleep together) are significantly more likely to have male initiation rites and couvade than societies without such exclusive arrangements (Whiting 1962).

Whether the males who form a primary cross-sex optative identity express their envy of, and identification with, females in couvade or male initiation rites appears to be determined by a second set of conditions. Thus male initiation rites occur more frequently in patrilocal societies, while couvade is more likely to be practiced in matrilocal societies. It appears that in societies with exclusive mother-infant arrangements, later patrilocal residence, in which kin-related males are grouped together, creates a conflicting secondary optative identity for the young boy. This conflict in primary and secondary identities appears to be resolved in part by initiation rites, which symbolically remove the young boy's clinging femininity and reward masculine behavior. In matrilocal societies, on the other hand, no such conflict is created, so that the male envy of women is more directly acted out in an imitation of female childbearing. (See Young 1962, for a contrary view of the functions of male initiation ceremonies.)

In order to test some of these hypotheses more directly, Whiting and his students have begun research in specific cultures that present internal contrasts relevant to identification theories. These studies have found the composition of the family in which the infant and young child is reared to be related to a number of variables, including math-verbal differences (L. K. Carlsmith 1964), individual participation in the ritual of couvade (Munroe 1964), interpersonal behavior (Longabaugh 1962), and psychological tests of sex identity (D'Andrade 1962). Generally the results of these studies are congruent with the hypothesis that optative identity and related behaviors are influenced by identification with significant others, and that the person with whom the child identifies is strongly influenced by the physical presence or absence of family members.

SEX DIFFERENCES IN FANTASY AND COGNITION

Perhaps the most complete cross-cultural investigation of sex difference in fantasy is Colby's study of dreams. From a collection of 1,853 reported dreams from 75 "tribal" societies, Colby selected one dream from each subject (366 males and 183 females), and coded each dream for the presence or absence of nineteen "qualities." For example, the quality "wife" was scored as present if the dream contained either the words "my wife" or "his wife" or "brother's wife" or "Felicia" when it was known that Felicia was the dreamer's wife. The following table presents the results of this study.

TABLE 6

Sex Differences in Fantasy: Dream Qualities Reported by Subjects from 75 Tribal Societies

(from Colby 1963)

Male Preferred Qualities			Female Preferred Qualities		
Quality	Total no. of dreams	M/F ratio	Quality	Total no. of dreams	F/M ratio
grass	11	5.0[a]	husband	25	10.5
coitus	23	3.3	clothes	21	2.7
wife	37	2.6	mother	37	1.9
weapon	60	2.0	father	40	1.7
animal	179	1.6	child	61	1.6
death	121	1.5	home	52	1.6
red	16	1.5	female figure	198	1.3
vehicle	83	1.4	cry	29	1.1
hit	70	1.4	male figure	317	1.01
ineffectual attempt	14	1.2			

[a] That is, the quality "grass" appeared in five times as many men's dreams as women's. Since there were twice as many men as women in the sample, we had to double the number of women's dreams to obtain true ratios.

Colby's initial hypothesis, based on work with American subjects, was that males would dream more about qualities associated with "female mating choice" and "intensified penetration of space," while females would dream more about "male mating choice objects." Generally, cross-cultural results support this hypothesis, although some modification in the definition of these categories was necessary.

One question with respect to these findings is whether these male-female differences in visual images are due to the expression of "body imagery" or to the fact that these visual images are reinforced in the daily performance of sex-typed activities. In other words, as a result of the division of labor, are males more likely to have higher frequencies of rewarding activities relating to such objects as dead animals, weapons, wives, and females more likely to have rewarding activities relating to clothes, husbands, children, and the like? The fact that male-female differences in dreams correspond roughly to these differences in daily activities could then be the result of simple contiguity. However, to the extent that physiological sex differences affect the reinforcement values of external events, sex differences in fantasy (or any other behavior) would be found despite identical external environmental conditions. This double confounding of stimulus conditions, in which males and females inhabit somewhat different internal *and* external environments, makes ambiguous the interpretation of many sex differences in fantasy productions.

Turning to the Rorschach data and other projective-test materials on sex differences in fantasy, a somewhat surprising picture of sex differences emerges. In general, females appear to have a better psychological adjustment than males. The following quotes from Lindzey's (1961) review of cross-cultural applications of projective tests may be taken as indicative:

The natives of Montserrat (Abel and Metraux 1959) as a whole are characterized by strong unconscious dependency needs, a lack of repression, free expression of affect, a practical non-abstract orientation toward the outer world, and little understanding of inner psychological processes. When the females are compared with males, they share unconscious dependency needs but show more of a tendency to "accept and cling to objects" and are more imaginative and creative in their inner life. Adolescents seem generally to have more anxiety than adults, but the female adolescent seems better able to cope with this anxiety than the male. (p. 225.)

A comparison of the two profiles (male and female Menomini Rorschach responses) displayed a number of differences and supported the conclusion that there is a "picture of disturbance, tension, and diffuse anxiety, and decrease in emotional controls among modal males that is not represented among the females." (p. 237; Lindzey is quoting here from Spindler and Spindler 1958, pp. 223–24.)

When male and female subjects born in China are compared (on Rorschach profiles, Abel and Hsu 1949), the females display greater flexibility, somewhat more freedom in expression of affect, and superior imaginative powers. . . . Of the American born (Chinese) subjects, the females appear to deal with their adjustment problems more directly and make less use of repressive mechanisms than the males. (p. 240.)

This point (projective tests provide hypothesis) is elaborated in a separate paper (Gladwin, 1953) discussing sex differences among the Trukese. Gladwin makes clear that after four years of contact with these people he returned home convinced that men were dominant and generally more secure than women, who appeared ". . . subservient, insecure, and afraid to express themselves in the presence of their lords and masters." (p. 306, Gladwin 1953). Much to his surprise, the analysis of the projective-test protocols suggested to Sarason that men were more anxious than women and less competent to deal with ambiguous or conflict situations. Prodded by this finding, Gladwin took a second look at the ethnographic data and found, again to his surprise, a considerable amount of information (incidence of suicide attempts, successful resistance to parental pressure in regard to marriage, male and female roles in adulterous relations, treatment of brother and sister at puberty separated by cultural decree, and so on) which supported Sarason's interpretation and forced a new formulation. (p. 273.)

Similar results appear in the Rorschach data from Tepoztlan, Mexico (Abel and Calabresi 1951) and also in the Ojibwa protocols (Hallowell 1955). One might speculate, then, that if these Rorschach results have some validity, the typical masculine prerogatives of deference, power, and sexual initiative may have some psychic cost. A number of investigators of sex differences have commented that men seem to have greater difficulty adjusting to their roles. The more frequent cultural institutionalization of male homosexuality, and the greater severity of male initiation rites (J. Brown 1963) would seem to support this notion.

Another factor that may be related to the greater anxiety found for males on the Rorschach involves the effects of acculturation on men. That is, since men typically occupy the public, political, and instrumental roles in a society, rapid social change, especially when externally imposed, would seem more likely to disturb the adjustment of men than women (Hallowell 1952). L. S. Spindler (1962), in a study of Menomini women, concludes that male-female differences on the Rorschach can be related directly to differences in role adjustment produced by acculturation. Most of the males had been forced to conform to "white" values and standards, while only the "elite" group of Indian women had to face such pressures. However, the degree to which acculturation is responsible for the greater male anxiety among the other societies mentioned above cannot be estimated from present information.

SUMMARY AND IMPLICATIONS

In all known human populations males differ from females not only in primary sex characteristics, but also in secondary characteristics, males tending, on the average, to have greater height, more massive skeletons, a higher ratio of muscle to fat, more body hair, etc. However, these differences hold only within particular populations; sex typing on the basis of secondary characteristics from unknown populations is extremely unreliable.

The division of labor by sex involved in subsistence and other activities is strongly influenced by primary and secondary sex characteristics: generally males tend to perform those activities that are physically strenuous, dangerous, involve long periods of travel, and demand a high level of cooperation.

Specialization by sex in activities generalizes from those activities that are differentially conditioned by physical differences to activities which are anticipatory or similar to the more directly conditioned activities. These sex differences can be seen in the division of labor, in the manufacture of various objects, in sex differences in socialization, and perhaps even in fantasy.

Sex bias in forms of social organization, such as rules of residence and types of descent groups, is related to subsistence activities and the division of labor by sex; the sex which performs or initiates the basic subsistence activities is more likely to control the property that is involved in these activities, and more likely to reside together and to form a descent group.

The cross-cultural mode is that males are more sexually active, more dominant, more deferred to, more aggressive, less responsible, less nurturant, and less emotionally expressive than females. The extent of these differences varies by culture. And in some cultures some of these differences do not exist (and occasionally the trend is actually reversed). These differences are related to and presumably influenced by which sex controls economic capital, the extent and kind of division of labor by sex, the degree of political "authoritarianism," and family composition.

Maleness and femaleness are institutionalized as statuses in all cultures. Such statuses become psychological identities for most individuals. Usually individuals learn to want to occupy the sex status they are assigned; however, special cultural conditions can affect the degree to which one sex envies the status of the other. Male envy of female status appears to be increased by paternal absence, and is culturally institutionalized in rites such as the couvade and male initiation ceremonies or in special transvestite statuses.

In fantasy dreams male and female differences can be seen as expressions of body imagery or as reflections of culturally institutionalized differences in activities and their reinforcement contingencies.

In projective tests (such as the Rorschach) males from a number of cultures have been found to be more insecure and anxious than females. This, if true, might be due to the greater stress and danger involved in male roles, or to the effects of acculturation, which appears to disrupt the cultural adjustment of males more than females.

In this chapter we have considered some of the very complex mechanisms that play a part in the development of sex differences in all human societies. To understand these mechanisms, it might be helpful to imagine an experiment in which two groups of randomly selected male albino rats are subjected to conditions in which the activities, reinforcement contingencies, and classes of discriminative stimuli are made as different for each group as possible. Would not any operant response measure, such as amount of exploratory behavior, resistance to temptation, or horizontal eye movements during dreaming, be likely to show group differences? These differences would not always be large, but they would probably always be consistent. Finding out exactly which set of experimental conditions was responsible for creating these differences might often be both complex and tedious.

This hypothetical laboratory world differs from the human cultural environment in three major respects. First, the activities, reinforcement contingencies, discriminative stimuli, etc., of the woman's world are not as different as possible from those of the man's world; there is considerable overlap. Second, because of the genetic biological differences between human males and females, some of the differences on various response measures will be innately determined rather than learned. (Indeed, the very fact that some of the present biological sex differences exist may be due to selective factors operating as a result of cultural universals in the division of labor.) Third, in human societies, these differences compound into complex causal chains, resulting in sets of institutional structures that "act back" on the conditions that created them in the first place, sometimes amplifying the original conditions, sometimes elaborating them in a variety of ways. This chapter has attempted to describe some of these phenomena, emphasizing the cultural and social factors that seem to have contributed to the institutionalization of sex differences.

REFERENCES

Abel, Theodora M., and R. A. Calabrese. (1951) The people [Tepoztecans] from their Rorshach tests. In O. Lewis (ed.) *Life in a Mexican village: Tepoztlan restudied*. Urbana: University of Illinois Press.

——, and F. L. K. Hsu. (1949) Some aspects of personality of Chinese as revealed by the Rorshach test. *Rorshach Res. Exch., 13*, 285–301.

——, and Rhoda Metraux. (1959) Sex differences in a Negro peasant community, Montserrat, B.W.I. *J. prog. Tech., 23*, 127–33.

Aberle, D. F. (1961) Matrilineal descent in cross-cutting perspective. In Schneider and Gough (eds.), *Matrilineal kinship*. Berkeley: University of California Press.

Barry, H. III, Margaret K. Bacon, and I. I. Child. (1957) A cross-cultural survey of some sex differences in socialization. *J. abnorm. soc. Psychol., 55*, 327–32.

Brown, Judith K. (1963) A cross-cultural study of female initiation rites. *Amer. Anthrop., 65*, 837–53.

Burton, R. V., and J. W. M. Whiting. (1961) The absent father and cross-sex identity. *Merrill-Palmer Quart., 7* (2), 85–95.

Carlsmith, Lyn. (1964) Effect of early father absence on scholastic aptitude. *Harvard educ. Rev., 34*, 3–21.

Colby, K. M. (1963) Sex differences in dreams of primitive tribes. *Amer. Anthrop., 65*, 1116–21.

D'Andrade, R. G. (1962) Paternal absence and cross-sex identification. Unpublished doctoral dissertation, Harvard University.

Ford, C. S., and F. Beach. (1951) *Patterns of sexual behavior*. New York: Harper & Bros.

Gladwin, T. (1953) The role of man and woman on Truk: A problem in personality and culture. *Transactions of the New York Acad. Sci.*, Ser. II, *15*, 305–9.

Gouldner, A. W., and R. A. Peterson. (1962) *Notes on technology and the moral order*. Indianapolis: Bobbs-Merrill.

Hampson, J. L. (1965) Determinants of psychosexual orientation. In F. Beach (ed.), *Sex and behavior*. New York: John Wiley & Sons.

Hollowell, A. J. (1955) *Culture and experience*. Philadelphia: University of Pennsylvania Press.

La Barre, W. (1954) *The human animal*. Chicago: University of Chicago Press.

Lindzey, G. (1961) *Projective techniques and cross-cultural research*. New York: Appleton-Century-Crofts.

Linton, R. (1942) Age and sex categories. *Amer. Sociol. Rev., 7*, 589–603.

Longabaugh, R. H. W. (1962) The description of mother-child interaction. Ed.D. thesis, Harvard University.

Mead, Margaret. (1935) *Sex and temperament.* New York: William Morrow, and Mentor.

——. (1949) *Male and female.* New York: William Morrow.

Munroe, R. L. (1964) Couvade practices of the Black Carib: a psychological study. Unpublished Ph.D. thesis, Harvard University.

Murdock, G. P. (1935) Comparative data on the division of labor by sex. *Social Forces, 15,* 551–53.

——. (1949) *Social structure.* New York: Macmillan Co.

——. (1957) World ethnographic sample. *Amer. Anthrop., 59,* 664–87.

——. (1959) *Africa: its peoples and their culture history.* New York: McGraw-Hill.

Romney, A. K. (1965) Variations in household structure as determinants of sex-typed behavior. In F. Beach (ed.), *Sex and behavior.* New York: John Wiley & Sons.

Simmons, Leo W. (1945) *The role of the aged in primitive society.* New Haven: Yale University Press.

Spindler, Louise S. (1962) Menomini women and cultural change, memoir 91. *Amer. Anthrop., 64.*

——, and G. D. Spindler (1958) Male and female adaptations in culture change. *Amer. Anthrop., 60,* 217–33. (Study revised for B. Kaplan, ed., *Studying personality cross-culturally.*)

Spiro, M. E. (1956) *Kibbutz: venture in utopia.* Cambridge: Harvard University Press.

——. (1958) *Children of the kibbutz.* Cambridge: Harvard University Press.

Stephens, W. N. (1963) *The family in cross-cultural perspective.* New York: Holt, Rinehart & Winston.

Washburn, S. L., and I. DeVore (1961) Social behavior of baboons and early man. In S. L. Washburn (ed.), *Social life of early man.* Chicago: Aldine.

Whiting, Beatrice B. (ed.). (1963) *Six cultures: studies of child rearing.* New York and London: John Wiley & Sons.

Whiting, J. W. M. (1962) Socialization process and personality. In F. K. Hsu (ed.), *Psychological anthropology.* Homewood, Ill.: Dorsey Press.

——, and I. I. Child. (1953) *Child training and personality development.* New Haven: Yale University Press.

Young, F. W. (1962) The function of male initiation ceremonies. *Amer. J. Sociol., 67,* 379–96.

Zelditch, M., Jr. (1955) Role differentiation in the nuclear family: a comparative study. In T. Parsons and R. F. Bales (eds.), *Family, socialization and interaction process.* Glencoe, Ill.: The Free Press.

Afterword

SANFORD M. DORNBUSCH
Stanford University

This essay is the response of one seminar participant—the lone sociologist—to the papers in this volume. All the members of the seminar contributed to the ideas presented here, but this chapter is simply one person's attempt at synthesis.

The areas of greatest novelty for me are the new modes of observation now available for the study of sex hormones and primate sexual differentiation. As new research techniques develop they may permit us to ask new questions of the empirical world and sharpen the answers to old questions. Hamburg and Lunde's description of new methods of hormonal analysis, for example, suggests that prenatal hormones may have developmental importance in producing sexual differentiation at a later stage in the life cycle when no hormonal differences can be observed. The observation of primates in the field permits study of the relationship between sexual dimorphism, differences in physical size, and degree of sexual differentiation. A review of current findings in these areas would not be particularly informative, but the potential for exciting research is obvious.

The field study of primates indicates that immature male primates generally behave more aggressively, engage in rougher play, and use large-muscle movements more than immature females. Immature females are more likely to look at and touch the newborn, seek to handle infants, and engage in grooming. Fights among adult-male primates are fiercer and occur less often than fights among females. Field studies also show that grooming, which serves to pacify, is employed most often by females of those species in which aggression is the basis of group organization (Marler 1965). These differences suggest evolutionary significance with respect to the defense and survival of the primate group and the nurturance of the helpless young.

Hamburg and Lunde's review of experimental studies of primates supports the results of field observations. Young males are more likely to threaten and engage in rough play, while young females are more likely to be passive and to withdraw. The link between sex differences in behavior and sex hormones is provided by their report of Young's research. Young gave the male sex hormone androgen to pregnant monkeys. The female offspring of these monkeys, when compared to a control group, were more likely to threaten, initiate action, and engage in rough play, and were less likely to withdraw from threat or from play.

It is unfortunate that the relationship between hormonal secretions and human behavior has not yet been well studied. Measurements of primate behavior in the field are more reliable than measurements of the behavior of humans who have been given sex hormones. For humans, we have only clinical impressions without adequate controls. The separation of disciplines, with corresponding gaps in training, probably accounts for the failure of physiologically oriented researchers to employ scientific standards in the study of behavior. Since studies of castrates and hermaphrodites show that sexual experience and the assignment of a sex are dominant influences in human behavior, the impact of sex hormones is likely to be seen in small behavior changes that demand careful measurement.

The primate and hormone studies suggest areas for further research. Although sex differences in aggression have been studied extensively, we know very little about the even greater sex differences in large-muscle movements. We do not know the effects of the interaction of these two phenomena. Perhaps the sex differences in muscle movements are responsible in part for the differences in aggression. And we have barely begun to study the learning of aggressive behavior in primates. Even though primates have only a rudimentary culture, aggressive behavior is partly a product of their social experiences. Baboons associated in infancy with the dominant males at the center of the baboon band are more aggressive than baboons raised on the periphery (DeVore and Jay 1963).

Let us now turn our attention toward humans. We note that only females can have babies or nurse them at the breast. These essential differences between the sexes may be elaborated both physiologically and socially. Physiologically, the male and female hormones associated with reproduction and lactation may have secondary effects, producing sex differences in other spheres, such as aggression. Socially, for the survival of the species, groups must not assign tasks to females that prevent their acting as mothers. Hunting societies, for example, show greater sexual differentiation in task assignment than other societies. This may be in part based upon sexual dimorphism, the fact that the male has greater size and strength. It is also possible that the differentiation is based upon the lack of female mobility. In other words, men become warriors and hunters not just because they are strong, but because they are not pregnant or breast feeding (Jacobs 1964).

D'Andrade's paper points out that the institutional subordination of women is more complete than would be expected solely on the basis of differences in the average level of dominance or aggression. There is a process of extension of the occupational division of labor which produces an institutional status of maleness and femaleness in every society. The result is a social devaluation of women. Zelditch et al. (1965) have analyzed the manner in which an evaluated diffuse status characteristic, such as sex, leads to differences in evaluation of behavior. Activities performed by women are evaluated less highly *because* they are performed by women.

Turning from society to the individual, Mischel and Kohlberg examine the development of sex identity and the learning of sex-patterned behavior. There is, of course, a basic conflict between Kohlberg's cognitive-developmental view that the child first learns his sex and then selects his repertoire of behavior, and Mischel's social-learning view that the child's sex identity is a product of previously learned behavior. Only research can resolve this theoretical conflict. Kohlberg predicts a relationship between the cognitive development of sex identity and a tendency to imitate same-sex models. A pilot study on a small sample has failed to find this relationship, but the results may not be reliable (Leifer 1966). Since both approaches have a common emphasis on the social basis of learning sexually appropriate behavior, we will focus on their similarities, rather than their differences.

Ascription by sex is not hard to explain. There are few other social bases for distinction among the newborn. But if no distinctions are made, each child must be trained to take part in every type of activity. Therefore it is of considerable advantage for a society to classify infants into categories based on the probability that members of that category will engage in a specific set of adult activities. A great difference in these probable future activities permits sharp differences in anticipatory training, emphasizing in one category what is ignored in another. Only sex, kinship, and skin color can be ascribed for an infant with relative certainty that he will remain in these categories for the rest of his life. This volume focuses on sex as an ascribed status that is associated with differences in behavior from childhood to death.

Since sex is an ascribed status, as well as a biological fact, the society can begin anticipatory socialization in the early years. Just as a military academy prepares a young man for a career as an officer, so early socialization prepares the child for his mature sex role. It is easy to overemphasize this basis for sexual differentiation. Maccoby's paper on intellectual functioning provides an opportunity to assess the extent of anticipatory socialization. Some sex differences, such as the greater conformity of girls, are at least in part the product of direct socialization. But socialization is a very complex process, and it is not always obvious how the different socialization practices that parents direct toward boys and girls produce the outcome we see in sex-typed behavior. For example, in a study of differences in the reactions of mothers and fathers to aggression and dependency behavior in male and female children (Rothbart and Maccoby 1967), mothers were found to be more permissive of both these behaviors in their sons, while fathers were more permissive of these behaviors in their daughters. Other studies have found more direct connections between socialization of the two sexes and sex-typed behavior, although the research is meager. Other sex differences, such as field dependency, are not directly taught but result from the interaction of various mediating processes. As a further complication, members of the society may be unaware of the existence of major sex differences such as those found in spatial ability, and it is difficult to conceive of a social group providing anticipatory socialization to mold individuals into a sex-typed pattern that they are unaware exists. In sum, sex-linked patterns of behavior may not be directly based on socialization practices, and use of anticipatory socialization as an explanatory notion requires empirical evidence of its utility.

The failure of a simple anticipatory-socialization model is linked to variability in the meaning of the sex role it is used to explain. To begin with a sociological conception, society defines a role—a particular position in the social system that has a set of normative expectations associated with it. Certain behavior is expected from the occupants of a role, and deviation from that behavior is punished. The occupants are passive incumbents, and the established normative expectations are supraindividual. Unfortunately, this conception of role has been found to be oversimplified. Within an organization, there is far from complete consensus on the normative expectations for a role or position (Gross et al. 1958). Role occupants in part create their roles in interaction with others.

At the other extreme, a role may be seen as the personal creation of the individual who occupies it, a product of both personal and social forces (G. A. Kelly 1955). This extreme psychological position throws out role as an explanatory concept. The way the person behaves *is* the role. Expectations may develop, but there is no normative element; deviation from the role merely changes its characteristics. "The role of wife in the Davis household" is merely another name for Mrs. Davis's behavior, providing a satisfactory concept only for those unable to recognize a tautology.

The social psychologist is wise to take the middle path. Roles are socially defined, but they differ on the degree of consensus with respect to normative expectations. If in Syria there is considerable agreement that husbands should prepare Arab coffee and wives should make Turkish coffee (Sweet 1960), then, assuming proper socialization, predictions about which sex will make which kind of coffee will do better than chance. We must not assume that the presence of these norms, per se, causes the normative behavior. Instead, we must demonstrate that the shared norms influence the socialization practices, thereby linking role behavior with normative expectations (Blake and Davis 1964).

Let us now look specifically at the concept of sex role. It is clearly a general role that interacts with other roles, such as student or athlete. It interacts with age to produce an age-sex structure in our society that includes infant, boy, girl, young man, young woman, old man, and old woman (Linton 1936). Maccoby has noted the discontinuity of sex differences in intellectual functioning. One study sees the male's higher rate of alcoholism as a function of the greater discontinuity between the roles of the male child and adult (McCord and McCord 1960). Such interaction effects do not make anticipatory socialization impossible, but they certainly make it more difficult.

There is a relatively low level of consensus on sex roles in American society. This lack of consensus is the result of a rapid rate of social change and the presence of considerable subgroup differentiation. Negro wives are more likely than white wives to have power in the family (Pettigrew 1964), and lower-class wives are expected to be more subservient than middle-class wives (Brim et al. 1962); there are even regional differences in the willingness of girls to "play dumb" in order to please their dates (Komarovsky 1946, Wallin 1950). Role consensus is likely to be reduced as members of these diverse subgroups interact with one another. Perhaps the often-noted relationship between homogeneity of social background and marital success is a product of shared role perceptions.

Accordingly, there is so much uncertainty about which adult roles the child will play that anticipatory socialization is very difficult. It is impossible to socialize for all contingencies. All that early socialization can do is lay a foundation that is compatible with the most probable later experiences (Brim 1963).

Many scales of masculinity and femininity do not use the concept of sex role that has been developed here. They define as sex-linked any behavior on which the two sexes show mean differences. The differences in the average behavior may be sex-linked because of some physiological factor, a difference in socialization, or, very often, a totally unexpected product of both these factors, as in the case of female superiority in grammar, spelling, and word fluency. If girls like books more than boys do, then a book-loving boy is less masculine by definition. If boys like dogs and girls like cats, then a boy who likes cats is more feminine.

Unfortunately, such masculinity-feminity scales are often mistakenly thought of as measures of basic sexuality. This is the fallacy of misplaced concreteness. These scales attempt to measure behavior that may be closely related to social or physiological differences; naturally these tests include material that reflects the current taste in recreation, clothing, or colors. One study using such measures showed that both men and women become more masculine as they age (E. L. Kelly 1955); an earlier study, however, found both males and females growing more feminine with age (Terman and Miles 1936). The explanation given for the new trend toward masculinity is the increased mechanization of our society, particularly the increased use of household appliances. We are far from masculinity or femininity as measures of sex role when these qualities can be affected by the presence or absence of washers and dryers in the home.

The seminar participants also agree that the expression of preferences should not be equated with sex-typing. Females prefer to be males more than males prefer to be females (Brown 1958), but this does not indicate that these unhappy females are unable to engage in behavior appropriate to their sex. The preference for the male role may explain why male deviation from the prescribed sex-role is more harshly penalized than female deviation (Faris 1952). The tomboy is more acceptable than the sissy. When females deviate they are attempting to take on the preferred role, whereas deviating males are attacking the preference order for the sexes.

This difference in society's reaction to deviance may be the basis for the tendency of males to learn sex-linked behavior more quickly than females. It also helps to explain the erroneous conclusions reached by researchers who use preferences as their only measure of masculinity or femininity. Young girls will choose to play with boys' toys in an experiment more often than boys will choose girls' toys. This is not a relative failure of female socialization, but merely an expression of the greater latitude for deviation granted to females by the society (Hartley 1964).

The lower status of the female acts as a modulator of performance in many areas. The self-conception of females is less resistant to experimental pressure toward devaluation of the self. This lack of ego defense is present even for the performance of tasks that have no previous sex-linkage (Cohen 1965). We have here a social-psychological correlate of the institutionalized dominance that D'Andrade noted. Since societies do differ in the relative difference in status between men and women, studies are needed of the relation between degree of male dominance and such variables as preference for the other sex, or self-confidence.

Male dominance as a cultural theme should have effects upon interpersonal relations in marriage. The degree of agreement on male dominance between husbands and wives is correlated with their perception of marital happiness (Jacobson 1952). Even more striking is the study which found that marital satisfaction was related to the wife's ability

to perceive her husband's expectations. Their happiness was not correlated with agreement on various aspects of family living or with the
husband's perception of the wife's expectations (Stuckert 1963). Here
is clear evidence of the dominance of the male.

We must go on to note that despite this institutionalized dominance,
sex roles vary tremendously in modern societies like the United States.
As one author puts it, "Every home is different from every other home,
every marriage, even within the same class in the same clique, contains
contrasts between the partners as superficially striking as the difference
between one New Guinea tribe and another." (Mead 1949, p. 187.) Subgroups within our society also differ with respect to sexual differentiation. For example, Negro females are more likely than white females to
assume some of the functions of the head of the household. This is believed to be linked to the Negro male's occupational experiences, which
lower his self-confidence, and to the Negro female's high rate of participation in the labor force, which raises her relative status (Pettigrew
1964).

There are also subcultural differences associated with social class. In
the United States and France there is greater segregation of husband
and wife activities in lower-class family life than in middle-class family
life (Dobriner 1963, de Lauwe 1962). A close-knit network of social
relationships with relatives and friends seems to increase such role segregation in the lower class (Bott 1957). No such tendency has been
found for a middle-class group (Udry and Hall 1965). Even within the
blue-collar group, there are subcultural differences. Higher-skill blue-
collar males are more egalitarian than lower-skill blue-collar males.
Therefore, when the wife comes from a higher status blue-collar family
than her husband, there is more marital maladjustment than when she
comes from the lower-status group (Komarovsky 1964).

Faced with such cultural complexity, it is particularly unfortunate
that, as Maccoby notes, we have only a few studies concerned with sexual
differentiation throughout the life cycle. One result of such research
proved both intriguing and puzzling. Our group spent many hours of
agony trying to understand why adult males are more likely than adult
females to retain their adolescent rank order with respect to aggression.
These findings are reversed for dependency. Perhaps, because aggression is linked to males and dependency associated with females, the rank
order among individuals is better preserved for that which is socially

approved. Yet, no one knows why such a relationship should be found. To make explanation even more difficult, variation in the inappropriate area of behavior has been found to be a better predictor of other behavior than variation in the approved area of behavior (Kagan and Moss 1962). For a girl, an aggression score predicts other behavior better than a dependency score. For a boy, dependency is a better predictor. Further research in this area will necessarily improve our theories of socialization, deviance, and reactions to deviance.

Kohlberg has reviewed the instrumental-expressive distinction, and he notes again the failure of a simple model to explain the complex variations in sexual differentiation. He concludes that power, not the Parsonian distinction, is the basic variable. Unfortunately, a recent research survey on power in the family concludes that we cannot cumulate research findings at this time because of the many diverse operational definitions that have been employed. Family power structure does not remain stable when the task or decision-making situations are varied (Zelditch 1964). Experimental studies of conformity illustrate this same complex interaction. Many studies have attempted to find whether women or men are more likely to conform to social pressure. The results are ambiguous, showing (depending on the task) that women are either as likely as, or slightly more likely than, men to conform. This slight or nonexistent difference is dwarfed by the sex differences in the bases of conformity. Men's conformity is part of a general orientation toward task performance, while women's conformity is more likely to be based on a desire for smooth interaction with other participants (Bass 1961). Under certain circumstances, the female concern with social interaction may lead to a more successful task performance than the male concentration on the task. One experimental study used a task that required coalition formation for success. Males tended to use exploitative strategies, while females tended to use accommodative techniques. For this particular task, females outperformed males (Bond and Vinacke 1961). We may draw a moral from such studies: field studies of family power in modern societies will be productive only insofar as they carefully analyze results in terms of specific types of tasks.

One of the few replicated findings on family power is the increase in the wife's power when she works (Blood and Wolfe 1960). For whole societies, D'Andrade has noted the relationship between women's participation in subsistence activities and their relative status. A similar finding comes from a study of social change during the Industrial Revolution in Great Britain: women and children who were employed in the new textile industries gained new status (Smelser 1959). The depression of the 1930's showed the impact of similar forces when unemployed men were found to lose status in their households (Bakke 1940).

One study, partially replicated, indicates than an ideological variable —the degree of endorsement by the wife of the ideology of male dominance—mediates the impact of the wife's working upon power in the home. To the surprise of the researcher, the increase in power of the employed wife occurred only for those women who either endorse male dominance or completely reject it. Wives who work and partially reject male dominance have less power than nonworking wives (Hoffman 1963). Another example of the power of ideology is the finding that working mothers do not, by working, seem to create disadvantages for their children, but these mothers do express guilt feelings about the harm they are sure they are doing to their children (Yarrow et al. 1962).

This does not mean that the mother's work has no impact upon her children. Daughters of working mothers do not sex-type behavior as much as daughters of nonworking mothers (Hartley 1960). One group of researchers reported a tendency for the mother's working to affect sons and daughters in opposite ways, although there were no clear effects on children in general (Siegel et al. 1963). It is important, however, that we do not view children as learning sex-appropriate behavior solely on the basis of the behavior of their parents. Apparently, the consensus on sexual differentiation within any society is high enough to permit children to develop sex-appropriate behavior without relation to the particular degree of sexual differentiation exhibited by the parents (Smith 1964).

It is appropriate at this point to note that we are moving away from the type of sexual difference in behavior summarized by Hamburg and Lunde or D'Andrade. Hormonal differences between the sexes may precipitate differences in aggression or nurturance behavior. These provide the building blocks for evolutionary development. Similarly, the subsistence activities of preliterate societies demand a rudimentary sexual division of labor for survival. As we move toward modern industrial societies, with their subgroup differentiation, the impact of human values begins to overshadow differences in innate predispositions or ability to perform social functions. When pregnant women can drive automobiles, occupational differentiation need no longer reflect the mobility of males.

Sexual differentiation increasingly depends on social definitions that do not depend upon biological forces (Mead 1949). As one author puts it:

All societies prescribe different attitudes and activities to men and to women. Most of them try to rationalize these prescriptions in terms of the physiological differences between the sexes or their different roles in reproduction. While such factors may have served as a starting point for the development of a division, the actual ascriptions are almost entirely determined by culture. (Linton 1936.)

We need not endorse this extreme conclusion of cultural determinism to observe the increase in the relative importance of social forces.

Fashions in what is considered womanly are now possible, since sexual differentiation has moved further from evolutionary necessity. In the Soviet Union three out of four physicians are women; in the United Kingdom one in six, and one in sixteen is a female in the United States (Degler 1964). In 1930 one-half of all professional and semiprofessional workers in the United States were women, while today only about one-third are. There has been an increase in absolute numbers, but proportionally females are not holding their own. Today four out of five professional women are in just seven fields: teaching, nursing, music, social work, accounting, auditing, and library work (Alpenfels 1962). The relative decline in professionalism among American women is matched by a similar decline in educational achievement. In the 1930's two out of every five B.A.'s and M.A.'s, and one of every seven Ph.D.'s, were earned by women. The proportions have declined to one in three for the B.A. and M.A., and one in ten for the Ph.D. (President's Commission on the Status of Women 1963).

In the United States at present, it is the fashion for women to have a low level of occupational commitment. About seventy per cent of female teachers view teaching only as an adventure (Mason et al. 1959). A study of student nurses found that sixty per cent felt that having a career was important, but only one-fourth said they would be very much displeased if they should marry and never work at nursing (Goldsen and White). Currently, only one-third of all married women work, although they constitute a majority of all female workers (Peterson 1964). Most women work in low-paid occupations and earn less than men in the same occupation. Both men and women share an ideology that is antagonistic toward the idea of women in high-status jobs (Keniston and Keniston 1954).

The defensive quality of the current ideology is shown by the myths used to explain the current occupational differentiation by sex. Women are supposedly more likely to be sick, to be absentees, and to quit their jobs. In fact, men lose more work days through illness than women do, the sex rates for absenteeism are identical, and only the rates for quitting show women markedly higher. Even this latter result cannot be used to defend keeping women out of high-status jobs, for the quit rates turn out to be purely a function of the skill level of the job. When the researchers control for skill level, the sex difference disappears (Peterson 1964).

Why are myths about masculinity and femininity believed and sustained—even in the face of evidence to the contrary? Clearly, both sexes must have a fairly high degree of emotional investment in the current sex-role ideology. At the same time, however, this ideology does change —from generation to generation, from society to society. Sex-roles, which were once based on evolutionary necessity, have become highly elaborated cultural products. And as we have seen again and again in this volume, it is difficult to separate the cultural product from its biological base. At several points, we simply lack evidence on crucial matters. For example, we do not know enough about the behavioral consequences of variations in the timing and concentrations of sex hormones in human beings. We also lack detailed observational data on the interactions between parents and children, and the conditions that affect the degree to which parental behavior varies with the sex of the child. And again we do not know whether or not, or in what ways, a given socialization practice will produce different results in children with different biological characteristics. Despite the magnitude of the task of accumulating evidence on these matters, it is hoped that today's generation of researchers will undertake it, so that tomorrow's ideology may reflect increased understanding of the forces that shape men and women.

REFERENCES

Alpenfels, Ethel. (1962) Women in the professional world. In Beverly Cassara (ed.), *American women: the changing image*. Boston: Beacon Press.

Bakke, E. W. (1940) *The unemployed worker*. New Haven, Conn.: Yale University Press.

Bass, B. M. (1961) Conformity, deviation, and a general theory of interpersonal behavior. In I. A. Berg and B. M. Bass (eds.), *Conformity and deviation*. New York: Harper & Brothers.

Blake, Judith, and K. Davis. (1964) Norms, values, and sanctions. In R. E. L. Faris, *Handbook of modern sociology*. Chicago: Rand McNally.

Blood, R. O., and D. M. Wolfe. (1960) *Husbands and wives*. Glencoe, Ill.: Free Press.

Bond, J. R., and W. E. Vinacke. (1961) Coalitions in mixed-sex triads. *Sociometry, 24,* 61–75.

Bott, Elizabeth. (1957) *Family and social network*. London: Tavistock.

Brim. O. G., Jr. (1963) Socialization through the life cycle. Paper given at Conference on Socialization Through the Life Cycle, Social Science Research Council, New York, May 16–18, 1963.

————, D. C. Glass, D. E. Lavin, and N. Goodman. (1962) *Personality and decision processes*, Stanford: Stanford Univ. Press.

Brown, D. S. (1958) Sex-role development in a changing culture. *Psychol. Bull., 55,* 232–42.

Cohen, B. P. (1965) Unpublished studies for the Laboratory for Social Research, Stanford University.

Degler, C. N. (1964) Revolution without ideology: the changing place of women in America. *Daedalus, 93,* 653–70.

de Lauwe, M. J. C. (1962) The status of women in French urban society. *Int. Soc. Sci. J., 14,* 26–65.

DeVore, I., and Phyllis Jay. (1963) Mother-infant relations in baboons and langurs. In Harriet L. Rheingold (ed.), *Maternal behavior in animals*. New York: John Wiley.

Dobriner, W. M. (1963) *Class in suburbia*. Englewood Cliffs, N.J.: Prentice-Hall.

Faris, R. E. L. (1952) *Social psychology*. New York: Ronald.

Goldsen, R. K., and R. F. White. A study of professional attitudes toward work: the case of nursing. Unpublished paper, Department of Sociology, Cornell University, no date.

Gross, N., W. S. Mason, and A. W. McEachern. (1958) *Explorations in role analysis*. New York: John Wiley.

Hartley, Ruth E. (1960) Children's concepts of male and female roles. *Merrill-Palmer Quart., 6,* 83–91.

————. (1964) A developmental view of female sex-role definition and identification. *Merrill-Palmer Quart., 10,* 3–16.

Hoffman, Lois W. (1963) Parental power relations and the division of household tasks. In F. I. Nye and Lois W. Hoffman (eds.), *The employed mother in America.* Chicago: Rand McNally.

Jacobs, M. (1964) *Pattern in cultural anthropology.* Homewood, Ill.: Dorsey Press.

Jacobson, A. H. (1952) Cited in R. E. L. Faris, *Social psychology,* New York: The Ronald Press.

Kagan, J., and H. A. Moss. (1962) *Birth to maturity: a study in psychological development.* New York: John Wiley.

Kelly, E. L. (1955) Consistency of the adult personality. *Amer. Psychologist, 10,* 659–81.

Kelly, G. A. (1955) *A theory of personality: the psychology of personal constructs.* New York: W. W. Norton.

Keniston, Ellen, and K. Keniston. (1964) An American anachronism: the image of women and work. *Amer. Scholar, 33,* 355–75.

Komarovsky, Mirra. (1946) Cultural contradictions and sex roles. *Amer J. Sociol., 52,* 184–89.

————. (1964) *Blue collar marriage.* New York: Random House.

Leifer, Aimee D. (1966) The relationship between cognitive awareness in selected areas and differential imitation of a same-sex model. Unpublished M.A. thesis, Department of Psychology, Stanford University.

Linton, R. (1963) *The study of man.* New York: Appleton-Century-Crofts.

Marler, P. (1965) Communication in monkeys and apes. In I. DeVore (ed.), *Primate behavior.* New York: Holt, Rinehart & Winston.

Mason, W. S., R. J. Dressel, and R. K. Bain (1959). Sex role and the career orientations of beginning teachers. *Harvard educ. Rev., 29,* 370–83.

McCord, W., and Joan McCord. (1960) *Origins of alcoholism,* Stanford: Stanford University Press.

Mead, Margaret. (1949) *Male and female.* New York: William Morrow. (The quotation in the text was taken from p. 187 of the New American Library Mentor edition, 1955.)

Peterson, Esther. (1964) Working women. *Daedalus, 93,* 671–99.

Pettigrew, T. F. (1964) *A profile of the Negro American,* Princeton: D. Van Nostrand Company.

President's Commission on the Status of Women. (1963) *American women.* Superintendent of Documents, Washington, D.C.

Rothbart, Mary K., and Eleanor E. Maccoby. (1967) Parent's differential reactions to sons and daughters. *J. Pers. soc. Psychol.,* in press.

Siegel, Alberta E., Lois M. Stolz, Ethel A. Hitchcock, and Jean Adamson. (1963) Dependence and independence in children. In F. I. Nye and Lois W. Hoffman (eds.), *The employed mother in America,* Chicago: Rand McNally.

Smelser, N. (1959) *Social change in the industrial revolution.* Berkeley: University of California Press.

Smith, C. (1966) The development of sex role concepts and attitudes in father-absent boys. Unpublished master's thesis, University of Chicago.

Stuckert, R. P. (1963) Role perception and marital satisfaction—a configurational approach. *Marriage and Family Living, 25,* 415–19.

Sweet, Louise E. (1960) Tell Togaan: a Syrian village. Anthropological Papers, Museum of Anthropology, University of Michigan, No. 14. Ann Arbor: University of Michigan Press.

Terman, L. M. and Catherine C. Miles. (1936) *Sex and personality,* New York: McGraw-Hill.

Udry, J. R., and Mary Hall. (1965) Marital role segregation and social networks in middle-class middle-aged couples. Paper presented at Annual Meeting of Pacific Sociological Association, April 1965, Salt Lake City, Utah.

Wallin, P. Cultural contradictions and sex roles: a repeat study. *Amer. Sociol. Rev., 15,* 288–93.

Yarrow, Marian R., Phyllis Scott, Louise de Leeuw, and Christine Heinig. (1962) Child-rearing in families of working and non-working mothers. *Sociometry, 25,* 122–40.

Zelditch, M., Jr. (1964) Family, marriage and kinship. In R. E. L. Faris (ed.), *Handbook of modern sociology.* Chicago: Rand McNally.

———, J. Berger, and B. P. Cohen. (1965) Stability of organizational status systems. Technical Report Number 10, Laboratory for Social Research, Stanford University.

Annotated Bibliography

Annotated Bibliography

Compiled by Roberta M. Oetzel

The chief findings of the studies listed in this Bibliography are set forth in summary form in the Classified Summary of Research in Sex Differences, pp. 323–51, under the headings Aggression, Dependency, Social Reinforcement, etc.

Abel, H., and R. Sahinkaya. Emergence of sex and race friendship preferences. *Child Develpm.*, 1962, *33*, 939–43.
  Measures: Children were presented with several sets of pictures; each set showed either a girl and a boy or a Negro and white child of the same sex. S's were asked which child of each pair they would choose for a friend. Subjects: 48 boys and girls, white, aged 4 and 5. Results: Both sexes preferred their own sex for friends. In the choice of race, 4-year-olds showed no significant differences in choice of friend. Five-year-olds showed a significant preference for their own race. When the sex comparison was made, boys preferred their own race, but this preference was not significant for girls.

Aberle, D. F., and K. D. Naegele. Middle-class fathers' occupational role and attitudes toward children. *Am. J. Orthopsychiat.*, 1952, *22*, 366–78.
  Measures: Interviews with fathers. Subjects: The fathers of 29 boys and 27 girls—all upper-middle-class professional and business men. Results: Fathers expected sons to go to college and then into business or a profession, but did not consider these goals as crucial for daughters. The expectation was for them to marry rather than have careers. Fathers were asked what behaviors in their children gave them concern or pleasure. For boys, the behaviors were lack of responsibility and initiative, poor school work, insufficient aggressiveness, athletic inadequacy, overconformity, excitability, excessive tearfulness, homosexual play, and "childish" behavior. Girls were mentioned in these categories also, but much less frequently. Disobedience ran high in concern for children of both sexes. Girls were to be pretty, sweet, affectionate, and nice. The authors feel fathers have more definite ideas of what a boy needs for successful adult role than they do for girls.

Adams, Elsie B., and I. G. Sarason. Relation between anxiety in children and their parents. *Child Develpm.*, 1963, *34*, 237–46.
  Measures: 4 anxiety scales administered to children and to parents: the Test Anxiety

Scale, Need for Achievement, Lack of Protection Scale, and the TMAS. Subjects: 72 male and 60 female 12th-grade students and their parents. Results: On all scales except Need for Achievement, girls had significantly higher scores than boys. Mothers also tended to be higher than fathers except in achievement. Girls' scores were significantly positively related to their mothers' scores on all 4 tests but not related to fathers' scores. Boys' scores were significantly related to mothers' scores on the Lack of Protection and TMAS scales, and to fathers' scores on the TMAS.

Adams, James P. Adolescent personal problems as a function of age and sex *J. genet. Psychol.*, 1964, *104*, 207–14.
   Measures: Questionnaire administered by teachers containing these questions: (1) What is your biggest personal problem? (2) How might you solve it? (3) What is the biggest problem for your peers? (4) How might it be solved? Subjects: Approximately 4,000 boys and girls, 10–19 years, from over 30 schools. Results: Boys reported more financial and school problems than girls; girls related more interpersonal and family problems than boys. Both saw peers as having fewer school problems and more interpersonal problems than they reported for themselves. There was a tendency for extrinsic solutions to problems to increase with age for both sexes, and intrinsic solutions to decrease with age for girls but remain fairly constant for boys. Both sexes suggested more extrinsic solutions for their peers than for themselves.

Alexander, V. E. Sex differences in 7th grade problem solving. *Sch. Sci. Math.*, 1962, *62*, 47–50.
   Measures: The Arithmetic Reasoning Test of the SRA Achievement Series, Grades 6–9. Also measures of understanding verbal concepts, general reasoning ability, quantitative skill, general reading skills, problem-solving reading skills, and interpretation of quantitative materials. (The tests consisted of verbal reasoning problems.) Subjects: 320 boys and 303 girls in 7th grade. Results: Arithmetic-reasoning test scores slightly favored girls when I.Q. was allowed to vary, but with I.Q. held constant boys did slightly better. Neither difference was significant.

Allen, V. L., and R. S. Crutchfield. Generalization of experimentally reinforced conformity. *J. abnorm. soc. Psychol.*, 1963, *67*, 326–33.
   Measures: S's were placed in a group-pressure situation which they were led to believe that 4 other S's of the same sex had agreed on an incorrect judgment. E reinforced the wrong group consensus by saying it was right on trials involving one kind of judgment: either perceptual judgments or vocabulary-meaning judgments. E then recorded the degree to which S conformed on these items, and the degree to which the conformity generalized to other kinds of judgments, such as attitudes and opinions on which there was no feedback. Subjects: 40 male and 40 female college students. Results: Women conformed more than males, and their conformity generalized to other kinds of judgments to a greater extent than males.

Ames, L. B., and Frances L. Ilg. Sex differences in test performance of matched girl-boy pairs in the 5-to-9-year-old age range. *J. genet. Psychol.*, 1964, *104*, 25–34.
   Measures: Subjects were matched in boy-girl pairs according to WISC I.Q., age in months, and socioeconomic status. Four tests were applied: the Gesell Incomplete Man, the Lowenfeld Mosaic Test, the Rorschach, and Monroe's Visual III. Subjects: An entire kindergarten division (81 children), one first-grade class (26 children), and one second-grade class (29 children). Tests were administered to subjects for 3 consecutive years. Results: For all 3 groups of subjects at every age, girls were superior to boys in terms of maturity of response and performance.

Anastasi, Anne, and Rita D'Angelo. A comparison of Negro and white preschool children in language development and Goodenough Draw-a-Man I.Q. *J. genet. Psychol.*, 1952, *81*, 147–65.

Measures: Goodenough Draw-a-Man Test, and a recording and analysis of 60 spontaneous responses in a standard test situation. Analysis of length and maturity of statements made. Subjects: 100 children, age 4½ to 5½. Half were white and half Negro, with an equal proportion of girls and boys in each race group. Subject primarily of lower class, with some from racially mixed, some from unmixed residential areas. All were in day nurseries. Results: On the Draw-a-Man Test the significant variation was sex, with girls being superior. In language, sex-by-race was the significant interaction: white girls were superior to white boys, while Negro boys were superior to Negro girls.

Anastasi, Anne, and J. P. Foley. *Differential psychology.* New York: Macmillan Co., 1949.

Chapters 18 and 19 include a review of sex-difference studies.

Anderson, C. C. A developmental study of dogmatism during adolescence with reference to sex differences. *J. abnorm. soc. Psychol.*, 1962, *65*, 132–35.

Measures: Rokeach's Dogmatism Scale, and CTMM or Otis intelligence scores. Subjects: 280 8th-graders, 142 10th-graders, 163 11th-graders, and 183 12th-graders. Results: There was no significant sex difference on dogmatism scores, but the sex-by-intelligence interaction was significant. Intelligent girls were much more dogmatic than intelligent boys. Sex differences in low intelligence subjects were not as prominent.

Anderson, I. H., B. O. Hughes, and W. R. Dixon. The rate of reading development and its relation to age of learning to read, sex, and intelligence. *J. educ. Res.*, 1957, *50*, 481–94.

Measures: Gates Primary Reading Tests at lower levels, Stanford Reading Test for 6th-graders. The reading rate was plotted from 1st to 6th grade. Subjects: 107 boys and 102 girls in 6th grade. The average I.Q. was 120 on the Stanford-Binet. Results: Girls learned to read earlier than boys, but the rate of development after that was the same for the two sexes. No sex comparison at 6th grade presented.

Andrieux, C. Contribution à l'étude des différences entre hommes et femmes dans la perception spaciale. *L'année psychologique*, 1955, *55*, 41–60.

Measures: Several tests of spatial orientation and localization, including the Gottschalt Figures Test, were given. Subjects: Students in Parisian normal schools; average age for the 50 males was 19, and for the 45 females was 18.3. Results: Significant sex differences were found on the Gottschalt Figures, with men doing better.

Bach, G. R. Father-fantasies and father-typing in father-separated children. *Child Develpm.*, 1946, *17*, 63–80.

Measures: Doll-play observation with a house and family group. Subjects: 10 boys and 10 girls, 6–10 years, of average I.Q., lower-middle-class, who had been separated from father for 1–3 years because of the war. Also a matched father-present control group. Results: The experimental group used father-doll less, but still frequently; they showed more stereotyped, affectionate relations with father and less aggression from or to father. Their play resembled that of normal girls. The girls showed even less father-aggression than most girls do.

Bach, G. R. Young children's play fantasies. *Psychol. Monogr.*, 1945, *59*, No. 2.

Measures: Observation of children's behavior in standardized doll play of teacher and school children. Subjects: 20 boys and 15 girls in preschool. Results: Boys' fantasies were more often socially unacceptable. Boys showed more hostile-aggressive acts. Girls did more verbal commanding. Girls used more themes of affection, socially approved themes.

Balint, M. Individual differences of behavior in early infancy, and an objective method for recording them: I, Approach and the method of recording. II, Results and conclusions. *J. genet. Psychol.*, 1948, *73*, 57–59; 81–117.
   Measures: Recording of frequency of sucking of bottle-fed babies on a Jacquet polygraph. **Subjects:** 100 infants from birth to 9 months of age. 53 boys and 47 girls. Most subjects were hospitalized for illness. **Results:** No sex differences on basic frequency. However, girls show a higher proportion of quivering motions of the tongue while nursing. There is also some slight evidence that the characteristic individual pattern of boys was less stable than girls.

Balow, I. H. Sex differences in first grade reading. *Elem. Eng.*, 1963, *40*, 303–6.
   Measures: Gates Primary Reading Tests administered in February of first grade and the Gates Reading Readiness Tests at the beginning of first grade. **Subjects:** 151 boys and 151 girls in first grade. **Results:** Girls were significantly better in both reading readiness and reading achievement in first grade. The reading readiness differences appeared to be a function of the ability to see similarities and differences between words.

Bandura, A. Influence of models' reinforcement contingencies on the acquisition of imitative responses. *J. Pers. soc. Psychol.*, 1965, *1*, 589–95.
   Measures: S observed a film of a model performing aggressive acts, and either being rewarded, punished, or not sanctioned for the behavior. Then S was introduced to a free-play situation which included the Bobo doll that had been the object of the aggression in the film. Observers scored the number of imitative aggressive acts performed. Then E returned and rewarded S for each aggressive act he could reproduce. **Subjects:** 33 boys and 33 girls, aged 42–71 months. **Results:** Boys imitated significantly more aggressive acts than girls. Children performed aggressive acts more when rewarded than they displayed spontaneously. This was true of girls under all three conditions of consequences to the model and of boys who saw the model punished. However, there were no differences between spontaneous imitation and rewarded imitation for boys who saw the model rewarded or receive no consequences.

Bandura, A., Dorothea Ross, and Sheila A. Ross. Transmission of aggression through imitation of aggressive models. *J. abnorm. soc. Psychol.*, 1961, *63*, 575–82.
   Measures: Observation of imitation of aggressive behavior displayed by a model. The child was given a task to do in a room in which an adult model (sex of model was varied) displayed distinctive aggressive behavior toward a Bobo doll. The child was then given attractive toys to play with for about two minutes, after which they were taken away. The child then was taken into another room with a Bobo doll and other toys, and allowed to play. An observer recorded aggressive behavior—verbal and physical. **Subjects:** 36 boys and 36 girls, aged 37 months to 69 months, with mean age of 52 months. **Results:** The aggressive-model group showed significantly more imitative aggression, verbal and physical. Aggressive groups showed more nonimitative aggression than the nonaggressive model group. Boys produced more imitative physical aggression than girls, but there were no differences in verbal aggression. Among children exposed to male models, boys showed more imitation than girls did; with a female model girls showed more verbal imitative aggression and more nonimitative aggression than boys. The latter was not significant.

Bandura, A., Dorothea Ross, and Sheila A. Ross. Imitation of film-mediated aggressive models. *J. abnorm. soc. Psychol.*, 1963, *66*, 3–11.
Measures: S's were exposed to aggressive adult models, either live, live on film, or cartooned on film. Then they played after mild frustration; and amount of imitative and nonimitative aggression was observed. Subjects: 48 boys and 48 girls, aged 35 to 69 months. Results: Boys exhibited more total aggression, imitative aggression, aggressive gun play, and nonimitative aggression. Subjects exposed to the male model exhibited more aggressive gun play. Interaction of sex-of-subject and sex-of-model indicated that sex appropriateness of the models' behaviors was influential.

Bandura, A., Dorothea Ross, and Sheila A. Ross. Vicarious reinforcement and imitative learning. *J. abnorm. soc. Psychol.*, 1963, *67*, 601–67.
Measures: S's were exposed to a movie in which (1) a model was aggressive, and then was either rewarded or punished, or (2) the model was active but nonaggressive, or (3) no model was presented. Then they were allowed to play with toys similar to the model's; and imitative and nonimitative aggression was recorded. Subjects: 40 boys and 40 girls, aged 38–63 months. Results: Boys exhibited both more total and more nonimitative aggression. Boys showed much less aggression when exposed to a punished model or no model. Girls showed less nonimitative aggression only with the nonaggressive model.

Barber, T. X., and D. S. Calverley. "Hypnotic-like" suggestibility in children and adults. *J. abnorm. soc. Psychol.*, 1963, *66*, 589–97.
Measures: S's were individually tested on the Barber Suggestibility Scale, which measures suggestibility to hypnotic-like phenomena. Subjects: 724 subjects, aged 6 through 22. Elementary school, high school, college, and nursing students made up the sample. Results: Suggestibility decreased with age. No sex difference.

Barratt, E. S. The space-visualization factors related to temperament traits. *J. Psychol.*, 1955, *39*, 279–87.
Measures: 10 space tests: the Barratt-Furchter Chair-Window Test A and Test B; Thurstone Flag Test; Thurstone's Figure Test and Card Test; Minn. Paper Form Board; Differential Aptitude Test; Industrial Aptitude Survey; Guilford-Zimmerman Aptitude Survey; Spatial Orientation; and Guilford-Zimmerman Spatial Visualization. Subjects: 103 female and 96 male college students. Results: The mean scores were significantly higher for men than women on eight of the ten tests. The factor composition for male and female subjects was different. The males showed clear differences in types of spatial factors, while women had a more general, undifferentiated space factor.

Barrows, G. A., and M. Zuckerman. Construct validity of three masculinity-femininity tests. *J. consult. Psychol.*, 1960, *24*, 441–45.
Measures: Guilford-Zimmerman Temperament Survey M-F Scale, the MMPI M-F Scale, and the Strong Vocational M-F Scale were given, and correlations run between (1) the scores of the scales and (2) the scores of the scales and intellectual and interest tests. Subjects: 2,296 male employees of a large Canadian firm. Results: Correlations among the three M-F scales were all in the .30's. The G-Z and Strong masculinity scores correlated positively with quantitative ability, while the MMPI correlated negatively with all intellectual measures.

Barry, H., Margaret K. Bacon, and E. L. Child. A cross-cultural survey of some sex differences in socialization. *J. abnorm. soc. Psychol.*, 1957, *55*, 327–32.
Measures: Ratings of ethnographers' reports of child-rearing practices in primarily nonliterate cultures. Subjects: 110 cultures. Results: 82% of the cultures press girls

more than boys to become nurturant, 87% press boys more to achieve, and 85% press boys more to be self-reliant. 35% want girls to be more obedient, while 62% do not differentiate sexes on this variable. 61% press girls more in responsibility training.

Baruch, Dorothy W., and J. Annie Wilcox. A study of sex differences in preschool children's adjustment coexistent with interparental tensions. *J. genet. Psychol.*, 1944, *64*, 281–303.

Measures: Psychiatric interviews with parents to determine areas of conflict in the marriage. The children were observed and rated on general adjustment in preschool. Subjects: 76 children and their parents. Children aged 1 yr. 6 mos. to 5 yrs. 7 mos. Results: Five areas of parental conflict were found to be significantly related to children's maladjustment. Lack of sexual satisfaction, ascendance-submission conflicts, and lack of consideration were related to boys' adjustment. Lack of sexual satisfaction, lack of consideration, lack of affection were related to girls' adjustment. Lack of ability to talk over differences was the 5th area, related to the total group's adjustment. The proportion of maladjusted boys vs. girls coexistent with tensions was not significant, although girls' index of maladjustment was more highly related to tensions than boys'. Thus girls seemed more affected by parents' tensions than boys.

Bauermeister, M., S. Wapner, and H. Weiner. Sex differences in the perception of apparent verticality and apparent body position under conditions of body tilt. *J. Pers.*, 1963, *31*, 394–407.

Measures: S's stood in a frame that tilted their bodies up to 90 degrees to the left and right. The room was darkened, and each S adjusted a luminescent rod to (1) his perception of verticality and (2) his perception of the slant of his body. Subjects: 40 male and 40 female adults. Results: There were no sex differences in perception of verticality. In perception of body tilt, women perceived their body axes as tilted more in the direction of the tilt, and more in the direction of the initial position of the luminescent rod, than did men.

Bayley, Nancy. Comparisons of mental and motor test scores for ages 1–15 months by sex, birth order, race, geographical location, and education of parents. *Child Develpm.*, 1965, *36*, 379–411.

Measures: Bayley's Scales of Mental and Motor Development. Subjects: 1,409 infants, ages 1–15 months. Results: No sex differences on either mental or motor scales.

Bayley, Nancy. Mental growth during the first 3 years: a developmental study of 61 children by repeated tests. *Genetic Psychol. Monogr.*, 1933, *14*, 1–92.

Measures: The Bayley Developmental Scales. Subjects: 61 children, 1 month to 3 years. Results: No significant differences, although boys showed slight superiority in sensorimotor skills during the first 8 months.

Bayley, Nancy. *Studies in the development of young children.* Berkeley: Univ. of Calif. Press, 1940.

Measures: X-ray of skeleton. Subjects: The same sample as the Bayley standardization groups: children 1 month to 3 years. Results: Girls' bones are more mature at birth and develop faster than boys'.

Bayley, Nancy, and E. S. Schaefer. Correlations of maternal and child behaviors with the development of mental abilities: data from the Berkeley Growth Study. *S.R.C.D. Monogr.*, 1964, *29*, 63–79.

Measures: Intelligence test scores from birth to 18 years, observation of behavior during testing, and observer's ratings of child's and mother's behavior in the first 3 years and in the years 9–14. Subjects: Children from the Berkeley Growth Study. Results:

Girls' I.Q.'s were more stable over time and correlated more highly with parents' intellectual ability than boys' I.Q.'s. Boys' I.Q.'s were more closely related to mothers' behavior in the first 3 years, even when measured many years later. Girls showed correlations between I.Q. and mothers' behavior at the time the I.Q. was measured, but little correlation when I.Q. and mothers' behavior were assessed at different ages.

Bayton, J. A., Lettie J. Austin, and Kay R. Burke. Negro perception of Negro and white personality traits. *J. Pers. soc. Psychol.*, 1965, *1*, 250–53.
Measures: S's were given the Guilford-Zimmerman Temperament Survey, which measures 10 temperament traits. They rated Negro and white men and women, with each S rating only one of these four groups. Subjects: 240 Negro subjects at Howard University. Results: 4 traits—general activity, ascendance, objectivity, and personal relations—differentiated race but not sexes, with whites given higher ratings on all four. Sociability was higher for women than men with no race differences. No differences were found at all on thoughtfulness. Males were higher on masculinity, and Negro males gave whites higher ratings on masculinity, while Negro females saw Negroes as more masculine. Males saw males as more friendly, while women saw females as more friendly. Negro males were seen as less restrained than white males, but there was no difference between Negro and white females. Males were seen as more emotionally stable, and whites were seen as more stable.

Beach, F. A. Neural and chemical regulation of behavior. In H. F. Harlow and C. N. Wolsey (eds.), *Biological and biochemical bases of behavior*. Madison: Univ. of Wisconsin Press, 1958.
The prime emphasis of the chapter is on neural and chemical regulation of sexual behavior. The sex act can be divided into two parts, arousal and copulation. These two aspects of the sexual act may be governed by different mechanisms. Experience can influence sexual behavior only insofar as the neocortex controls that behavior. Primates show much greater cortical control, and thus greater learning effects and individual differences, than lower mammals. Males among the lower mammals are more controlled by the cortex than females. Male sexual arousal in lower mammals can be modified by experience more than can female arousal.

Becker, W. C., D. R. Peterson, Zella Luria, D. S. Shoemaker, and L. A. Hellmer. Relations of factors derived from parent-interview ratings to behavior problems of five-year-olds. *Child Develpm.*, 1962, *33*, 509–35.
Measures: Interviews with parents were rated on 71 scales. These scales were factor-analyzed separately for mothers and fathers. The relationship of these factors to ratings by parents and teachers on conduct problems and personality problems was explored. Subjects: 36 boys and 35 girls and their parents. The children were in kindergarten. Results: Degree of hostility in both parents and use of physical punishment is related to aggressive behaviors in children. Girls who are moderately punished by mothers were the most aggressive in school. For boys in school and boys and girls at home, the relation of aggression to mother's hostility and physical punishment was linear. Boys who were moderately punished by fathers were less aggressive at home and somewhat less so at school. Aggression in girls at school and home tended to be linearly related to father's hostility and physical punishment.

Beier, E. G., et al. Responses to the human face as a standard stimulus: a reexamination. *J. consult. Psychol.*, 1957, *21*, 165–70.
Measures: Response of like or dislike to photos of persons varying in age and sex. Subjects: 60 male and 60 female college students. Results: Both sexes preferred persons of their own age or younger; but boys were relatively more accepting of older people, and girls were more accepting of younger persons (children 2–5). The latter

was the largest difference found. There was no difference found in preference for one sex over the other.

Beller, E. K. Dependency and autonomous achievement striving related to orality and anality in early childhood. *Child Develpm.*, 1957, *28*, 287–315.

Measures: Rating scales and nursery summaries on dependency, achievement striving, and orality and anality. Subjects: 51 emotionally disturbed children between 28 and 74 months of age. Results: The data were not analyzed by sex except in relation to the structure of the scales. Autonomous achievement striving and dependency correlated in opposite directions for the two sexes. When the most severely disturbed children were removed, the correlation was .41 for boys, —.45 for girls.

Beller, E. K. Personality correlates of perceptual discrimination in children. Progress Report, 1962.

Measures: Observer ratings on dependency, autonomous achievement striving, and aggression. The Embedded Figures Test was administered. Subjects: 13 boys and 14 girls, 66–75 months of age, middle-class families. Results: Boys were significantly higher on aggression. Embedded figures did not correlate significantly with any dependency scale. It correlated positively and significantly with several independence scales (completes activities, gets work satisfaction, and total independence). The aggression scales all correlated significantly in a negative direction with EFT for boys, but the correlations were not significant for girls. The investigator speculated that only at the higher levels of aggression does one get a relationship between impulse control and EFT.

Beller, E. K., and P. B. Neubauer. Sex differences and symptom patterns in early childhood. *J. Child Psychiat.*, 1963, *2*, 414–33.

Measures: Data on symptomatology of children brought to the clinic, collected from parents in diagnostic interviews. Subjects: 55 boys and 55 girls, aged 2–5 years, of urban middle-class and lower-middle-class families. Result: Parents reported significantly more hyperaggression, hyperactivity, lack of bowel control, and speech disturbances for boys. Girls were reported to have significantly more problems of overdependence, emotional overcontrol, bowel retention, and sibling rivalry.

Beller, E. K., and J. LeB. Turner. A study of dependency and aggression in early childhood. From progress report on NIMH project M-849, 1962.

Measures: Trained participant observer ratings on a seven-point scale of dependency, autonomous achievement striving (AAS), and aggression. Subjects: A clinical group consisting of 41 boys and 48 girls, and a nonclinical group made up of 48 boys and 43 girls. The children were preschoolers, matched for age. Results: On the dependency scales, girls were significantly higher on seeking physical contact and seeking physical nearness. There were no significant differences on the other dependency scales of seeking help, recognition, or attention. This was true of both clinical and nonclinical groups. On AAS there were no sex differences on any of the subscales. In aggression, the clinical group showed boys significantly higher on all subscales. In the nonclinical group, boys were significantly higher in threatening, destroying, and attacking children. There were no significant differences on derogation, attacking adults, or the combined attacking-adults-and-children score in the nonclinical group.

Bendig, A. W. Age-related changes in covert and overt anxiety. *J. genet. Psychol.*, 1960, *62*, 159–63.

Measures: Cattell's IPAT Anxiety Scale, a self-administered scale that contains 40 anxiety items—20 obvious and 20 hidden. This scale gives an overt, a covert, and a total anxiety score. Subjects: 104 men and 115 women in undergraduate and graduate school. Results: No significant sex differences.

Bendig, A. W. Age, sex, and the Manifest Anxiety Test. *J. consult. Psychol.,* 1954, *18,* 16.

Measures: 50-item version of the Taylor Manifest Anxiety Scale. Subjects: College undergraduates. Results: Women were a little higher, but no significant sex differences were found.

Bennett, D. H. Perception of the upright in relation to body image. *J. ment. Sci.,* 1956, *102,* 487–506.

Measures: S's were seated in a darkened room and presented with a luminous rod within a luminous frame. This is the Witkin Rod and Frame Test. S's were asked to indicate when the rod was upright. Subjects: 25 men and 25 women in a normal adult group, and 4 other groups of hospitalized mental patients. Results: Women made more errors in the Rod and Frame Test. Men showed a rightward tendency and women a leftward tendency in righting the rod.

Bennett, E. M., and L. R. Cohen. Men and women: personality patterns and contrasts. *Genet. Psychol. Monogr.,* 1959, *59,* 101–55.

Measures: S's were given lists of adjectives from which they had to pick the three that most or least described themselves. In other lists they picked words to describe their motivations or their values. Subjects: 1,300 persons, aged 15–64. Results: Many sex differences were found. A general summary indicated that women felt greater benevolence toward social activities and greater social orientation. Women felt greater social propriety including greater social morality and honesty. Women felt greater personal satisfaction, but greater personal inadequacy of functioning and lack of personal protection. Women felt greater covert hostility but less overt aggressiveness. Men felt greater personal capacity and need for attainment, and a greater need for being uncompromising and ruthless. Men saw the world as more socially hostile.

Bennett, G. K., et al. Differential aptitudes tests manual, 3d ed. New York: Psychol. Corp., 1959.

Verbal and numerical scores on the DAT show little difference between the sexes. The largest differences are in space and mechanical ability, with boys ahead; and on clerical, spelling, and sentences, with girls ahead.

Bernard, J. Prediction from human fetal measures. *Child Develpm.,* 1964, *35,* 1243–48.

Measures: Heart rate, fetal movements recorded by kymograph, birth size, birth weight, postnatal heart rate. Subjects: Approximately 100 cases from the early Fels study. Results: Fetal heart rate did not predict sex of fetus. Sex differences in total fetal activity did not appear, although males did produce more quick (kicking) movements. Males were longer and heavier at birth.

Berry, J. L., and B. Martin. GSR reactivity as a function of anxiety, instructions, and sex. *J. abnorm. soc. Psychol.,* 1957, *54,* 9–12.

Measures: Sarason Text Anxiety Scale was used to obtain groups of high-anxious and low-anxious subjects. Then a tone followed by a shock was used to condition GSR. Subjects: College students—20 male and 30 female high-anxiety S's, and 30 male and 30 female low-anxiety S's. Results: Women showed greater GSR reactivity in all conditions. The conditions were also manipulated to give high apprehension arousal ("sometime during this experiment you will get one much stronger shock"), reassurance ("you will soon become accustomed to the shock, and it won't be too bad"), and neutral ("this is the shock you will receive"). Males showed less conditioning with reassurance than with apprehension arousal, while females showed less conditioning with apprehension arousal than with reassurance.

Bieri, J., et al. Sex differences in perceptual behavior. *J. Pers.*, 1958, *26*, 1–12.
Measures: (1) Witkin's Embedded Figure Test (EFT). (2) A modified Rorschach.
(3) The Barron-Welsh Art Scale (to measure preference for complex or simple figures). (4) The External Construct Score (to measure the tendency to perceive and categorize other people in terms of concrete and superficial characteristics, or in terms of motivational and internal traits). (5) Guilford's Bricks Test (to measure spontaneous flexibility, "how many things can you do with a brick?"). (6) Verbal and math aptitude on the Scholastic Aptitude Test (SAT). Subjects: 62 female and 50 male college undergraduates. Results: Mean differences. Males were superior in the EFT at the .01 level. They were also superior on math SAT, although there were no significant differences on the verbal SAT (women were somewhat superior). On the Rorschach, females showed fewer nonhuman movement responses, fewer FC and Sum C (color) responses, and more F responses—the latter two not reaching the .05 level. Sex differences in correlations were also discussed.

Bing, Elizabeth. Effects of childrearing practices on development of differential cognitive abilities. *Child Develpm.*, 1963, *34*, 631–48.
Measures: Primary Mental Abilities Test and other abilities tests to find subjects with higher verbal than nonverbal ability and subjects with higher nonverbal than verbal ability. Questionnaire and interviews to measure parents' socialization practices when the child was small; and an observed interaction situation between mother and child in which child worked on tasks and mother could give help or withhold it. Subjects: 60 boys and girls, of which 16 boys and 16 girls were low verbal, and 16 boys and 12 girls were high verbal. S's were matched for total I.Q. Results: Generally, for boys, the early parental behavior reported in interview and questionnaire was more highly related to verbal skill than were the current interaction variables. The reverse was true for girls. Maternal stimulation and interaction were important in producing high verbal ability in boys. For girls, mother's high interaction rate in the present-day interaction situation was conducive to high verbal ability. Mothers of high-verbal girls were more intrusive with help, suggestions, and criticism. There were no mean differences on the variables between the sexes.

Boehm, Lenore, and M. L. Nass. Social class differences in conscience development. Progress report, Jan. 30, 1960.
Measures: Piaget-type interviews with children in which 4 stories were told to measure attitudes toward (1) aggression, (2) material values, (3) lying, and (4) ingratiation of authority and authority dependence. Protocols were scored for 3 Piaget levels of morality. Subjects: Children 6–11 years old from working-class and middle-class families. Results: No sex differences, although there was some tendency for girls to be more "mature."

Book, W. F., and J. L. Meadows. Sex differences in 5,925 high school seniors in 10 psychological tests. *J. appl. Psychol.*, 1928, *12*, 58–81.
Measures: A standardized intelligence test made up of 10 subtests: rote memory, logical selection, arithmetical ability, opposites, logical memory, word completion, moral classification, dissected sentences, practical information, and analogies. Subjects: High school seniors, nearly all over 16 yrs. The performance of these S's was compared with that of Pressey's S's (9 to 16 yrs.), who took the same test. Results: From 9 to 16 girls were superior in total score; boys were superior after 16. Authors feel that there are no real differences in ability. Girls were superior up to 16 because of accelerated maturation, while boys were superior after 16 because more dull boys than girls drop out of school. In the subtests, boys excelled from ages 9 to 23 in arithmetic skills and practical information; girls excelled at all ages in opposites, logical memory, and dissected sentences. There was greater variability among boys than girls.

Borgatta, E. F., and J. Stimson. Sex differences in interaction characteristics. *J. soc. Psychol.*, 1963, *60*, 89–100.

Measures: Groups of 5 persons of the same sex discussed 4 topics for 80 minutes. Interaction was scored on categories adapted from Bales. Subjects: College students, 31 male groups and 8 female groups. Results: No differences in overall interaction. A higher percentage of the interaction was concerned with common social acknowledgments and the categories of drawing attention and clarifying in male groups than in female groups. Female groups had a higher percentage of disagreement interaction than male groups. Differences in factor structure for the sexes were also found.

Borstelmann, L. J. Sex of experimenter and sex-typed behavior of young children. *Child Develpm.*, 1961, *32*, 519–24.

Measures: Brown's It Scale, Toy Preference Test, and the Pictures Test. All 3 of these tests were used to measure sex-appropriate activity or toy choice. Sex of child, sex of E on initial testing, and sex of E on retest were systematically varied. Subjects: 64 nursery school children, 3 yrs. 4 mos. to 5 yrs. Eight male and eight female E's were used. Results: Sex of E had no significant effect on toy choice for either boys or girls. Boys made significantly more sex-appropriate toy choices.

Bradway, Katherine P., and Clare W. Thompson. Intelligence at adulthood: a twenty-five-year followup. *J. educ. Psychol.*, 1962, *53*, 1–14.

Measures: Stanford-Binet given at preschool age, adolescence, and adulthood. The WAIS was also given in adulthood. Subjects: 111 adults between the ages of 27 and 32. Results: The correlation between preschool S-B I.Q. and adult S-B was .59; with the WAIS it was .64. The correlation between adolescent S-B and adult S-B was .85; with the WAIS it was .80. The mean I.Q. on the Stanford-Binet showed an increase of 11 points from adolescence to adulthood. This was a 20-month gain in mental age beyond age 16. Males exhibited significantly more I.Q. gain from adolescence to adulthood than girls. Bright girls were less likely to increase I.Q. than less bright girls or any boys. Girls tested significantly higher on I.Q. at both younger ages, and insignificantly higher at the adult testing. Education was not related to I.Q. change.

Brim, O. G. Family structure and sex role learning by children: a further analysis of Helen Koch's data. *Sociometry*, 1958, *21*, 1–16.

Measures: Teachers' rating on the Fels Behavior Rating Scales and the Calif. Behavior Rating Scale. The traits were then rated as either instrumental (masculine) or expressive (feminine). Subjects: Same as the Koch (1956) study (children, aged 5 and 6). Results: Children with cross-sex sibs showed more opposite-sex characteristics than those with same-sex sibs. The differences were greater if the sib was older. Girls with cross-sex sibs did not show fewer feminine characteristics, but boys with sisters were low in masculine traits. Age differences between the sibs did not affect the amount of opposite-sex-typing.

Brim, O. G., D. C. Glass, D. E. Lavin, and N. Goodman. *Personality and decision processes.* Stanford: Stanford Univer. Press, 1962.

Measures: A self-administered Decision Process Test was given to parents to discover how they evaluated and made decisions about four child-rearing problems. In addition, a large number of personality tests were given, including (1) TMAS, (2) a satisfaction-in-interpersonal-relations test, (3) a test of parental concern about child rearing, (4) the Parental Attitude Research Instrument (PARI), (5) a test for desire for certainty, (6) general personality tests including scales on autism, cycloid tendency, emotionality, interest in philosophizing and puzzles, dominance, nervousness, persistence, self-confidence, self-sufficiency, orderliness, meticulousness, impulsivity, and rhythymia, (7) a test of epistemological and instrumental beliefs, (8) an independence-of-judgment test. Subjects: A total of 96 couples, from lower and middle class. Each couple had a son in 4th, 5th, or 6th grade. **Results:** On decision processes there were no significant sex differences in the middle class. In the lower class the only difference was that women were more swayed by immediate than long-range outcomes of decisions. In personality measure, middle-class men were higher on autonomy, less satisfied with interpersonal relations, and less optimistic. Women were more anxious, less confident, less self-sufficient, and more nervous. Females had greater need for certainty. Men were more concerned with children's work habits and more interested in philosophy and puzzles. There were no sex differences in personality in the lower class.

Brodbeck, A. J. Learning theory and identification: IV, Oedipal motivation as a determinant of conscience development. *J. genet. Psychol.*, 1954, *84*, 219–27.
> **Measures:** Children were given a series of personality traits and asked to say if these characterized their mother or father. Then they took another test in which they made moral evaluations of the traits. A positively evaluated trait that had been attributed to the same-sex parent gave a point for identification. **Subjects:** Rural school children, age 10–14. **Results:** Both sexes identified more with the same-sex parent at age 10. Both sexes increased the amount of identification with the other sex up to age 14. By then girls were equally identified with both parents, and boys more with the mother. Mother was evaluated equally by children of both sexes; father more favorably by boys.

Bronfenbrenner, U. Some familial antecedents of responsibility and leadership in adolescents. In L. Petrullo and B. M. Bass (eds.), *Studies in leadership.* New York: Holt, 1960.
> **Measures:** A Parent Activities Inventory (listing dimensions of parent-child relations derived from Parson's instrumental-expressive dichotomy) administered to the child; and teachers' ratings of the child's responsibility and leadership. **Subjects:** 192 adolescents (10th-graders), chosen equally from 4 SES levels and an equal number of each sex. **Results:** Girls received more affection, attention, and praise than boys, especially from fathers. Boys received more pressure and discipline, especially from fathers. Through all SES groups, the father's techniques were similar. However, the mother's techniques varied with social class, becoming more domineering, materialistic, and rejecting with lower SES. In lower SES families, mothers were more influential and fathers less so with all children. On responsibility girls were rated higher than boys by teachers. Responsibility and leadership correlated negatively with parental rejection and neglect in both sexes. In boys, high responsibility correlated with greater presence, nurturance, affection, and companionship, especially from mother, and with greater discipline and authority from father. These relationships were reversed for girls.

Brown, D. G. Masculinity-femininity development in children. *J. consult. Psychol.*, 1957, *21*, 197–202.
> **Measures:** The It Scale for Children. **Subjects:** 303 boys and 310 girls between 5½ and 11½. **Results:** Up to 5th grade, boys showed more masculine preferences than girls did feminine. Girls showed equal preference for both roles in kindergarten, masculine preference in 1st through 4th grade, and then shifted to feminine preference in 5th grade.

Buckingham, B. R., and J. MacLatchy. The number abilities of children when they enter grade one. *Yearb. Nat. Soc. Stud. Educ.*, 1930, *29* (II), 473–549.
> **Measures:** Counting and number identification. **Subjects:** 1,000 first-grade entrants, aged 6 to 6½. **Results:** 9 out of 11 comparisons favored girls, with CR's from 1.03 to 2.90.

Burton, R. V., Eleanor E. Maccoby, and W. Allinsmith. Antecedents of resistance to temptation in 4-year-old children. *Child Develpm.*, 1961, *32*, 689–710.

Measures: Interviews with mothers to determine child-rearing practices, and mother's perceptions of the child. The child was asked to play a throwing game in which he got points toward an attractive prize. The child played alone, and amount of cheating was observed. Subjects: 40 boys and 37 girls, all aged 4. Results: The antecedents of resistance to cheating were different for the two sexes. Girls who cheated tended to have a warm home atmosphere where withdrawal of love as a disciplinary technique, lenience about cleanliness, and readiness to answer questions about sex were found. These variables tended to be correlated with resistance to cheating in boys.

Buss, A. H. Physical aggression in relation to different frustrations. *J. abnorm. soc. Psychol.*, 1963, *67*, 1–7.

Measures: S was asked to act as E in a concept-learning task. He was to present stimuli and administer reward and punishment to a victim. Punishment consisted of a shock, and S could choose the strength of the shock to be administered. The stronger the shock, the greater the aggression of S. In the experiment S was frustrated by being told that his reward would depend on how fast his victim learned the task. The victim always learned much too slowly to earn the reward for S. Half the men and half the women S's had a male victim and the other half a female victim. Subjects: 160 college students. Results: Men were significantly more aggressive than females. Men administered more punishment to male than female victims, while women administered equal amounts to male and female victims.

Buss, A. H., and T. C. Brock. Repression and guilt in relation to aggression. *J. abnorm. soc. Psychol.*, 1963, *66*, 345–50.

Measures: S's who were opposed to giving shock were required to give shock to experimental victims. Before administering shock, S read a communication saying that shock was either beneficial (positive communication) or that it was harmful in its effect (negative communication). Subjects: 47 women and 34 men. Results: S's recalled the negative communication less well than the positive communication. Guilt was assessed by questionnaire after the experiment, and women were significantly more guilty than men. Female victims aroused more guilt than male victims.

Byrne, D. Parental antecedents of authoritarianism. *J. Pers. soc. Psychol.*, 1965, *1*, 369–73.

Measures: The F Scale and the Traditional Family Ideology Scale were administered to S's and their mothers and fathers. Subjects: 49 male and 59 female college students. Results: All 4 correlations between F scores and TFI scores of fathers and sons were significant. Mothers' F score correlated with F score of children of both sexes. No other correlations were significant for mothers or daughters.

Campbell, Elise H. The social sex development of children. *Genet. psychol. Monogr.*, 1939, *21*, No. 4.

Measures: Observers' ratings of behavior of the sexes toward each other during recreation club sessions. Subjects: 112 children aged 5–17, average I.Q. and SES. Results: Girls were more advanced at all ages in social sex development. They moved from nondifferentiation to boy-hating to interest in boys at younger ages than boys made the corresponding advancements.

Carey, Gloria L. Reduction of sex differences in problem-solving by improvement of attitude through group discussion. Unpublished dissertation, Stanford University, 1955.

Measures: Reasoning problems were given before and after a discussion group aimed at improving attitudes toward problem-solving. An attitude questionnaire was given on problem-solving before and after discussion. Subjects: 96 college students. Results: Women had poorer attitudes than men toward problem-solving. There were no changes in attitude from before to after discussion, but women's performance on the problems improved significantly after discussion. This was not true for men.

Carlson, Rae. Identification and personality structure in preadolescents. *J. abnorm. soc. Psychol.*, 1963, *67*, 566–73.

Measures: A questionnaire administered to S asked him to make statements about himself and about his ideal self. The same questionnaires were sent to S's parents, who were asked to state their concepts of an ideal child and to predict their child's self-description. Subjects: 25 girls and 18 boys in 6th grade. Results: Girls' ideal self-ratings and that of their parents were more similar (congruent) than boys'. Parental accuracy (similarity between predicted child's self-rating and actual self-rating) and parental acceptance (similarity between parents' rating of ideal child and the parents' prediction of the child's self-rating) were higher for boys than for girls.

Carlson, Rae. Stability and change in the adolescent's self-image. *Child Develpm.*, 1965, *36*, 659–66.

Measures: A self-descriptive questionnaire in which S described himself and his ideal self in terms that could be classified as social interests and skills or personal, nonsocial interests. Self-esteem was measured by the correspondence between ideal and real self. Kelly's Role Construct Repertory Test was also given. Here S nominated people for various roles. Subjects: 49 children in 5th and 6th grades, retested six years later in 11th and 12th grades. These were volunteer subjects; some of the original sample had moved away or did not reply. 33 girls and 16 boys were studied. Results: There were no sex differences at the earlier age in personal versus social orientation, but in high school, girls were significantly more socially oriented than boys. There were no sex differences in self-esteem.

Carment, D. W., F. S. Schwartz, and L. G. Miles. Participation and opinion changes as related to cohesiveness and sex of subjects in two-person groups. *Psychol. Rep.*, 1964, *14*, No. 3, 695–702.

Measures: Three sets of male-and-female pairs of S's were studied. In one set, both members of each pair were told that they should like each other. In the 2d set, one was told the above and the other was told that there was no reason to believe he would get along with the other. In the 3d set, both members were given the negative preinstruction. The dependent measures were the amount of participation and extent of opinion change during and after an informal debate. Subjects: An equal number of male and female students selected from an introductory psychology course. Results: Males spoke more than females. Most opinion change took place among favorably predisposed males paired with unfavorably predisposed opponents. Females were less affected than males by favorable preinformation, whereas the difference between unfavorably predisposed males and females, irrespective of the nature of their opponents' predispositions, was not marked. Male S's emitted more positive statements than females. Males made more neutral statements than females. Females were not significantly affected by their own instruction or that of their opponent.

Carrier, N. A., K. D. Orton, and L. F. Malpass. Responses of bright, normal, and EMH children to an orally administered Children's Manifest Anxiety Scale. *J. educ. Psychol.*, 1962, *53*, 271–74.

Measures: WISC intelligence scores and an oral CMAS. Subjects: Eleven 14-year-old children in four groups: 32 bright children (I.Q. 120–150), 31 normals (I.Q. 90–110), 27 noninstitutionalized mentally handicapped (I.Q. 50–80), and 17 institutionalized mentally retarded (I.Q. 50–80). **Results:** I.Q. was negatively related to anxiety. Girls tended to be higher on anxiety, but only among noninstitutionalized mentally retarded girls was it significant.

Carter, L. B. The effects of early school entrance on the scholastic achievement of elementary school children in the Austin public schools. *J. educ. Res.,* 1956, *50,* 91–103.

Measures: Metropolitan Achievement tests (arithmetic, spelling, reading, English) in grades 2–6. **Subjects:** 50 children who were 6 years and over, and 50 children who were under 6, when entering 1st grade. **Results:** Underage children were poorer than normal-age children in achievement at all grade levels. Underage boys were more affected than underage girls.

Castaneda, A., and B. R. McCandless. The children's form of the Manifest Anxiety Scale. *Child Develpm.,* 1956, *27,* 317–26.

Measures: CMAS. **Subjects:** 386 children in 4th, 5th, and 6th grades. **Results:** Girls scored significantly higher (p = .005). They scored higher on the lie scale as well. The lie scale has items, such as "I am never angry," that indicate a tendency to deny or falsify the scale.

Chaplin, J. P. Sex differences in the perception of autokinetic movement. *J. gen. Psychol.,* 1955, *52,* 149–55.

Measures: Presentation of various illuminated figures in a totally dark room. S told the E when he saw movement, how much he saw, and the direction of movement. **Subjects:** 52 male and 51 female college students. **Results:** Women saw significantly less movement than men, both in terms of latency and extent. There was no difference in direction. When asked after the experiment, women believed the light did not move, while men were sure it really had moved.

Chateau, J. Le test de structuration spaciale Tib. I. S. *Travail hum.,* 1959, *22,* 281–97.

Measures: A new test of spatial ability consisting of embedded figures of different difficulty levels. **Subjects:** 753 males and 429 females, aged 10 to adulthood. (There were several studies done, and this is the total sample size.) **Results:** Males do significantly better than females.

Cheek, Frances E. A serendipitous finding: sex roles and schizophrenia. *J. abstr. soc. Psychol.,* 1964, *69,* 392–400.

Measures: 48 minutes of recorded interaction between father, mother, and schizophrenic young adult coded with variation of the Bales interaction categories. This interaction was compared to that of families with nonpsychotic young adults under similar conditions. **Subjects:** 67 convalescent young adult schizophrenics (40 male, 27 female), and 56 nonpsychotic young adults (31 male and 25 female). **Results:** No significant difference in total interaction appeared between normal and schizophrenic subjects as a group. However, female schizophrenics were higher than female normals in total interaction. Male normals were higher than male schizophrenics. Thus, male schizophrenics tended to be withdrawn and inactive, while female schizophrenics tended to be overactive.

Cieutat, V. J. Sex differences in verbal operant conditioning. *Psychol. Rep.,* 1964, *15,* 259–75.

Measures: Groups of 3 same-sex S's discussed various topics for 50 minutes while time spent talking was recorded for each S. A base rate was recorded, and then either a male or a female E entered the group as a conditioner. E either positively

rewarded talking by attentiveness, or negatively reinforced talking by inattention.
Subjects: 144 college students in first study, and 96 in the second. Results: In
the first study only male E's were effective reinforcers; only female E's were effective
in the second.

Clark, W. W. Boys and girls—are there significant ability and achievement differences? *Phi Delta Kappan*, 1959, *41*, 73–76.
    Measures: California Test of Mental Maturity and California Achievement Test.
    Subjects: A stratified sample of 75 boys and 75 girls from all 48 states, matched on
    age, from grades 3, 5, and 8. Results: On the CTMM the only significant differences
    were at the 3d-grade level, in language mental age, numerical reasoning, and verbal
    concepts. Boys were superior in all three. On the CAT, there were no differences in
    reading vocabulary, reading comprehension, and arithmetic reasoning. In arithmetic
    fundamentals, girls were better in grade 8. In mechanics of language, girls did better
    at grades 5 and 8, and they did better in all three grades on spelling.

Clifton, Marguerite A., and Hope M. Smith. Comparison of expressed self-
concepts of highly skilled males and females concerning motor performance.
Percept. Motor Skills., 1963, *16*, 199–201.
    Measures: Subjects performed 4 motor tasks: running, catching, throwing, and
    standing broad jump. No comments on performance were made. S's then took a Per-
    ception Checklist on which they evaluated their performances. Subjects: 36 males
    and 49 females, all highly skilled athletes. Results: Females rated themselves much
    less favorably on standing broad jump than males, although their performance was
    objectively good.

Colby, K. M. Sex differences in dreams of primitive tribes. *Amer. Anthro.*, 1963,
65, 1116–22.
    Measures: Analysis of dreams from a cross-cultural collection of dreams reported by
    primitive people. The dreams were analyzed and placed into one of 19 categories.
    Subjects: One dream each from 366 men and 183 women representing 75 tribes was
    used. Results: Men dreamed more of wife, weapon, coitus, death, and animals;
    women dreamed more of husband, mother, clothes, and female figure. There were no
    significant differences on father, child, hit, vehicle, cry, grass, ineffectual attempt,
    red, home, or male figure. The only overlap between these significant differences and
    those of a previous American-European sample was on wife and husband.

Cole, D., S. Jacobs, Bea Zubok, Beverly Fagot, and E. Hunter. The relation of
achievement imagery scores to academic performance. *J. abnorm. soc. Psychol.*,
1962, *65*, 208–11.
    Measures: Four TAT cards were used to elicit achievement imagery. College Board
    scores and school grades were examined to pick overachievement and underachieve-
    ment. There were 2 separate studies. Subjects: College students. In one study group,
    23 honors students were matched with 23 average students on the basis of College
    Board scores, sex, years of college, and other variables. In the other study, 130
    freshmen were tested, and their grades at the end of the semester inspected for dis-
    crepancies from College Board predictions. Results: No significant differences were
    found between overachieving and underachieving women on achievement imagery.
    For men, there was a significant negative relationship between actual achievement
    and achievement imagery in the first study, and in the second study the results were
    in the same direction, although the final sample size was too small to be significant.

Coleman, J. S. *The adolescent society*. Glencoe, Ill.: The Free Press, 1961.
    Measures: Questionnaires administered to students, teachers, and parents; inter-
    views; and data from school files. Subjects: Students in 10 Illinois high schools; the

schools were chosen to be representative of social class, size of school, and other demographic variables. Results: Girls had higher school grades than boys, and less variability among grades; that is, a boy with a B average had more A's and C's, while a girl had mostly B's. This was felt to be a result of double pressures on the girl, who feels that she should be a good girl and do what her parents and teachers want, but also feels that it is unfeminine and poor for popularity to be a brilliant student. This was further borne out by the fact that boys who were named as best scholar by others were more likely to want to be thought of as a brilliant scholar than girls so named. Also, the boys named best scholar had higher I.Q. scores than girls named best scholar, even though the mean I.Q. of girls was higher than that of boys.

Corah, N. L. Differentiation in children and their parents. *J. Pers.*, 1965, *33*, 300–308.
Measures: The Children's Embedded Figures Test and the Draw-a-Person Test measured differentiation in children; and the Embedded Figures Test and Draw-a-Person measured differentiation for parents. Subjects: 60 families, half with boys and half with girls between 8 and 11 years. Results: Boys' differentiation correlated positively with fathers' differentiation, while girls' differentiation correlated positively with mothers' differentiation.

Cosentino, F., and A. B. Heilbrun, Jr. Anxiety correlates of sex-role identity in college students. *Psychol. Repnts.*, 1964, *14*, 729–30.
Measures: 80-item aggression questionnaire (R. Sears) was used. Only 12 items related to aggression anxiety were scored. An adjective check list and the Taylor Manifest Anxiety Scale were used as well. Subjects: 85 male, 156 female, college students. (Mean age of males 19.9, and females 19.5.) Results: (1) The direction and magnitude of the relationship between aggression anxiety and sex-role identity were essentially the same at 20 years as at 12 years (see Sears's earlier work with 12-year-olds). At each level, greater femininity was associated with greater aggression anxiety for both males and females. (2) A more feminine sex-role identity in either sex involved more than a latent disposition to respond with greater anxiety to aggression cues. More feminine males and females were more manifestly anxious, presumably in response to a wider range of cues.

Costello, C. G., and H. M. Brachman. III: Cultural and sex differences in extroversion and neuroticism reflected in responses to a Children's Personality Inventory. *Brit. J. educ. Psychol.*, 1962, *32*, 254–57.
Measures: The Junior Maudsley Personality Inventory, which measures extroversion and neuroticism. Subjects: 261 male and 248 female Canadian high school children, and 304 male and 230 female British high school children. All were between 14 and 16 years of age. Results: No sex differences were found on extroversion, but females were higher than males on neuroticism. There was also a significant tendency for girls to acquiesce more than boys (items were all agree-disagree type). However, it was not possible to determine whether this was due to higher neuroticism scores.

Cox, F. N. A second study of four family variables. *Child Develpm.*, 1963, *34*, 619–30.
Measures: Children were asked to respond to a questionnaire reporting on parental socialization techniques. From this, ratings were made on 4 family variables: love (parents' behavior is child-oriented, developmentally appropriate, and child-respecting), social restriction (child's activities and companions are restricted), household duties and responsibilities (child is assigned or assumes chores), and family cohesion (family does things together). Subjects: 362 boys and girls in 4th and 5th grades in Canberra, Australia. Results: Only correlations among variables are given. There are no significant correlations among the 4 variables for boys, but for all girls in both grades, love is significantly correlated with household duties.

Crandall, J. E. Some relationships among sex, anxiety, and conservatism of judgment. *J. Pers.*, 1965, *33*, 99–107.

Measures: The Taylor Manifest Anxiety Scale was used to pick high and low anxiety groups. Pettigrew's Category Width Test (CWT) and a word evaluation test (WET) in which S rated words for pleasantness were given. For each test, extreme responses indicated less conservatism. Subjects: 20 men and 20 women in the high-anxiety condition and the same number in the low-anxiety condition. Results: Men were more conservative on the WET and women on the CWT. High-anxious men were more conservative than low-anxious men, while low-anxious women were more conservative than high-anxious women.

Crandall, V. J., Rachel Dewey, W. Katowsky, and Anne Preston. Parents' attitudes and behaviors and grade-school children's academic achievements. *J. genet. Psychol.*, 1964, *104*, 53–66.

Measures: Stanford-Binet I.Q., California Achievement Test, and interviews with both parents to assess general socialization variables of affection, rejection, and nurturance. Also interviews to assess parents' specific attitudes toward achievement. Subjects: 20 boys and 20 girls in each of three grades, 2d, 3d, and 4th. Results: Mean sex differences are not given. The only significant correlations between general child-rearing variables and the child's academic achievement were between girls and their mothers: girls who were achievers had mothers who were less affectionate and less nurturant. Of 18 significant correlations between academic competence and parents' specific attitudes toward achievement, only three involved boys.

Crandall, V. J., W. Katkowsky, and Anne Preston. Motivational and ability determinants of young children's intellectual achievement behaviors. *Child Develpm.*, 1962, *33*, 643–61.

Measures: TAT measures of n. Achievement; CMAS; measures of relative value of intellectual success over physical, creative, or mechanical skills; expectation of success in a task; achievement standards; attribution of responsibility for performance in self or others; S-B I.Q.; reading and arithmetic scores on the CAT; amount of competition in intellectual play activities. Subjects: 20 boys and 20 girls in the 1st, 2d, and 3d grades. Above-average I.Q.'s. Results: No sex differences in mean scores except that girls value intellectual attainment over other areas of competence more than boys, and that girls take the blame for intellectual failure rather than projecting blame as boys do. Bright boys expected to exceed in new tasks more than less bright boys ($r = .62$), while brighter girls expected to fail ($r = .41$).

Crandall, V. J., S. Orleans, et al. The development of social compliance in young children. *Child Develpm.*, 1958, *29*, 429–44.

Measures: Behavioral observations of social compliance in nursery school or day camp and at home. Subjects: Nursery school children and 6-, 7,- and 8-year-olds. Results: No sex differences in amount of social compliance.

Crandall, V. J., and Alice Rabson. Children's repetition choices in an intellectual achievement situation following success and failure. *J. genet. Psychol.*, 1960, *97*, 161–68.

Measures: Children were given 2 puzzles to work and allowed to finish only one of them. They were then allowed to choose whether they would like to do more work on the completed or the uncompleted task. The children were also rated on many behavior variables by observers who watched their free play. The 6 variables were: (1) achievement efforts in free play, (2) seeking help from peers, (3) seeking help from adults, (4) seeking approval from peers, (5) seeking approval from adults, and (6) withdrawal from threatening situations. Subjects: 30 children 3–5 years old, and 29 children 6–8 years old. The children were members of the Fels Institute Longitudinal Study. **Results:** On repetition choice there were no significant sex differences at nursery school age, but boys in grade school chose to repeat the failed puzzle significantly more frequently than did grade school girls. The difference was created by an increase in failure choices by boys. Girls did not change with age. In behavior ratings, there were no significant sex differences at nursery school age. At the older age, however, there were sex differences in all variables except achievement efforts. Girls significantly more often asked help and approval from adults than help from peers. The trend was for girls to ask approval from peers also, but this was not significant. Girls withdrew from threat significantly more often than boys.

Crandall, Virginia C., W. Katkowsky, and V. J. Crandall. Children's beliefs in their own control of reinforcements in intellectual-academic achievement situations. *Child Develpm.*, 1965, *36*, 91–109.
> **Measures:** The children's Intellectual Achievement Responsibility Test, which asks the child whether positive and negative rewards for intellectual performance are a result of his own effort or are the result of other people's intervention. Also grades and achievement scores in school. **Subjects:** 923 children in grades 3 to 12. **Results:** No sex differences up to grade 5. From grade 6 on, girls take responsibility for their own performance significantly more than boys. Scores on this test tended to correlate with young girls' achievement in school and with older boys' achievement. (High self-responsibility was associated with higher achievement.)

Crudden, C. H. Form abstraction by children. *J. genet. Psychol.*, 1941, *58*, 113–29.
> **Measures:** Children were trained to discriminate between pairs of simple pictures. When they touched the correct figure, they received an auditory reward, such as a bell ringing or a cat meowing. Then the figures were embedded in a complex geometrical figure, and ability to abstract the correct figure for the reward was measured. **Subjects:** 30 boys and 35 girls, aged 5 yrs. 5 mos. to 6 yrs. 6 mos. **Results:** Girls were somewhat better at abstracting the figures, although the difference was not significant.

Crutchfield, R. S. Conformity and character. *Amer. Psychologist*, 1955, *10*, 191–98.
> **Measures:** Conformity to the judgments of others. S's made decisions on perception and attitudes by flipping a switch in a small cubicle. Each S received false information about the judgments of others. **Subjects:** 59 college undergraduates, 19 male and 40 female. Another study used 50 female college graduates in their 40's. And still another studied 50 professional men. **Results:** Among the college group, women were significantly more conforming. However, the older women were significantly less conforming than the professional men. The men in this study were less selected in I.Q. and professional success than the women. The investigator felt this might be the reason the differences ran in the direction they did among the older subjects.

Cunningham, J. D. Einstellung rigidity in children. *J. exper. child Psychol.*, 1965, *2*, 237–47.
> **Measures:** Water-jar problems and an alphabet maze were administered under standard, no-time-limit conditions, under speed conditions, and under stress conditions (first working on an unsolvable problem). Some of the problems could be solved a short way by breaking the set to solve in a standard fashion. **Subjects:** 734 children between the ages of 7 and 12. **Results:** A nonsignificant trend for boys to be less susceptible to set was found. In ability to overcome set, boys were superior in the water-jar problems under standard conditions. No other sex differences in breaking set were found.

Dahlstrom, W. G., and G. S. Welsh. *An MMPI handbook.* Minneapolis: Univ. of Minnesota Press, 1960.

Measures: The masculinity–femininity scale on the MMPI was standardized on a group of male homosexuals, normal men, and normal women. The items cover five content areas: ego sensitivity, sexual identification, altruism, endorsement of culturally feminine occupations, and rejection of culturally masculine occupations. Twenty-three items on the scale came from the Terman M–F scale, while the rest (37) came from the original MMPI pool.

Davidson, Helen H., and D. Balducci. Class and sex difference in verbal facility of very bright children. *J. educ. Psychol.,* 1956, *47,* 476–80.

Measures: Total number of words, number of unusual words, and number of adjectives and adverbs in responses to 4 Rorschach cards. Subjects: 10 girls and 10 boys of a lower SES group, and 10 boys and 10 girls from upper-middle class. The mean I.Q. for boys was 143, while the mean for girls was 135. Results: No significant differences although boys were superior in all 3 measures. This was probably because boys were higher in I.Q.

Davidson, K. S., and S. B. Sarason. Test anxiety and classroom observations. *Child Develpm.,* 1961, *32,* 199–210.

Measures: Test Anxiety Scale for Children and the Defensiveness Scale for Children (both self-administered). The former measures anxiety about school, the latter, willingness to admit feelings about anxiety, shame, aggression, etc. There were also teacher and observer ratings on personality variables. Subjects: 40 boys and 37 girls in second grade. Results: No differences on the tests are given. The observer reliabilities were higher for boys than for girls. The correlations with personality variables were quite different for the sexes. In total, the TASC was the best predictor of personality for boys, while the DSC was the important predictor for girls. High TASC girls were dependent, didn't hide emotions, were sensitive, and were immature. High TASC boys were independent, hid emotions, had difficulty communicating, were submissive, cautious, ambitious, inactive, *not* underachieving, paid attention, had strong consciences and were responsible. High DSC boys were not sensitive and were forgetful. High DSC girls had difficulty communicating, were not well liked, daydreamed, underachieved, learned slowly, forgot, didn't pay attention, were masculine, and were not responsible.

Davis, Edith A. *The development of linguistic skill in twins, singletons with siblings, and only children from age 5–10 years.* Minneapolis: Univ. of Minnesota Press, 1937.

Measures: Recording of 50 remarks in a play session with an adult. Subjects: Twins, singletons, and only children at ages 5½, 6½, and 9½. The total sample was 436 subjects. Socioeconomic class was distributed among classes. Results: At all ages girls were superior despite the fact that the toys used in the play session were boys' toys. They were superior in articulation, word usage, and length, complexity, and grammatical correctness of sentences. Most of the sex differences were greater for low SES than for upper SES children. No significance tests were given in this study.

Dawe, Helen C. An analysis of 200 quarrels of preschool children. *Child Develpm.,* 1934, *5,* 139–56.

Measures: Observation of free play and recording of why fights were started, who started them, what was the response, how fight was resolved, how children adjusted afterward, and duration of quarrel. Subjects: 19 girls and 21 boys in nursery school, age 25 to 60 months. Results: Boys were involved in more quarrels than girls. Children quarreled more frequently with their own sex.

Day, Ella J. The development of language in twins. I: A comparison of twins and single children. *Child Develpm.*, 1932, *3*, 179–99.

Measures: Recording of 50 responses in room with an adult. Subjects: 80 pairs of twins, ages 2 to 5, with varied socioeconomic backgrounds. The average I.Q. of the subjects was below the general average. Results: Girls used longer sentences at most ages. The differences were greatest at 5 years, second greatest at 2 years. No significance tests were given.

de Jung, J. E., and W. J. Meyer. Expected reciprocity, grade trends, and correlates. *Child Develpm.*, 1963, *34*, 127–39.

Measures: Children rated their peers on how much they would like to have them available to talk to when they were unhappy (need-succorance situation). They then estimated on a similar scale how they thought others would rate them. Subjects: 408 children in grades 5 through 12. Results: There was an age trend toward increasing expectation that others would rate self as self rates the other. At all age levels girls were more likely to expect that a given peer would give them the same rating that they gave the peer. This was true although there was no sex difference in accuracy of guessing how the person would actually rate the child.

DeLucia, Lenore A. The toy-preference test: a measure of sex-role identification. *Child Develpm.*, 1963, *34*, 107–17.

Measures: Toys were presented to college students for rating on a nine-point scale of masculinity–femininity. From these ratings, toys were paired and pictures of them given to children along with a picture of a boy or girl. The child was asked to tell which toy the pictured child would prefer. Toys differing in degree of sex appropriateness were paired. Subjects: 113 children of each sex, ranging in age from kindergarten through 4th grade. Results: There was a progressive increase in choice of sex-appropriate toys for both sexes from kindergarten through 3d grade. In 4th grade there was a slight reversal of the trend. Boys made more sex-appropriate choices at all ages. This difference was small in kindergarten and became larger with age. Sex-by-grade interaction was significant.

Dember, W. N., F. Nairne, and F. J. Miller. Further validation of the Alpert-Haber Achievement Anxiety Test. *J. abnorm. soc. Psychol.*, 1962, *65*, 426–27.

Measures: The Alpert-Haber Achievement Anxiety Scale and the Mandler-Sarason Achievement Anxiety Test were given and correlated with grades in introductory psychology. Subjects: 25 male and 39 female college students. Results: The Alpert-Haber Scale correlated negatively and the Mandler-Sarason Scale correlated positively with course grades for men, but the correlations were not significant for women.

Devereux, E. C., U. Bronfenbrenner, and G. J. Suci. Patterns of parent behavior in the United States of America and the Federal Republic of Germany: a cross-national comparison. *Int. soc. Sci. J.*, 1963, *14*, 2–20.

Measures: A group-administered questionnaire to assess child's perception of parental socialization practices having to do with punishment, responsibility training, and nurturance. Subjects: 40 boys, 32 girls in each country; all were 6th-graders and matched pairs. Results: German children reported more of all kinds of parental behavior than American children. German fathers were more active than American fathers in direct discipline and expression of affection. American mothers were more active in disapproval and pressure for achievement than German mothers. Combining countries, the only sex difference in how parents handle children was deprivation of privileges, with boys receiving more of this treatment. Children received more attention from same-sex parent; this was more marked in the American sample.

DeVore, I., and Phyllis Jay. Mother-infant relations in baboons and langurs. In H. Rheingold (ed.) *Maternal behavior in mammals.* New York: Wiley and Sons, 1963.

Measures: Field observation. Subjects: Separate social groups, one of langurs and one of baboons. Results: In baboons, sexual dimorphism is pronounced, with females ranking well below males in the dominance hierarchy. In langurs, sexual dimorphism is less pronounced, and the status of females is somewhat higher. In baboons, the early infant period is characterized by intense mother-child relations and protection from adult males. The infant has no sibling relationships since females have infants only every two years. There is always a large peer group in which the baboons are socialized. The dominance level of the mother affects the infant's emotional make-up and speed at which it is weaned. The dominant mothers achieve faster weaning. Among langurs, the early mother-infant relation is also very intense. However, adult males are not interested in the infants, and the first contact the male infants have with adult males is at about 10 months. This is a very tense experience for the infant. These animals are socialized by the peer group much as the baboons are. In both baboons and langurs there are sex differences in aggressiveness apparent at about 4 months. Females are less active and more passive in their play activities. In langurs, the juveniles split into separate sex groups for play.

Diggory, J. A. Sex differences in the organization of attitudes. *J. Pers.*, 1953, 22, 89–100.

Measures: 10 Thurstone-type attitude scales on church, war, Negroes, communism, criminals, law, birth control, influence of God on conduct, censorship, and capital punishment. Subjects: 75 male and 103 female college students. Results: Mean differences were significant only on church and God, with females more favorably disposed toward religion. Factor analysis brought out 2 factors with different loadings for the sexes. One of these was a religious factor and the other was nonreligious-social. Attitudes toward war, communism, and law are loaded higher on the religious factor for women than for men. On the whole, intercorrelations were higher for women than for men.

Digman, J. M. Principal dimensions of child personality as inferred from teacher's judgments. *Child Develpm.*, 1963, 34, 43–60.

Measures: Teachers were given an adjective checklist to rate personality traits of their children. The responses were factor-analyzed. Subjects: 102 children of mixed racial composition in grades 1 and 2. Results: 11 first-order factors and 3 second-order factors were extracted. One of the first-order factors was a sex factor. When the factors were intercorrelated, sex correlated with hostility (boys more negativistic, untrustworthy, aggressive, noisy), social confidence (boys more gregarious, confident, and adventurous), and parental harshness (girls' parents more dominating, overprotecting, rejecting). Sex was also the 3d second-order factor.

Douvan, Elizabeth. Independence and identity in adolescence. *Children*, 1957, 4, 186–90.

Measures: Structured 1- to 4-hour interview with each subject. Only the areas of establishing independence and occupational choice are discussed in this article. Subjects: 2 national samples of adolescents. One consisted of 1,045 boys aged 14–16 and the other of 1,925 girls from 10 to 18. Results: Boys were more likely to admit having broken rules, and they were more likely to consider parental rules as external controls rather than to have internalized them. They were likely to consider rules as means of keeping out of trouble, while girls thought of them in terms of guidance and safety. When asked what they would like to change about themselves, boys stressed internal personality changes while girls stressed looks and popularity. Fewer girls than boys had plans for the future that had been worked out in a realistic manner.

Douvan, Elizabeth. Sex differences in adolescent character processes. *Merrill-Palmer Quart.*, 1960, *6*, 203–11.
Measures: Ratings of variables were made from a 4-hour individual interview with each subject. Variables discussed in this article consist of a composite index of internalization of moral standards; an index of development of interpersonal skills and sensitivity as independent variables; and measures of ego development such as energy level, self-confidence, time perspective, achievement, and autonomy as dependent variables. Subjects: Two nationwide surveys of boys and girls, 14–16 years old. Results: Internalization of moral standards predicts a large number of other ego measures in boys but not in girls, while development of interpersonal skills predicts high ego development in girls but not in boys. Thus, for mature ego development, the internalization of standards is more important for boys while the development of interpersonal skills is more important for girls.

Droppleman, L. F., and E. S. Schaefer. Boys' and girls' reports of maternal and paternal behavior. *J. abnorm. soc. Psychol.*, 1963, *67*, 648-54.
Measures: 26 scales describing components of parental nurturance and control were administered to children. Separate forms were used for mothers and fathers. Subjects: 85 boys and 80 girls, 7th-graders in a suburban middle-class parochial school. Results: Mothers were reported significantly higher than fathers on the expression of affection scale, and also on most of the love and nurturance scales. Mothers were higher on scales measuring psychological control for girls and many of those scales for boys. Boys reported fathers higher than mother on the physical-control variables of punishment and strictness. Girls rated parents equal on these scales. Boys reported fathers higher than mothers on hostility scales of nagging and irritability, while girls reported parents equal. Girls reported fathers higher than mothers on neglect and ignoring, while boys reported parents equal. Both sexes clearly described the opposite-sex parent as granting more autonomy (Extreme Autonomy and Lax Discipline scales). Sex differences in overall reporting: girls reported more love and nurturance from both parents than boys did. Both boys and girls received equal amounts of psychological control from mothers, but boys received more from father than girls did. Boys received more physical control, hostility, neglect, and ignoring from both parents.

Duggan, Lucy. An experiment on immediate recall in secondary school children, *Brit. J. Psychol.*, 1950, *40*, 149–54.
Measures: 3 tests of immediate recall: numbers, words, and objects. In each case each item was presented separately, and 11 or 12 were shown altogether. The child wrote down all he had seen or heard. Subjects: 106 boys and 117 girls, 14–16 years old, in Britain. Results: Girls were better at object and word memory, while boys were better at numbers. Within the sexes, girls were better at words and objects than they were at numbers. Boys did equally well at numbers and words.

Dunsdon, M. I., and J. A. Fraser-Roberts. A study of the performance of 2,000 children on four vocabulary tests. *Brit. J. stat. Psychol.*, 1957, *10*, 1–16.
Measures: Four oral vocabulary tests from WISC, Terman-Merrill Intelligence Test, and Mill Hill A and B Vocabulary Scales. Subjects: A random sample (3%) of all the children age 5–15 in Bristol, England. Total sample of 2,000. Results: At all ages, boys' norms were about one word higher than girls' norms. When all 4 tests were combined, boys' norms at age 5 were 19 words, girls' 16. At age 7, boys' norms were 33 words, girls' 30. At age 9, boys averaged 46 and girls 43 words. At age 11 boys averaged 58 and girls 55 words, and at age 14 yrs. 11 mos. boys averaged 81 words and girls 75.

Durrett, Mary E. The relationship of early infant regulation and later behavior in play interviews. *Child Develpm.*, 1959, *30*, 211–16.

> Measures: Observation of doll play in the manner of P. S. Sears. Subjects: 60 children, 4–6 years. All professional families. Results: Boys significantly higher in total aggression. Boys higher in physical aggression (p = .01). Girls higher in verbal aggression (p = .01).

Edgerton, H. A., and S. H. Britt. Technical aspects of the fourth annual Science Talent Search. *Educ. Psychol. Meas.*, 1947, *7*, 3–21.

> Measures: Science Aptitude Examination. Subjects: 1,970 boys and 776 girls in high school completed all of the data necessary for the contest. Results: Girls' scores on the exam were significantly lower than boys', despite the greater selectivity.

Edmonds, W. S. Differences in the verbal ability of socioeconomically depressed groups. *J. educ. Res.*, 1964, *58*, 61–64.

> Measures: SCAT Verbal Ability scores. Subjects: 1,239 11th-grade students from economically depressed schools, lower-class and lower-middle-class families. Results: No overall sex differences in verbal skill, and no difference between sexes within social class.

Eichorn, Dorothy H., and Nancy Bayley. Growth in head circumference from birth through young adulthood. *Child Develpm.*, 1962, *33*, 257–71.

> Measures: Repeated measurements of head circumference from birth to 29 years. Subjects: 37 boys and 37 girls from the Berkeley Growth Study. Results: The mean head circumference was greater for males at all ages. The rate of increase was greater for males up to 15 months, and for females from 15 months to 12 years. Circumference increases for a longer period in males than in females, continuing at least until 21 years.

Emmerich, W. Parental identification in young children. *Genet. Psychol. Monogr.*, 1959, *60*, 257–308.

> Measures: Questionnaires to parents and interview sessions with children. The children were given a structured doll-play session in which a doll representing the child was presented in company with a mother or father doll. The child was asked how the parent would respond to the child, and the response was rated on a nurturance-control scale. Then the parent doll was replaced by a baby doll, and the subject was asked to tell E how the child doll would react to the baby's behavior. This also was rated on nurturance-control. The measure of child's identification with a parent was the similarity of child's response to baby, and the subject's perception of the parent's response to him. Subject: 31 children in nursery school aged 3 yrs. 7 mos. to 5 yrs. 1 mo. The children had no siblings. Results: Boys significantly more often selected the like-sex parent for identification, while the difference was not significant for girls. Boys saw fathers as more controlling and mothers as more nurturant, but the difference in child's perception of his two parents was not significant for girls. Boys increased significantly in their own controlling behavior with age, but girls did not. From parent questionnaires there was a slight but not significant tendency for mothers to be more nurturant, and fathers more controlling, with daughters than with sons.

Emmerich, W. Variations in the parent role as a function of the parent's sex and the child's sex and age. *Merrill-Palmer Quart.*, 1962, *8*, 1–11.

> Measures: Questionnaires to parents to assess the amount of nurturance (reward for positive behavior and dependency) and restrictiveness (punishment for negative behavior) they show toward children. The two were combined as a measure of power. Subjects: Middle-class parents with children age 6–10. Results: Mothers were more nurturant and less restrictive toward all children. Parents exerted more power toward like-sex children.

Emmett, W. C. Evidence of a space factor at 11 and earlier. *Brit. J. Psychol., Stat. Sec.,* 1949, *2,* 3–16.

Measures: Moray House Space Test, which requires spatial judgment of 2- and 3-dimensional figures. Also a verbal I.Q. test given to some of the sample. Subjects: About 4,000 girls and 4,000 boys in England, aged about 10 to 11½. Results: Boys were significantly better at space, more so in 3-dimensional than 2-dimensional tasks; girls were slightly superior in verbal I.Q. tests.

Erickson, E. H. Sex differences in the play configurations of pre-adolescents. *Amer. J. Orthopsychiat.,* 1951, *21,* 667–92.

Measures: Children were asked to construct a scene from an exciting movie. Blocks, toy furniture, cars, and dolls were presented to them. Subjects: 157 11-year-olds, 161 12-year-olds, and 150 13-year-olds. Children were from the California Guidance Study. Results: Use of play space was analyzed. Boys' play constructions were characterized by the use of height and downfall, motion and its channelization or arrest; girls built static interiors that were open, simply enclosed, or blocked and intruded upon. Boys emphasized the outdoors, girls the indoors. The differences were interpreted from a psychoanalytic viewpoint in terms of body imagery and psychosexual development.

Eron, L. D. Relationship of TV viewing habits and aggressive behavior in children. *J. abnorm. soc. Psychol.,* 1963, *67,* 193–96.

Measures: Mothers and fathers reported how much S watched TV and what his favorite programs were. Programs were rated for aggressiveness by independent raters. S's aggressiveness was measured by a reputation test in which classmates reported who in the class was aggressive. Subjects: 277 boys and 245 girls whose fathers were interviewed, and 875 children whose mothers were interviewed. All were 3d-graders. Results: Boys who preferred aggressive TV shows were significantly more aggressive than boys who preferred low-aggressive shows. In boys, length of time watching TV was negatively related to aggression. There were no significant relationships between TV habits and aggression for girls.

Eron, L. D., L. O. Walder, R. Toigo, and M. M. Lefkowitz. Social class, parental punishment for aggression, and child aggression. *Child Develpm.,* 1963, *34,* 849–67.

Measures: Reputation test to measure aggression. Interviews with both parents to assess degree and type of punishment for aggression. Occupational index of SES to divide sample into high, medium, and low SES groups. Subjects: 206 girls and 245 boys in 3d grade. Results: Aggression of child was positively related to punishment for aggression. Upper-class children were more aggressive than lower-class. Social class interacted with father's punishment, so that only when SES was held constant did father's punishment lead to greater aggressiveness. Mother's punishment overrode SES and did not interact. Low SES girls were more severely punished for aggression to peers than high SES girls. There was no SES difference for aggression to parents.

Exline, R. V. Effects of need for affiliation, sex, and the sight of others upon initial communications in problem-solving groups. *J. Pers.,* 1962, *30,* 541–56.

Measures: Groups of S's were picked on the basis of n. affiliation on the French Insight Test. They were put in groups with a task to do, and allowed to communicate only by notes. Some groups could see all members of the group, and others were isolated. They had the choice of giving and receiving personal or task-relevant information. Subjects: 16 groups of 3 men and 16 groups of 3 women. All were college students. Half of the groups were made up of n. affiliation, and half low n. affiliation persons. Results: Women significantly more often chose to give personal information as the first communication, and this was more true in visible groups than in non-visible groups. N. affiliation was not significantly related to this variable.

Exline, R. V. Explorations in the process of person perception: visual interaction in relation to competition, sex, and need for affiliation. *J. Pers.*, 1963, *31*, 1–20.
Measures: N. affiliation was measured by the French Insight Test. Competition was manipulated by having members of 3-man groups try to persuade the others to adopt their views or just discuss without choosing. During the discussion observers recorded the instances in which 2 of the subjects looked each other directly in the eye. Subjects: All groups were adults. There were 16 three-man groups of each sex, half of which were high n. affiliation and half low. Each of those was divided into high or low competition conditions. Thus there were 4 cells in the analysis of variance. Results: Women interacted visually significantly more than men. N. affiliation did not have a significant main effect. High n. affiliation subjects interacted less under high competition than under low competition, and this finding was reversed for low n. affiliation subjects. This interaction effect was much greater for women than for men.

Exline, R., D. Gray, and Dorothy Schuette. Visual behavior in a dyad as affected by interview content and sex of respondent. *J. Pers. soc. Psychol.*, 1965, *1*, 201–9.
Measures: S was interviewed by a male or female interviewer under conditions of embarrassment (E asked personal questions) or neutral affect (neutral questions). Some S's were told to try to conceal their real feelings and others were not so instructed. E maintained eye contact with S at all times. The amount of time S met E's glance and maintained mutual eye contact was measured. Subjects: Women and men in college: 40 S's of each sex. Results: Women maintained eye contact significantly more often than men under all conditions.

Farnsworth, P. R. The effects of role-taking on artistic achievement. *J. Aesthetics art Criticism*, 1960, *18*, 345–49.
Measures: A questionnaire asking subjects to judge whether activities having to do with the arts were masculine or feminine interests. Different types of music, art, sculpture, literature, drama, and ballet were included, and in each field activities were specified as appreciating, performing, or creating the art form. Subjects: 103 men and 86 women college undergraduates. Results: Jazz was judged the most masculine and ballet the most feminine activity. In general, both sexes agreed that the performance and appreciation aspects of the arts are more feminine, the creative aspects more masculine.

Fauls, Lydia B., and W. D. Smith. Sex-role learning of 5-year-olds. *J. genet. Psychol.*, 1956, *89*, 105–17.
Measures: Presentation of 3 sets of paired pictures; each set depicted a child of the same sex as the subject doing a masculine activity and a feminine activity. Each S was asked to tell his own activity preference, what the mother of the child preferred him to do, and what the child's father preferred. Subjects: Middle-class children, age 4 yrs. 9 mos. to 5 yrs. 9 mos. Some S's were only children, others had siblings. Results: Both sexes chose sex-appropriate activities more often than inappropriate activities. Boys' preferences corresponded more to perceived paternal preferences than girls' preferences did to fathers' preferences, but there was no sex difference in similarity of perceived maternal preference and child's preference. Only children chose sex-appropriate behavior more often than children with older like-sexed siblings.

Feldhusen, J. F., and T. Denny. Teachers' and children's perceptions of creativity in high- and low-anxious children. *J. educ. Res.* 1965, *58*, 442–47.
Measures: General Anxiety Scale for Children was administered to 77 S's, and high- and low-anxious children were picked from this. These groups then took a check-list test measuring self-perception of creative interests. Teachers rated S's on the scale as well, and S's were given 5 paper-and-pencil tests measuring divergent thinking skills. Subjects: 20 high- and 20 low-anxious children, half boys and half girls, in grades 7,

8, and 9. Results: Girls were more anxious than boys. There were no differences between the sexes on the divergent thinking tests. Low-anxious girls rated themselves as significantly less creative than high-anxious girls or either group of boys. Teachers rated low-anxious boys as significantly more creative than any of the other three groups.

Feshbach, S. The catharsis hypothesis and some consequences of interaction with aggressive and neutral play objects. *J. Pers.*, 1956, *24*, 449–62.
Measures: (1) Teachers' ratings of aggressiveness (high- and low-aggressive boys and girls were categorized on this basis). (2) Observer ratings of aggressiveness during free play—rated as thematic, fantasy, or peer-directed. Subjects: 30 boys and 31 girls ranging from 5 to 8 years. The children were from high socioeconomic levels and had high I.Q.'s. Results: Boys were significantly higher than girls on teachers' ratings of aggression. High- and low-aggressive boys and girls were put into groups; some groups were given aggressive toys and told aggressive stories, and others were given neutral toys and stories. Aggressive-toy groups showed more inappropriate (nonthematic) aggressive play than did neutral-toy groups. Sex differences on observations were not reported. After four 50-minute sessions of play, teachers rated the children again. On a cathartic hypothesis, the high-aggressive children should show less aggression. This was not confirmed. However, the low-aggressive boys were rated higher on aggression after aggressive play sessions. This did not occur for girls.

Fischer, J. L. Typical dreams in Japanese children. Paper delivered at annual meeting, Amer. Anthro. Assn., Chicago, 1962.
Measures: A dream questionnaire in which S was asked if he could remember having a dream on 32 different themes. Subjects: 465 boys and 438 girls who took the questionnaire at school, and 40 boys and 43 girls who took it at home. Average age was about 12. Results: Boys in school reported more dreams interpreted as indicating anxiety than did those taking the test at home. Girls taking the test at school reported fewer anxiety dreams than the "at home" girls. The investigator suggests that girls are more confined and criticized at home than boys, who are favored by the culture. At school the sexes are treated the same. Thus school is less anxiety-provoking than home for girls, more so for boys.

Fisher, G. M., T. R. Risley, and A. B. Silverstein. Sex differences in the performance of mental retardates on the Wechsler Adult Intelligence Scale. *J. clin. Psychol.*, 1961, *17*, 170.
Measures: Wechsler Adult Intelligence Scale. Subjects: 400 mental retardates, aged 16 to 64. Results: When compared with the standardization sample, 3 of the original sex differences did not appear: arithmetic, digit symbol, and block design.

Fisher, S. Sex differences in body perception. *Psychol. Monogr.*, 1964, *78*, N. 14.
Measures: Ability to tolerate aniseikonically induced distortions in the appearance of the body was measured. Skin resistance of different parts of the body and Barrier and Penetration scores from the Rorschach were used as measures of definitiveness of body boundaries. A Body Prominence score was reached by asking S to name 10 things presently in his awareness and counting the body parts involved. A body-focus questionnaire asked S to report how clearly he was aware of different parts of his body. S reported how his image looked when distorted by a mask of the opposite sex. Subjects: Multiple groups of college students. Results: Women perceived less aniseikonically induced distortion in their legs, and hence were considered more anxious about their legs than men. No other differences were found. Women had higher Rorschach Barrier scores, and hence had more definite body boundaries. Men were more disturbed than women by changes caused by the opposite-sex mask.

Fishman, J. A. *1957 supplement to College Board scores, No. 2.* New York: College Entrance Examination Board, 1957.
Measures: Scholastic Aptitude Test. Subjects: High school subjects tested during the academic year 1956–57. The number tested ranged in the thousands. Results: Boys were superior on math and girls on verbal. Boys averaged about 55 points higher than girls on the math norms, while girls averaged about 8 to 10 points higher on the verbal section. Because of the large N's, all differences were significant.

Fitt, A. B., and C. A. Rogers. The sex factor in the Cattell Intelligence Tests, Scale III. *Brit. J. Psychol.*, 1950, *41*, 186–92.
Measures: Cattell Intelligence Tests, Scale III. Subjects: 641 college students. Results: Significant differences in mean I.Q. in favor of girls were found. The material on the test is primarily verbal.

Flory, C. D. Sex differences in skeletal development. *Child Develpm.*, 1935, *6*, 205–12.
Measures: Roentgenograms of 6,500 subjects from birth to maturity. Results: Growth rates were related to sex. Girls were more mature at birth, 1 year ahead at school age, 1½ years ahead at age 9, and 2 years ahead at the average age of onset of puberty. High school girls were two years ahead of boys in skeletal development. Girls were also ahead in physiological maturity, dentation, acquisition of locomotor ability, onset of procreative ability, and completion of physical growth.

Franck, Kate, and E. Rosen. A projective test of masculinity-femininity. *J. consult. Psychol.*, 1949, *13*, 247–56.
In this test, S is given a series of incomplete drawings to finish. The finished drawings are then rated according to masculinity or femininity. Men expand the stimulus outward, build it upward, emphasize angles, rely on strength of simple lines, and prefer oneness. Women leave the stimulus area open, elaborate within the area, draw round or blunt shapes, and prefer twosomes. These differences are interpreted in terms of sexual function and body characteristics.

French, J. W. *A study of emotional states aroused during examinations.* College Entrance Examination Board, Research and Development Reports. R.B.-61-6, March, 1961.
Measures: The SAT was administered with the usual instructions to some subjects, and with more relaxed instructions to others, to determine the effect of test conditions on performance. Subjects: About 300 high school seniors. Results: For girls there was a slight but significant improvement in math scores relative to verbal scores in the anxiety situation, while this condition did not affect boys' scores.

Gainer, W. L. The ability of the WISC subjects to discriminate between boys and girls of average intelligence. *Calif. J. educ. Res.*, 1962, *13*, 9–16.
Measures: Wechsler Intelligence Scale for Children. Subjects: 100 boys and 100 girls between ages of 6 and 12. I.Q.'s ranged from 90 to 109. Results: Neither full-scale, verbal, nor performance scores showed sex differences. Comprehension showed significant differences in favor of boys, while coding was significant in favor of girls. No other subtest gave sex differences that were significant. These other tests were: information, arithmetic, similarities, vocabulary, digit span, picture completion, picture arrangement, block design, object assembly, and mazes.

Gallagher, J. J., and Mary Jane Aschner. A preliminary report on analyses of classroom interaction. *Merrill-Palmer Quart.*, 1963, *9*, 183–93.
Measures: Tape recordings were made of 5 consecutive sessions in 12 classes of in-

tellectually superior children. At each session, 2 observers took extensive notes on classroom activities; thought units in these sessions were scored for cognitive memory, convergent thinking, divergent thinking, and evaluative thinking. Subjects: Junior high school students in 12 classes of intellectually superior children. In this report, 10 boys and 9 girls from one social studies classroom are studied. Results: Boys were consistently more fluent verbally in all expressive areas. In divergent thinking and in total production the difference between boys and girls was significant at the .10 level, and in the other 3 areas the significance level approximated .10. The proportion of total interaction falling in each of the four areas was similar in boys and girls.

Gansl, Irene. Vocabulary: its measurement and growth. *Arch. Psychol.*, 1939, No. 236.
Measures: A 100-item vocabulary test. This study reports the standardizing test data. Subjects: The population of two New York City schools (about 600 subjects), grades 3–8. Results: Boys slightly but fairly consistently outperformed girls at each grade level. Boys did better in 10 out of 14 comparisons made.

Gardner, D. B., and M. K. Swiger. Developmental status of two groups of infants released for adoption. *Child Develpm.*, 1958, *29*, 521–30.
Measures: Calif. Infant Scale for Motor Development and Gesell Developmental Schedules. Subjects: 128 infants ranging in age from 4 to 92 days, with a mean age of 31.6 days. Results: Boys exceeded girls at the .05 level in overall length and in head circumference, and at the .10 level in weight. The other measures favored males but were not significant.

Gardner, R. W., et al. Cognitive control. *Psychol. Issues*, 1959, *1*, No. 4.
Measures: A battery of tests was given to measure 6 different cognitive control functions. Subjects: 30 male and 30 female adults. The average age of women was 27.4, and of men 23.7. This was a significant difference in age. Results: Significant differences were found on the Rod and Frame Test, the Embedded Figures Test (these two in favor of men), the Picture Sorting Test, the Object Sorting Test, and the Apparent Movement Test. The direction of differences on the last 3 tests was not given. Factor analysis was done separately by sex. The correlations for women were generally higher than for men. Factor structure differed for the sexes.

Gardner, R. W., et al. The stability and generality of cognitive attitudes. Final Progress Report, 1961.
Measures: Object-sorting task, with degree of abstraction of categories scored. Subjects: 10 boys and 10 girls, age 9 yrs. to 10 yrs. 9 mos., from Kansas, and 18 boys and 11 girls of the same age and socioeconomic level from Mexico. Results: No differences in level of abstraction in the Kansas study, but girls were significantly lower in preferred level of abstraction in the Mexican sample.

Gatewood, M. C., and A. P. Weiss. Race and sex differences in newborn infants. *J. Genet. Psychol.*, 1930, *38*, 31–49.
Measures: Observation of body movements under control and stimulus conditions (light, sound, holding the nose). Subjects: 78 infants, 0–10 days old: 16 male whites, 20 female whites, 20 male Negroes, and 16 female Negroes. Results: (1) Males were less active than females. (2) Under stimulus conditions males increased the amount of respiratory changes (rapid breathing, sighing, etc.) over the control-condition rates much more than females (white male 364%, Negro male 331%, Negro female 122%, white female 148%). (3) Vocalization was greater in females. (4) Body jerking was more frequent among males.

Gellert, Elizabeth. Power relationships of young children. *J. abnorm. soc. Psychol.*, 1961, *62*, 8-15.

Measures: Observation of dominance, submission, and resistance to domination in play between 2 children. Each dyad was homogeneous with respect to sex. Subjects: Nursery school children. Results: Girls initiated more of all three types of acts during the three 20-minute play sessions. The sex difference was not significant.

Gesell, A., et al. *The first 5 years of life.* New York: Harper, 1940.

Measures: Gesell Developmental Scales. Subjects: Standardizing population, age birth to 5 years. Results: Walking boards (age 3–6)—girls walked more slowly and made more errors. Throwing—boys showed superiority as early as 3½, and by 5 years were clearly advanced in stance and throwing. Block building—at 18 months boys built more blocks in a vertical direction than girls, while girls built more blocks horizontally. However, differences in block building dropped out when the task was definitely assigned. There were no differences on the Kuhlman-Terman Geometric Form Recognition Tests or other form-recognition tests. In drawing a man, girls included more details than boys, and the same was true of the incomplete-man drawing test. Girls were better at drawing a circle at 18 months and 2 years, but there were no differences on drawing a cross. Counting—girls counted higher and erred less at ages 2–6. Girls developed earlier in aesthetic sense (on the aesthetic comparison test). Comparison of weights—boys were superior. Naming pictures—girls named more pictures than boys at 18 months, but by 3 years this difference dropped out. Tells sex—girls were a little more likely to say they were boys. Girls dressed themselves at a younger age.

Getzels, J. W., and J. J. Walsh. The method of paired direct and projective questionnaires in the study of attitude structure and socialization. *Psychol. Monogr.*, 1958, *72*, No. 1.

Measures: S's completed sentences written in the third person, and after a time interval completed the same sentences written in the first person. Areas of content were family, personal, and social attitudes. The measure was the difference in number of socially unacceptable attitudes endorsed in the first and third person. Subjects: 428 boys and 485 girls, aged 8 to 13, from various social classes; 11% of the sample was Negro. Results: Children gave more socially acceptable responses when the sentences were written in the first person, and this discrepancy increased with age. Girls showed greater discrepancy than boys. Boys had more unacceptable attitudes in their personal protocols than girls.

Gewirtz, J. L., and D. M. Baer. Deprivation and satiation of social reinforcers as drive conditions. *J. abnorm. soc. Psychol.*, 1958, *57*, 165–72.

Measures: Effectiveness of social reinforcers on changing behavior during a game after social deprivation, satiation, and neither of these. Deprivation meant leaving the child alone for 20 minutes. Subjects: 102 middle-class children from 1st and 2d grade. Results: No sex differences in the effects of the independent variable. Also no difference due to S-E cross-sex interaction (only a female E was used).

Gewirtz, J. L., et al. A note on the similar effects of low social availability of an adult and brief social deprivation on young children. *Child Develpm.*, 1958, *29*, 149–52.

Measures: Experiment No. 1: Number of dependency bids made by children while painting, under high and low availablity of an adult. No. 2: Amount of behavior change observed in children playing a game, with (1) social reinforcement after 20 minutes of social deprivation, and (2) no deprivation. Subjects: 4–6-year-olds in the first study, 3–6-year-olds in the second study. Results: In both studies the difference between conditions (that is, greater effect of social reinforcement after deprivation) was greater for cross-sex E–S combinations, especially for boys. The rank order of differences was boys with women, girls with men, girls with women, boys with men. The only significant change in behavior after deprivation was boys with women E's.

Gill, Lois J., and B. Spilka. Some nonintellectual correlates of academic achievement among Mexican-American secondary school students. *J. educ. Psychol.,* 1962, *53,* 144–49.

Measures: A modification of Shoben's Parent Attitude Survey was given to parents; Gough's CPI, the Siegel Manifest Hostility Scale, and the Jewell Anxiety Adaptation Scale were given to S's. Subjects: 15 boys and 15 girls in each of 2 groups—overachievers and underachievers. All were Mexican-Americans in junior and senior high school, matched on I.Q. (between 90 and 110), age, grade, and sex. Results: High-achieving girls and low-achieving boys tended to come from mother-dominated homes. Boys were significantly higher on manifest hostility and girls were significantly higher on conformity achievement (conforming to rules). The sex difference on conformity came within the high-achieving group. There was no difference between the sexes in the low-achieving groups.

Goda, S., and B. C. Griffith. Spoken language of adolescent retardates and its relation to intelligence, age, and anxiety. *Child Develpm.,* 1962, *33,* 489–98.

Measures: A set of 25 pictures was used to elicit verbal responses. The subject made one response to each picture. The responses were scored for sentence length, completeness, and type. WISC I.Q. and CMAS were also given. Subjects: 106 adolescents aged 13 to 21. All were residents of institutions for retardates. I.Q.'s ranged from 45 to 85. Results: Girls tended to be more advanced than boys in language, although this was significant only in tense variability. Girls were more anxious than boys.

Goldstein, M. The relationship between coping and avoiding behavior and responses to fear-arousing propaganda. *J. abnorm. soc. Psychol.,* 1959, *58,* 247–52.

Measures: Sentence Completion Test to pick subjects with specific stress reactions. S's were given a sentence stem with sexual or aggressive implications and asked to complete the sentence. High scores were obtained by giving a highly emotion-charged or personal-reference ending to the sentence. Such people are called copers (with anxiety material), while those who deny the emotional implications are called avoiders. These groups were then subjected to highly threatening and neutral propaganda. Subjects: 350 freshman in high school. Avoiders and copers were selected separately for each sex. Results: There were significant differences in both mean and standard deviation in favor of women. Women were more likely to give an emotional response and were more variable in responses. There was no difference between the sexes on susceptibility to persuasion.

Gollin, E. S. Organizational characteristics of social judgment: a developmental investigation. *J. Pers.,* 1958, *26,* 139–54.

Measures: S's were shown a silent movie of a boy in 4 situations. In 2 situations he did something ethically "good," and in 2 he was bad. The children were asked to tell about the boy and what they thought of him. The children's descriptions were then rated to determine the number of attempts made to integrate diverse behavior into an explanatory concept. Subjects: 712 boys and girls in 3 age ranges: 10 yrs., 13 yrs., and 16 yrs. I.Q. ranged from 80 to 135. Results: At the upper 2 age groups, girls tended to make more inferences and give more explanatory concepts than boys did. At 10, less than 5% of the children attempted to make inference of concepts.

Goodenough, Evelyn W. Interest in persons as an aspect of sex differences in the early years. *Genet. psychol. Monogr.,* 1957, *55,* 287–323.

Measures: Parent interviews, the drawings of children who were asked to make something, and spontaneous remarks made by children while playing a mosaics game. Subjects: 40 children from the Gesell nursery school, age 2–4. All upper SES. Results: Girls drew more persons and mentioned them more than boys. Parents were concerned about having children sex-typed, and fathers were more concerned than mothers. Boys were reported sex-typed earlier than girls (i.e., opposed to girls' occupations) by parents. Parents expected girls to be more interested in persons than boys. The following traits were sex-typed by parents: for boys, masculine interests, masculine expressive movements (e.g., a swagger), aggression, obstinacy, power, and suppression of emotion; for girls, feminine interests, feminine expressive movements, gentleness, submission, sensitivity and emotion, social awareness, coquetry, and affection.

Goodenough, Florence L. The emotional behavior of young children during mental tests. *J. Juv. Res.*, 1929, *13*, 204–19.
Measures: Testers rated children on shyness, negativism, and distractibility during standard mental tests. Lack of shyness meant leaving mother and coming willingly to be tested. Subjects: 990 children, 13 months to 6 years, from various social classes. Results: No sex differences for the group as a whole. However, the trend of improvement with age in all variables started at a later age in boys than it did in girls. Girls started improving at 18 months, boys not until 30 months. Lower-class boys were the least shy of all.

Goodstein, L. D., and L. Goldberger. Manifest anxiety and Rorschach performance in a chronic patient population. *J. consult. Psychol.*, 1955, *19*, 339–44.
Measures: Taylor Manifest Anxiety Scale. Subjects: 84 male and 55 female institutionalized psychiatric patients with various disorders. Results: Women were significantly more anxious than men in all diagnostic categories.

Goolishian, H. A., and A. Foster. A note on sex differences on the W-B Tests. *J. clin. Psychol.*, 1954, *10*, 298–99.
Measures: W–B Test, Form I. Subjects: 190 males and 202 females, average age about 30. Outpatients in a psychiatric clinic. Results: The males had a mean I.Q. 5 points higher than the females, a difference significant at the .01 level. All of the differences on the test favored males except digit symbol. Of the others, comprehension, digit span, arithmetic, picture completion, block design, verbal I.Q. and performance I.Q. were significant. Arithmetic and verbal I.Q. were the largest differences.

Gordon, J. E., and E. Smith. Children's aggression, parental attitudes, and the effects of an affiliation-arousing story. *J. Pers. soc. Psychol.*, 1965, *1*, 654–59.
Measures: S engaged in structured doll play before and after being read a story aimed at arousing affiliation motivation. In the doll play, S's doll was frustrated and challenged by another doll, and the amount of aggressive response was measured. Mothers of all S's were interviewed to determine maternal strictness, permissiveness for aggression, and use of physical punishment. Subjects: 24 nursery school children, and 24 children aged 6–7. Results: Affiliation arousal decreased aggression in the younger children but not in 6–7-year-olds. Boys displayed more aggression than girls in the first doll play session. No sex differences are given for the second session. Mothers of girls and boys did not differ in permissiveness for aggression, general strictness, or use of physical punishment. Strictness of mother was positively correlated with aggression in girls and negatively related to aggression in boys. Parental permissiveness for aggression was associated with low aggression in girls only if the girls were physically punished; this relationship was not found for boys. The more strict a girl's mother, the more aggressive the girl if she was physically punished. Strict mothers led to nonaggressive sons, especially if they were not physically punished.

Gough, H. G. Identifying psychological femininity. *Educ. psychol. Measmt.*, 1952, *12*, 427–39.

Measures: Gough Femininity Scale. Results: The items were made up to have minimum face validity and maximum empirical validity. The scale has 58 items falling into the following areas: (1) acceptance of traditional occupational roles and hobbies and acceptance of clean white-collar work, (2) social sensitivity, (3) timidity in both social and physical situations, (4) compassion and sympathy, (5) lack of interest in the abstract political and social world, (6) lack of braggadoccio and hyperbole, (7) pettiness and irritability, (8) niceness and acquiescence.

Gray, Susan W. Masculinity-femininity in relation to anxiety and social acceptance. *Child Develpm.*, 1957, *28*, 203–14.

Measures: (1) A masculinity-femininity measure on which classmates rated each other on a 5-point scale from very ladylike to tomboy for girls and very masculine to unmasculine for boys. (2) A reputation test to get at social acceptance in 5 areas: leadership, practical intelligence, aggression, withdrawal, and popularity. (3) The CMAS. Subjects: 34 boys and 27 girls in 6th and 7th grades in a laboratory school. The subjects were mostly high in social class. Results: High anxiety was associated with appropriate sex-typing in both sexes. In the 5 social-acceptance categories there was a tendency toward greater social acceptance with high masculine sex-typing in boys, but appropriate sex-typing in girls did not lead to more social acceptance, and it sometimes led to less acceptance. This tendency was seen in 3 of the categories. Practical intelligence and aggression had no significant relationships with sex-typing.

Gray, Susan W. Perceived similarity to parents and adjustment. *Child Develpm.* 1959, *30*, 91–107.

Measures: Osgood's adjective-pairs rating of self, mother, and father were used to assess perceived similarity. This was the measure of identification. Measures of adjustment were (1) a who-are-they test of reputation with peers, and (2) a masculinity-femininity scale on which peers rank one another. Subjects: Upper-middle-class boys and girls in 5th through 8th grade. Results: Perceived similarity to father went with favorable acceptance by peers in boys, but girls who identified with mother were seen less favorably.

Gray, Susan W., and R. Klaus. The assessment of parental identification. *Genetic psychol. Monogr.*, 1956, *54*, 87–114.

Measures: Allport-Vernon-Lindsey Study of Values as filled out by self, as father would, as mother would; mother and father also filled it out. Subjects: 34 women and 28 men from a southern college. Results: Greater similarities, both tested and perceived, were found between child and like-sexed parent. Women were more like mothers than sons were like fathers, bost tested and perceived.

Green, Elise H. Friendships and quarrels among preschool children. *Child Develpm.*, 1933, *4*, 236–52.

Measures: Behavioral observation of children's free play, particularly quarrels and friendships. Subjects: 40 nursery school children. Results: Boys quarreled more than girls. Boy-boy interaction led to most quarrels, boy-girl next, and girl-girl least.

Greenstein, F. I. Sex-related political differences in childhood. *J. Politics*, 1961, *23*, 353–71.

Measures: A questionnaire about political knowledge and interest was administered. Subjects: 337 boys and 332 girls in 4th through 8th grades. Results: Girls tended to know less about politics and be less interested in it. Both sexes were more likely to ask father than mother for advice on politics. There were no differences between boys and girls on questions of whether they planned to vote and be involved in civic activities when they grew up.

Grinder, R. E. Parental child-rearing practices, conscience, and resistance to temptation of 6th grade children. *Child Develpm.*, 1962, *33*, 803–20.
Measures: Interviews with mothers about child-rearing techniques and observation of children's behavior from the Sears, *Patterns of child rearing* study. At the age of 11–12, the children played a target-shooting game in which they tallied their own scores to try to earn a prize. Whether the child resisted the temptation to cheat in order to get a prize was observed. Subjects: 70 boys and 70 girls, aged 11 and 12 from the original Sears sample. Results: Mothers' reports on child's conscience development at age 5 were positively correlated with resistance to temptation at age 12. In particular, resistance to temptation was correlated with voluntary confession of transgression at age 5 in girls and with confession on questioning in boys. Earlier child-rearing antecedents of resistance to temptation in boys were: high standards of neatness and orderliness, and high standards of obedience. In girls the correlates were more specific: pressures in weaning, bowel training, and sex training.

Grinder, R. E. Relations between behavioral and cognitive dimensions of conscience in middle childhood. *Child Develpm.*, 1964, *35*, 881–91.
Measures: Piaget's questions measuring moral realism and immanent justice (immature forms of moral development) were administered, and children were put in an experimental setting to observe conformity to rules and resistance to temptation. They were asked to play a shooting game alone, with "M-and-M's" the reward for a certain score. Scores had to be falsified to receive any candy. Subjects: 106 boys and girls from 2nd, 4th, and 6th grades. Results: There was no sex differences on any of the measures. Moral realism and immanent justice were associated with younger children of both sexes. Resistance to temptation was not related to age, and conformity to rules was related only in girls, with older girls following rules better.

Grinder, R. E., and Judith C. Spector. Sex differences in adolescents' perceptions of parental resource control. *J. genet. Psychol.*, 1965, *106*, 337–44.
Measures: S's reported whether they felt mother or father was more in control of resources generally desirable to teenagers. Subjects: 19 boys and 19 girls from each of three grades, 9, 10, and 12. Results: Boys were more likely to see father as controller of resources, while girls were more likely to see mother as controller.

Guetzkow, H. An analysis of the operation of set in problem-solving behavior. *J. genet. Psychol.*, 1951, *45*, 219–44.
Measures: A set of problems that required a complex method of solution was presented. This set was followed by similar problems in which either the same complex method or a simpler solution was possible. The number of complex solutions used on these problems was a measure of susceptibility to set. Then a final problem, which could only be solved by the simple method, was given to measure ability to overcome set. A similar analysis was made of the Maier 2-string problem. Subjects: College students. Results: There was no sex difference in susceptibility to set, but men were significantly superior to women in ability to overcome set.

Haan, Norma. The relationship of ego functioning and intelligence to social status and social mobility. *J. abnorm. soc. Psychol.*, 1964, *69*, No. 6, 594–605.
Measures: Ratings were made on the basis of intensive interviews with subjects in a longitudinal study. Also, childhood and adult social-status ratings were available. Subjects: 49 men, 50 women, about 37 years of age at time of latest measurement. Results: For both men and women, upward mobility was positively associated with ability to make appropriate provisions for impulse control. However, men controlled

and modulated impulse (substitution and suppression), while women expressed impulse (sublimation). Male's impulse control was further elaborated by interpersonal empathy and capacity to tolerate ambiguities. Female mobility was related to individualistic expressiveness or to coping cognitively. Regression was found highly incompatible with upward mobility for men. The presence or absence of defense mechanisms was not an important associate of mobility of women. Intelligence was moderately predictive of social mobility for women, but was not related to mobility for men.

Haggard, E. A. Socialization, personality, and academic achievement in gifted children. *Sch. Rev.*, 1957, *65*, 388–414.
Measures: Parent interviews and questionnaires, personality tests, grades, achievement tests, and intelligence tests. Subjects: 45 children, studied longitudinally from grades 3 to 7. All were gifted children who came from professional families and were attending the Laboratory School of the University of Chicago, which stresses high achievement. Results: Relatively more boys than girls were high achievers in reading, while more girls were high achievers in spelling and language arts. Other variables were not reported in terms of sex differences.

Hall, C. A modest confirmation of Freud's theory of a distinction between the superego of men and women. *J. abnorm. soc. Psychol.*, 1964, *69*, 440–42.
Measures: People reported their dreams, which were then coded for themes of aggression toward a victim or misfortune befalling the main character. Subjects: 3,049 dreams collected from young adults. Results: Women had dreams in which there was a victim of aggression significantly more often than men, while men had more dreams where someone was the victim of misfortune with no clear aggressive intent. The results were explained in terms of Freud's hypothesis that women's superegos are less internalized than men's.

Hall, C., and B. Domhoff. A ubiquitous sex difference in dreams. *J. abnorm. soc. Psychol.*, 1963, *66*, 278–80.
Measures: Dream narratives collected from a wide variety of subjects. Subjects: Males and females, 2 years through 80 years, all types. Results: Men dream more about men than about women, while women dream equally often about men and women.

Hammer, M. The relationship between recalled type of discipline in childhood and adult interpersonal behavior. *Merrill-Palmer Quart.*, 1964, *10*, 143–45.
Measures: The Shutz Fundamental Interpersonal Relations Orientation Behavior Test, and a self-report scale measuring need for inclusion in interpersonal situations. S's were also asked what type of discipline they received in childhood. Types of discipline were interactive (involved being with others, such as spanking and reasoning) and noninteractive (being banished from social group). Subjects: 119 male and 81 female college students. Results: Girls who received interaction discipline showed greater need for social inclusion than noninteraction-disciplined girls. There were no differences for boys.

Hammes, J. A. Judgment of emotional facial expressions as a function of manifest anxiety and sex. *Percept. mot. Skills*, 1964, *17*, 601–2.
Measures: S's evaluated a series of 18 female faces on two dimensions, pleasantness-unpleasantness and danger-aggression threat. Subjects: 40 college students differing in degrees of manifest anxiety. Results: Females rated pleasant and unpleasant faces at more extreme ends of the scale than did males. Females also saw the faces as more dangerous, aggressive, and threatening than males did.

Harlow, H. F., and R. R. Zimmerman. Affectional responses in the infant monkey. *Science, 130,* (3373), 421–32.

> **Measures:** Observation in captivity. **Subjects:** Rhesus monkeys. **Results:** By 2 or 3 months, differences between the sexes were evident. Threat responses were most frequently male to male, then male to female, female to female, and rarely female to male. Females withdrew from rough contact play. Differences in which sex the monkey mounts did not occur until 6 months.

Harmatz, M. G. The effects of anxiety, motivating instructions, success and failure reports, and sex of subject upon level of aspiration and performance. Unpub. master's thesis, Univ. of Washington, 1962.

> **Measures:** High- and low-anxiety subjects were picked on the basis of the Sarason Test Anxiety Scale. Subjects performed on a digit-symbol task, under high or low motivation conditions and with either success or failure fed back. **Subjects:** 32 high- and 32 low-anxiety subjects. **Results:** Under conditions of low task motivation, males react to failure feedback by raising their performance scores on the second test. Females lowered their scores. Scores of failure females decreased sharply compared to the scores of success females, which increased sharply.

Harper, F. B. W., K. Hoving, Gretchen Holm, Joanna Lasso, and R. Dubanoski. Young children's yielding to false adult judgments. *Child Develpm.,* 1965, *36,* 175–83.

> **Measures:** Children were asked to find the geometric figure the same size as a standard after two adults gave wrong judgments. Yielding to adult pressure was the measure. **Subjects:** 56 boys and 56 girls in grades 1 and 2. Half of each sex was paired with male stooges and half with female stooges. **Results:** Sex differences were not significant, although girls tended to yield more.

Hartley, Ruth E. A developmental view of female sex-role definition and identification. *Merrill-Palmer Quart.,* 1964, *10,* 3–16.

> **Measures:** Preferences for feminine role activities. **Subjects:** 40 girls, 8 and 11 years. Matched groups of upper-middle and lower-middle class. **Results:** Upper-middle-class girls preferred a narrower range of feminine behaviors. They rejected feminine work roles such as cleaning and washing dishes, while the lower-class girls accepted these activities. The writer suggests that a variety of complex cognitive processes add to sex-role learning, and that acceptance of masculine toys at a young age suggests broad role definition rather than masculine striving.

Hartley, Ruth E. Children's concepts of male and female roles. *Merrill-Palmer Quart.,* 1960, *6,* 84–91.

> **Measures:** Projective questions and pictures to study children's perceptions of male and female roles and attitudes toward women working. **Subjects:** Children, 5, 8, and 11 years old. **Results:** Both sexes perceived the woman's role as primarily domestic, while the man was given the work function. Boys and girls felt that both mother and father feel sad when they have to leave home to go to work.

Hartley, Ruth E. Sex-role pressures and the socialization of the male child. *Psychol. Rep.,* 1959, *5,* 457–68.

> **Measures:** Interviews with boys. **Subjects:** 41 boys, 8 and 11 years old. **Results:** The study found that many of the boys were rigidly antiwomen in an anxious attempt to be masculine. Boys were expected to be "not sissies" even though their models and those they must obey are women. The study found 4 major configurations of masculine identification: (1) overstriving with hostility toward women and rigidity about male

and female activities; (2) overstriving with rigidity but no hostility; (3) a tendency to give up the struggle; (4) a successful, well-balanced role adoption with clear differentiation of roles but flexibility in applying them.

Hartley, Ruth E., and F. P. Hardesty. Children's perceptions of sex roles in childhood. *J. genet. Psychol.*, 1964, *105*, 43–51.
Measures: S's were asked in individual sessions whether mostly boys or girls did, or played with, the items in the Role Distribution Series (57 items). S also was asked to tell what boys most need to know and be able to do, and what girls must be able to do. Subjects: 91 girls and 40 boys, aged 8 and 11. Results: Each sex claimed more items for itself than the other sex attributed to it. 17 items were clearly assigned to girls, 23 to boys, and 6 to both sexes. Boys tended to be aware of the roles of both sexes, while girls were more clearly aware of their own than boys' role.

Hartley, Ruth E., and A. Klein. Sex-role concepts among elementary-school-age girls. *Marriage and fam. Living*, 1959, *21*, 59–64.
Measures: The subjects sorted descriptions of typical adult activities into male, female, and non-sex-typed groups. They also sorted them into things they would or would not enjoy doing when they grew up. Some of the children were interviewed. Subjects: Twenty-seven 8- and 11-year-old girls, and eleven 8- and 11-year-old boys from middle and upper-middle classes. Results: Out of 133 items, the girls sex-typed 70 on the average. A group of elementary school teachers (men and women) sex-typed an average of 67. The difference was not significant, and the agreement on which items belonged in which group was substantial. Thus girls had about the same perception of sex roles as adults. In choosing what they would like to do, girls rejected most male items, and they looked forward to most feminine items. Rejections of feminine items tended to follow class lines, e.g., telephone operator and beautician were rejected by these middle-class children. The boys agreed well with the girls, and disagreement was mostly in de-sex-typing some feminine activities involved in the home. The percentage of sex-typed items differed little with age, but whether mother worked was important. The children of working mothers sex-typed few items.

Hartshorne, H., and M. A. May. *Studies in deceit.* New York: Macmillan Co., 1928.
Measures: Situational tests in school, home, and at a party to determine incidence of cheating. Also questionnaires to measure lying. Subjects: Large sample of children in grades 3–12. Results: Girls cheated significantly more on take-home test, party tests, and lie test. However, the results of the lie test may indicate something other than pure cheating. Although one would have to be a saint to answer all its questions in a socially approved manner, the girls may have been more socially conforming than the boys.

Hartshorne, H., M. A. May, and J. B. Maller. *Studies in service and self control.* New York: Macmillan, 1929.
Measures: 5 tests of cooperation and persistence, such as choosing between keeping and sharing, doing things for others, and actually working on a task for self and then for others. Subjects: About 400 children of each sex in grades 5–8. Results: Girls more cooperative and persistent with critical ratio of 1.9, which approaches significance. Also measured persistence by seeing how long children work on one puzzle before turning to another. Girls higher, but not significant. In self-control (working on a task in the presence of distracting stimuli) girls were significantly superior. Teacher ratings and guess-who reputation tests were also used. In all but self-control the girls were given credit for much more moral superiority than they actually showed.

Hartup, W. W., and E. D. Keller. Nurturance in preschool children and its relation to dependency. *Child Develpm.*, 1960, *31*, 681–89.

Measures: Observation of nurturance and dependency in nursery school. Subjects: Children 3 yrs. 2 mos. to 4 yrs. 2 mos., and another group 4½ to 5 yrs. 7 mos. Results: No sex differences. Nurturant behavior was positively correlated with active dependency bids (seeking help and physical affection), but negatively related to passive "being near."

Hartup, W. W., and Y. Himino. Social isolation vs. interaction with adults in relation to aggression in preschool children. *J. abnorm. soc. Psychol.*, 1959, *59*, 17–22.

Measures: Observation of aggression in doll play after 10 minutes of isolation and after 10 minutes of interaction with E. Two E's of each sex were used. Hypothesis: isolation leads to frustration, which in turn leads to aggression. Subjects: 55 preschoolers. Results: There was more aggression with isolation. Significant sex differences in amount of aggression (with boys higher) were found. Boys were more aggressive with a male E. There were no stable differences among E's for girls.

Hartup, W. W., and Shirley G. Moore. Avoidance of inappropriate sex-typing by young children. *J. consult. Psychol.*, 1963, *27*, 467–73.

Measures: Observation of children's behavior when presented with attractive opposite-sex-typed toys and unattractive neutral toys. Latencies and amount of time spent playing with the 2 types of toys, with and without a female E present, were recorded for boys and girls. The It Scale was also given. Subjects: 4 groups of boys and 4 groups of girls, chosen on the basis of age. The youngest group was 3 yrs. 2 mos. to 4 yrs. 4 mos. The oldest group was 7 yrs. to 8 yrs. 2 mos. There were 69 boys and 78 girls in all. Results: Both sexes significantly more often chose neutral toys. Age was a significant factor for boys, with older boys more often avoiding opposite-sex-typed toys. Boys were also less likely to play with opposite-sex toys if E was present. Age and E's presence were not significant for girls. Correlations with It Scale were low.

Hattwick, Laberta A. Sex differences in behavior of nursery school children. *Child Develpm.*, 1937, *8*, 343–55.

Measures: Nursery school teachers' ratings of whether behaviors had or had not occurred in the last few months. Each child received a score that was an average of 3 teachers' ratings. Subjects: 283 boys and 296 girls, aged 2–4½, in 2 public nursery schools. Results: Boys showed significantly more "negativistic" behavior—grabbing toys, attacking others, ignoring teacher requests, wasting time. Boys also asked unnecessary help more frequently than girls. There were more speech defects among boys (not significant). Boys also laughed, squealed, and jumped around a great deal more than girls, were more tense at rest, stayed awake during nap time, broke toys, rushed into danger, and handled sex organs more than girls. Girls avoided play, were jealous, stayed near adults, dawdled at meals, sucked thumb, feared high places, avoided risks, refused to eat, and twisted hair more than boys. Girls were high on withdrawing introversion. Nervous mannerisms and bed wetting were not related to sex. Main conclusion: Boys were aggressive extroverts, while girls were withdrawing and introverted.

Hauer, H. J. Frustration in neonates: an investigation of the relationship between frustration tolerance of neonates and frustration tolerance of their parents. *Dissert. Abstr.*, 1955, *15*, p. 1,914.

Measures: Change in heart beat when the bottle is taken away after one minute of feeding. In the parents, the change in pulse rate after trying to solve an unsolvable problem was measured. Subjects: 17 males and 17 female neonates and their parents.

Results: No sex differences in response to frustration. However, there was a high correlation between infant's reactions and those of the mother.

Havighurst, R. J., and Fay F. Breese. Relation between ability and social status in a midwestern community. III: Primary mental abilities. *J. educ. Psychol.*, 1947, *38*, 241–47.
Measures: PMA. Subjects: All 13-year-olds in a midwestern city of 6,000. Results: No sex differences on verbal ability. Girls did better on number, word fluency, reasoning, and memory subtests. Boys excelled in space.

Havighurst, R. J., and L. L. Janke. Relations between ability and social status in a midwestern community. I: 10-year-old children. *J. educ. Psychol.*, 1944, *35*, 357–68.
Measures: Minnesota Paper Form Board, Stanford-Binet, and a mechanical abilities test, one for boys and one for girls. Subjects: 10-year-olds. Results: The only sex difference was that boys did better on the Form Board.

Heathers, G. Emotional dependence and independence in nursery school play. *J. genet. Psychol.*, 1955, *87*, 37–57.
Measures: Observation of nursery school play to get scores on 10 dependence-independence variables. These consisted of 4 emotional dependence variables (clinging or seeking attention from teacher or from peers), 3 measures of nondistractibility, and 3 measures of self-assertion. Subjects: Twenty 2-year-olds and twenty 4–5-year-olds. Results: No significant sex differences.

Hebb, D. O. Behavioral differences between male and female chimpanzees. *Bull. Canad. psychol. Assn.*, 1946, *6*, 56–58.
Measures: Observation of chimps in controlled situations with experimenters who (1) just stood and greeted the animal, (2) came disguised as a "timid man," or (3) came as a "bold man." Subjects: 30 adolescent and adult chimps, 8 males and 22 females. Results: The male showed more aggressive behavior, but there were no differences in friendly behavior. The female was more likely than the male to appear friendly and then show aggressive behavior. The female showed more aggression than males toward the timid man.

Heilbrun, A. B. Parental model attributes, nurturant reinforcement, and consistency of behavior in adolescents. *Child Develpm.*, 1964, *35*, 151–67.
Measures: S's rated their parents on 9 traits considered sex-typed. The degree to which a parent received high ratings on appropriate sex items gave a measure of parental sex-role modeling. Each S then reported on how he would behave in 8 interpersonal situations. The correspondence between behavior in the different situations gave a measure of role consistency. S also took the Edwards Personal Preference Schedule, and then rated the items in it for social desirability. The correspondence between his choices for himself and his choice of socially desirable items comprised a measure of SV-SB consistency. S also rated parents for nurturance. Subjects: 61 male and 63 female college students. Results: Mothers were seen as more nurturant toward their children than were fathers, and this difference was significantly greater for male children than female. More masculine fathers were less nurturant than feminine fathers, but there was no difference between feminine and masculine mothers. Males with nurturant fathers were higher in role consistency, while the relationship was curvilinear for girls and mothers (high role consistency went with moderate maternal nurturance). Females with feminine mothers had higher SV-SB consistency than females with low feminine mothers, while the relation was curvilinear for boys with masculine fathers.

Heilbrun, A. B. Social value: social behavior consistency, parental identification and aggression in late adolescence. *J. genet. Psychol.*, 1964, *104*, 135–46.

Measures: The Edwards Personal Preference Schedule was administered twice, once with S making choices for himself and once with S rating the social desirability of the items. The correspondence between the two was the measure of SV-SB consistency. S also described himself and his parents in terms of the 15 needs in the Heilbrun Need Scales. Similarity between self and parent description was the measure of identification. Appropriateness of the identification model was assessed by determining whether the descriptions of the similar parent were appropriate to the sex of the subject. S was also scored for aggression on three measures: the aggression scale from the Need Scales, the EPPS Aggression Scale, and the Ma scale of the MMPI. Subjects: 69 male and 63 female college students. Results: No relationship was found between identification and SV-SB consistency. Appropriately identified females were less aggressive than inappropriately identified females. Appropriately identified males were more aggressive, but this was not significant.

Heilbrun, A. B. Sex differences in identification learning. *J. genet. Psychol.*, 1965, *106*, 185–93.

Measures: S took the Adjective Check List, and this was rated for 15 Murray-type needs. S then stated whether each of the 15 needs better described his mother or his father. S's similarity to each of his parents was then assessed. Subjects: 427 college students, some of whom had applied for student counseling. Results: For adjusted S's, males showed more similarity to father than females to mother. Females showed no more similarity to mother than to father. Maladjusted males were more similar to their mothers, and maladjusted females were more like mother than father.

Heilman, J. D. Sex differences in intellectual abilities. *J. educ. Psychol.*, 1933, *24*, 47–62.

Measures: Stanford Achievement Test. Subjects: About 400 boys and 400 girls, aged 10 years. Results: Girls were significantly superior in spelling. Girls were higher in language usage, boys in nature study, science, and arithmetic reasoning. There were no differences in variability.

Heimann, R. A., and Q. F. Schenk. Relations of social class and sex differences to high school achievement. *Sch. Rev.*, 1954, *62*, 213–21.

Measures: Henson-Nelson Tests of Mental Maturity and the average of academic grades. Subjects: 120 sophmore high school students in two SES levels, III and IV. Results: Girls and high SES children were significantly higher in grade average. They were also higher on the I.Q. test.

Henry, A. F. Sibling structure and perception of the disciplinary roles of parents. *Sociometry*, 1957, *20*, 67–74.

Measures: Questionnaires that revealed which parent S felt to be the principal disciplinarian in the home, and whether S had older or younger siblings. Subjects: 1,335 Massachusetts high school children, age 13–21, 63% Catholic. Another sample consisted of 391 college students and 226 high schoolers in the South, age 15–25, 86% Protestant. Results: First-born children were more likely to see father as disciplinarian. Size of family was not controlled. Females were more likely to see mother as disciplinarian than males.

Herzberg, F., and M. Lepkin. A study of sex differences on the Primary Mental Abilities Test. *Educ. psychol. Measmt.*, 1954, *14*, 687–89.

Measures: PMA. Subjects: High school seniors, 16–18 years old. Results: At all 3 ages boys were higher in space at the .01 level, and girls were higher on word fluency at .05 level. At age 17 girls were higher on verbal and reasoning. There were no differences on total score or number ability.

Hess, R. D., and Judith V. Torney. Religion, age, and sex in children's perceptions of family authority. *Child Develpm.*, 1962, *33*, 781–89.
Measures: Questionnaire item asking whether father is boss, mother is boss, or both are equal in the family. Subjects: 1,861 children aged 7–15. Results: Boys significantly more often see father as boss, while girls significantly more often see both parents as equal.

Hetherington, E. Mavis. A developmental study of the effects of sex of the dominant parent on sex-role preference, identification, and imitation in children. *J. Pers. soc. Psychol.*, 1965, *2*, 188–94.
Measures: Parental dominance was measured by having parents discuss and agree on a solution to several child-rearing problems. Discussions were taped and scored for dominance of parent. Father-dominant and mother-dominant families were selected on this basis. The children in the study were then tested for sex-role preference (It Scale). They were given an imitation-measuring task where they could imitate mother's or father's behavior. And a rating list of adjectives was given to friends of the parents and teachers of the children to rate parents and children so that the objective similarity of parent and child could be assessed. Subjects: 36 boys and 36 girls at each of three age levels: 4–5, 6–8, and 9–11. Results: Girls developed preference for their sex role at a later age than boys. When father was dominant, appropriate sex roles were found, but interaction effects indicated that this was only significant for boys. Boys from mother-dominant homes were more feminine. Older children were more like parents than younger children. Children were more likely to resemble the dominant parent, and this was particularly true when mother was dominant. Boys were more similar to the dominant parent, but for girls, father dominance led to equal identification with both parents. In father-dominant homes, girls identified more with father than in mother-dominant homes, but identification with mother was not affected by which parent was dominant. Children imitated the dominant parent more than the passive parent, but their were no differences in imitation of mothers or fathers by either sex. Girls imitated more than boys. The only meaningful correlations among sex-typing measures were for older girls in father-dominant homes.

Hicks, D. J. Imitation and retention of film-mediated aggressive peer and adult models. *J. Pers. soc. Psychol.*, 1965, *2*, 97–100.
Measures: S observed a film in which an adult male or female, or a peer male or female, performed distinctive aggressive acts. After mild frustration, observers recorded S's imitative aggressive acts. Six months later, S was again allowed to play and imitate, and was then asked to recall the model's actions after the 6-months interval. Subjects: 30 boys and 30 girls, aged 41 to 76 months. Results: Boys imitated significantly more aggressive acts than girls. The male peer had the most effect on shaping immediate behavior, while the adult male model had the most effect on retention.

Hill, K. T. Relation of test anxiety, defensiveness, and intelligence to sociometric status. *Child Develpm.*, 1963, *34*, 767–76.
Measures: Children's ratings on preference for peers for play and work companions; CMAS; I.Q.; socioeconomic status; and a defensiveness scale. Subjects: 39 boys and 45 girls in 3d grade. All working-class families. Results: Boys favored low-anxious girls as companions, while girls preferred high-anxious boys. Boys preferred low-defensive girls, while the correlation was low for girls' preference for boys.

Hill, K. T., and H. W. Stevenson. Effectiveness of social reinforcement following social and sensory deprivation. *J. abnorm. soc. Psychol.*, 1964, *68*, 579–84.
Measures: S's were subject to one of three deprivation conditions: isolation in a fairly dark room, exposure to a nonsocial movie without social company, or exposure to the same movie with E present and making comments to S about the movie. Then S took part in marble-dropping game with social reinforcement for performance. E's were male. Subjects: 36 boys and 36 girls aged 5–7. Results: Sensory deprivation (the dark room) produced a greater effect on the rate of boys' operant conditioning than it did on girls'. Boys' conditioning rate was generally higher than girls'.

Hobson, James R. Sex differences in PMA's. *J. educ. Rec.*, 1947, *41*, 126–32.
Measures: Primary Mental Abilities. Subjects: A large sample of 8th and 9th graders. Results: Boys were significantly higher than girls on the spatial subtest. Girls were significantly higher on word fluency, reasoning, and visual reasoning. Boys slightly exceeded girls in verbal, and girls did slightly better in number.

Hoffman, M. L., and H. D. Salzstein. Parent practices and child's moral orientation. Paper presented at Am. Psychol. Assn., 1960.
Measures: Interviews with children to determine whether they had (1) internalized conscience, and (2) whether conscience was conventional (rigid adherence to religious precepts or law) or humanistic (allowance for intent, helping others, etc.). Interview consisted of stories in which the child decided which of 2 crimes was worse, and 2 story completions after which the child told how someone felt after doing something wrong. Children were also asked how parents would respond to the 4 transgressions. Subjects: A small sample of 7th-grade children. Results: No sex-differences were found in parent attitudes when conventional and humanistic groups were compared. But when another group, which had externalized rather than internalized control, was compared to the 2 internalized groups, sex differences in parental attitudes appeared. Parents of boys with internalized controls were high on affection from mother and child-centered in father interaction, high on guilt induction and low on power assertion and withdrawal of love. Girls differed only on withdrawal of love, with internalizing girls receiving more withdrawal of love.

Honzik, Marjorie P. Biosocial aspects of thumbsucking. *Amer. Psychologist*, 1948, *3*, 351–52.
Measures: Incidence of thumbsucking. Subjects: Children 21 months to 18 years from the Berkeley Guidance Study. Results: At 21 months 40% of the girls and 18% of the boys sucked their thumbs.

Honzik, Marjorie P. Sex differences in the occurrence of materials in the play constructions of preadolescents. *Child Develpm.*, 1951, *22*, 15–35.
Measures: Children were asked to construct a scene from an exciting movie. Blocks, toy furniture, cars, dolls, and toy animals were provided. Subjects: 11–13-year-olds from the Berkeley Guidance Study, 468 children in all. Results: Boys used significantly more blocks, vehicles, and persons in uniform than girls. Girls used more persons in ordinary dress and furniture than boys.

Honzik, Marjorie P. A sex difference in the age of onset of the parent-child resemblance in intelligence. *J. educ. Psychol.*, 1963, *54*, 231–37.
Measures: Education of parents was correlated with the California preschool intelligence scales and the Stanford-Binet I.Q. scores of children. Subjects: 124 Berkeley Guidance Study children in the guidance group and 124 control children from that study. A large group of siblings of these children was also studied. Results: There was an increasing positive correlation between child's I.Q. and parents' education with age. Girls' I.Q. correlation with parental education became significant around age

3, while boys' correlations were not significant until age 5 or 6. There was a slight tendency for cross-sex correlations (mothers' educations with son's I.Q.'s, and father's educations with daughters' I.Q.'s). to be higher than same-sex correlations.

Honzik, Marjorie P., and J. P. McKee. The sex difference in thumbsucking. *J. Pediatrics*, 1962, *61*, 726–32.
Measures: In the 1st study infants were observed during developmental tests and thumbsucking noted. In the 2d study, mothers filled out questionnaires on thumbsucking. In the 3d study, mothers were interviewed to collect data on thumbsucking. Subjects: In the first sample there were 62 boys and 34 girls suspected of brain damage, and 54 boys and 34 girls who were normal. All children were 8 months old. In the second sample there were 373 boys and 370 girls, aged 2–4, in nursery school. In the third sample there were 248 children from the California Guidance Study, aged 21 months to 12 years. Results: No differences in the 8-month-old children were found. In the second sample, girls sucked their thumbs more at each of the three age levels. In the third sample, girls were more frequent thumbsuckers in all age levels from 21 months to 12 years.

Hovland, C. I., I. J. Janis, et al. *Personality and persuasibility*. New Haven: Yale Univ. Press, 1959.
Measures: Opinion was assessed, S was exposed to persuasive communication, and then opinion was reassessed. The amount of change in opinion was the measure of persuasibility. Subjects: High school students. Results: Two studies, one by Janis and Field and one by B. T. King, found girls more susceptible to persuasion. In another study, in which the experimenter tried to influence choice in 1st-graders, Abelson and Lesser found no sex differences. Low self-esteem and vivid imagery correlated with high persuasibility in boys but not in girls. Sex role seemed to outweigh individual personality differences in girls.

Hughes, Mildred C. Sex differences in reading achievement in the elementary grades. *Suppl. Educ. Monogr.*, 1953, No. 77, 102–6.
Measures: Chicago Reading Test, Van Wageman-Dvorak Diagnostic Examination of Silent Reading Abilities, Huelsman Word Discrimination Test, Primary Mental Abilities. Subjects: 100 children of each grade level, 3–8. Results: Girls were superior through grade 4, and then the differences were no longer significant or consistent. No differences were found on total PMA score.

Hurlock, E. B. The suggestibility of children. *J. genet. Psychol.*, 1930, *37*, 59–74.
Measures: Margaret Otis Group Test of Suggestibility for Children. Subjects: 404 children in public school. Both Negro and white. Average age 13. Results: Boys of each race were less suggestible than girls of the same race. The difference approaches significance. However, the difference was small.

Imanishi, K. Social organization of subhuman primates in their natural habitat. *Current Anthrop.*, 1960, *1*, 393–407.
Measures: Field observation. Subjects: Primates. Results: Dominant females had dominant offspring. Subordinate females had trouble weaning their infants, who were also subordinate. Females in general were subordinate to males.

Irwin, O. C., and H. P. Chen. Development of speech during infancy: curve of phonemic types. *J. exp. Psychol.*, 1946, *36*, 431–36.
Measures: The sounds uttered in 30 breaths were recorded in phonetic alphabet. The mean number of phonemic types was the measure used. Subjects: 95 infants, 1–30 months old. Results: The curves for separate sexes were identical in the 1st year, and then diverged with girls superior. No significance tests were given.

Iscoe, I., and Joyce A. Carden. Field dependence, manifest anxiety, and socio-metric status in children. *J. consult. Psychol.*, 1961, *25*, 184.

> Measures: CMAS; sociometric popularity ratings; Embedded Figure Test. Subjects: 11-year-old boys and girls, 16 boys and 14 girls. Results: Rank-order correlation of .57 between field dependence and sociometric status for girls, and a significantly neg-ative −.51 for boys. CMAS was not related to sociometric status in boys, but highly anxious girls were significantly less popular. CMAS and field dependence were not correlated in boys, but field dependent girls were less anxious (−.60).

Iscoe, I., Martha Williams, and J. Harvey. Modifications of children's judgments by a simulated group technique: a normative developmental study. *Child Develpm.*, 1963, *34*, 963–78.

> Measures: Children counted clicks of a metronome heard on earphones. They heard the judgments of 3 other children (stooges) before they gave their own report, and the amount of conformity to group pressure was measured. Subjects: 32 males and 32 females in each of 4 age groups, 7, 9, 12, and 15 years. Results: Females and younger children were more conforming than males and older children. However, at age 15 the sex difference was reversed with boys slightly more conforming than girls.

Iscoe, I., Martha Williams, and J. Harvey. Age, intelligence and sex as variables in the conformity behavior of Negro and white children. *Child Develpm.*, 1964, *35*, 451–60.

> Measures: Children counted clicks of a metronome heard on earphones. They heard the judgments of 3 other children (stooges) before they gave their own report, and the amount of conformity to group pressure was measured. Subjects: Negro and white children, aged 7, 9, 12, and 15, in segregated schools. 64 males and 64 females in each racial group. White children in this study were also reported on in a previous study (see Iscoe et al. 1963). Results: There was a significant sex-by-race interaction: white girls conformed more than Negro girls and both groups of boys; Negro girls less than Negro boys. There were no differences between Negro and white boys.

Jahoda, G. Sex differences in preferences for shapes: a cross-cultural replication. *Brit. J. Psychol.*, 1956, *47*, 126–32.

> Measures: McElroy's Picture Preference Test in which children chose between 12 pairs of rounded and angular designs. Subjects: 858 boys and girls in Accra, Africa, from 11 to 19 (age is estimated since exact ages are not kept in Accra). Results: Sex differences were found, but they were smaller than those found in the Scottish study (see McElroy 1954). Significant differences in only 5 instead of 11 out of 12 items were found. When analyzed by age, boys did not change, but girls became increas-ingly more interested in rounded shapes. The interpretation given was psychoanalytic.

Janke, L. L., and R. J. Havighurst. Relations between ability and social status in a midwestern community. II: 161 year-old boys and girls. *J. educ. Psychol.*, 1945, *36*, 499–509.

> Measures: Minnesota Paper Form Board; Stanford-Binet; and a mechanical abili-ties test for boys and one for girls. Subjects: 16-year-olds. Results: No significant sex differences.

Jegard, Suzanne, and R. H. Walters. A study of some determinants of aggression in young children. *Child Develpm.*, 1960, *31*, 739–47.

> Measures: Projective test to measure guilt and anxiety over aggression. Children were placed in high and low frustration situations. The measure was number of hits and time elapsed before hitting a punch toy after frustration. Subjects: Children 4 yrs. 10 mos. to 6 yrs. 8 mos. Results: Few differences in the experimental variables. Boys were significantly higher in total aggression. Guilt scores were not broken down by sex.

Jersild, A. T., and F. V. Markey. Conflicts between preschool children. *Child Develpm. Monogr.* No. 21, 1935.

Measures: Observations of children in nursery school and kindergarten and recording of pertinent data on quarrels. Subjects: 54 children aged 2–5 years. Results: Boys engaged in more conflicts and "won" more quarrels than girls. Girls seemed to engage in more verbal conflict (not significant) than boys. Boys were more likely to be the aggressor and girls the victim. Boys showed more personal acts of attack and defense. No significant differences in amount of quarreling with like- or opposite-sex peer. However, boys won more and were the aggressors more in mixed conflicts. Boys used more language in quarreling with girls than with other boys.

Jersild, A. T., and Ruth Ritzman. Aspects of language development: the growth of loquacity and vocabulary. *Child Develpm.*, 1938, *9*, 243–59.

Measures: Stenographic recording of 9 hours of nursery school conversation, spread over 3 days. The child was observed for the full morning play session. Subjects: 43 boys and 45 girls, aged 18–71 months. SES and I.Q. were quite high in the sample (mean I.Q. 132). Results: Girls consistently excelled in number of words used and number of different words used (vocabulary). However, the ratio of different words to total output shows no difference. Differences are small and not significant.

Johnson, B. L. Children's reading interests as related to sex and grade in school. *Sch. Rev.*, 1932, *40*, 257–72.

Measures: Detailed record of reading during a month as kept by subjects. Subjects: 888 boys and 968 girls, grades 6–11. Results: The biggest difference was in scientific articles and newspaper sports sections, boys reading these more. Boys also read more crime and national news. Girls read the children's page, society news, the home page, and advertisements more than boys. In books, boys read adventure stories; girls read stories of home, school, and children.

Johnson, Marian M. Sex role learning in the nuclear family. *Child Develpm.*, 1963, *34*, 319–33.

This is a theoretical paper in which results of several studies are discussed in the light of a new theory of identification. Parsons' instrumental-expressive dimension is considered the major component of the difference between masculine and feminine sex roles. It is proposed that the father is the primary source of sex-role differentiation for both sexes. The father is expressive in his relations with daughters and both expressive (affectionate) and demanding with sons. The demands for excellence lead to the instrumental attitude, which females lack. Thus males have both instrumental and expressive components in their personalities, while females have only expressive components. Mothers are expressive to children of both sexes.

Jones, M. C. The development of early behavior patterns in young children. *J. genet. Psychol.*, 1926, *33*, 537–85.

Measures: Observation of infants in standard Gesell-like situations. Subjects: 365 subjects from Well Baby Clinics. Age range from near birth to 10 months. Mixed sex and race. Results: Boys were precocious in smiling (in response to an adult smile) but the difference was probably not significant. Girls were slightly superior in reaching for objects. There were no differences in eye coordination, sitting, blinking, or thumb opposition.

Jourard, S. M. Identification, parent-cathexis, and self-esteem. *J. consult. Psychol.*, 1957, *21*, 375–80.

Measures: Questionnaires to measure perceived similarity between S's personality and his parents', his attachment to them, and his self-esteem. Subjects: 56 males and

56 female college students. Results: No sex differences were found in parent S's saw as most similar to themselves or were closer to.

Jourard, S. M., and Patricia Richman. Factors in the self-disclosure inputs of college students. *Merrill-Palmer Quart.*, 1963, *9*, 141–48.

Measures: Disclosure output and disclosure input were measured by asking S to rate how much he had revealed about himself to significant others on selected personal topics, such as what he dislikes about himself, and what his biggest disappointment in life was. S then rated how fully the other person confided in him on these topics (disclosure input). Significant persons used were mother, father, best like-sex friend, and best opposite-sex friend. Subjects: 58 male and 51 female unmarried college undergraduates. Results: Females had higher mean input and output ratings than males. This was significant for output to mother, same-sex friend, and total output, and for input from mother, opposite-sex friend, same-sex friend, and total input. Women confided in same-sex friend, mother, opposite-sex friend, and father, in descending order. Men confided most in same-sex friend, and then in opposite-sex friend, mother, and father, in that order.

Kagan, J. The child's sex role classification of school objects. *Child Develpm.*, 1964, *35*, 1051–56.

Measures: Children were taught the concepts of masculine objects, feminine objects, and farm objects by learning to associate nonsense syllables with these objects. Then they were given new items and asked to apply these concepts to them. The new items included 8 school objects along with other neutral and farm items. Subjects: 240 2d-grade children and 65 3d-grade children. Results: Four of the school items (blackboard, book, page of arithmetic, and school desk) were labeled feminine more often than masculine by 2d-graders. This was more marked among girls than boys. Pencil and map were labeled masculine by both sexes at 2d-grade level, while library and school building were not sex-typed. Third-grade girls continued labeling the four items as predominantly feminine, while 3d-grade boys tended to label more of them as masculine. Girls also tended to label dangerous animals (lion and alligator) as masculine.

Kagan, J., and M. Freeman. Relation of childhood intelligence, maternal behaviors, and social class to behavior during adolescence. *Child Develpm.*, 1963, *34*, 899–911.

Measures: Ratings of interviews with adolescents, self-ratings by subjects, and ratings from observer reports of mother's behavior when the child was young. Also S-B I.Q. at 3½, 5½, and 9 years. Subjects: 30 boys and 20 girls from the Fels longitudinal study. Results: Daughters with higher I.Q. scores had mothers who encouraged them to excel during ages 4–7. This was not true of boys. Girls who rejected traditional feminine sex roles had slightly higher I.Q. scores than traditionally sex-typed girls. Acceptance, affection, and protection during early years was predictive of conformity and dependence for boys; severe discipline and restrictiveness was predictive of these characteristics for girls.

Kagan, J., and Judith Lemkin. The child's differential perception of parental attributes. *J. abnorm. soc. Psychol.*, 1960, *61*, 440–47.

Measures: Individual interviews to determine the child's perceptions of parents with respect to nurturance, punitiveness, source of fear, and competence. Questions were asked about a make-believe family and about the child's own family. Subjects: 32 boys and 35 girls, 3 to 6 years of age. Results: Boys and girls chose like-sex parent as a model to emulate and as the person they liked best. Girls labeled father both more punitive and more affectionate than boys did. Girls wanted to be like mother, but saw father as wiser and stronger.

Kagan, J., and H. A. Moss. *Birth to maturity.* New York: John Wiley, 1962.
Measures: (1) Ratings made from protocols from observations and tests of subjects during childhood; (2) interviews and ratings of subjects in adulthood, and a battery of personality assessment tests consisting of TAT cards, W-B Intelligence Test, tachistoscopic presentation of pictures depicting aggression and dependency, a self-rating inventory, and other instruments. Subjects: 89 adults, aged 20 to 29, from the Fels longitudinal sample. Results: Correlations from age 6–10 to adulthood indicated that dependency is a more stable trait in women than in men, and that aggression is more stable in men than in women. Achievement motivation was equally stable in the sexes. Men recognized tachistoscopic presentations of aggressive pictures faster than women, and they rated themselves as more aggressive on a self-report measure. Women recognized dependency pictures faster than men. Intercorrelations showed striking differences between the sexes on many variables.

Kagan, J., H. A. Moss, and I. E. Sigel. Conceptual style and the use of affect labels. *Merrill-Palmer Quart.,* 1960, *6,* 261–78.
Measures: S's sorted human-figure drawings into "go together" groups, which were subsequently scored as descriptive, abstract, relational, or egocentric; these categories were then broken down into subcategories according to the affect shown. The Rorschach was also modified and scored for movement; the TAT was scored for attributing affect to characters, the tachistoscopic presentation of pictures was scored for affect, ratings of introspection were made for each subject (ability to talk about his own feelings, motives, etc.), and the Wechsler Bellevue I.Q. given. Subjects: Male and female college students. Results: Only correlations were given. The intercorrelations of the affect responses were high and approximately equal for both sexes. High-affect categories correlated highly with verbal I.Q. in women and performance I.Q. in men. The correlations with the other I.Q. component were positive in both sexes but lower.

Kass, N. Risk in decision making as a function of age, sex and probability preference. *Child Develpm.,* 1964, *35,* 577–82.
Measures: Three simulated slot machines with probabilities of one, one-third, and one-eighth. S had his choice of odds. Subjects: 52 preschool and elementary school children, evenly divided by sex. Results: Boys made the greater number of responses on the machines that involved more risk, those with intermediate and low probabilities. Girls made more responses on the machine that paid off each time.

Kates, S. L. Suggestibility, submission to parents and peers, and extra-punitiveness, intropunitiveness, and impunitiveness in children. *J. Psychol.,* 1951, *31,* 233–41.
Measures: Sentence completions to determine tendency to submit to the demands of father, mother, friend, or club. Subjects: Thirty-one 3d-graders, lower-middle class. Results: No sex differences in submission to any of these influences.

Katowsky, W., Anne Preston, and V. J. Crandall. Parents' achievement attitudes and their behavior with their children in achievement situations. *J. genet. Psychol.,* 1964, *104,* 105–21.
Measures: Interviews with parents to assess the degree to which the parent participated with the child and instigated the child's participation in four achievement areas: intellectual, physical, artistic, and mechanical. Parents were also interviewed to assess their own standards and expectation of success in achievement in these areas. Subjects: 20 boys and 20 girls from 2d, 3d, and 4th grades, and their parents. Results: Parents' expectations and satisfactions with their own achievement in intellectual and artistic pursuits were more likely to be expressed in behavior with daughters than with sons, particularly by fathers. Parents' expectations for physical skill

and mechanical achievement were more likely to be translated into behavior with sons than with daughters, especially by mothers.

Keller, E. D., and V. N. Rowley. Junior high school and additional elementary school normative data for the Children's Manifest Anxiety Scale. *Child Develpm.*, 1962, *33*, 675–81.
> Measures: CMAS. Subjects: 213 boys and 202 girls in 7th, 8th, and 9th grades. 165 boys and 146 girls in 4th, 5th, and 6th grades. Results: The sex difference at the junior high level was significant at the .01 level with girls scoring higher. The difference was not significant at the elementary school level.

Kelman, H. C., and Janet Barclay. The F Scale as a measure of breadth of perspective. *J. abnorm. soc. Psychol.*, 1963, *67*, 608–15.
> Measures: The California F Scale to measure authoritarian personality. Subjects: 282 college freshmen, all Negro. Results: Females were significantly higher than males. In males, older subjects were lower than younger ones, but this was not true for females.

Kennedy, W. A., and R. S. Lindner. A normative study of the Goodenough Draw-a-Man Test on southeastern Negro elementary school children. *Child Develpm.*, 1964, 35, 33–62.
> Measures: Goodenough Draw-a-Person Test, Stanford-Binet, and California Achievement Test. The Goodenough was scored according to Goodenough's norms; new weights were used to make it correlate better with the S–B. Subjects: 1,800 Negro school children in grades 1–6. Stratified sampling. Results: Using Goodenough's scoring, there were no significant sex differences, although the girls were slightly higher. With the revised scoring there were no sex differences.

Kessen, W., E. J. Williams, and J. P. Williams. Selection and test of response measures in the study of the human newborn. *Child Develpm.*, 1961, *32*, 7–23.
> Measures: Observation to determine amount of mouthing, hand–mouth contact, crying, and movement. Movies as well as on-the-spot observation were used. Subjects: 50 newborns during their first 5 days of life in the hospital. Results: No sex differences.

Klausmeier, H. J., and W. Wiersma. Relationship of sex, grade level, and locale to performance of high I.Q. students on divergent thinking tests. *J. educ. Psychol.*, 1964, *55*, 114–19.
> Measures: Seven tests yielding 10 divergent thinking scores: object uses, word uses, plot titles, expressional fluency, plot questions, object improvement, and sentence improvement. Four tests requiring convergent thinking: current events, work-study skills, problem-solving judgment, and analogies. Subjects: 160 children, grades 5 and 6, Lorge-Thorndike I.Q.'s of over 115. Results: Girls had higher mean scores on object uses (flexibility); expressional fluency; plot titles (fluency); plot questions and object improvement. Boys had higher mean scores in current events, problem-solving, and analogies.

Klausmeier, H. J., and W. Wiersma. The effects of I.Q. level and sex on divergent thinking of seventh grade pupils of low, average, and high I.Q. *J. educ. Res.* 1965, *58*, 300–302.
> Measures: Subjects were divided into high, low, and average I.Q. groups on the basis of the Otis Quick Scoring Mental Ability Test. Seven tests of divergent thinking and 4 tests of convergent thinking were administered. Subjects: 240 7th-grade students. Results: Girls were significantly better at three divergent thinking tasks: expressional fluency, plot questions, and object improvement. Boys were superior to girls on the divergent task (plot titles, cleverness), and on two convergent tasks, current

events and analogies. No differences were found on problem-solving judgment, work-study skill, or any other divergent tasks.

Knights, R. M. Test anxiety and defensiveness in institutionalized and noninstitutionalized normal and retarded children. *Child Develpm.*, 1963, *34*, 1019–26.
Measures: Test Anxiety Scale for Children and the Defensiveness Scale for Children. Subjects: 127 institutionalized and 179 noninstitutionalized children. 50 of the institutionalized children were mentally retarded and 77 were normal. 78 noninstitutionalized children were retarded and 101 were normal. Retarded children had mental ages of at least 9 years. Normal children were 5th-graders. Results: Institutionalized normals had higher anxiety than noninstitutionalized normals. Retarded children had higher anxiety than normals. Girls were more anxious than boys, particularly among normals. Boys scored higher than girls on the DSC.

Koch, Helen L. The relation of "primary mental abilities" in 5- and 6-year-olds to sex of child and characteristics of his siblings. *Child Develpm.*, 1954, *25*, 209–23.
Measures: Primary Mental Abilities, primary level. Subjects: Grade school children, aged 5 and 6. All from 2-child families. Results: On verbal, boys were consistently ahead, significantly so only when child was first-born with sibs 2–4 years younger. No differences were found on perceptual speed, on quantitative or spatial, or on total score. The study did not consider the motor subtest.

Koch, Helen L. Sissiness and tomboyishness in relation to sibling characteristics. *J. genet. Psychol.*, 1956, *88*, 231–44.
Measures: Teachers' ratings of sissiness and tomboyishness (activities, interests, and attitudes of the opposite sex) taken from the Calif. Behavior Inventory for nursery school children. Subjects: 192 boys and 192 girls, aged 5 and 6, matched on SES, residence, and age. All S's came from 2-child families. Results: Sex of sibling was not a significant variable. None of the independent variables were significant for girls (sex of sib, ordinal position, and age differences between sibs.) For boys, ordinal position and age differences were significant. Boys with a slightly older (2 years) sister were more sissyish. Among second-born boys, sissiness increased as spacing decreased regardless of sex of sib. With first-born boys, it decreased as distance increased but then rose at the four-year age gap. Ordinal differences were great, with first-borns lower than second-borns in sissiness when the sib was a girl 2 to 4 years old. The order was reversed with the 6-year age gap.

Kohlberg, L., and E. Zigler. The impact of cognitive maturity on the development of sex-role attitudes in the years 4–8. *Genet. Psychol. Monogr.*, 1966, in press.
Four experiments were done:
(1) Measures: The It Scale for Children and a peer-preference scale. Subjects: 62 children aged 3–8. Results: On peer-preference boys became more same-sex oriented up to age 6, and then less so. Girls became less same-sex oriented with age.
(2) Measures: Recording of verbal dependency statements to male and female adults in a design-making task. Subjects: 72 children, aged 3–8. Results: No significant sex differences in total dependency displayed. Boys changed from opposite-sex orientation at age 4 to same-sex orientation at 7. Bright boys did just the opposite. Average girls remained slightly same-sex oriented, bright girls slightly masculine, in sex-typing.
(3) Measures: Same as Experiment 2. Subjects: 24 4th-graders with mean age 9 yrs. 11 mos. Results: These children were oriented toward the opposite sex.
(4) Measures: Doll-play session in which the child imitated or showed attachment to either mother or father. Subjects: 58 children, aged 3–8. Results: Average intelli-

gence boys became father-oriented with age; bright boys remained father-oriented throughout the age range. Average girls were oriented first to mother, then to father. Bright girls remained neutral.

Kohn, A. R., and F. E. Fiedler. Age and sex differences in the perception of persons. *Sociometry*, 1961, *24*, 157–64.

Measures: Each subject rated significant others in his life (mother, father, self, favorite teacher, friend, sibling) on 20 bipolar items of personality description. Subjects: 120 subjects divided into groups of college seniors, college freshmen, and high school freshmen. Results: Older subjects made more distinctions among people. Women made fewer distinctions than men and generally evaluated others more favorably.

Kohn, M. L., and Eleanor E. Carroll. Social class and the allocation of parental responsibility. *Sociometry*, 1960, *23*, 378–92.

Measures: Mother, father, and child were interviewed at home, and the amount of parental support (encouraging the child to turn to him and offering help) and constraint (setting limits) was measured. Subjects: 400 families, 200 middle-class and 200 working-class, chosen on the basis of Hollinghead Index of Social Position. Results: Middle-class mothers felt fathers should be equally as supportive as mothers, and fathers agreed with them in relation to sons. Fathers were less supportive of daughters, feeling that this was mother's responsibility. Lower-class mothers wanted fathers to be directive, but lower-class fathers did not feel that either constraint or support was their duty—child-rearing was the mother's job.

Kostick, M. M. A study of transfer: sex differences in the reasoning process. *J. Psychol.*, 1954, *45*, 449–58.

Measures: A questionnaire made up of questions on science and home economics. Some items were on information, others on principles, and still others on deduction from previously given information. Subjects: 600 high-schoolers, age 15–17 years, and in the 11th grade. A third of these were matched on reading comprehension, I.Q., and achievement. Results: Boys were significantly better at the deduction items in both science and home economics, despite lower information scores in home economics.

Krippner, S. The relationship between MMPI and WAIS masculinity-femininity scores. *Personnel and Guidance J.*, 1964, *42*, 695–98.

Measures: WAIS and MMPI M–F scales. Subjects: 50 male college students. Results: Low but significant positive correlations were found for M–F scores from the 2 tests.

L'Abate, L. Personality correlates of manifest anxiety in children. *J. consult. Psychol.*, 1960, *24*, 342–48.

Measures: Children's Manifest Anxiety Scale and Rogers' test of personality adjustment. Also teachers' ratings of maladjustment. Subjects: 49 boys and 47 girls, grades 4–8. Rural southern school. Results: No differences on amount of anxiety. It was expected that boys would use more alloplastic (acting out), and girls more autoplastic, defenses against anxiety. The only confirmation was that girls used daydreaming more as a defense than did boys.

Labrant, Lou L. A study of certain language developments of children in grades 4–12 inclusive. *Genet. Psychol. Monogr.*, 1933, *14*, 387–491.

Measures: Children were given a topic to write about during a 20-minute period. Subjects: 482 children in classes 4–9, 504 children in classes 9–12. Mean I.Q. was approximately average. Many of the children were from rural areas. Results: Girls greatly exceeded boys in number of words written. Girls exceeded boys in mean words per clause and in number of subordinate clauses, but these differences were very slight.

Lagrone, C. W. Sex and personality differences in relation to fantasy. *J. consult. Psychol.*, 1963, *27*, 270–72.

Measures: S's wrote down their most typical daydream or fantasy, and how they felt about it. These responses were rated for need and content. Subjects: 96 women and 123 men in college. Results: The first-ranked need for women was affiliation, and the content area was marriage and family. For men, the most frequent need was new experience, and the content area was money and possessions.

Lambert, P. Mathematical ability and masculinity. *The Arith. Teach.*, 1960, *7*, 19–21.

Measures: MMPI masculinity–femininity scale, and 2 arithmetic tests: the American Council on Education Arithmetic Examination and a basic skills test. Subjects: Group I contained 10 female and 70 male college students enrolled in advanced math and physics courses. Group II contained 292 college seniors in practice teaching. Results: There was no correlation between arithmetic proficiency and M–F, and for males there was no difference in masculinity between math majors and non-math majors. For women, contrary to hypothesis, math majors were significantly more feminine than non-math majors.

Landreth, Catherine. Four-year-olds' notions about sex appropriateness of parental care and companionship activities. *Merrill-Palmer Quart.*, 1963, *9*, 175–82.

Measures: S's were shown 2 sets of 3 drawings, one set depicting a child in situations demanding parental care and one depicting situations demanding parental companionship. S's were then shown 2 insets, one picturing mother, the other picturing father fulfilling the child's need in each of the 6 situations. S's chose one of the insets in response to the questions: "Who helps (or plays with) a boy (or a girl for girl subjects)?" and "Who helps (or plays with) you?" Subjects: Preschool children from Berkeley, California, and Wellington, New Zealand. Professional and manual-workers' families were represented. Results: Mother was chosen more often than father for both care and companionship. For care alone, more children more often chose the mother than the father in all the cells except the Berkeley boy professional group. For companionship alone, only the Wellington girl professional group preferred mother. Girls more than boys chose the mother for companionship, but only significantly in the Wellington manual group. Comparing the Berkeley and Wellington professional groups, sex differences were greater in the Berkeley children's choices of mother for care but not for companionship. Mother was chosen for giving care more than for giving companionship in all but the 2 professional boy groups.

Landy, D. *Tropical childhood*. Chapel Hill: Univ. of North Carolina Press, 1959.

Measures: Observation; mother and father questionnaires about child training; doll-play sessions. Subjects: Children in a lower-class rural Puerto Rican village. Results: Boys and girls were treated quite differently. There was a strict sex-role and labor division for boys and girls. Girls helped mother and were restricted in play areas and activities, while boys ran errands and were not restricted in play space. Boys were allowed to play rough games and even have tantrums as long as clear antisocial aggression did not occur. Girls were required to play quiet games. Boys were allowed to go naked more than girls. Boys were given many duties and much responsibility from age 7 on. Girls had chores, but much less was expected of them. Girls' burdens were supposed to begin when they married, and then their work was very heavy. Girls were toilet-trained earlier and more severely than boys. Boys were less restricted in making noise. Obedience expectations were stricter for boys than girls—by both parents. Boys received both more punishment and more indulgence for misbehavior. Despite sex-role training, doll play showed children using child doll more than parental doll, and the author felt this showed less identification with parental figures. This behavior differed from the behavior of U.S. children. A tentative explanation for this was that socialization was generally slower than it was in the U.S. The children were toilet trained and taught other habits at later ages than in the U.S.

Lansky, L. M., V. J. Crandall, J. Kagan, and C. T. Baker. Sex differences in aggression and its correlates in middle-class adolescents. *Child Develpm.*, 1961, *32*, 45–58.

Measures: Interviews to determine expressed criticism and reported aggression toward parents, anxiety about lack of achievement, and amount of conformity to authority. Presentation of a modified Rorschach to measure aggression and sex anxiety. A self-rating inventory to measure aggression, desire for acceptance, identification with mother and father. A story-completion test to measure severity of moral standards and defense against guilt. The Gough Femininity Scale. The French Test to measure n. achievement, n. dependence, n. autonomy, and n. affiliation. Subjects: 54 children of the Fels study, aged 13–18, 32 boys and 22 girls. Results: Boys were significantly ahead in reported aggression toward father, self-rated aggression, n. independence-autonomy, and severity of moral standards. Girls exceeded boys in n. affiliation, anxiety about sex (self-rated), Gough Femininity, and accepting responsibility (as a defense against guilt). The intercorrelations among aggression variables were higher for boys than girls, but there were higher correlations of aggression with other variables for girls. Thus in girls, criticism of mother went with high n. ach., low identification with mother, high latency for perceiving female sex symbols on Rorschach, low needs for acceptance, and low severity of moral standards. In boys the correlations were with Rorschach aggression, which went with high n. dependence, and low conformity to authority.

Lansky, L. M., and G. McKay. Sex role preferences of kindergarten boys and girls: some contradictory results. *Psychol. Reps.*, 1963, *13*, 415–21.

Measures: The It Scale for Children. Subjects: 20 boys and 16 girls, aged 60–73 mos. Results: Boys were more masculine and girls feminine, as expected. The boys' scores were more widely distributed than the girls' scores.

Larson, L., and R. H. Knapp. Sex differences in symbolic conceptions of the deity. *J. proj. Tech. pers. Assessment*, 1964, *28*, No. 3, 303–6.

Measures: Method of symbolic equivalences: subject indicates degree to which a series of stimuli (7 ink blots) symbolize a general concept (deity). Subjects ascribe certain attributes to the symbol, the concept itself. Blots were rated in terms of benevolence and potency. Subjects: 20 men and 20 women, of religious denominations with a comparatively orthodox viewpoint. Age range of men 15–54 years, women 15–58 years. Mean ages were 25.00 for men and 28.00 for women. Results: Men exhibited a consistent pattern through the series while women significantly more often moved from lower to higher means on "B" or benevolence scale. Little differentiation was found on the "P" or potency scores. Fear of God was more characteristic of males than females.

Lazowick, L. M. On the nature of identification. *J. abnorm. soc. Psychol.*, 1955, *51*, 175–83.

Measures: Taylor Manifest Anxiety Scale; and the Osgood Semantic Differential involving the three factors of evaluation, activity, and potency. Subjects: 418 college students. Results: No significant sex differences on the TMAS. From each sex group, the highest 10% and lowest 10% on TMAS were given the semantic differential. Their parents were also given this test. It was found that low-anxious S's had semantic differentials more similar to their parents than high-anxious S's. This was stronger for men than women. Men in general showed more identification with parents than women. Both sexes showed less perceived identification (ratings of self and parent by the subject himself) than actual identification (similarity between S and his parent's rating) toward the parent of the opposite sex. The writer felt that this last finding was a result of cultural sex stereotypes, which make people deny identification with opposite-sex parents.

Lee, L. C. Concept utilization in preschool children. *Child Develpm.*, 1965, *36*, 221–27.
Measures: Children had to learn the concepts of color, size, number, form, analysis (something different about part of the object), and sex type. They learned by having to find the non-instance among three small toys presented to them. There were several sets of 3 for each concept. Subjects: 45 boys and 45 girls, aged 3 yrs. 6 mos. to 6 yrs. 5 mos. Results: Analysis of variance showed sex a significant variable, with girls doing better than boys on the task. Older children also did better. There were no significant interactions between sex and age or concept.

Lefkowitz, M. M. Some relationships between sex role preference of children and other parent and child variables. *Psychol. Reps.*, 1962, *10*, 43–53.
Measures: A preference-for-activities test constructed by the author, with separate forms for boys and girls. Parental interviews were obtained to discover which parent disciplined the child, how nurturant each parent was, and the social class of the family. CTMM I.Q., the Draw-a-Person Test, and an aggression score from peer ratings were also correlated with sex-role preference. Subjects: 421 boys, 403 girls from 3d and 4th grades. Only parents of 3d-graders were interviewed (570 fathers and 713 mothers). Results: Boys who had strong sex-role preferences had more nurturant mothers, were disciplined by both parents, were of higher social class, and tended to be slightly more intelligent than boys with less defined sex-role preferences. These boys drew male figures first in figure drawing. Relationships were not found for highly sex-typed girls. Mean aggression scores did not relate to sex-typing in either sex.

Levin, H., and R. R. Sears. Identification with parents as a determinant of doll play aggression. *Child Develpm.*, 1956, *27*, 135–53.
Measures: Observation of doll-play aggression; parent interviews to measure (1) who punishes, (2) how much, (3) superego development. Subjects: Nursery school children: the *Patterns of child rearing* sample (see Sears et al. 1957). Results: In boys, identification with the male role led to high aggression. In girls, a severely punishing mother was the greatest predictor of aggression.

Levy, D. M., and S. H. Tulchin. The resistant behavior of infants and children, II. *J. exper. Psychol.*, 1925, *8*, 209–24.
Measures: Observers recorded the resistant behavior of children during mental testing. Subjects: 57 boys and 53 girls, aged 6 months to 53 months. Results: Boys clung to their mothers more than girls. Girls attempted to hide more. The most intense resistive reactions, such as struggling and screaming, reached their peak at 18 months for girls and at 30 months for boys.

Lezine, Irene, and Odette Brunet. Présentation d'une echelle française de tests du premier age. *Ann. Med. Psychol.*, 1950, *108*, 499.
Measures: Developmental tests similar to those of Gesell, standardized on French children. Subjects: Children 1 month to 4 years. Results: From 4 months to 4 years, girls were superior in verbal and postural tests. Boys were superior to girls in handling objects from 8 months on.

Lindzey, G., and M. Goldberg. Motivational differences between males and females as measured by the TAT. *J. Pers.*, 1953, *22*, 101–17.
Measures: Group-administered TAT (8 cards), which were then rated on aggression,

sex, achievement, abasement, nurturance, narcissism, and verbal responsiveness. **Subjects:** 74 pairs of male and female college students. **Results:** Boys were significantly higher on sex responses, and girls were significantly higher on abasement, nurturance, and verbal responsiveness.

Lipsitt, L. P., and N. Levy. Electroactual threshold in the human neonate. *Child Develpm.*, 1959, *30*, 547–54.

> **Measures:** Shock administered to the foot. **Subjects:** 18 male and 18 female infants in the first 4 days of life. **Results:** Two studies were run. The first used the same infants over 4 days and found significant sex differences. The female pain threshold was lower than that of the males on all 4 days. The second study used different S's for each day. The sex differences were in the same direction on the first 3 days and reversed on the fourth. Differences were not significant in this second study.

Livson, N., and Wanda C. Bronson. An exploration of patterns of impulse control in early adolescence. *Child Develpm.*, 1961, *32*, 75–88.

> **Measures:** Comprehensive clinical descriptions, taken from all the material available on the Berkeley Guidance Study children. These descriptions were Q-sorted by 2 clinical psychologists. These were then cluster-analyzed to give 4 clusters: ego control, ego strength, social adjustment, and emotional expansiveness. Then the 2 types of ego control (undercontrolling, acting on impulse; and rigid, overcontrolling, inflexible) were used to set up 4 groups of children: high impulsivity, high overcontrolling; low impulsivity, high overcontrolling; low impulsivity, low overcontrolling (undercontrol); and high impulsivity, low control. **Subjects:** 40 children (20 boys and 20 girls), aged 11 to 13 years. **Results:** Extreme impulsivity and undercontrol make for poor adjustment in girls but for moderate adjustment in boys. Ego strength and social adjustment are related more to overcontrol in boys and to impulsivity in girls—negative in both sexes.

Long, J. M. Sex differences in academic prediction based on scholastic, personality, and interest factors. *J. exp. Educ.*, 1964, *32*, 239–48.

> **Measures:** High school grades, the SCAT Test, the Diagnostic Reading Test, English Training Test, Kuder Preference Record, and the Guilford-Zimmerman Temperament Survey were used in a multiple regression equation to predict college grades. **Subjects:** 113 female and 303 male college freshmen. **Results:** High school GPA was very important in prediction for both sexes. For women, verbal skill and interest patterns were more important; for men, quantitative skills and personality factors were important predictors.

Lord, F. E. A study of spatial orientation of children. *J. educ. Res.*, 1941, *34*, 481–505.

> **Measures:** Children (1) named the directions in which an arrow pointed (N., S., etc.), (2) indicated the direction in which known cities lie and whether buildings in known areas were on north or south sides of streets, which way streets ran, etc., and (3) kept track of directions during an actual car trip. **Subjects:** 173 boys and 144 girls in grades 5–8 in rural Michigan. **Results:** On a composite score of these 3 measures, boys were significantly superior.

Loughlin, L. J., H. A. O'Connor, M. Powell, and K. M. Parsley. An investigation of sex differences by intelligence, subject-matter area, grade, and achievement level on three anxiety scales. *J. genet. Psychol.*, 1965, *106*, 207–15.

> **Measures:** The Children's Manifest Anxiety Scale, Test Anxiety Scale for Children, and the General Anxiety Scale for Children. S's were subdivided into groups on the basis of the CTMM, the California Reading Test, and the California Arithmetic Test. On the basis of I.Q. and achievement scores, over-, under-, and average achievers were separated into groups. **Subjects:** 2,651 boys and 2,369 girls in grades 4–8. **Results:**

Girls had significantly higher anxiety scores on all three scales. Sex differences for subgroups indicated that the largest differences were for average-intelligence children and average achievers. Fifth grade is the year of maximum sex differences; 8th grade shows the least differences. Overachievers and children with high I.Q.'s show fewer sex differences in anxiety.

Luchins, A. S., and Edith H. Luchins. *Rigidity of behavior.* Eugene: Univ. of Oregon, 1959.

Measures: Water-jar problems with complex and simple solutions. The measure analyzed was S's ability to break set in order to find the simpler solutions. Subjects: 274 girls and 209 boys in elementary school, and 40 male and 40 female college students. Results: Girls were more susceptible to set in elementary school. The difference in college was in the same direction but not significant.

Luria, Z., Miriam Goldwasser, and Adena Goldwasser. Response to transgression in stories by Israeli children. *Child Develpm.,* 1963, *34,* 271–80.

Measures: Story completions in which the child wrote the ending to stories depicting transgression on the part of a child. Number of confessions of the deed was the measure. Subjects: 24 boys and 22 girls living in an Israeli kibbutz (where children do not live with parents). 14 boys and 12 girls in moshavoth (Israeli communities where children live with parents). These were compared with a group of Jewish American children and a group of Gentile American children. All were 11–13 years old. Results: There were no sex differences within any of the Jewish groups. Among the Gentiles, girls confessed much more than boys (p = .01). The American boys were more similar to the Jewish groups.

Lynn, D. B. Sex-role and parental identification. *Child Develpm.,* 1962, *33,* 555–64.

This theoretical paper analyzes the process of sex-role identification in boys and girls, and postulates different characteristics that boys and girls should show as a result of the different behaviors required for male and female identification. Lynn feels that the girl learns her role by personal relationship and imitation. The boy learns his sex role by defining the goal, restructuring the field, and abstracting principles. From this, the following hypotheses are derived: (1) Females should have higher n. affiliation than males; (2) Females should be more dependent on external context and more reluctant to deviate from the given; (3) Males should surpass females in problem-solving skills; (4) Males should be more concerned with internalized moral standards than females; (5) Females should be more receptive to the standards of others than males. The author cites evidence from the literature which tends to substantiate all 5 hypotheses.

Lynn, D. B., and W. L. Sawrey. The effects of father-absence on Norwegian boys and girls. *J. abnorm. soc. Psychol.,* 1959, *59,* 258–62.

Measures: Interviews with mothers, and semi-structured doll play. Subjects: 40 children of sailors and 40 father-present children, aged 8 to 9½. Results: Father-absent boys seemed to be less mature than either controls or girls. The experimental boys chose the father doll more than control boys. From mother interviews, experimental boys showed more compensatory masculinity. Experimental boys had poorer peer adjustments than girls or controls. Experimental girls showed more dependence on the mother in a fantasied separation situation than either controls or experimental boys.

Lynn, D. B., and W. L. Sawrey. Sex differences in the personality development of Norwegian children. *J. genet. Psychol.,* 1962, *101,* 367–74.

Measures: Interviews with mothers, structured doll play, and drawing a family. Subjects: 80 Norwegian children in 2d grade and their mothers. Half the families had fathers who were sailors, while the others had fathers present. Results: Mothers stressed achievement of positive goals in their hopes for their sons' futures and avoidance of bad influences for their daughters' futures. Girls drew the like-sex parent larger, first, and more detailed significantly more often than boys; they also chose the like-sex parent more often in doll play. On the other hand, girls were less likely to choose a like-sex peer as a playmate. The investigators feel that girls may prefer boys' role activities while still identifying with like-sex parent.

McCandless, B. R., C. B. Bilous, and H. L. Bennett. Peer popularity and dependence on adults in preschool age socialization. *Child Develpm.*, 1961, *32,* 511–18.
Measures: Observation of dependency bids and popularity in the nursery school. Subjects: 26 white and 36 nonwhite nursery school children, aged 3½ to 5. Results: Boys initiated significantly more conflicts than girls, and girls showed less resistance to conflict. Girls changed the activity they were engaged in more frequently after conflict. Popularity and emotional dependency were negatively correlated, more so for girls than for boys. No sex differences in total dependency bids or in instrumental dependency were found. Girls showed more emotional dependency, the differences being a result of more frequent requests for teacher to solve conflicts. Mothers did not intervene more in girls' conflicts than in boys' (this was a rather unreliable measure). There were no sex differences in popularity.

McCarthy, Dorothea. Language development of the preschool child. *Inst. Child Welf. Monogr.*, No. 4, Minneapolis: Univ. of Minn. Press, 1930.
Measures: Recording of 50 consecutive utterances of the child. Subjects: 67 boys and 73 girls, aged 18 months to 54 months, stratified by socioeconomic class. Results: Seven age groups were reported, 7 out of 7 showed a higher proportion of incomprehensible utterances in boys than in girls. Girls showed a higher mean number of words per response. In grammar, girls used simple sentences and sentences with phrases earlier than boys did. Girls used a greater number of different words. They also used more adjectives, conjunctions, and other advanced speech forms at a younger age.

McClelland, D., et al. *The achievement motive.* New York: Appleton-Century-Crofts, 1953.
Measures: TAT's scored for achievement motivation under relaxed conditions and under achievement arousal. Arousal was accomplished by introducing academic competition on an "intelligence test" in one experiment and competition for social approval and acceptability in another study. Subjects: College students. Results: Under relaxed conditions girls showed higher n. ach. than boys. The rise in n. ach. under achievement arousal by academic competition was significant for men, but women were not affected. However, when achievement motivation was aroused by social reward, women showed a significant increase, while men did not.

McConnell, T. R. Suggestibility in children as a function of chronological age. *J. abnorm. soc. Psychol.*, 1963, *67,* 286–89.
Measures: S's made judgments on paper about perceptual stimuli projected on the classroom screen after receiving erroneous suggestions that came from E or were attributed to large numbers of children the child's age. Susceptibility to the suggestion was measured, and one composite measure was compiled. Subjects: 290 children in grades 1–12. Results: Conformity to the erroneous suggestions decreased with age. No sex differences in conformity were found.

McDonald, F. J. Children's judgments of theft from individual and corporate owners. *Child Develpm.*, 1963, *34,* 141–50.
Measures: Children were given 2 stories involving theft of similar items. One of each pair was a theft from a corporate owner and the other was from an individual. The

child was asked to state which crime was the worse and why. Reasons given were scored in one of 10 categories. **Subjects:** 792 children, 8–15 years old. **Results:** Only 14% of the children gave reasons associated with corporate vs. individual owners. 50% of the sample said both actions were equally wrong because stealing is categorically wrong. Girls were significantly more likely to give this response than boys. Boys were significantly more likely to give reasons for the seriousness of the action in terms of the value of the object stolen.

McDonald, R. L., and M. D. Gynther. Relationship of self and ideal-self descriptions with sex, race, and class in southern adolescents. *J. Pers. soc. Psychol.*, 1965, *1*, 85–88.
Measures: Interpersonal Check List on which S rated himself and his ideal self on a list of adjectives. Tests were rated for 2 dimensions. **Subjects:** 261 Negro and 211 white high school seniors in segregated schools. **Results:** Males rated themselves and their ideal selves as more dominant than females, while females rated themselves as higher on the love dimension. Negro students rated themselves as higher on both the love and dominance dimensions than did white students.

McElroy, W. A. A sex difference in preference for shapes. *Brit. J. Psychol.*, 1954, *45*, 209–16.
Measures: A set of 12 pairs of pictures, one of each pair made up of curved lines and the other of straight, angular lines. Subjects were asked to choose which of each pair they preferred. **Subjects:** 380 boys and 399 girls aged 9–12, and 33 children aged 11–13. The children were Scottish. **Results:** Boys preferred round shapes, and girls preferred angular shapes (.001 level). Considering children under and over 12, boys preferred round shapes significantly more after than before 12, but there was no difference with age for girls.

McGuire, Carson. Sex role and community variability in test performances. *J. educ. Psychol.*, 1961, *52*, 61–73.
Measures: CAT; STEP social studies and science; STEP listening; clerical aptitude; mechanical reasoning from DAT; vocabulary completion; Gestalt transformation (ability to use an object in a different way); and four tests of perceptual closure mutilated words, Gestalt completion, short words, and copying). Tests of dotting and discrimination reaction time. They also gave the IPAT junior personality quiz, CMAS, Brown-Holzman survey of study habits and attitudes. **Subjects:** 144 junior high students, divided equally by sex and socioeconomic class (3). **Results:** No differences on the CAT reading achievement, either vocabulary or comprehension. On the CAT language achievement, and in the subdivisions of mechanics and spelling, girls excelled. There were no differences in arithmetic fundamentals or reasoning. There were no differences in social studies of science. In DAT clerical aptitude, girls excelled, and boys excelled in mechanical reasoning on the DAT. Girls were superior in vocabulary completion, short words, dotting, and DRT reaction time. On personality tests the girls were emotionally sensitive, surgent or talkative and excitable, high in socialized morale or acceptance of school and cultural standards, low in independent dominance, tolerant and slow to anger; they also valued teachers positively. Boys were the opposite: tough-minded, serious or disurgent, reacting negatively to learning tasks and school authority, independent, impatient, and less appreciative of teachers. There were no differences on the CMAS, on self-inadequacy, on any CYS family-tension scales such as authoritarianism, negative social orientation, etc., or on emotional stability, sociable, withdrawn, adventurousness, or energetic-conformity.

McHugh, Ann F. Sexual identification, size, and associations in children's figure drawings. *J. clin. Psychol.*, 1963, *19*, 381–82.
Measures: Subjects were instructed to draw human figures, and then to indicate sex, age, and activity of figures. **Subjects:** 626 children (320 girls, 306 boys), grades 1–6

in 2 elementary schools in the same community; white and English-speaking. Results: Both sexes tended to draw same-sex figure first. This tendency was significantly greater for girls at ages 7 and 10, for boys at 11. The tendency to draw the same-sex figure larger was significant for girls at all ages (7–11), and for boys at 8 and 11. The tendency to make the male figure older was significant for girls at ages 7 and 8, and for boys at age 8. The significant difference in activities of female figures was found at age 10, with girls making the figure more static and boys making it more active.

McKee, J. P., and F. B. Leader. The relationship of socioeconomic status and aggression to the competitive behavior of preschool children. *Child Develpm.,* 1955, *26,* 135–42.
  Measures: Observation of pairs of children in a structured play situation. Each child was given a set of blocks to build with while the E watched through a one-way screen. Subjects: 112 children, 3–4 years old, divided equally by sex, age, and social class (middle and lower). Results: Boys slightly higher on competition. No clear sex differences in aggression. (The authors felt that the situation called forth primarily verbal aggression, and this they felt might account for the lack of sex differences.)

McKee, J. P., and A. C. Sherriffs. The differential evaluation of males and females. *J. Pers.,* 1957, *25,* 356–71.
  Measures: Sarbin's Adjective Check List, previously rated for favorable or unfavorable evaluation of the items. Also a separate question: "Are men or women superior in worth?" Subjects: Several samples of about 50 men and 50 women. Results: Both men and women felt men were more worthwhile. Both men and women rated the two sexes with more positive than negative adjectives, but men received greater number of positive ratings.

McKusick, V. A. On the X chromosome of man. *Quart. Rev. Biology,* 1962, *37,* 69–175.
  This article reviews what is known about the X chromosome, including a list of traits which are X-linked. Mutation, the sex ratio, selection, consanguinity, and evolution are discussed as they relate to the X chromosome.

McManis, D. L. Pursuit-rotor performance of normal and retarded children in four verbal-incentive conditions. *Child Develpm.,* 1965, *36,* 667–83.
  Measures: S's performed 5 trials a day for 5 days on a pursuit-rotor with E either giving praise, reproof, no comments, or encouraging the child to be more competitive. After the 5 trials on the last day, S was told he could take more trials if he wanted, and his response was used as a measure of persistence. S always performed under the same incentive condition. Subjects: 24 normal boys and 24 normal girls (5th to 6th grades), and 48 retarded children (I. Q. 58–85). Results: No sex differences in accuracy of performance, although boys' accuracy was somewhat more affected by treatment (praise and competition giving greater accuracy). Boys persisted longer after the trials were over.

McNeil, J. D. Programmed instruction versus usual classroom procedures in teaching boys to read. *Amer. educ. Res. J.,* 1964, *1,* 113–19.
  Measures: Word-recognition tests were given to assess learning after a programmed learning course in reading for kindergarteners and after 4 months of 1st grade instruction in reading by a female teacher. Questionnaires to the teachers and interviews with the children were also given to assess teachers' differential treatment of the sexes in reading instruction. Subjects: 132 public school kindergarten children, with 93 of these followed up in 1st grade. Results: Boys were significantly better than girls in kindergarten, but these same boys were inferior to girls after 1st grade in-

struction. From the questionnaires to teachers and pupil interviews it was found that boys received more negative admonitions than girls and were rated more negatively on motivation and reading readiness. Boys also were given less opportunity to read than girls.

McNemar, Q. *The revision of the Stanford-Binet Scale: an analysis of the standardization data.* Boston: Houghton Mifflin, 1942.

Measures: 1937 revision, Stanford-Binet, the provisional form used in revising. **Subjects:** Children 2–18 years old. **Results:** At young ages (about 2–4) girls were better at picture memories, counting, paper folding, and buttoning. From about 3–5 they were better at aesthetic comparisons, matching objects, and paper folding. At later ages they were better at tying a bow tie, age discrimination, copying a bead chain from memory, one of the Minkus Completions, and one of the codes. Boys were better at picture absurdities from ages 4–9 and 9–17, and this was highly significant. They were better at orientation at each age in which it appeared, at block counting (7–12), ingenuity (11–17), plan of search (13–18), arithmetical reasoning (11–18), and at one only of several tests of opposite analogies, comprehension, and abstract words. These last three were probably content-specific. Total score gives girls an edge up to age 5½ and boys a slight edge from 5½ on up.

McNemar, Q., and L. M. Terman. Sex differences in variational tendency. *Genet. psychol. Monogr.*, 1936, *18*, No. 1, 1–65.

Measures: Many studies dealing with physical measurement, mental tests, and achievement tests were reviewed to find differences in variation between the sexes. The standard deviation is the statistic investigated whenever possible. **Subjects:** A large number of standardization samples for tests and measurements. **Results:** In anthropometric data there are no differences up to age 10. From age 10 to 14 girls show significantly more variation. From 14 on, boys show more variability. Achievement tests show no consistent differences. Verbal I.Q. tests such as the Stanford-Binet show significantly more male variability, the standard deviation being about one I.Q. point greater on the average for males.

Maccoby, Eleanor E. The taking of adult roles in middle childhood. *J. abnorm. soc. Psychol.*, 1961, *63*, 493–503.

Measures: Self-report scales measuring rule enforcement with peers, acceptance of rule enforcement from others, and several aspects of dependent-nurturant behavior. These measures were correlated with measures of child-rearing techniques taken when the child was 5. **Subjects:** 165 children from the original Sears et al. (1957) study. The children were 12 at the time of this follow-up. **Results:** Boys who tended to make others follow rules also tended to accept rule enforcement from others. This was not true for girls. Boys high on rule enforcement tended to be high on prosocial aggression and low on antisocial aggression. The correlations with aggression were similar for girls but weaker. High rule-enforcing boys were rated "good" in classroom behavior by teachers, but there was no relationship between these variables for girls. In looking at correlations with child-rearing antecedents, the clearest sex difference is that rule enforcement is positively related to parental strictness in boys, and to punitiveness in girls.

Maccoby, Eleanor E., and W. C. Wilson. Identification and observational learning from films. *J. abnorm. soc. Psychol.*, 1957, *55*, 76–87.

Measures: Movies with more than one main character were shown to children, and questionnaires were administered afterward. The tests determined which character the child identified with, and how much of the content of that character's actions and words and the cues relevant to his actions the child remembered. **Subjects:** 7th-grade children in 3 public schools, from various socioeconomic levels. Results: Boys chose the boy, and girls chose the girl for identification. Boys remembered aggressive content better than girls, provided the boy was the agent. Girls remembered boy-girl interactions best, provided the girl was the agent.

Maccoby, Eleanor E., W. C. Wilson, and R. V. Burton. Differential movie-viewing behavior of male and female viewers. *J. Pers.*, 1958, *26*, 259–67.
Measures: Eye movements of S's were observed as they watched scenes in which only the male and female leads of entertainment films were on the screen. The time spent watching each character was recorded. Subjects: 24 male and 24 female young adults. Results: Women spent proportionately more time than men watching the female lead, and men spent more time watching the male lead.

Malpass, L. F., Sylvia Mark, and D. S. Palermo. Responses of retarded children to the Children's Manifest Anxiety Scale. *J. educ. Psychol.*, 1960, *51*, 305–8.
Measures: CMAS. Subjects: 53 institutionalized mentally retarded children with mean I.Q. of 63 and mean age of 11½. 41 mentally retarded children living at home and attending special classes (average age 11½ and average I.Q. 68). 63 normal 11-year-olds with mean I.Q. of 110. Results: The retarded groups had higher CMAS scores than the normals. There were no sex differences in CMAS scores for the normal children or the institutionalized children. The other retarded group showed sex differences: the boys were significantly less anxious than either group of retarded girls or the institutionalized boys.

Marshall, H. R., and B. R. McCandless. Sex differences in social acceptance and participation of preschool children. *Child Develpm.*, 1957, *28*, 421–25.
Measures: Sociometric choices: teachers' ratings of popularity in school; observation of popularity and dependency. Subjects: Nursery school children. Results: No differences in dependency on teacher or popularity, but girls were higher on the sociometric test. Negative relationship between dependency and popularity in both sexes, with girls higher.

Mason, W. A., et al. Sex differences in affective-social responses of rhesus monkeys. *Behavior*, 1960, *16*, 1–2.
Measures: Observation. Subjects: Rhesus monkeys. Results: Female monkeys are more likely to threaten an outside observer than are male monkeys.

Mellone, Margaret A. A factorial study of picture tests for young children. *Brit. J. Psychol.*, 1944, *35*, 9–16.
Measures: A battery of 14 picture tests including digit-symbol, absurdities, memory span, series completion, analogies, block counting, directions, "which line doesn't belong," completion, picture arrangement, reversed similarities, and mazes. Subjects: About 500 boys and girls aged 6–7 in Edinburgh. Results: Boys were significantly better at block counting and mazes. A factor analysis was done with an arithmetic and reading test thrown in. In both sexes the first factor was a g factor and the second was a scholastic one defined by reading and arithmetic. A clear space factor also emerged for boys but not for girls.

Meltzer, H. Sex differences in children's attitudes to parents. *J. genet. Psychol.*, 1943, *62*, 311–26.
Measures: Children were asked to associate to the thought of their mothers and fathers. The first 10 associations were tabulated and categorized by content and affect. Subjects: 76 boys and 74 girls, aged 9–16, representing a variety of socioeconomic groups. Results: Girls gave more emotional responses than boys, and mothers evoked

more pleasant feeling tone than fathers for both sexes. Girls gave more acceptance responses to both parents than boys. Girls gave more hostile responses to mother than father, and boys gave more hostile responses to father than mother.

Mendel, Gisela. Children's preferences for differing degrees of novelty. *Child Develpm.*, 1965, *36*, 453–65.

Measures: Children were permitted to play with a group of 8 toys for a few minutes. Then each child was given his choice of playing with one of several other groups of 8 toys, differing in novelty (what per cent of the toys was identical to the 8 habituated toys). Teachers also rated children on anxiety. Subjects: 60 experimental and 60 control children, aged 3 yrs. 7 mos. to 5 yrs 6 mos. Results: Older children, boys, and less anxious children preferred greater novelty than did younger children, girls, and more anxious children. There were no sex differences in anxiety.

Menyuk, Paula. Syntactic structures in the language of children. *Child Develpm.*, 1963, *34*, 407–22.

Measures: Recording and syntactic analysis of children's speech in 3 situations: responses to Blacky pictures, conversation with an adult, and role playing with other children. Subjects: 48 nursery school and 48 1st-grade children, aged 3–7. Results: There were no differences in degree of syntactic complexity between the sexes.

Meyer, W. J. Social needs and heterosexual affiliations. *J. abnorm. soc. Psychol.*, 1959, *59*, 51–57.

Measures: A sociometric instrument asking the child whom he would most and least like to have around: (1) to meet succorance needs, and (2) for play-mirth needs. The scale was a five-point scale. Subjects: 212 girls and 175 boys in grades 5–12 in a rural community. The children were predominantly lower-middle class. Results: Boys preferred boys, and girls preferred girls, for both situations throughout the age range. The relative ratings for the two sexes remained constant for both boy and girl raters on succorance and for boy raters on play-mirth. However, girls gave boys increasingly higher ratings on ability to fulfill their play-mirth needs after the 7th grade.

Meyer, W. J., and A. W. Bendig. A longitudinal study of the Primary Mental Abilities Test. *J. educ. Psychol.*, 1961, *52*, 50–60.

Measures: PMA and the Myers–Ruch High School Achievement Test (a one-hour exam.). Subjects: 49 boys and 51 girls in an industrial town, lower-middle class. They were tested in 8th grade and again in 11th grade. The high school achievement test was given in 11th grade. Results: There were no significant differences on any subtests at 8th-grade level. At that level all but space favored girls (V, R, N, W). Space favored boys. At age 16 the same direction of differences was found, but now W, V, R, and N were significant in favor of girls. Space still did not significantly relate to sex differences. The average retest correlations were higher for boys than girls, this difference being extremely noticeable when correlations of differences between subtest scores were considered. The median correlation for boys was .55; for girls it was .08.

Meyer, W. J., Barbara Swanson, and Nancy Kauchack. Studies of verbal conditioning: I, Effects of age, sex, intelligence, and "reinforcing stimuli." *Child Develpm.*, 1964, *35*, 499–510.

Measures: S was asked to make up sentences using one of two verbs presented to him for each sentence. One word was hostile and the other was neutral. In the sex-comparison study, S was reinforced for using the hostile word by female E saying "good." Subjects: Three studies were done, but only the first investigated sex differences. This study involved 20 boys and 20 girls each from grades 4 and 6 in the experimental group and an equal number in the control group. Results: No sex differences were found in rate of conditioning to use of hostile verbs.

Miele, J. A. Sex differences in intelligence: the relationship of sex to intelligence as measured by the Wechsler Adult Intelligence Scale and the Wechsler Intelligence Scale for Children. *Dissert. Abstr.*, 1958, *18*, 2,213.
    Measures: WISC and WAIS. Subjects: The standardization population for both tests, consisting of 850 males and 850 females between the ages of 16 and 64, and 1,100 males and 1,100 females between the ages of 5 and 15. Results: No differences on total score on either test. On the vocabulary subtests, no differences ages 5–7, boys superior ages 8–15, and women superior on the WAIS vocabulary. On arithmetic, no differences ages 5–7, males superior but not significant ages 8–15, and males superior at all ages on the WAIS. Males superior at all ages except 5–7 and 55–64 in block design. In digit symbol, females were superior at all ages. On picture completion, males were superior after age 7. On the WISC, boys were superior on comprehension and mazes. On the WAIS, males were superior on information and females on similarities.

Miller, A. Sex differences related to the effect of auditory stimulation or to stability of visually fixated forms. Presented at APA meeting, Aug. 30, 1962, St. Louis, Missouri.
    Measures: Latency and amount of apparent change in 3 triangle forms that were fixated for a period of time while a continuous tone was introduced. Subjects: 18 men and 18 women college students. Results: Women showed longer latency before movement and greater stability than men. Explanation offered: women fuse experiences from 2 modalities so the triangle is stable like the tone. Men do not: they alternate attention from one modality to another. Authors give this as an alternate explanation of sex differences in rod and frame.

Milton, G. A. The effects of sex-role identification upon problem-solving skill. *J. abnorm. soc. Psychol.*, 1957, *55*, 208–12.
    Measures: Terman-Miles M-F scale; MMPI M-F scale; a behavior M-F scale; a verbal and a math aptitude test. Also a test of problem-solving skill. Subjects: 63 males and 66 females in college. Results: Men were significantly better at problem solving. The MMPI and behavior M-F did not correlate significantly with problem solving in either sex. The Terman-Miles M-F test did, with more masculine subjects excelling at problem solving. In a multiple regression equation this M-F test contributed significantly to the prediction of problem-solving skill within both sexes. Math aptitude also contributed to the regression equation for both sexes; verbal ability did for males only.

Minuchin, Patricia. Emergent patterns of sex difference in a study of children. Paper presented at New York State Psychological Assoc., 1963.
    Measures: WISC, Kuhlmann-Anderson Intelligence Test; achievement-test scores; specially derived problems for solving; fantasy story telling similar to the TAT; writing letters about self; play sessions; self-rating on competence and popularity; Draw-a-Person Test, and other assessments of interpersonal orientation and self-image. Subjects: 57 boys and 48 girls, aged 9, who attended two traditional and two modern schools. Results: On the WISC, girls were better at coding and boys at object assembly. No overall differences in achievement or I.Q. were found. Special problems requiring resourcefulness, restructuring and flexibility, fluidity, and processing and utilization of data showed no sex differences. Girls were more preoccupied with achievement in fantasy stories, although boys saw themselves as better at school work. On the fantasy stories, girls were more imaginative. Boys showed more aggres-

sion in play sessions and in fantasy. Boys were ambivalent about sex membership and more favorable toward their own sex. Girls were more socially oriented.

Minuchin, Patricia. Sex role concepts and sex typing in childhood as a function of school and home environments. Paper presented at American Orthopsychiatric Assoc., Chicago, 1964.
Measures: A wide range of cognitive, self-report, and projective measures of sex-typing, ability, interpersonal orientation, and self-image were given (see Minuchin 1963). Parent interviews were also conducted. Subjects: 57 boys and 48 girls, aged 9, from two traditional and two modern schools. Children were also classified by home atmosphere, modern or traditional. Results: Sex-typing was less clear, especially for girls from modern schools. Differences in favor of boys in problem solving, and in favor of girls in WISC coding, were found in traditional schools but not in modern schools. Boys from modern schools and modern homes displayed less aggression in play sessions than boys from traditional schools and homes.

Mitchell, A. M. *Children and movies.* Chicago: Univ. of Chicago Press, 1929.
Measure: Children quizzed about preferences for 10 movie subject categories. Subjects: About 10,000 children, aged 10 to 18. Results: 5 categories showed significant differences: boys preferred adventure, war, and westerns; girls preferred romance and tragedy.

Moffitt, J. W., and R. Stagner. Perceptual rigidity and closure as functions of anxiety. *J. abnorm. soc. Psychol.*, 1956, *52*, 354–57.
Measures: TMAS was given, and high and low scorers were chosen. These groups were made up equally of males and females, and were divided on an experimental variable, induction of anxiety. The experimental group was told that the tests might reveal neurotic personality traits; the control group was not threatened. The tests given were perceptual: a brightness-contrast test, the McGill Closure Test, an incomplete-figure-closure test, a tolerance-for-ambiguity test, and a perceptual-stability test based on an Ames distorted-room situation. Subjects: 40 high and 40 low TMAS-scoring college students, half male and half female. Results: There was no sex difference on the TMAS. The only significant sex difference was that women responded more to the experimental manipulation of anxiety in the closure test. They responded with greater closure than men in the threat condition.

Monmouthshire Education Committee. Report of a survey of reading ability in Monmouthshire, part I. Newport, Monmouthshire, England. Education Department, County Hall.
Measures: Vernon Graded Word Test. Subjects: About 5,000 children, aged 7–8 and 10–11. Results: There were more retarded readers among boys than girls.

Moore, Shirley G. Displaced aggression in young children. *J. abnorm. soc. Psychol.*, 1964, *68*, 200–204.
Measures: S's played a card game by which they lost or won chips from cards; some cards were plain, and some had drawings of a child of the same sex as S. In high frustration condition S lost chips to the card with the child on it. In the low frustration condition he came out even on chips, and in the control condition he came out even, winning from the child card. Then S was asked to play a shooting game where he could choose whether to shoot at a card with a figure of high or low similarity to the card used in the chip game. Subjects: 68 boys and 40 girls, aged 4 yrs. 7 mos. to 6 yrs. 2 mos. Results: Girls tended to prefer the low similarity card, while boys preferred the high similarity card (p = .07). Treatment conditions showed slight effects and only for boys.

Moore, Shirley, and Ruth Updegraff. Sociometric status of preschool children related to age, sex, nurturance-giving, and dependency. *Child Develpm.*, 1964, *35*, 519–24.

> **Measures:** Each S was asked to point to 4 children he liked and four he disliked from pictures of his nursery school peers. Then he had to tell whether he liked or disliked each of the other children in the school. Nurturant and dependent behavior in the school was observed. **Subjects:** 31 boys and 31 girls, aged 3 yrs. 2 mos to 5 yrs. 6 mos. **Results:** Sex was not related to popularity. Children tended to like same-sex children better than opposite-sex children. Sex differences in dependency and nurturance were not explored.

Moore, T., and L. E. Ucko. Four to six: constructiveness and conflict in meeting doll play problems. *J. child Psychol. Psychiat.*, 1961, *2*, 21–47.

> **Measures:** A structured doll-play session in which the child was asked to tell what would happen in domestic situations. Such situations as children fighting, not enough food for all the family, a child's lapse in toilet-training were used. The children's responses were scored as to constructiveness of solution, punitiveness, aggression, passivity, or failure to respond (avoiding the problem). Anxiety of the child was also scored. **Subjects:** 54 boys and 61 girls tested at age 4 and again at age 6. Children were residents of London. **Results:** Girls exceeded boys in constructiveness at both ages. Girls gave more punitive responses at age 4, but boys increased to the same level by age 6. Boys gave more aggressive responses at both ages. Boys failed to respond more at both ages. When anxious, boys were more likely to give aggressive responses while girls gave more passive responses or did not respond at all. The investigators concluded that boys cope less well than girls. Girls may give more socialized, constructive responses.

Moriarty, Alice. Coping patterns of preschool children in response to intelligence test demands. *Genet. Psychol. Monogr.*, 1961, *64*, 3–127.

> **Measures:** The Stanford-Binet and the Merrill-Palmer Performance Tests were administered. From observation, ratings were made on aspects of the child's orientation and adjustment to testing. 11 variables were rated, for example, cooperation, accepting own limits, tension. **Subjects:** 32 preschool children. **Results:** Girls initially tended to meet the unfamiliar situation more adaptively, orienting quickly to directions and tasks. However, as the tasks became more difficult, this sex difference was reversed, and girls became less integrated and more evasive than boys.

Mussen, P., and E. Rutherford. Parent-child relations and parental personality in relation to young children's sex-role perferences. *Child Develpm.*, 1963, *34*, 589–607.

> **Measures:** It Scale for Children was used to measure children's sex-typing. A doll-play session was administered to measure the child's perception of mother and father as nurturant, punitive, and powerful (nurturant and punitive). Mother interviews were made to assess various aspects of socialization practices, and parents filled out the femininity and self-acceptance scales from the California Personality Inventory. Parents also reported whether they encouraged their children to play sex-appropriate games. **Subjects:** 29 high-feminine girls and 28 low-feminine girls, and 24 high-masculine boys and 22 low-masculine boys, all in 1st grade. **Results:** High-masculine boys saw their fathers as more nurturant and somewhat more punitive than low-masculine boys. High-feminine girls saw mother as more nurturant, but not more punitive than low-feminine girls. Perception of opposite-sex parent from doll play was not significant. CPI variables and encouragement of sex-typed games were not significantly related to sex-typing in boys. In girls, mother's self-acceptance and father's encouragement of sex-typed games were significantly related to femininity.

Muste, Myra J., and D. F. Sharpe. Some influential factors in the determination of aggressive behavior in preschool children. *Child Develpm.*, 1947, *18*, 11–28.

Measures: Behavioral observation of aggression and response to aggression in paired children in standardized play situations. **Subjects:** 30 children, 2 yrs. 10 mos. to 5 yrs. 4 mos., in a college nursery school and a working-class nursery school. **Results:** Boys showed more total aggressive responses, but the difference was unreliable. It was consistent but small. In interaction, boy-boy combinations were the most aggressive, boy-girl next, and girl-girl least. In response to aggression, boys used counteraggression and active resistance most; girls used active resistance and verbal resistance most. Girls used more verbal aggressive techniques.

Nakamura, C. Y. Conformity and problem solving. *J. abnorm. soc. Psychol.*, 1958, *56*, 315–20.

Measures: A problem set consisting of 10 straightforward problems and 10 problems needing restructuring before solution was given. An analogies test was also administered, and the subjects were observed in a conformity situation in which S could report his perceptions accurately or go along with a rigged consensus. **Subjects:** 64 men and 77 women undergraduates. **Results:** Men were significantly higher in general intelligence. With this partialed out, men were still significantly better at both kinds of problems. Women were more conforming. There were significant negative correlations between performance on both kinds of problems and conformity in men. I.Q. was also negatively related to conformity in men. These correlations were negative but not significantly so for women.

Nakamura, C. Y., and F. F. Ellis. Methodological study of the effects of relative reward magnitude on performance. *Child Develpm.*, 1964, *35*, 595–610.

Measures: S played a lever-pressing game with marbles as the reward. Two levels of reward, high and low, were used. Both speed of lever pressing and persistence of pressing after extinction trials had begun were measured. Teachers also rated children on task persistence; and high and low task-persistence groups were used at each reward level. **Subjects:** 14 boys and 14 girls in kindergarten, and 14 boys and 14 girls in 3d grade. **Results:** Teachers tended to rate girls as more persistent than boys (no significance test given). In kindergarten, girls were more persistent during extinction trials than boys in the high reward condition. There were no sex differences for low reward or rate of lever pushing or for 3d grade children.

Newbigging, P. L. The relationship between reversible perspective and embedded figures. *Canad. J. Psychol.*, 1954, *8*, 204–8.

Measures: 5 reversible figures including the Necker cube were presented, and S was asked to try to reverse the figure as often as possible. The number of perceived reversals was measured. The Embedded Figures Test was also given. **Subjects:** 26 male and 26 female college students. **Results:** Men perceived significantly more reversals and did significantly better on the Embedded Figures Test.

Norman, R. D. Sex differences and other aspects of young superior adult performance on the Wechsler-Bellevue. *J. consult. Psychol.*, 1953, *17*, 411–18.

Measures: W-B test. **Subjects:** 85 males and 68 females, average age 23.5 for males and 22.3 for females. All were college students. The mean I.Q. equated for the two sexes, 127.5 for males and 126.8 for females. All total I.Q.'s were over 120. **Results:** Males were significantly superior on verbal, and females superior on performance. These differences were a result of a large difference in favor of males on arithmetic and females on digit-symbol. These were the only significant differences among subtests. Vocabulary favored females but was not significant.

Norman, R. D., Betty P. Clark, and D. W. Bessemer. Age, sex, I. Q., and achievement patterns in achieving and nonachieving gifted children. *Except. Child,* 1962, *29,* 116–23.

Measures: CTMM, CAT, and a predicted achievement level based on the CTMM. Groups were picked on the basis of a discrepancy between predicted achievement and actual performance as measured by the CAT. Subjects: 5,000 6th-grade children were tested; children with an I.Q. of 130 or more constituted the sample. There were 125 boys and 90 girls in this sample. Results: There were significantly more boys than girls with I.Q.'s over 130 in the total population. Boys were more variable in the discrepancy scores calculated from CTMM and CAT scores. Girls were more likely to overachieve than to underachieve. On the CAT, there were significant differences in favor of girls on mechanics of English, spelling, and reading vocabulary. Boys did not excel as expected in math.

Northby, A. S. Sex differences in high school scholarship. *Sch. and Soc.,* 1958, *86,* 63–64.

Measures: Rank order of scholarship. Subjects: June 1958 graduates of 83 Connecticut high schools. Results: Girls were much more successful: twice as many girls as boys were in the top decile; twice as many boys were in the bottom decile.

Oetzel, Roberta M. Sex typing and role adoption. Unpub. manuscript, Stanford University, 1961.

Two independent scales, one a masculinity scale and one a femininity scale, were constructed by submitting a list of personality descriptions to college students and to 5th-grade students for rating on masculinity and femininity. Items rated high on femininity were chosen for the masculinity scale. These scales were then presented to several classes of 5th-graders who nominated their peers for the items they felt described each child in the class. The final scales differentiated between the sexes in the appropriate direction and were highly reliable. The correlation between the two scales was low and insignificant.

Osborne, R. T., and Wilma B. Sanders. Variations in graduate record examination performance by age and sex. *J. Gerontol.,* 1954, *9,* 179–85.

Measures: Graduate Record Examination. Subjects: U. of Georgia graduate students, 1,173 men and 634 women aged 19–65, with a mean age of 31.76. Results: Men were significantly higher on mathematics and science, especially physics and chemistry. Women were significantly superior on literature and fine arts. Men were slightly superior in social science.

Paivio, A. Audience influence, social isolation, and speech. *J. abnorm. soc. Psychol.,* 1963, *67,* 247–53.

Measures: S's were administered the CASI, CMAS, and test-anxiety scales; and from these, children high and low on exhibitionism and on audience anxiety were picked. These groups were divided into two conditions—isolation and no isolation—before being asked to tell stories to an experimenter. Length of stories and speech errors made during delivery were recorded. Subjects: 80 children, 4th and 5th grades. Results: No differences as a result of exhibitionism. High audience-anxiety children gave shorter stories under isolation conditions, but not under no-isolation conditions. Boys spoke longer than girls.

Paivio, A. Childrearing antecedents of audience sensitivity. *Child Develpm.,* 1964, *35,* 397–416.

Measures: S took the Children's Audience Sensitivity Inventory and wrote a composition on why he either did or did not like to recite before the class. Parents filled out questionnaires on socialization practices such as use of praise and punishment, training in performing before an audience, parental sociability. Subjects: 2 studies: 192

children (grades 3–4) in the first, and 233 children (grades 3–5) in the second. Results: In general, parental practices related more to sons' than to daughters' sensitivity to audiences. This was particularly true of the relation between high use of reward, low use of punishment, and low sensitivity to audiences. Other sex differences included the finding that mother's sociability was negatively related to audience sensitivity in both boys and girls, but father's sociability was related only to sons' scores. Specific training in audience-oriented skills made girls less sensitive to audiences, but not boys.

Palermo, D. S. Racial comparisons and additional normative data on the Children's Manifest Anxiety Scale, *Child Develpm.*, 1959, *30*, 53–57.
   Measures: Children's Manifest Anxiety Scale. Subjects: 61 Negro boys, 75 Negro girls, 207 white boys, and 187 white girls in 4th, 5th and 6th grades. Results: Negroes scored higher than white children of the same sex. Girls scored significantly higher than boys in both racial groups.

Patel, A. S., and J. E. Gordon. Some personal and situational determinants of yielding to influence. *J. abnorm. soc. Psychol.*, 1960, *61*, 411–18.
   Measures: S's were given a vocabulary test with words of varying difficulty. The test booklet had some answers circled, 50 circled wrong and 11 right. The first four words were circled right to instill confidence. The S's were told that another class had taken the test and that they should ignore the marks. The other class was alternately described as one year ahead or one year behind the S's class in school. The number of wrong suggestions copied was the measure. Subjects: Boys and girls in 10th, 11th, and 12th grades. Results: Girls took more suggestions than boys, particularly when the source was high prestige (an older class). With lower prestige sources (younger class) the 10th grade girls were more suggestible but approached the boys on resistance to suggestion by 12th grade.

Patterson, G. R., R. A. Littman, and W. C. Hinsey. Parental effectiveness as reinforcers in the laboratory and its relation to child rearing practices and child adjustment in the classroom. *J. Pers.*, 1964, *32*, 180–99.
   Measures: S's were placed in a marble-dropping game with mother or father. The parent tester tried to change behavior by verbal reinforcement. Mothers were interviewed to assess warmth, permissiveness, and concern about child-rearing. Teachers also rated children on a number of dimensions from behavior in the classroom. Subjects: 41 families with 19 boys and 22 girls, ages 5 to 9. Results: Main effects of mother, father, or sex of child were not significant in effectiveness of conditioning. However, fathers were more successful in conditioning daughters than sons, and mothers were more successful with sons. Boys and girls conditioned more by same-sex parent came from permissive homes, while those conditioned more by opposite-sex parent came from restrictive (and, for boys, cool) homes. There were correlations between conditionability and teachers' ratings for girls—high-conditionable girls were seen as relaxed and nonaggressive—but not for boys.

Peisach, Estelle C. Children's comprehension of teacher and peer speech. *Child Develpm.*, 1965, *36*, 467–80.
   Measures: Children were asked to fill in missing words deleted from teachers' and children's speech. The children were from diverse social backgrounds. Subjects: 64 1st-grade and 127 5th-grade children. Results: No sex differences in 1st grade. At 5th-grade level, lower-class girls were superior at this language-comprehension task, while there were no sex differences among middle-class children.

Penney, R. K. Reactive curiosity and manifest anxiety in children. *Child Develpm.* 1965, *36*, 697–702.
   Measures: Children's Reactive Curiosity Scale (RCS), a paper-and-pencil test (to

measure curiosity), the Children's Manifest Anxiety scale, and the Peabody Picture Vocabulary Test (to measure I.Q.). Subjects: 178 children in grades 4, 5, and 6. Results: Girls had higher CMAS scores than boys. Correlation between I.Q. and CMAS was negative in girls and not significant for boys. No sex differences on RCS were given.

Peterson, D. G. *Minnesota Mechanical Ability Tests.* Minneapolis: Univ. of Minn. Press, 1930.

Measures: Minn. Mechanical Ability Tests. Subjects: 7th-grade boys and girls, and college sophomores, male and female. Results: On the Minn. assembly test, which involves putting together mechanical gadgets, boys and men were quite superior. On the Minn. form board the difference was in the same direction but much smaller. In the Minn. spatial-relations test (putting odd-shaped pieces in a form board as quickly as possible) and in card sorting and packing blocks there were no differences in the college group; but 7th-grade girls were better.

Pettigrew, T. F. The measurement and correlates of category width as a cognitive variable. *J. Pers.*, 1958, *26*, 532–44.

Measures: Questionnaire to measure category width—given the average statistic, what is the largest and smallest measurement recorded? Subjects were given a choice of extreme measurement describing categories of different widths. Subjects: College students. Results: There were significant differences between the sexes, with women having narrower categories. The scale also correlated positively with scores on the quantitative section of the ACE. (Broad categories were associated with high math scores.)

Phillips, B. N. Sex, social class, and anxiety as sources of variation in school achievement. *J. educ. Psychol.*, 1962, *53*, 316–22.

Measures: CTMM, CAT, Castaneda-McCandless Anxiety Scale, teachers' grades, social-class index based on income, occupation, and education. Subjects: 759 7th-grade students. Results: Girls were higher in achievement and in anxiety than boys. In anxiety the difference was only significant in the lower class. There were no significant sex differences in anxiety in the middle class. I.Q. was more correlated with achievement in boys than in girls. High anxiety was associated with poor achievement in girls and slightly higher achievement in boys, particularly in the lower class.

Phillips, B. N., E. Hindsman, and C. McGuire. Factors associated with anxiety and their relation to the school achievement of adolescents. *Psychol. Rep.*, 1960, *7*, 365–72.

Measures: Factor analysis of 19 variables including some from the IPAT Junior Personality Quiz, the CTMM, a scholastic-motivation variable, the Castaneda-McCandless Anxiety Scale, peer acceptance, and other measures. The 6 factors extracted (separately by sex) were correlated with objective achievement-test scores and teachers' grades. Subjects: 634 boys and 608 girls, all 7th-graders. Results: The 1st 5 factors were the same for both sexes: (1) self-criticism and guilt, (2) frustration with generalized aggression, (3) effective verbal ability, (4) anxious hostility to age-mates, and (5) anxious hostility toward school. The 6th factor was independent sociability and interests for females, and aggressive self-assurance for males. The correlations of these factors with achievement indicated that effective verbal ability was more highly correlated in boys than in girls, and that the 2 factors, anxious hostility toward school and anxious hostility toward age-mates, were more highly negatively correlated with achievement in girls than in boys.

Pintler, Margaret H., Ruth Phillips, and R. R. Sears. Sex differences in the projective doll play of preschool children. *J. Psychol.*, 1946, *21*, 73–80.

Measures: Three 20-minute sessions of doll play. Subjects: 20 boys and 20 girls in preschool, aged 3 yrs. 2 mos. to 6 yrs. 3 mos. Results: Girls showed more stereotyped thematic play, while boys were higher in aggression, nonhuman thematic play, and number of theme changes.

Pock, J. C. Some problems in evaluating the impact and function of education. Mimeo. copy, 1963.

Measures: A self-report religiousness scale developed for the Cornell Values Study was given. It attempts to measure on a 5-point scale the degree to which divine sanction is part of the respondent's values. Subjects: 2,513 alumni of a small college. 433 had some college, 1,226 had B.A.'s, 456, M.A.'s, and 398, doctorates. Results: Women were significantly more religious than men. In both sexes there was a tendency for amount of education to be negatively related to religiousness. This tendency was much stronger in women and was significant only for women. The biggest change in religiousness came for women who held graduate degrees.

Poffenberger, T., and D. Norton. Sex differences in achievement motive in mathematics as related to cultural change. *J. genet. Psychol.*, 1963, *103*, 341–50.

Measures: Students' reports of high school grades in algebra and other subjects, their liking for math, and their perceptions of grades parents expected them to get. Subjects: 208 male and 188 female college freshmen entering college fall 1955, and 309 male and 460 female college freshmen entering college fall 1960. Results: Study assumed that the reports for 1960 (a post-Sputnik year) would reflect an increased emphasis on math and science achievement. Prediction, following McClelland, was that this "arousal condition" will affect boys more than girls. Both boys and girls had better overall grades in 1960 than in 1955, but boys showed greater increase. In algebra grades, there were no significant sex differences in either year, but boys showed a greater increase in 1960. (Both sexes had significantly higher algebra grades in 1960 than in 1955.) In both 1955 and 1960, boys liked math better than girls. Girls' liking for math was identical in 1955 and 1960. Boys increased their liking for math significantly between 1955 and 1960. In 1955 boys and girls did not differ in their perceptions of either mother's or father's expectations for math grades. In 1960 boys felt that both mothers and fathers expected higher math grades of them than girls did. In 1960 both sexes felt parents expected higher grades in math than in 1955, but boys' expectations increased more.

Porteus, Barbara D., and R. C. Johnson. Children's responses to two measures of conscience development and their relation to sociometric nomination. *Child Develpm.*, 1965, *36*, 703–11.

Measures: S responded to stories of moral transgressions. In "A" type stories the hero or heroine yields to temptation. The amount of guilt, restitution, and confession that S attributes to this person is the measure of moral development. In "C" type stories the themes are immanent justice, moral realism, the necessity and efficacy of severe punishment; the measure of moral development was the number of times S rejected these concepts. The Differential Aptitude Test was used as a measure of I.Q., and intelligence was controlled in analysis. Subjects: 235 9th-grade students. Results: Girls were more mature in conscience development in both measures. There was a significant correlation between the two measures for boys but not for girls.

Porteus, S. D. The measurement of intelligence: 643 children examined by the Binet and Porteus tests. *J. educ. Psychol.*, 1918, *9*, 13–31.

Measures: Porteus mazes and Binet test (Goddard and Stanford revisions). Subjects: 200 girls and 253 boys. Results: Girls did significantly less well than boys on the Porteus maze. They tested closer to their Binet age, while boys were likely to score above their Binet age.

Pratt, K. C. A note upon the relation of activity to sex and race in young infants. *J. soc. Psychol.*, 1932, *3*, 118–20.

Measures: Stabilimeter to measure geenral activity. Subjects: 70 infants up to 2 weeks old. **Results:** No significant sex or race differences in general activity, although boys were slightly less active.

Pustell, T. E. The experimental induction of perceptual vigilance and defense. *J. Pers.*, 1957, *25*, 425–38.

Measures: Tachistoscopic presentation of 4 geometric symbols on a card, 4 cards giving all positions to the 4 symbols. All 4 symbols were the same brightness, but S was required to tell which of the 4 positions looked lighter to him. Then 16 cards were used for training, with one card lighter than the others. S was shocked severely whenever a particular symbol was lighter. Finally, the 1st cards were again presented, and the proportion of times the shocked symbol was seen as lighter was measured. If that proportion was greater than chance, vigilance was inferred. **Subjects:** 12 males and 12 female college students. **Results:** 12 out of 12 males used vigilance. 9 out of 12 women used defense. The authors attributed this to the fact that women were more anxious over the shock; therefore it acted as a drive. For men only moderate anxiety was aroused, and it became a cue for vigilance. When questioned and observed, women were passive and resigned to their fate. Men actively tried to avoid their fate, even though it was not possible in the situation.

Raaheim, K. Sex differences on problem-solving tasks. *Scandinavian J. of Psychol.*, 1963, *4*, 161–64.

Measures: The F Test, which measures ability to list uses or functions of common objects; the O Test, which requires listing of implements that serve a function or naming the missing implement in a problem; and the Pea Problem, which involves finding a way to transfer peas from one container to another. **Subjects:** 87 students, 15–16 years old, were given the F Test. 51 college students were given the O Test and the Pea Problem. **Results:** No significant differences on the F Test or the Pea Problem. Women were significantly superior on the O Test.

Rabban, M. Sex-role identification in young children in two diverse social groups. *Genet psychol. Monogr.*, 1950, *42*, 81–158.

Measures: Choice of boy or girl toys, being like a boy or girl doll, and wishing to be a mama or papa. **Subjects:** 300 children, 30 months to 8 years. **Results:** No differences among 3-year-olds. Above this age, boys made more masculine choices than girls made feminine choices.

Rebelsky, Freda G., W. Alinsmith, and R. E. Grinder. Resistance to temptation and sex differences in children's use of fantasy confession. *Child Develpm.*, 1963, *34*, 955–62.

Measures: Story completions to determine fantasy confession to deviation administered before and after a game in which cheating was possible and necessary to win. **Subjects:** 138 6th-grade children—69 boys and 69 girls from the *Patterns of child rearing* sample. **Results:** Boys cheated more than girls. Girls confessed in their story completions more than boys. Confession was a better indication of resistance to cheating in girls than in boys. The greater use of confession in girls was felt to be a result of the more dependent, affiliational needs of girls.

Reese, H. W. Manifest anxiety and achievement test performance. *J. educ. Psychol.*, 1961, *52*, 132–35.

Measures: CMAS; PMA; an arithmetic speed test. The arithmetic test scores were correlated with CMAS, PMA partialed out. **Subjects:** 539 students, grades 4 and 6. **Results:** Significance of mean differences was not reported. The correlation of CMAS with performance was negative, and there was no sex difference in correlation.

Reese, H. W. Sociometric choices of the same and opposite sex in late childhood. *Merrill-Palmer Quart.*, 1962, *8*, 173–74.

Measures: S's rated each of their classmates on a five-point scale from "best friends" to "dislike." Popularity with the opposite sex was investigated as a function of popularity with the same-sex peers. Subjects: 36 girls and 48 boys from the 5th grade. Results: Girls liked boys who were popular with other boys. Boys' acceptance of girls was less clearly related to girls' popularity with other girls.

Rempel, H., and E. I. Signoi. Sex differences in self-rating of conscience as a determinant of behavior. *Psychol. Reps.*, 1964, *15*, 277–78.
Measures: S rated himself on a 7-point scale for the degree to which conscience determined his behavior. Subjects: 55 males and 42 females in college. Results: Females were more likely to rate themselves high in conscience as a determinant of behavior than were males.

Richards, T. W., and O. C. Irwin. Plantar responses of young children. *Univ. Iowa Stud. Child Welfare*, 1935, *11*, 7–146.
Measures: Observation of plantar response after stroking the foot. Subjects: 97 infants, 1–12 days old. Results: Males were slightly ahead in total responses. Females showed more extension of smaller toes, flexion, and mixed responses. None of the differences were significant.

Richardson, S. A., A. H. Hastorf, and S. M. Dornbusch. Effects of physical disability on a child's description of himself. *Child Develpm.*, 1964, *35*, 893–907.
Measures: Children were asked to describe themselves. Descriptions were recorded and coded into scoring categories such as personality traits, physical description, activities, and abilities. Subjects: 63 handicapped and 63 nonhandicapped boys, and 44 handicapped and 65 nonhandicapped girls in a summer camp for underprivileged children. White, Negro, and Puerto Rican children. Results: Handicapped girls talked about nonphysical recreation more than normals, but this was not true of boys. Handicapped girls talked more than nonhandicapped girls about others' giving aid, but this was not true for boys. Handicapped boys were more concerned with aggression than handicapped girls.

Richardson, S. A., A. H. Hastorf, N. Goodman, and S. M. Dornbusch. Cultural uniformity in reaction to physical disabilities. *Am. soc. Rev.*, 1961, *26*, 241–47.
Measures: Children were presented with pictures of children of their own sex who represented different physical disabilities. There was an able-bodied child, a child with a crutch and leg brace, a child in a wheel chair, a child with a missing hand, a child with a facial disfigurement, and an obese child. The subjects were asked to rank-order the pictures according to their liking for each pictured child. Subjects: Approximately 600 children (some handicapped) from different ethnic groups and social classes. The children were 10 and 11 years old. Results: Although both boys and girls ranked the social handicaps of facial disfigurement and obesity lower than the functional disabilities, the mean rank for these social handicaps was lower for girls than for boys. Boys ranked the functional handicaps lower than girls.

Rie, H. E. An exploratory study of the CMAS Lie Scale. *Child Develpm.*, 1963, *34*, 1003–17.
Measures: Children's Manifest Anxiety Scale, and the lie scale constructed for it. Subjects: 344 children in grades 1–7. Results: Slight but consistent differences between the sexes, significant only at 10-year level, were found. Girls were higher in manifest anxiety. Differences on the lie scale were quite small.

Riggness, T. A. GSR during learning activities of children of low, average, and high intelligence. *Child Develpm.*, 1962, *33*, 879–88.
Measures: Measurement of GSR base level, variability of base level, and combined height of peaks and number of peaks for a 15-minute period, during which the child performed 3 tasks: counting, piling pennies, and teaching addition. Subjects: 20

children of each sex in each of 3 intelligence-level groups: 50–80, 90–110, and 120 up. **Results:** Of the 3 groups, the bright children tended to be more reactive. Boys tended to have lower base-line GSR level (a lower initial-arousal level).

Rosenberg, B. G., and B. Sutton-Smith. The measurement of masculinity and femininity in children. *Child Develpm.*, 1959, *30*, 373–80.
    Measures: 181 games were presented to children to determine play preferences. Those games that differentiated the sexes were then given to 2 cross-validation groups to determine whether sex differences were significant. **Subjects:** 183 children in 4th through 6th grades in the first presentation; the cross-validation groups consisted of 75 boys and 92 girls and 199 boys and 207 girls in grades 4–6. **Results:** More games were found to be feminine than masculine. A total possible score on the masculine scale was 56, and on the feminine scale 116. On cross validation the boys' means differed significantly in the expected direction from the girls' means on both scales. Boys preferred forceful physical contact, dramatization of conflict between male roles, propulsion of objects through space, and complex team games. Girls preferred dramatization of static activity, verbal games, ritualistic noncompetitive games, choral and rhythmic games, and games with a central role for one player.

Rosenberg, B. G., and B. Sutton-Smith. The measurement of masculinity and femininity in children: an extension and revalidation. *J. genet. Psychol.*, 1964, *104*, 259–64.
    Measures: A scale-measuring game and pastime choices of boys and girls. **Subjects:** 928 boys and 973 girls in grades 3–6. **Results:** The scale was somewhat revised on the strength of the new sample, and was found to differentiate boys and girls adequately. The scale continues to be used as a measure of masculinity-femininity.

Rosenberg, B. G., and B. Sutton-Smith. The relationship of ordinal position and sibling sex status to cognitive abilities. *Psycho. Sci.*, 1964, *1*, 81–82.
    Measures: ACE Psychological Examination, which measures ability in quantitative and linguistic tasks. **Subjects:** 125 male and 252 female college students from two-sibling families. **Results:** Males performed better on the quantitative and females on the linguistic sections of the test. For males, having a sister tended to increase linguistic scores. This was not true for girls.

Rosenblith, Judy F. Learning by imitation in kindergarten children. *Child Develpm.*, 1959, *30*, 69–80.
    Measures: Children were asked to work Porteus Mazes before and after watching an adult perform the task. After the before measure, the subjects were divided into four performance-level groups. Half of each of these were female and half male. Some groups had a male, and some had a female leader to imitate, while a third group, the control, had no leader. Before the mazes the leader either played with the subject for 10 minutes, or played 5 minutes and then withdrew from interaction for 5 minutes. The dependent variable was the amount of improvement on the mazes after watching the leader. **Subjects:** 120 kindergarten children, middle class. **Results:** (1) Having the leader was more effective than merely having more trials. (2) The male leader was generally more effective. (3) Boys showed more improvement than girls, and girls were less sensitive to experimental manipulation. (4) Constant attention was better than withdrawal of attention except for boys with a male leader.

Rosenblith, Judy F. Imitative color choices in kindergarten children. *Child Develpm.*, 1961, *32*, 211–23.
    Measures: A second report on the experiment described above (Rosenblith 1959), with the dependent variable being matched dependent behavior—imitating the leader's choice of colored pencil. **Subjects:** 80 kindergarten children, middle-class and upper-middle-class groups, excluding the control group reported in the 1959 article.

Results: Boys improved on maze performance more than girls. Girls were slightly more likely to imitate color. There was also a withdrawal of attention for 5 of a 10-minute play session by the adult, and the girls were more likely to match color with attention than with withdrawal of attention; low-performance boys showed a non-significant tendency for attention to produce more imitation. High-performance boys imitated more with withdrawal of attention. Sex of leader vs. sex of child: for boys, same-sex leader was more influential; for girls, attention, regardless of sex of leader, was important. For both sexes together, attentive opposite-sex leaders were more effective than withdrawing opposite-sex leaders. For same-sex leaders, attention or withdrawal gave no difference.

Rosenblith, Judy F. The modified Graham Behavior Test for Neonates: test-retest reliability, normative data, and hypotheses for future work. *Biologia Neonatorum*, 1961, *3*, 174–92.
> **Measures:** The maturation scale from the Graham Behavior Test for Neonates. This scale measures lifting head, pushing against something with the feet, strength of grasp, reaction to auditory stimuli, reaction to cotton held over the nose, etc. **Subjects:** Infants during the first 4 days of life. **Results:** No significant sex differences.

Rosenblith, Judy F. Tactile sensitivity and muscular strength in the neonate. To be published in *Child Develpm.*
> **Measures:** Behavioral tests consisting of tactile-adaptive items (reaction to cotton over nose, e.g.), motor items (prone head reaction, strength of grasp, etc.), and irritability. Also electrotactual stimulation. **Subjects:** 43 males and 46 females in the first 4 days of life. **Results:** Boys were higher on the motor scale, and girls had lower tactual thresholds. However, these differences were not significant. When birth weight was held constant, the motor differences dropped out. The most quantitative motor item, strength of grip, showed girls slightly stronger than boys when weight was held constant. Chubbiness (ratio of weight to length) was correlated with electrotactual sensitivity. It correlated –.35 for 16 males and –.12 for 16 females.

Rosenblum, S., and R. J. Callahan. The performance of high-grade retarded, emotionally disturbed children on the Children's Manifest Anxiety Scales and Children's Anxiety Pictures. *J. clin. Psychol.*, 1958, *14*, 272–75.
> **Measures:** CMAS and CAP (pictures that children may see as threatening or not—a TAT-type projection test). **Subjects:** 19 boys and 14 girls, high-grade mental defectives, institutionalized and extremely disturbed. **Results:** Girls tended to be higher on CMAS (p = .01), but not on the CAP.

Rosenthal, R., R. L. Mulry, G. W. Persinger, Linda Vikan-Kline, and Mardell Grothe. Emphasis on experimental procedure, sex of subjects and the biasing effects of experimental hypotheses. *J. proj. Tech. Pers. Assessment*, 1964, *28*, 470–73.
> **Measures:** Naive experimenters were trained to administer a standardized series of photographs of faces to S's. S rated the pictures on degree of success or failure the person had been experiencing. E's were told that half their subjects would probably react one way and half the opposite way. Degree of influence of E on S's judgments was measured. **Subjects:** College students. **Results:** Male E's influenced their subjects according to the bias given them. Female E's influenced female S's in the direction of their biases, but they influenced male S's in the opposite direction.

Rothaus, P., and P. Worchel. Ego-support, communication, catharsis, and hostility, *J. Pers.*, 1964, *32*, 296–312.
> **Measures:** An index of behavioral hostility (BIHS) was administered to pick high- and low-hostile subjects. E then administered an intelligence test to groups of S's in a way calculated to provoke hostility. S's were then given either a catharsis session

to ventilate feelings, catharsis with ego support from confederates, catharsis with communication to E, or no catharsis. S's hostility to E was measured (before and after); S's were tested at an aiming task after catharsis, and given six TAT cards after catharsis to measure aggression anxiety. Subjects: 192 college students, half male and half female and half high- and half low-hostility subjects. Results: Men were more hostile to E before and after the treatment conditions. Women had higher aggression-anxiety scores on the TAT than men (measured by the amount of impersonal aggression expressed).

Rothbart, Mary K., and Eleanor E. Maccoby. Parents' differential reactions to sons and daughters. *J. Pers. soc. Psychol.*, 1967, in press.

Measures: Parents listened to a taped child's voice addressing a series of remarks to a parent. In some cases S was told the voice was that of a girl; in others, that of a boy. S's were asked to respond to the demands as though the child was their own. A questionnaire measure of sex-role differentiation was also given. Subjects: 32 fathers, 98 mothers of nursery school children. Results: Fathers were more permissive of both aggression and dependency from daughters; mothers were more permissive of both kinds of behavior from sons.

Rowley, V. N., and F. Beth Stone. Changes in children's verbal behavior as a function of social approval, experimenter differences, and child personality. *Child Develpm.*, 1964, 35, 669–76.

Measures: Teachers rated S's on Peterson's Problem Checklist, which contains two types of problems: inhibition and acting out. S's were chosen for two groups: high inhibition and low acting out and low inhibition and high acting out. These children were divided between male and female E's and placed in a conditioning experiment. S made up sentences using personal pronouns, one of which was rewarded by E. Subjects: 24 boys and 24 girls, 4th-graders. Results: Analysis of variance indicated no significant effects on rate of conditioning as a function of sex of E, sex of S, or the interaction between them. Other variables were not analyzed by sex.

Ruebush, B. K., and H. W. Stevenson. The effects of mothers and strangers on the performance of anxious and defensive children. *J. Pers.*, 1964, 32, 587–600.

Measures: High and low anxiety and defensiveness groups were picked on the basis of scores on the Defensiveness Scale for Children and the Test Anxiety Scale for Children. S performed two tasks with either his own mother or a female stranger as social reinforcer: a marble-dropping game and an embedded figures game (EFG), which involved finding an object in a complex familiar scene. Subjects: Three groups of 32 children in 2d grade. Results: Boys performed at a higher rate than girls in the marble game, while girls performed better on the EFG. On the marble game high-anxious, low-defensive girls made more responses than the comparable group of boys, while low-anxious, low-defensive boys made more responses than the girls in that group.

Ruebush, B. K., and R. R. Waite. Oral dependency in anxious and defensive children. *Merrill-Palmer Quart.*, 1961, 7, 181–90.

Measures: Subjects were given the Sarason Test Anxiety Scale for Children, the Defensiveness Scale for Children, and the Holtzman Inkblot Test. The inkblot test was rated for direct, obvious expressions of oral dependency, and for indirect, less obvious expressions of oral dependency. Subjects: Extreme groups were chosen from a pool of 261 boys and 253 girls in 4th grade. Six groups of 12 subjects each were selected for the study: low-anxious, low-defensiveness boys and girls; high-anxious, low-defensiveness boys and girls; and low-anxious, high-defensiveness boys and girls. Results: In an analysis of variance in which anxiety and sex were independent variables (all children having low defensiveness scores), boys with high anxiety were high in direct dependency, but this was not true for girls. Using this same set of subjects, there was a significant sex difference in indirect dependency with girls higher. In an analysis of variance studying defensiveness and using all low-anxious children, high-defensive boys were more expressive of indirect dependency than low-defensive boys, while low-defensive girls were more expressive of indirect dependency than high-defensive girls. There were no differences among these subjects on direct dependency.

Russell, D. G., and E. G. Sarason. Test anxiety, sex, and experimental conditions in relation to anagram solution. *J. Pers. soc. Psychol.*, 1965, *1*, 493–96.
Measures: S's were selected for high or low anxiety by the Test Anxiety Scale. They solved anagram problems under conditions of high or low motivation and under conditions of being asked to verbalize solution processes while working or not being asked to verbalize. Subjects: 24 males and 24 females high in anxiety and 24 of each sex low in anxiety. All college students. Results: High anxiety males and low-anxiety females performed at a faster rate than low-anxiety males and high-anxiety females. This was particularly clear in the verbalization condition.

Samuels, F. Sex differences in reading achievement. *J. educ. Res.*, 1943, *36*, 594–603.
Measures: Kuhlman-Anderson Intelligence Test; Monroe Aptitude Test of reading readiness; teachers' ratings of reading readiness after 2 weeks of 1st grade; Gates Primary Reading Test at the end of 1st grade; and reading grades in 1st grade. Subjects: 216 boys and 237 girls in 1st grade in Arizona schools. Children went into special reading groups on the basis of readiness ratings and tests. Results: Girls were significantly superior in mental age, I.Q. scores, drawing test scores, teachers' ratings, and the Monroe Aptitude Test. They were also significantly superior in Gates Reading Test and in reading grades. Because of the superior intelligence of the girls, 100 matched pairs of girls and boys were made up on the basis of mental age (with chronological age loosely controlled). Girls remained superior but not significantly so on the Monroe Aptitude Test, but they remained significantly superior on the Gates Test and teachers' grades. The last two were achievement measures.

Sanford, R. N., M. Adkins, R. B. Miller, and E. A. Cobb. Physique, personality, and scholarship. *Monogr. Soc. Res. Child Develpm.*, 1943, *8*(1).
Measures (1) Teachers' ratings of children's displayed needs. (2) E's ratings of same. (3) Tabulation of need themes on the TAT. Subjects: 48 children, ages 5–14, studied for 3 years. Results: (1) By teachers' ratings, n. exposition, n. aggression, and n. construction were the most masculine, while n. nurturance, n. succorance, and n. sentience were the most feminine needs. (2) Final staff ratings—a synthesis of all known data—made n. play, n. construction, and n. understanding the most masculine, and n. defendence, n. retention, and n. rejection the most feminine needs. (3) In TAT tabulation, aggression was 1st in rank order for both sexes, but it was much higher in boys. Girls scored higher than boys at all ages in n. affiliation, n. deference, n. cognizance, n. blame-avoidance, n. exhibition, and infavoidance. Most differences were greatest during middle childhood.

Santostefano, S. A developmental study of the cognitive control, "leveling-sharpening." *Merrill-Palmer Quart.*, 1964, *10*, 343–60.
Measures: S's were presented with 2-second exposures of a series of line drawings in which the drawing gradually changed. In one series, a drawing of a wagon was presented, and lines were gradually subtracted from the drawing. In another series, lines were gradually added to complete an incomplete drawing of a wagon. In a third series, a circle gradually changed in size. S was asked to tell each time he thought the picture had changed and in what way. Earliest correct perception of a change and number of correct perceptions of change were computed as a measure of sharpening.

Not perceiving changes was interpreted as leveling. Subjects: 10 boys and 10 girls from each age group, 6, 9, and 12 years. Groups approximately matched on I.Q. and visual acuity. Results: Wagon subtraction, the measure presented to S's first, gave best results. Younger children and girls tended to level more than older children and boys. The sex differences were not significant with the other two series.

Sarason, I. G. Test anxiety and intellectual performance. *J. abnorm. soc. Psychol.*, 1963, *66*, 73–75.
Measures: The Test Anxiety Scale and a "need for achievement" scale were correlated with School and College Ability Test scores (SCAT). Subjects: 219 11th-grade and 241 12th-grade students. Results: Test Anxiety scores correlated negatively with SCAT scores, more so in females than in males. The "need for achievement" scale did not correlate significantly with SCAT scores.

Sarason, I. G., V. J. Ganzer, and Judith W. Granger. Self-description of hostility and its correlates. *J. Pers. soc. Psychol.*, 1965, *1*, 361–65.
Measures: A paper-and-pencil hostility scale was administered, and then in one study S unscrambled sentences that had both a hostile and a neutral solution. In another study S was tested for recall of hostile trait descriptions of someone else. In a third study S recalled parent-child relationships from his own childhood. Subjects: Varying number of college students in each of the three studies. Results: Women were higher on the hostility scale, but significance tests are not given. Women made significantly fewer hostile sentences in the first study. In the third study high-hostile S's saw their parents as less affectionate and close. The correlations were generally higher for women than for men, although correlations for both sexes were in the same direction on the variables.

Sarason, I. G., and M. G. Harmatz. Test anxiety and experimental conditions. Unpublished manuscript, 1965.
Measures: S participated in a serial-learning task with either a male or female E and with motivating conditions involving neutral instructions, high-achievement-motivating instructions, or low-achievement instructions. S's were divided into high and low anxiety groups on the basis of the Test Anxiety Scale. E also varied comments (good, or try harder) during testing. Subjects: 72 male and 72 female high school sophomores. Results: Anxiety was a significant variable, with low-anxious S's performing better than high-anxious S's. Complex sex-by-anxiety-by-condition interactions were found. The male experimenter was more effective than the female E in terms of performance of S's of both sexes.

Sarason, I. G., and M. G. Harmatz. Sex differences and experimental conditions in serial learning. *J. Pers. soc. Psychol.*, 1965, *1*, 521–24.
Measures: S's were assigned to groups on the basis of anxiety scores, measured by the Test Anxiety Scale. Four conditions were established for a serial-learning task: a green light came on periodically to indicate either above-average, average, or below-average performance, or no light was flashed at all. Subjects: 60 male and 60 female college students. Results: Under neutral motivational conditions, women performed better than men. Under all three light conditions men performed better than women. There were no differences among the three light conditions.

Sarason, S. B., K. S. Davidson, F. F. Lighthass, R. R. Waite, and B. K. Ruebush. *Anxiety in elementary school children.* New York: Wiley and Sons, 1960.
Measures: General Anxiety Scale for Children and the Test Anxiety Scale for Children. Subjects: A large number of children in elementary school tested in several different studies of anxiety. Results: Girls consistently scored higher. However, high anxiety in boys showed higher correlations and more consistent patterning when relationships with other variables were reviewed.

Schaefer, E. S., and Nancy Bayley. Maternal behavior, child behavior, and their intercorrelations from infancy through adolescence. *SRCD Monogr.*, 1963, *28*, No. 3.

Measures: Observation, interviews, and ratings of children and mothers from infancy to adolescence. Subjects: 61 children from the Berkeley Growth Study. Results: A large number of relationships are reported between maternal behavior and child behavior at different ages. There is evidence that maternal behavior during child's early childhood predicts child's later behavior better for boys than girls. For instance, early mother behavior on the love-hostility dimension predicts task-oriented behavior and social behavior in boys at age 9–12, while the r's are much lower for girls. Also, early maternal behavior on automony-control dimension predicts several personality variables for boys at adolescence, but there are no significant correlations for girls.

Scheidel, Thomas M. Sex and persuasibility. *Speech Monogr.*, 1963, *30*, No. 4, 353–58.

Measures: A 2-part attitude scale was administered before and after a persuasive 11-minute speech. The scale, "An Attitude Scale for Empirical Studies in Communication Research," was constructed by the author. A speech-retention test was given as well. Subjects: 242 college students (104 men, 138 women) in undergraduate speech courses. Results: Women were found to be significantly more persuadable than men; they were found to transfer the persuasive appeal significantly more than men, and found to retain significantly less of the speech content than men.

Schiller, Belle. Verbal, numerical, and spatial abilities of young children. *Arch. Psychol.*, 1934, No. 161.

Measures: A battery of 4 verbal, 3 numerical, and 5 spatial-manipulation tests. Verbal tests consisted of vocabulary, analogies, sentence completion, and reading. Numerical tests were made up of number series, arithmetic reasoning, and computation. Spatial tests contained the Otis (directions, associations, mazes, picture sequence, similarities), the Beta (mazes, cube analysis, X-O series, digit-symbol, picture completion, geometrical construction), the International (cubes, association, similarities, faces, mazes, rhythms, analogies, and narratives), the Draw-a-Man test, the Pintner-Paterson Scale (5-figure, casuist, Knox cube, Healy A). Subjects: 189 boys and 206 girls in 3d and 4th grade. All of Jewish parentage. Results: Arithmetic reasoning, Otis, and Army Beta favored boys, and the differences were significant. Draw-a-Man favored girls, and there were no differences on the verbal tests. The spatial factor did not consistently favor boys.

Schmuck, R., and E. Van Egmond. Sex differences in the relationship of interpersonal perceptions to academic performance. *Psychol. in the Schools*, 1965, *2*, 32–40.

Measures: S's were placed in high and low I.Q. groups on the basis of a standardized I.Q. test. Teachers rated children on performance in class. Questionnaires, sentence-completion tests, and group interviews were given to S's to determine social-class affiliation, parents' attitudes toward school, S's satisfaction with the teacher, and child's perception of his peer status. Subjects: 18 elementary school classrooms, 4 junior high classrooms, and 5 senior high classrooms. Results: Although there were no I.Q. differences between the sexes, girls were better achievers than boys. Performance and social status were positively related in girls but not in boys. Perceived peer status was positively related to performance in both sexes. Satisfaction with the teacher was also positively related to performance in both sexes. Perceived support for school from parents was related to performance in girls but not in boys. When variables were held constant, satisfaction with teacher was the most important correlate of achievement in both sexes.

Schneidler, Gwendolen R., and D. G. Patterson. Sex differences in clerical aptitude. *J. educ. Psychol.*, 1942, *33*, 303–9.
> Measures: Minnesota Vocational Test for Clerical Workers. Subjects: A large group of children in grades 5–12. Results: At all age levels there was a large and significant difference in favor of girls. This was true of adults as well, although there were no sex differences among people actually employed as clerical workers.

Schopler, J., and N. Bateson. The power of dependence. *J. Pers. soc. Psychol.*, 1965, *2*, 247–54.
> Measures: 3 studies were run. In the first, S's were asked to volunteer for a psychological experiment in which they would have to spend some time in a chamber at 125 degrees. The request came from a graduate student working on a dissertation under one of two conditions: a pressing deadline or no deadline. The former was high dependence on S, and the latter low dependence on S. In the second 2 studies, S made decisions for himself and a dependent fellow player in situations where the other person was either very dependent or only somewhat dependent on S for winning money in a game, and where S's yielding to the other person's need would cost him a little or a lot of money. Subjects: College students in each of the three studies. Results: In the first study women volunteered less than men. Women volunteered more when the graduate student was highly dependent, and men volunteered more when the student was less dependent. In the second and third studies, there were no sex differences when the risk of loss to S was high, but under lower risk of loss to S, females yielded more when the opponent was very dependent, and males yielded more when he was not quite so dependent.

Sears, Pauline S. Doll play aggression in normal young children: influence of sex, age, sibling status, father's absence. *Psychol. Monogr.*, 1951, *65* (6), iv, 42.
> Measures: Behavioral observation of children's aggressive acts in standardized doll play with dolls representing family members. Subjects: 150 preschoolers enrolled in day schools for working mothers. Results: Boys showed significantly more aggression than girls, particularly direct bodily injury. There was little difference in amount of verbal and mischievous aggression. Boys showed more aggression to father doll, and girls more to baby and girl doll.

Sears, R. R. Relation of early socialization experiences to aggression in middle childhood. *J. abnorm. soc. Psychol.*, 1961, *63*, 466–92.
> Measures: Self-administered aggression scales. Subjects: 6th-grade children who as kindergarteners had been part of the *Patterns of child rearing* sample. Results: Girls were higher on prosocial aggression and on aggression anxiety. Boys were higher on antisocial aggression. Gough's CPI femininity scale correlated positively with prosocial aggression and aggression anxiety, and negatively with antisocial aggression *within* sex. Aggression anxiety appeared to have different antecedents in the two sexes. In boys it was related to rapid socialization and high conformity in a love-oriented home. In girls it came from conflict caused by the excitation of aggressive tendencies that disrupted appropriate sex-typing.

Sears, R. R., Eleanor E. Maccoby, and H. Levin. *Patterns of child rearing.* Evanston, Ill.: Row, Peterson, 1957.
> Measures: Interviews with mothers of children, transcribed and rated on dimensions of child-rearing practices by raters familiar with the objectives of the study. Subjects: 379 mothers of kindergarten children. Results: There were no significant differences between the sexes on mothers' reports of aggression or dependency. Boys' mothers were more permissive of aggression toward parents and peers, and used more physical punishment. Parental punitiveness for aggression and permissiveness for aggression were both positively correlated with aggression in both sexes. There were significantly

more girls than boys reported as having highly developed consciences. Warmth and acceptance by mother were more important in fostering girls' conscience development than boys', while father's acceptance was more important in boys' conscience development.

Sears, R. R., Lucy Rau, and R. Alpert. *Identification and child rearing*. Stanford: Stanford Univ. Press, 1965.

Measures: Behavior observations and ratings in nursery school, observation of mother-child interaction, mother and father interviews, doll play. Child measures on aggression, dependency, sex-typing, adult role taking, and "conscience." Subjects: 40 nursery school children. Results: Boys were higher in almost all measures of aggression. They were higher in antisocial aggression and thematic aggression in doll play, in 7 out of 10 measures of aggression during free play, but in only two out of eight measures in mother-child interaction. Intercorrelations among various measures of aggression were higher for boys than girls. With respect to dependency, the only difference was in frequency of negative attention getting, in which boys exceeded girls. No differences were found in the number of dependent responses to peers or adults. Both sexes directed more dependent responses to like-sex peers. There were higher correlations among dependency measures (particularly behavior-unit observations) for girls than boys. On resistance to temptation there were no overall sex differences. In a test in which children were led to believe they had deviated from adult requests, girls showed more emotional upset than boys.

Sears, R. R., J. Whiting, V. Nowlis, and Pauline Sears. Some child rearing antecedents of aggression and dependency in young children. *Genet. psychol., Monogr.*, 1953, *47*, 135–234.

Measures: Teachers' ratings and behavioral observation of aggression and dependency of children. Subjects: 40 nursery school children. Results: On teacher ratings girls were significantly more dependent on teachers and more dependent in general than boys. There were no significant differences in either dependency or aggression by observation, although boys slightly exceeded girls in aggression. There were higher intercorrelations of dependency measures in boys than in girls. Negative attention getting was viewed as aggression in girls and as dependency in boys by the teachers. Dependency and aggression correlated positively with each other, partly as a result of activity level. Maternal punitiveness and current non-nurturance and frustration correlated positively with dependency in boys and negatively in girls. Frustration and aggression showed the same pattern, although differences were slight. The sex differences among correlations were significant in severity of maternal punishment for aggression and current aggression. Parental antecedents of aggression: the correlation between maternal punishment for aggression and aggression was positive for boys and curvilinear for girls.

Shaw, M. C., and D. L. White. The relationship between child-parent identification and academic underachievement. *J. clin. Psychol.*, 1965, *21*, 10–13.

Measures: Grade-point average was used to pick underachievers and overachievers. S's took the Sarbin Adjective Check List for self, mother, and father. Parents also took it for themselves and for their child. Similarity of self and parent was the measure of identification. Subjects: 114 children in grades 10 and 11; I.Q. of 110. Results: Boy overachievers identified more with father than boy underachievers. Girl overachievers identified more with mothers.

Shepler, B. F. A comparison of masculinity-femininity measures. *J. consult. Psychol.*, 1951, *15*, 484–86.

Measures: The M-F scale from the MMPI, the Terman-Miles M-F scale, the Strong Vocational Interest M-F scale, and the Franck test were given. Subjects: 57 male and 67 female college students. Results: All 4 scales showed sex differences at the .01

level. The 4 tests were intercorrelated, and the Strong, the MMPI, and the Terman-Miles scales all correlated with one another between .50 and .70 for both men and women. The Franck test did not correlate significantly with any of the other tests for either sex.

Sherriffs, A. C., and R. F. Jarrett. Sex differences in attitudes about sex differences. *J. Psychol.*, 1953, *35*, 161–68.
Measures: A checklist of behavior and personality traits. Men and women were asked to attribute these traits to males or females and to evaluate them for moral worth. Subjects: Adults. Results: Women were more likely to give extreme values (either positive or negative) to items than were men. There was a marked consistency in traits attributed to the sexes.

Shirley, Mary, and Lillian Poyntz. The influence of separation from mother on children's emotional response. *J. Psychol.*, 1941, *12*, 251–82.
Measures: Diary recordings of observation of children during an all-day examination away from mother. Subjects: Children aged 2–8. Results: Significance tests were not given, but the boys showed more frequent and more severe upset at being separated from mother than girls.

Siegel, A. E. Film-mediated fantasy aggression and strength of aggressive drive. *Child Develpm.*, 1956, *27*, 365–78.
Measures: Observation through one-way glass of a pair of like-sex children playing after they had seen an aggressive and a nonaggressive film. Subjects: 24 children aged 3 yrs. 9 mos. to 5 yrs. 1 mo. Results: No differences as a result of the experimental variable. However, boys showed more aggression in play (p = .0002). They also showed more guilt and anxiety in play.

Siegel, A. E., Lois M. Stolz, E. A. Hitchcock, and J. Adamson. Children of working mothers and their controls. *Child Develpm.*, 1959, *30*, 533–46.
Measures: Observation of children in kindergarten free play. Observations were coded by goal, i.e., into types of dependent-independent behavior such as aggression, conformity, and dominance. Subjects: 16 matched pairs of boys and 10 matched pairs of girls. Results: Sex differences were ambiguous because a different observer was used for each sex. However, a different rank order for the 9 behavior categories was found for the 2 sexes. Sociability, succorance, and aggression were the first 3 for boys; succorance, obedience, and sociability were the first 3 for girls. Obedience was 5th for boys, and aggression was 7th for girls. No significance tests were given.

Simpson, Margaret. Parent preferences of young children. *Teach. Coll. Contr. Educ.*, No. 652, 1935.
Measures: Informal interviews with children in which they were asked to indicate which parent they preferred, which gave them money, and which punished and played with them. They also told stories about pictures revealing parents' preferences and who punished them. Subjects: 250 boys and 250 girls, 50 in each age group from 5 to 9. The SES was lower middle class. Results: Both sexes preferred mother except for girls aged 6 years. From age 5 on up to age 9, father preference declined. Boys felt they were punished more by father than mother (that is, spanked). Girls reported that mothers spanked them more when directly questioned, but the stories to pictures gave the opposite result. Both sexes felt that the father played with them more, especially at 5 years.

Sinick, D. Two anxiety scales correlated and examined for sex differences. *J. clin. Psychol.*, 1956, *12*, 394–95.
Measures: Taylor Manifest Anxiety Scale, and Sarason and Mandler Test Anxiety

Questionnaire. **Subjects:** 50 women and 161 males, college freshmen. **Results:** On both tests women scored significantly higher.

Sinks, Naomi B., and M. Powell. Sex and intelligence as factors in achievement in reading in grades 4 through 8. *J. genet. Psychol.*, 1965, *106*, 67–79.

Measures: S's were given the California Test of Mental Maturity and the California Reading Test. S's more than 6 months ahead of the mean grade for their I.Q. group in reading achievement were considered overachievers, and those 6 months below were underachievers. The rest were average achievers. The percentage of male and female over- and underachievers for each grade level was computed. **Subjects:** 3,551 students in grades 4 through 8. **Results:** No consistent sex differences were found.

Smith, J. M. The relative brightness values of three hues for newborn infants. *Univ. Iowa Stud. Child Welfare, 12*, No. 1, 91-141.

Measures: Measures of amount of activity and crying in darkness and in the presence of red, blue, and green lights. Movement was recorded on a stabilimeter. **Subjects:** Twenty infants, 10 male and 10 female, 7, 8, and 9 days old. **Results:** Boys were significantly more active under all conditions than girls. Boys also cried more under all conditions. Girls showed more proportional decrease in activity and crying than boys did in the presence of all of the colors, with red showing the greatest difference. Boys showed no different reaction to red than they did to darkness.

Smith, Madorah E. Development of the sentence in children. *J. genet. Psychol.*, 1935, *46*, 182–212.

Measures: Recording of spontaneous conversations with adults and other children. **Subjects:** 305 children age 1½ to 5½. Average I.Q. slightly above average. **Results:** Girls' average sentence length was slightly longer than boys' at all ages except 5 years. At 2 years the difference was significant. At 2 years girls made fewer grammatical errors.

Smith, R. M. Sentence completion differences between intellectually superior boys and girls. *J. proj. Tech. Pers.*, 1963, *27*, 472–80.

Measures: A revision of the Rohde-Hildreth Sentence Completions Test. **Subjects:** 37 males and 45 females, all 12 years old and candidates for admission to a university high school sub-freshman program. **Results:** Males were consistently more positive concerning themselves, especially in the area of physical self. Females were more positive than males about family, mother, father, same sex, and other people. Females were not different from males in evaluating the opposite sex. Religion, work, and creativity were more positively evaluated by females than males.

Smith, S. Age and sex differences in children's opinion concerning sex differences. *J. genet. Psychol.*, 1939, *54*, 17–25.

Measures: Children indicated which sex possessed a greater degree of 19 desirable traits and 14 undesirable traits. Teachers indicated whether the item was desirable or not. **Subjects:** 100 boys and 100 girls in each age group from 8 to 15 years. **Results:** Both sexes gave themselves a more favorable rating than the opposite sex. However, boys became more favorable to themselves and less favorable to girls as age increased. Girls became more favorable to boys and less favorable to themselves as age increased.

Smock, C. D., and Bess G. Holt. Children's reactions to novelty: an experimental study of curiosity motivation. *Child Develpm.*, 1962, *33*, 631–42.

Measures: 4 sets of pictures representing types of perceptual conflict were presented. They represented stimulus ambiguity, stimulus incongruity, absence of stimulus support for conceptual structuring, and relative preference for the unknown. The child could elect to look at each picture as many times as he wished. A measure of perceptual rigidity was also given, and a preference for known vs. unknown toy test. Sub-jects: 22 boys and 22 girls in the first grade. Results: The girls were more rigid than boys (p = .10). Girls preferred the unknown toy and showed more curiosity with ab-sence of environmental structure. Boys were higher in curiosity on the other 3 types of perceptual conflict. In general boys were somewhat more curious.

Solkoff, N., A. T. Gibson, and G. S. Chandler. Effects of frustration on percep-tual-motor performance. *Child Develpm.*, 1964, *35*, 569–75.
Measures: Each S took the coding subtest from the Wechsler Intelligence Test for Children, and then another task was given under the following conditions. High frus-tration: a marble game was introduced with a prize to be gained at the end. The game was interrupted before completion so that the prize was not obtained. Low frustra-tion: S played a game for a short time and was interrupted, but with no knowledge of a prize lost or a goal unachieved. No frustration: S was taken out of the room for a short time and played no game. All S's then repeated coding. Subjects: 42 boys and 42 girls, aged 5 to 9 years. Results: Boys showed a decline in coding performance under high frustration and slight improvement under no frustration. Girls improved under high frustration conditions. The sex-by-condition interaction was significant.

Sommer, R. Sex differences in the retention of quantitative information. *J. educ. Psychol.*, 1958, *49*, 187–92.
Measures: 2 items from the W-B scales (what is the population of the U.S., and how far is it from New York to Paris), and 3 other questions (how many pints in a quart, how many teaspoons in a tablespoon, and what is the population of the town you live in). Some subjects were also given 2 paragraphs to read orally; the paragraphs con-tained both quantitative and nonquantitative information. Subjects: 156 mental pa-tients (who took only the W-B items), a group of American college students, and a group of Canadian college students. These last two groups were given all 5 informa-tion questions. Another group of 49 women and 27 men studying to be psychiatric nurses were given the paragraphs to read. Results: Men in all groups were superior in knowing the U.S. or Canadian population. They were superior in knowing N.Y. to Paris distance in 2 out of 3 groups. There was no difference in one group, and women were better in one group on pints in a quart. Women were better in both groups on teaspoons and men on town population. On the paragraphs, there was no difference on nonquantitative retention but men were significantly better at quantitative reten-tion.

Sontag, L. W. Physiological factors and personality in children. *Child Develpm.*, 1947, *18*, 185–89.
Measures: Measures of skin resistance, blood flow and variability, blood pressure, and heart rate and variability under baseline and stress conditions. The stress con-ditions were immersion of foot in cold water or tilting the person's head down at 45 degrees for 2½ minutes. Subjects: Fels study subjects: 12-year-olds. Results: Under the tilting condition, sex differences occurred: (1) girls showed more palmar con-ductance relaxation than boys, (2) girls showed greater diastolic blood pressure re-laxation, (3) girls had more reaction to stress in palmar conductance and systolic blood pressure, but not in diastolic pressure, (4) girls recovered in palmar conduc-tance, systolic pressure, and in diastolic pressure faster than boys, (5) girls adapted less to stress in palmar conductivity than boys. Summary: girls were more reactive to stress, relaxed more readily, and recovered more quickly.

Spache, George. Sex differences in the Rosenzweig P-F Study, Children's Form. *J. clin. Psychol.*, 1951, *7*, 235–38.
Measures: Rosenzweig Picture-Frustration Test, a projective test to elicit responses to frustration. Each response was scored extropunitive, intropunitive, or impunitive; whether aggression was vented in task-oriented ways, toward the other person, or

toward the situation; and whether the response conformed to group norms. Subjects: 50 boys and 50 girls in elementary school. Age mean was 9.3 with 36% 10 years old or older. Range was 6–13 years. Some of these children were referred for academic or personality difficulties. Results: With the planned scoring, no reliable sex differences were found. When the responses were separated into child–child vs. child–adult situations, sex differences appeared. Boys reacted personally and directed aggressiveness toward the other person in child–child interactions and in child–adult interactions. Boys showed more outward aggressiveness with children than with adults. Boys projected aggressiveness on the environment when dealing with adults, and on the other person when dealing with a child. Girls showed more direct aggressiveness to adults than boys did.

Spangler, D. P., and C. W. Thomas. The effects of age, sex, and physical disability upon manifest needs. *J. counsel. Psychol.*, 1962, *9*, 313–19.
Measures: Edwards Personal Preference Scale. Subjects: 20 physically disabled persons in each of 4 age ranges: 40 to 49, 50 to 59, 60 to 69, and 70 to 79. An equal number of physically normal persons were matched on age, sex, and SES. Each subgroup contained an equal number of men and women. Results: There were significant sex differences on 5 of the 15 manifest needs measured by the Edwards. Women were significantly higher on affiliation, nurturance, and succorance, while men were significantly higher on dominance and aggression.

Spivack, G., M. Levine, and B. Brenner. The Rorschach Index of Repressive Style and Scale-checking Style: a study of sex differences. *J. proj. Tech. pers. Assessment.*, 1964, *28*, No. 4, 484–90.
Measures: Prior to actual experiment, 141 male and female students were given the Rorschach Index of Repressive Style (RIRS) test. The subjects to be used were chosen on the basis of their scores on this test. Some weeks later, each subject was asked to make 10 art products and to use 11 semantic differential scales to show the meaning each piece had for him. Subject also had to rate himself on the semantic differential scales. Subjects: 48 subjects divided into four subgroups: a high and low repressed male group, and a high and low repressed female group. Results: There were no significant differences among any of the four groups in self-ratings. They differed in the way in which the two cognitive processes were organized. The males who produced rich and full verbal protocols on the RIRS test had a tendency to make careful and discriminating judgments. For females, the more fluid and rich the protocols, the greater tendency to make quick black and white decisions.

Stalnaker, J. M. Sex differences in the ability to write. *Sch. and Soc.*, 1941, *54*, 532–35.
Measures: The English test on the College Entrance Examination Board. Subjects: Over 6,000 high school students. Results: Girls were superior on this essay-writing test, even though boys were superior or equal on most other subjects on the test. When the Scholastic Aptitude Test was used as a control, the difference remained.

Stanford, Diane, W. N. Dember, and L. B. Stanford. A children's form of the Alpert-Haber Achievement Anxiety Scale. *Child Develpm.*, 1963, *34*, 1027–32.
Measures: Alpert-Haber Achievement Anxiety Scale, school grades, and I.Q. scores. Subjects: 61 3d-grade children. Results: No significant sex differences were found in achievement anxiety or its relationship to I.Q. or grades.

Staples, R. The responses of infants to color. *J. exp. Psychol.*, 1932, *15*, 119–41.
Measures: Munsell color discs presented against gray background. Brightness and saturation held constant. The length of time the very young infant looked at the light was recorded, while the number of times the older babies reached for the light was

recorded. **Subjects**: Group 1: infants 69–143 days old. Group 2: infants 5½ to 24 months old. **Results**: No sex differences in the first group. However, in the second group girls reached for the colored disc significantly more often than boys. The girls also showed more mature color preferences in a paired comparison situation. They showed a drop in preference for yellow at a younger age than boys, and they developed a discrimination between blue and green earlier.

Steiner, I. D., and E. D. Rogers. Alternative responses to dissonance. *J. abnorm. soc. Psychol.*, 1963, *66*, 128–36.

Measures: S was paired with a respected peer who gave judgmental responses dissonant with S's responses. S could conform or not to the peer's responses. After the judgments were done, S was tested to determine his tendency to under-recall the number of disagreements on judgments, devalue the importance of the judgments, or reject the peer as a respected person. All of these methods of reducing dissonance were put together to measure tolerance for dissonance. Those S's who used the dissonance-reducing methods least were relatively high in tolerance for dissonance. S's also received the TMAS. **Subjects**: 50 male and 50 female college students. **Results**: Males rejected the peer significantly more often than females. Females tolerated the dissonance more often than males. There were no differences on conformity, under-recall, or devaluing the test. Females who were high in anxiety tended to conform more and tolerate dissonance more, but this did not hold for males.

Stevenson, H. W. Social reinforcement with children as a function of CA, sex of E, and sex of S. *J. abnorm. soc. Psychol.*, 1961, *63*, 147–54.

Measures: A marble-dropping game was played in which S picked marbles from a bin and dropped them through a hole. A base rate of frequency of responding was established, and then social reinforcement was given by E. Change in rate of response was recorded, and sex of child and of E was varied. Six E's of each sex were used. **Subjects**: 252 boys and 252 girls chosen from three age ranges: 3–5, 6–8, and 9–11. **Results**: Women were significantly more effective as reinforcers for both sexes at the 3- to 5-year range. At age 6–8, women were significantly better reinforcers for boys than for girls. Men were better reinforcers for girls than boys at this age, but it was not significant. At age 9–11 there was no significant difference in reinforcement effectiveness between male and female E's.

Stevenson, H. W., and Sara Allen. Adult performance as a function of sex of experimenter and sex of subject. *J. abnorm. soc. Psychol.*, 1964, *68*, 214–16.

Measures: S was asked to drop marbles of different colors into holes matching the color. Rate of responding with and without verbal reinforcement was measured. **Subjects**: 8 male and 8 female experimenters each tested 8 men and 8 women. **Results**: Women responded at a higher rate both with and without reinforcement. Both sexes performed at a higher rate with E's of the opposite sex. Verbal reinforcement did not increase responding rate.

Stevenson, H. W., Rachel Keen, and R. M. Knights. Parents and strangers as reinforcing agents for children's performance. *J. abnorm. soc. Psychol.*, 1963, *67*, 183–86.

Measures: E reinforced S's performance in a marble-dropping game with verbal comments. For some S's, E was father; for others E was mother, a male stranger, or a female stranger. **Subjects**: 116 boys and 116 girls, aged 3 to 5. **Results**: Base rate was higher with male than female E's. Female E's and strangers were more effective in increasing rate of response than male E's and parents. Girls tested by females or mothers were the most effective reinforcement group, while boys tested by males were the least effective. Overall, girls responded at a somewhat higher rate than boys for the total experimental session.

Stevenson, H. W., and R. D. Odom. Interrelationships in children's learning. *Child Develpm.*, 1965, *36*, 7–19.

Measures: Five paper-and-pencil tasks: a paired-associates learning task (nonsense syllables and words), concrete discrimination task (learn which of the pictured objects is correct), abstract discrimination task (learn which of the abstract figures is right), concept formation (learn whether size, color, or shape is the relevant dimension), and anagrams (make as many words as possible from a long word). Subjects: 354 children in grades 4 and 5. Results: Girls did significantly better on paired associates. No other sex differences.

Stith, Marjorie, and Ruth Connor. Dependency and helpfulness in young children. *Child Develpm.*, 1962, *33*, 15–20.

Measures: Time-sampling observation of children in nursery school and kindergarten. Seven categories of helpful behavior and seven of dependent behavior were scored. Subjects: 30 boys and 35 girls, aged 38–75 months. Results: No significant sex differences, although boys were slightly higher in all categories.

Strange, F. B., and J. O. Palmer. A note on sex differences on the W-B Tests. *J. clin. Psychol.*, 1953, *9*, 85–87.

Measures: W-B Form I. Subjects: 145 male and 90 female adult outpatients in a psychiatric clinic. Mean age was 30.92 for men and 33.62 for women. Results: All subtests favored men except vocabulary, on which there was no difference. There was a significant sex difference in total I.Q., so it is difficult to conclude much about the subtest differences. This difference was significant at the .001 level. One can, however, notice that the largest differences were in information, comprehension, arithmetic, picture completion, and verbal I.Q.

Strong, E. K. *Vocational interests of men and women.* Stanford: Stanford Univ. Press, 1943.

Measures: The M–F scale from the Strong Vocational Interest Test. Subjects: Standardization sample of high school, college, and adult men and women. Results: Items that differentiate the sexes were compiled into a masculinity–femininity test. The items are all answered in terms of like or dislike for objects and activities. The items preferred by men included mechanical and scientific activities; physically strenuous, adventuresome activities; legal, political, and army occupations; selling activities; games like poker, chess, and billiards; and outdoor work. Men also felt more sure of themselves than women. Activities preferred by women included musical and artistic activities; literary activities; dealing with unfortunate and disagreeable people; entertainment involving fortune-tellers, full-dress affairs, entertaining others, social problems, movies; clerical work; teaching; social work; relating to merchandise; school subjects such as Bible study, botany, sociology, and philosophy; and planning for the immediate rather than the distant future.

Stroud, J. B., and E. F. Lindquist. Sex differences in achievement in the elementary and secondary schools. *J. educ. Psychol.*, 1942, *33*, 657–67.

Measures: Iowa Every-Pupil Testing Program for high school and the Iowa Every-Pupil Basic Skills Testing Program for grades 3–8. Subjects: Students in high school and grades 3–8 throughout the state of Iowa in the year 1932–39 for the high schoolers and 1940 for younger children. Results: With younger children, girls excelled in language, word study, reading-vocabulary, and reading comprehension, the difference being greatest for language. Boys excelled slightly but not significantly in arithmetic. At the high school level boys excelled in 10 out of 12 subjects. Girls excelled insignificantly in algebra and reading comprehension. In order of size of difference, boys excelled in general science, physics, contemporary affairs, American history, American government, economics, plane geometry, Latin, biology, and world history.

Stubbs, E. M. The effect of the factors of duration, intensity, and pitch of sound stimulation on the responses of newborn infants. *Univ. of Iowa Stud. Child Welfare*, 1934, *9*, No. 4, 75–135.
  Measures: Stabilimeter recording of activity levels and pneumograph recording of respiration changes in response to sound. Subjects: 75 infants in 3 experiments, age 1–10 days. Results: Girls showed greater response than boys on experiments with duration and pitch, but boys were more responsive in the experiment with intensity.

Stukat, K. G. *Suggestibility, a factorial and experimental analysis.* Stockholm: Almqvist and Wiksell, 1958.
  Measures: 9 tests of suggestibility including the body sway test and 2 other similar tests, leading questions, authority suggestions, and co-judge suggestions. Subjects: 319 children, ages 8, 10, 12, and 14; a group of young adults; and a group of neurotics. All in Sweden. Results: Most of the tests showed females more suggestible, although the differences were small. The largest differences were in the co-judge and contradictory tests, where personal influence was the greatest. The author felt this indicated woman's greatest need for conformity and dependency.

Sutton-Smith, B., and B. G. Rosenberg. Peer perceptions of impulsive behavior. *Merrill-Palmer Quart.*, 1961, *7*, 233–38.
  Measures: A self-report impulsivity scale measuring problems in control of motor activity, acting-out behavior, and social discomfort; and a shortened form of the Tuddenham Reputation Test, measuring peers' perceptions of the subjects. Subjects: 21 high-impulsive and 20 low-impulsive boys, and 25 high-impulsive and 35 low-impulsive girls, in the 4th, 5th, and 6th grades. Results: Peers saw more differences between high- and low-impulsive boys than they did between high-and low-impulsive girls. High-impulsive boys were seen as significantly less quiet, more quarrelsome, more chance-taking, more bossy, less bashful, more show-offish, and as leaders and fighters. Girls who were impulsive were seen as less quiet and more apt to take chances, act tomboyish, and show off. Mean difference comparisons between the sexes were not given.

Sutton-Smith, B., B. G. Rosenberg, and E. F. Morgan. Development of sex differences in play choices during preadolescence. *Child Develpm.*, 1963, *34*, 119–26.
  Measures: 180-item play inventory on which the child indicated likes and dislikes of various games and pastimes. Subjects: Approximately 1,900 children in grades 3–6. Results: As girls got older, they tended to choose more of both boys' and girls' games and pastimes. Boys also increased their range of interests, but entirely among masculine activities.

Sweeney, E. J. Sex differences in problem solving. Unpub. dissertation, Stanford University, 1953.
  Measures: A wide variety of problems including water-jar problems, arithmetic reasoning, trick and standard verbal-reasoning problems. Problem-solving ability and ability to overcome set was measured. Subjects: Several groups of college students. Results: Males did better on many of the reasoning tasks, especially tasks involving restructuring.

Swineford, Frances. A study in factor analysis: the nature of the general, verbal, and spatial bi-factors. *Supp. Educ. Monogr.*, 1948, N. 67.
  Measures: 3 tests of a general factor: a variation of the Woody-McCall Mixed Fundamentals Test (arithmetic), a series-completion test (number series), a verbal-deduction test. 3 tests of the verbal factor: word meaning, a general information test, and a reading comprehension test. 3 tests of a spatial factor: punching holes (imagine a folded paper with holes punched and draw what it would be like opened), a drawing test (draw mirror images of 24 geometric figures), and a visual-imagery test

(imagine a block of wood painted different colors on different sides and tell what sawed-off sections would be like). Subjects: 952 pupils, 5th–10th grades. Results: In the age range 12–14½ years, girls excelled at the .01 level in visual imagery. Although the significant level of punched holes was not given, the critical ratio is 1.84 in favor of boys, while the drawing test has a critical ratio of 1.98. Differences in general information and word meaning favored boys, but were not significant. The other tests favored girls but were not significant. Little difference was found in factor structure for the two sexes.

Tasch, Ruth J. The role of the father in the family. *J. exp. Ed.*, 1952, *20*, 319–61.
Measures: Interviews with fathers to find their conceptions of the father role—activities, discipline, support, etc. Subjects: 85 fathers with a total of 80 boys and 80 girls. Diversified SES. Most fathers were between 30 and 50 years, and the children ranged from newborn to 17 and older. Results: Activities in relation to sex of child showed more consistency than difference. However, fathers participated more in the daily care of girls, and were more concerned about their safety. (They seemed to see girls as more fragile and delicate.) They participated more in the development of motor abilities, skills, and interests of boys. In rough-and-tumble play, there was no sex difference at the preschool level. However, from age 6 onward fathers engaged in much more such play with boys than girls. Fathers were more likely to administer corporal punishment to boys than to girls. Fathers made distinctions between tasks for boys and girls: girls iron, mind siblings, and wash clothes; boys take out garbage and help father.

Taylor, Janet A. A personality scale of manifest anxiety. *J. abnorm. soc. Psychol.*, 1953, *48*, 285–90.
Measures: TMAS. Subjects: 1,971 college students, the normative sample. Results: Women had somewhat higher scores but the differences were not significant.

Templin, Mildred C. Certain language skills in children. *Inst. Child Welfare Monogr.*, No. 26. Minneapolis: Univ. of Minnesota Press, 1957.
Measures: Individual tests of articulation, sound discrimination, vocabulary (number of words known or used), and verbalization (length of remarks). Subjects: 60 children in each age category, 3, 3.5, 4, 4.5, 5, 6, 7, 8. Results: Girls tended to excel in articulation at the older ages (7 and 8), and boys generally did better in word knowledge. However, the differences were not great.

Terman, L. M. *Genetic studies of genius*, Vol. 1. Stanford: Stanford Univ. Press, 1925.
Measures: Anthropometric measures, psychological tests, school reports, and parent reports. Subjects: 352 boys and 291 girls with I.Q.'s over 130. Results: Significantly more boys than girls in the group. Parents noticed speech development earlier in girls than in boys. In school, boys were more likely to be weak in reading, girls in arithmetic.

Terman, L. M., and M. Lima. *Children's readings* (1st ed.). New York: Appleton, 1926.
Measures: Reading lists kept by the subjects for 2 months. Subjects: 511 gifted children and 808 average children, all aged 9–15. Results: Girls read 20 to 30% more books than boys. Girls read books of home and school life and emotional fiction. Boys read adventure and mystery stories.

Terman, L. M., and Catherine C. Miles. *Sex and personality*. New York: McGraw-Hill, 1936.
Measures: A paper-and-pencil multiple-choice test (910 items) consisting of 7 parts: word association, ink-blot association, information, emotional and ethical response,

interests, personalities and opinions, and introvertive response. **Subjects:** A large group of subjects varying in age from early adolescence to old age. Homosexuals, delinquents, and various occupations and education groups were included. **Results:** Items on which the sexes differed were retained; scores on the tests ranged from +200 to −100 for men and +100 to −200 for women in the general population. Mean score for men was +52 and for women it was −70. The scores correlated positively with I.Q.: the higher the I.Q., the more masculine for both sexes. Content of the differences: On word association women used domestic words, kind and sympathetic words, and clothes and color words, while men used scientific and business terms, excitement and adventure words, and food words. On ink blots, men gave machinery and science items, outdoor activities and adventure. Women gave domestic occupations, aesthetic experiences, and personal adornment. On the information test men knew more about aggressive and active bodily interests, politics, adventure, and business, economic, scientific, and physical facts. Women knew about domestic occupations, individual embellishment, etiquette, fiction, music, colors, and topics appealing to sympathy and maternal interest. In emotions and ethics, women showed more of all 4 emotions: disgust, pity, fear, and anger. The greatest differences were in disgust, pity, and fear. Women were more likely to censure small offenses, and the amount of censure did not increase with the severity of the crime in women as with men. Women showed more anger over school offenses and social vexations than over business and extra-domestic troubles. In interests, females liked indoor, artistic, and decorative occupations; men preferred adventure, body risk, and muscular-strength occupations. Males preferred predominantly male occupations, while females liked female and mixed occupations. Females had more likes and fewer dislikes than males. In personalities and opinions men preferred successful generals, sports heroes, and defiers of convention. Women preferred women, unfortunates, and philanthropists. In the test of introvertive response, women had tastes and habits of timidity, active sympathy, and care of appearance. They confessed weakness in emotional control and psychic abnormalities. They gave more introverted responses. Men had more habits involving adventure and courage.

Terman, L. M., and Leona E. Tyler. Psychological sex differences. In L. Carmichael (ed.), *Manual of child psychology* (2d ed.). New York: Wiley, 1954.
This chapter reviews a large number of studies on sex differences.

Toigo, R., L. O. Walder, L. D. Eron, and M. M. Lefkowitz. Examiner effect in the use of a near-sociometric procedure in the third grade classroom. *Psychol. Reps.,* 1962, *11,* 785–90.
Measures: A peer-nomination aggression score was computed by counting aggressive characteristics attributed to each S by his classmates. Three different male E's were used. **Subjects:** 5 classrooms tested by each of the 3 E's were examined. Seven boys and 7 girls from each classroom were used as S's for this analysis. All classrooms were 3d grade. **Results:** No effects of different E's on scores. Boys received higher aggression scores than girls.

Torrance, E. P. Factors affecting creative thinking in children: An interim research report. *Merrill-Palmer Quart.,* 1961, *7,* 171–80.
Measures: Children were asked to tell how toys could be improved in one study, and tell how scientific toys could be used in another. **Subjects:** Children in grades one through three in the first study, grades four through six in the second. **Results:** Boys became increasingly superior in grades one through three on this creativity measure. Boys were superior at the second task as well and liked it better in 1959, but this difference was less in 1960. (These data are discussed in more detail in Torrance 1962 and 1963.)

Torrance, E. P. *Guiding creative talent.* Englewood Cliffs, N.Y.: Prentice-Hall, 1962.
Measures: Children were asked to think of ways to improve various toys. Subjects: Children, grades 1–3. Results: In 1st and 2d grade, boys did better on fire truck and girls on nurse's kit. By 3d grade, boys were doing better regardless of toy presented.

Torrance, E. P. Changing reactions of preadolescent girls to tasks requiring creative scientific thinking. *J. genet. Psychol.*, 1963, *102*, 217–23.
Measures: Groups of 5 children were given a set of scientific toys, and asked to figure out how they worked and what they could be used for. Each child's contribution to the group, his enjoyment of the task, and his peers' ranking of the value of his contribution was assessed. The study was done 2 different years. Subjects: 32 boys and 36 girls in 1959, and 32 boys and 38 girls in 1960. All were 4th, 5th, and 6th graders. Results: In 1959 boys contributed significantly more to the task, enjoyed it more, and their contributions were valued more. In 1960 there were no differences in contribution or in liking for the task, although boys' contributions were still more highly valued.

Trembly, D. Age and sex differences in creative thinking potential. Paper presented at the American Psychological Association, 1964.
Measures: Measures of ideaphoria (or creative imagination) taken by asking S to write for 5 minutes on "What would happen if all plant life should suddenly disappear from the earth?" Subjects: A large sample of people of various ages. Results: Females at all ages scored higher than men.

Trumbull, R. A study of relationships between factors of personality and intelligence. *J. soc. Psychol.*, 1953, *38*, 161–73.
Measures: MMPI; PMA; Guilford-Martin factor-analytic personality test. Intercorrelations were done among all measures, getting 450 r's in all. Of these, 29 were significant. T-tests between groups were also done. Subjects: 87 college women, 49 high school girls, and 43 high school boys. Results: The t-tests showed that boys were superior to girls in space, the only significant PMA subtest difference between sexes. Girls were more masculine than boys were feminine, and they were also higher on hysteria, neurotic tendency, introversion, and depression. There were many differences in correlations as well.

Tuddenham, R. D. Studies in reputation: III, Correlates of popularity among elementary school children. *J. educ. Psychol.*, 1951, *42*, 257–76.
Measures: A "guess-who" reputation test was given to whole classes. Children nominated classmates for pairs of traits such as bossy, not-bossy. Subjects: Over 1,000 children in grades 1, 3, and 5. Results: An item cluster for boys which indicated that "real boy" was a Leader, Good at Games, and Takes Chances. This was stable through the 3 grades and seemed to indicate a consistent ideal sex role for boys. For girls the correlates of Acts Like a Little Lady changed as the age of the children changed. In 1st grade it correlated with being popular; in 3d grade with unassertiveness, and in 5th it was in no cluster and had zero correlation with popularity.

Tuddenham, R. D. Studies in reputation: I, Sex and grade differences in school children's evaluations of their peers. *Psychol. Monogr.*, 1952, No. 333, 1–39.
Measures: "Guess-who" reputation test (sociometric) given to classes of children. The items were paired ends of a dimension, for example: who is wiggly? and who is quiet? Subjects: 119 1st-graders, 692 3d-graders, and 628 5th-graders. These children were from the Berkeley Child Guidance Study. Results: Girls in general got more

favorable ratings than boys. The typical girl was rated as quiet, popular, full of fun, not quarrelsome, a good sport, "a little lady," good-looking, not a show-off, tidy, and friendly. The typical boy was seen as wiggly, quarrelsome, bossy, show-offish, takes chances, not bashful, good at games, and "a real boy." In rating others, both sexes tended to rate others more favorably than not, except when girls rated boys. As age increased, boys were seen more as real boys and girls less as little ladies. Girls tended to be given more votes than boys.

Tuma, E., and N. Livson. Family socioeconomic status and adolescent attitudes to authority. *Child Develpm.*, 1960, *31*, 387–99.
> Measures: Interviews and ratings from parents, teachers, and classmates. Subjects: 14–16-year-olds. Results: A slight tendency toward greater acceptance of authority by girls.

Tyler, F. B., Janet E. Rafferty, and Bonnie B. Tyler. Relationships among motivations of parents and their children. *J. genet. Psychol.*, 1962, *101*, 69–81.
> Measures: Interviews with parents and children to obtain ratings of their needs and expectancies. The needs were: (1) recognition-status, (2) love and affection, (3) dominance, (4) protection and dependency, and (5) independence. Subjects: 45 preschool children and their parents. Results: There was a stable positive cluster of recognition-status and dominance needs for all groups. For girls, independence needs are negatively related to other needs, while independence is either independent of or positively related to other needs in boys. For girls, love and affection needs are negatively related to independence and positively related to recognition-status. Love and affection are unrelated to independence and negatively related to recognition-status in boys. Mean differences on the variables did not appear.

Vance, T. F., and Louise T. McCall. Children's preferences among play materials as determined by the method of paired comparisons of pictures. *Child Develpm.*, 1934, *5*, 267–77.
> Measures: Paired comparisons of photos of toys, and recording of order and time of playing with actual toys. Subjects: 17 girls and 15 boys, 3 yrs. 6 mos. to 6 yrs. 4 mos. Results: Boys showed preference for woodwork, large blocks, and equipment requiring large-muscle activity; girls preferred housekeeping materials and materials for more passive play.

Vaught, G. M. The relationship of role identification and ego strength to sex differences in the rod and frame test. *J. Pers.*, 1965, 33, 271–83.
> Measures: Witkin's Rod and Frame Test (RFT) was used to measure field dependence. S's were also given the Gough Femininity Scale and the Barron Ego Strength Scale. Subjects: 90 male and 90 female college subjects. Results: Males were significantly more field independent than females. High femininity went with high field dependence in both sexes. High ego strength went with high independence.

Vinacke, W. E., and G. R. Gullickson. Age and sex differences in the formation of coalitions. *Child Develpm.*, 1964, *35*, 1217–31.
> Measures: S's played a simple counter game in which they moved counters around a board from start to home. Counters were given different weights; the weights determined the number of moves a player could make at each throw of the dice. S's could easily figure out what coalitions were necessary to win, and were allowed to make coalitions if they wished. Each game was played with three like-sex players. Subjects: 10 triads of each sex, ages 7 and 8; 10 triads of each sex, ages 14 to 16; and 30 triads of each sex at college level. Results: Younger children tended to form coalitions in an accommodative manner in which they tried to come to terms mutually satisfactory to all members—often splitting rewards 3 ways. Older boys became much more exploi-

tive and competitive, attempting to use power and coalitions to gain the most advantage for themselves. Women remained accommodative in playing technique. Thus adult males were different from both adult women and younger children in their playing techniques.

Walker, R. N. Body build and behavior in young children. *Child Develpm.*, 1963, *34*, 1–23.

Measures: Ratings of body build (standard scores for each age), parent adjective check list, and nursery school behavior scales (check list filled out by teachers). Subjects: 147 nursery school children, 82 boys, 65 girls, modal age 3 years. Results: On parent check list, boys were rated as more active and curious than girls. Endomorphy in girls was associated with "robust good adjustment" (e.g., loving, cooperative, relaxed, stable, expressive); endomorphy correlated with 32 behavior traits rated by parents. For boys endomorphy showed few correlations with behavior traits. Mesomorphy was not correlated with many behavior items for either sex; but for both sexes, the existing correlations indicate an association with high energy level, expressed in boys as bossy, bold, impudent, and destructive behavior. Ectomorphy correlated with different clusters of traits in the two sexes: ectomorphic girls tended to be tense, unstable, uncooperative, aggressively fault-finding, anxiously dependent, moody, and low in energy level. Ectomorphic boys tend to be socially reserved, unaggressive, affectionate, well-coordinated, and not easily discouraged.

Walker, R. N. Measuring masculinity and femininity by children's games choices. *Child Develpm.*, 1964, *35*, 961–71.

Measures: Modification of Rosenberg and Sutton-Smith's Games List, including their original F and M scales. Subjects: 419 Connecticut school children. Results: Large differences were found between the original Ohio sample and the Connecticut sample on F scores, small differences on M scores. Introducing a correction factor for total "likes" (response set) improved the discrimination of the test considerably.

Wallach, M. A., and A. J. Caron. Attribute criteriality and sex-linked conservatism as determinants of psychological similarity. *J. abnorm. soc. Psychol.*, 1959, *59*, 43–50.

Measures: Measure of width of category. S learned a category, and then was tested to see how much deviation from the norm he would permit in admitting new items to that category. The authors used geometric designs in which width of an angle was varied. Subjects: 78 sixth-grade school children. Results: Girls were much less likely than boys to allow wide deviations from the norm on the relevant attribute. Their category was narrower. Pettigrew's Category Width Questionnaire was also given to the sample, and girls had narrower categories on this test as well.

Wallach, M. A., and N. Kogan. Sex differences and judgment process. *J. Pers.*, 1959, *27*, 555–64.

Measures: (1) A probability and certainty test in which the subject estimated the probability of a given event occurring, and then estimated how sure he was of his answer (from very sure to not sure at all). (2) A dilemma-of-choice questionnaire in which the subjects played the role of advisor to a person with a choice between a sure thing and taking a risk for great rewards. The S was asked to advise the person how sure the risk must be before he should take it. Subjects: 225 males and 132 female college students. Results: Women were more conservative than men on all decisions except when they were very certain of their answers. Then they were more extreme. However, women were much less likely to be sure of their answers. Women were more conservative on the risky dilemma when it involved money, life, or football defeat. Men were more conservative when the reward was marriage or an artistic career.

Walter, D., Lorraine S. Denzler, and E. G. Sarason. Anxiety and the intellectual performance of high school students. *Child Develpm.*, 1964, *35*, 917–26.
Measures: Questionnaire composed of 4 scales: test anxiety scale, need for achievement scale, general anxiety scale, and a lack of protection scale. A test anxiety rating scale was also given, and intellectual performance was measured by the differential Aptitude Test and the grade-point average. Subjects: 282 10th-grade students. Results: None of the measures of anxiety were significantly related to grades or intellectual performance in boys. For girls, test anxiety was negatively related to both.

Walters, J., Doris Pearce, and Lucille Dahms. Affectional and aggressive behavior of preschool children. *Child Develpm.*, 1957, *28*, 15–26.
Measures: Observation of play and recording of affectional and aggressive contacts with other people in nursery school. Subjects: 124 nursery and kindergarten children, aged 2–5 years. Results: Boys were more aggressive. Boys of 2, 3, and 4 years chose other boys or adults more than girls for affectional contacts. Boys chose other boys most frequently for aggressive contacts also.

Walters, R. H., and Lillian Demkow. Timing of punishment as a determinant of response inhibition. *Child Develpm.*, 1963, *34*, 207–14.
Measures: Children were given a training session in which they were left alone with a dull book and told not to touch the attractive toys lying around. 2 groups were made up, one of which received aversive stimuli (a loud buzzer) as they reached toward toys, and the other of which received the stimulus only after touching a toy. The next day the same E took them from class and left them for 10 minutes in the same situation. Length of time before deviation was recorded. Subjects: 23 boys and 21 girls in kindergarten. Results: 6 children of each sex did not deviate at all during the 30-minute training session. These children were not punished at all. Of these children, significantly more girls than boys did not deviate on the second day of testing. This suggested to the writers that the effects of E's verbal instructions were longer lasting for girls than boys. There were no sex differences among the children who did receive punishment.

Weatherley, D. Self-perceived rate of physical maturation and personality in late adolescence. *Child Develpm.*, 1964, *35*, 1197–1210.
Measures: S's rated self as early, average, or late in physical maturation. Taylor Manifest Anxiety Scale, Edwards Personal Preference Schedule, and a measure of identification from perceived similarity to parents and friends were given. Subjects: 234 male and 202 female college students. Results: Late maturation was more of a handicap to males than to females. Late-maturing males were less dominant, in need of more succorance, against conformity, and anxious. For females, the only meaningful relationship was that late-maturing girls were more anxious.

Webb, A. P. Sex-role preferences and adjustment in early adolescents. *Child Develpm.*, 1963, *34*, 609–18.
Measures: Gough Femininity Scale; Cunningham's Classroom Social Distance Scale as a measure of social acceptance; Children's Manifest Anxiety Scale; and records of school attendance. Subjects: 161 girls and 156 boys from 7th, 8th, and 9th grades. From these, subgroups of each sex were chosen as high and low in all measures except femininity. Results: Femininity was not related to social acceptance in either sex. Anxiety was related significantly to femininity in girls, with high-anxious girls being more feminine. In boys there was a significant grade-by-anxiety interaction. Tests revealed that there was no significant relationship for 7th-grade boys, that in 8th grade low-anxious boys were less feminine, and that in 9th grade high-anxious boys

were less feminine. School attendance was related to femininity in both sexes, with high-feminine boys and girls having better attendance records.

Wechsler, D. *The measurement and appraisal of adult intelligence.* Baltimore: Williams and Wilkins, 1958.
Measures: Wechsler Adult Intelligence Scale. Subjects: The standardization sample of adults. Results: Men performed better than women on the information, arithmetic, and picture-completion subtests, while women did better on vocabulary, similarities, and digit symbol. From these differences an M-F scale was constructed.

Wechsler, D. *The measurement of adult intelligence.* Baltimore: Williams and Wilkins, 1941.
Measures: Wechsler Adult Intelligence Test. Subjects: The standardizing population. Results: The WAIS was standardized so that there is no significant difference on total I.Q. score, although women showed small but consistent superiority in total scores at all ages. Any tests showing large sex differences were eliminated.

Weider, A., and P. A. Noller. Objective studies of children's drawings of human figures: I, Sex awareness and socioeconomic level. *J. clin. Psychol.,* 1950, *6,* 319–25.
Measures: Group-administered Draw-a-Person test. Subjects: 153 children ages 8–10 from varied SES levels. Results: A larger proportion of girls than boys drew the like-sex parent first and larger.

Weider, A., and P. A. Noller. Objective studies of children's drawings of human figures: II, Sex, age, intelligence. *J. clin. Psychol.,* 1953, *9,* 20–23.
Measures: Draw-a-Person test, group-administered. Subjects: 210 boys and 228 girls, ages 8–12. I.Q. normally distributed. Results: Significantly more girls than boys drew own sex first and larger. Age was not a significant factor.

Weinstein, E. A., and P. N. Geisel. An analysis of sex differences in adjustment. *Child Develpm.,* 1960, *31,* 721–28.
Measures: Interviews with parents to assess home environment. From this, 12 variables such as physical punishment, amount of discipline, home quality, pleasurable relations with parents were extracted. The child was rated on madadjustment by teachers and given the California Test of Personality. Subjects: 220 boys and 190 girls between the ages of 9 and 15, all adopted children. Results: Boys were significantly higher on 4 of 7 measures of maladjustment, the largest differences being in control of aggression and conformity. Correlations of the 12 home environment variables with the 7 maladjustment variables indicate that there are higher relationships for boys than for girls. Boys seem more responsive to specific environmental variables.

Weller, G. M., and R. Q. Bell. Basal skin conductance and neontal state. *Child Develpm.,* 1965, *36,* 647–57.
Measures: Basal skin conductance records and observational count of activity level. Subjects: 40 newborn infants, aged 60 to 110 hours. Results: Females had significantly higher skin conductance, higher correlation between activity level and skin conductance, and were somewhat higher in activity level.

Wellman, Beth L., Ida Mae Case, G. Mengert, and Dorothy E. Bradbury. Speech sounds of young children. *Univ. Iowa Stud. Child Welfare,* 1931, *5,* No. 2.
Measures: Children were shown pictures of toys and activities and asked questions to elicit speech. Pronunciation was recorded in phonetics. Subjects: 204 children aged 2–6 with a mean I.Q. of 115.9. Results: Girls tended to be superior on consonants at

nearly all ages. Mean age differences between sexes at different age categories make conclusions difficult to draw.

Wesman, A. G. Separation of sex groups in test reporting. *J. educ. Psychol.*, 1949, *40*, 223–29.
Measures: Differential Aptitude Test. Subjects: 10th-graders. Results: Clerical, spelling, and sentences favored girls. Abstract reasoning slightly favored boys. Space relations and mechanical reasoning showed large differences in favor of boys. Verbal and numerical showed no differences.

White House conference on child health and protection, section III. The young child in the home. A survey of 3,000 American families. New York: Appleton-Century Co., 1936.
Measures: Standardized interviews with mothers in the home. Subjects: 2,779 white and 202 Negro families with 3,779 and 321 children respectively. The sample was stratified to be representative of U.S. population. Results: For physical punishment, no sex differences before school, then more boys than girls were spanked. Punishment in general was started at 1 year for two-thirds of the girls and three-quarters of the boys. After that there was no sex difference in amount of punishment. Most children were punished by both parents, but as age increased fewer boys were punished by mother only. The percentage of girls punished only by mother stayed constant (about 32%) while boys went from 32% at age 1 year to 19% at age 10–12. Girls learned bowel and bladder control earlier, and dressed themselves earlier. No difference appeared in feeding self. There were slight but consistent tendencies for boys to stutter more and for girls to suck thumbs more. There was no difference in the restriction of play area for the sexes. Girls tended to have a favorite playmate more than boys after age 4.

Whiteman, P., and K. P. Kosier. Development of children's moralistic judgments: age, sex, I.Q., and certain personal-experiential variables. *Child Develpm.*, 1964, *35*, 843–50.
Measures: Pairs of stories very similar to Piaget's stories were used to elicit moral judgments. S was asked to tell whether a child who broke 15 cups accidentally was better or worse than a child who broke one cup on purpose. Two other similar stories were used. Choice of the child with good intentions was considered a more mature response than choice of the child who did less damage. Teachers were asked to rate S's on Griffiths' questionnaire of problems revolving around the dimensions of aggression, nonconformity, and withdrawal. Subjects: 173 children, 7–12 years, of lower-middle socioeconomic level. Results: No significant sex differences, although girls gave a slightly higher percentage of mature responses.

Whiting, J., and Beatrice Whiting. Personal communication on a current research project, 1962.
Measures: Field observations of children in other cultures. Subjects: Children of various ages in 6 cultures—in particular, children 3–6 years old. Results: No significant differences in average factor score on succorance-sociability. Boys were significantly higher on factor loadings on physical aggression in all cultures. Girls were significantly ahead in affection factor loadings. Girls were significantly higher on responsibility. In 5 out of 6 cultures girls were higher than boys on succorance-sociability. In the Mexican culture, this was reversed and significant. In the other cultures the differences on succorance-sociability were not all significant.

Winkel, G. H., and I. G. Sarason. Subject, experimenter and situational variables in research on anxiety. *J. abnorm. soc. Psychol.*, 1964, *68*, 601–8.
Measures: High- and low-anxiety subjects were chosen on the basis of the Sarason Test Anxiety Scale. Subjects performed a serial-learning task, under neutral, achieve-

ment-oriented, or reassurance instructions. Half of the S's were run by high-anxious experimenters, half by low-anxious E's. Subjects: 144 college undergraduates served as S's, equally divided by sex. The E's were 24 male undergraduates. Results: Females performed better than males, but only when they were run by low-anxious E's.

Winker, J. B. Age trends and sex differences in the wishes, identifications, activities, and fears of children. *Child Develpm.*, 1949, *20*, 191–200.
   Measures: Questionnaires asking about wishes, identifications, figures, activities, fears. Subjects: 12 children aged 7 and 8, 12 children 11 and 12 years, and 12 children aged 15 and 16. The fathers of these children were dead. Results: Girls identified more with people they knew, boys with societal roles. Girls were more concerned with social relationships.

Wisenthal, M. Sex differences in attitudes and attainment in junior schools. *Brit. J. educ. Psychol.*, 1965, *35*, 79–85.
   Measures: I.Q. tests and achievement tests in school subjects. Teachers were asked to estimate what percentage of their boy and girl pupils exhibited various traits indicating a negative attitude toward school. Subjects: 1,164 boys and 1,085 girls, aged 7–11, in British girls', boys', and mixed schools. 44 teachers completed the questionnaire on attitudes. Results: Girls had higher I.Q.'s in this sample, although the I.Q. test used had been constructed to eliminate sex differences. Girls also had higher achievement records. Teachers rated girls as more favorable to school than boys.

Witkin, H. A. Sex differences in perception. *Trans. N.Y. Acad. Sci.*, 1949, *12*, 22–26.
   Measures: (1) Embedded figure test. (2) Rod and frame test (in a darkened room a rod within a frame was projected on the wall, and the S was required to adjust the rod to vertical as the frame was tilted). (3) A task requiring the adjustment of a tilting chair to upright when the room tilts. (4) A test of ability to stand straight without swaying in a dark room with a luminous cube swaying back and forth. (5) A test of ability to balance on a platform with the luminous cube moving as the only visual field. (6) A test of ability to locate the direction from which a story comes as the sound is moved from where E is reading to the other side of S's head   here visual and auditory cues were confounded. Subjects: A sample of adult men and women. Results: Women did less well on all tests. They relied on visual rather than gravity or auditory cues more than men, they could not balance as well with confusing visual field (although they improved with practice), and they did less well on embedded figures.

Witkin, H. A. Individual differences in ease of perception of embedded figures. *J. Pers.*, 1950, *19*, 1–15.
   Measures: Gottschaldt Figures, requiring the subject to find a simple design embedded in a more complex design. Subjects: 51 men and 51 women college students. Results: Women were significantly poorer at the task. They took more time than men in finding the figure and were more likely to be unable to find it within the five-minute time limit. Women were slightly more variable from trial to trial.

Witkin, H. A., R. B. Dyk, H. F. Faterson, D. R. Goodenough, and S. A. Karp. *Psychological differentiation.* New York: Wiley and Sons, 1962.
   Measures: Tests of field dependence (including the embedded figure test). Results: Citing a number of studies and unpublished theses, the authors concluded that there are consistent though small differences in mode of field approach between the sexes. Women are more field dependent. The differences are small compared with variations within sex, however. The findings have been generalized to children as young as 8 and to populations in Europe and in Hong Kong.

Witryol, S. L., and W. A. Kaess. Sex differences in social memory tasks. *J. abnorm. soc. Psychol.*, 1957, *54*, 343–46.

Measures: Three social memory tasks. Two of these required S to remember names of people in photographs. The 3d required memory of the name of people interviewed for a short time. Subjects: 103 male and 69 female college students. Results: Women were significantly superior in all three tasks. Age and I.Q. were not significant factors.

Witryol, S. L., D. J. Tyrrell, and Lynn M. Lowden. Five-choice discrimination learning by children under simultaneous incentive conditions. *Child Develpm.*, 1964, *35*, 233–43.

Measures: S's were asked to choose among nonsense drawings to obtain a reward. There were 5 drawings to choose from, each associated with a different reward: a penny, a charm, bubble gum, verbal reinforcement from E, or nothing. Choice of the different incentives was observed over a series of trials. Subjects: 20 boys and 20 girls, 10 years old. Results: Boys quickly established a preference for the penny and decreased the frequency of "nothing" choices. The other three rewards remained constant, with verbal somewhat lower than the others. Girls also decreased choice of "nothing," but their penny choices did not increase. Choice of verbal reinforcement increased for girls.

Woody, C. The arithmetical backgrounds of young children. *J. educ. Res.*, 1931, *24*, 188–201.

Measures: An individual test of arithmetical ability. Subjects: Nearly 3,000 children in kindergarten through 2d grade. Results: Boys were superior, but not significantly.

Wortis, Helen, M. Braine, Rhoda Cutler, and A. Freedman. Deviant behavior in 2½-year-old premature children. *Child Develpm.*, 1964, *35*, 871–79.

Measures: A developmental examination; the Cattell Test of Infant Intelligence; a test of gross motor development; a neurologic examination; an interview with the mother to determine a measure of deviant behavior (e.g., sleep disturbance, rocking, bad temper, head bumping or shaking, incomplete bowel control, and eating difficulties); and social variables assessed by reference to mother's social-status rating, mother's education, degree of family disorganization at time of birth, and mother's emotional disturbance. Subjects: lower-class Negro premature infants: 250 children, mean age 30 months. Results: Boys were higher on deviant behavior, even in the group that showed no abnormal neurological findings. The relations between deviant behavior, neurological abnormality, prematurity, poor motor development, and poor mental-test performance tended to be higher for boys than for girls.

Wozencraft, Marian. Sex comparisons of certain abilities. *J. educ. Res.*, 1963, *57*, 21–27.

Measures: The Kuhlman-Anderson Group Intelligence Test and the Cleveland Classification Test were used to divide subjects into high, average, and low I.Q. groups, called probable-learning-rate (PLR) groups in this study. These groups were tested for sex differences in chronological age, mental age, and Stanford Achievement Test subscores (paragraph meaning, word meaning, reading average, arithmetic reasoning, arithmetic computation, and arithmetic average). Subjects: 564 3d-grade and 603 6th-grade students. Results: No significant sex differences in mental age. In 3d grade, girls were significantly younger in the total group and the average PLR group. Boys were younger in the high PLR group. Girls were younger in the average and total groups in 6th grade. At 3d-grade level girls were significantly higher on all SAT subtests in the total and average groups. In the low groups girls were higher on word meaning and reading average. No differences in the high PLR group at 3d-grade level were found. Differences were less in 6th grade. For the total group, the arithmetic-reasoning and arithmetic-average subtests showed no difference, although all other differences favored girls. The average 6th-grade girls were better than boys in arithmetic computation and arithmetic average. No other comparisons were significant in the 6th grade.

Wright, D. S. A comparative study of the adolescent's concepts of his parents and teachers. *Educ. Rev.*, 1962, *14*, 226–32.
Measures: Semantic differential to get measures of perceptions of self, teachers, mother, father, and ideal self. Subjects: 105 adolescents. Results: Boys valued achievement, while girls valued personal relationships in their ideal-self descriptions.

Wrightsman, L. S. The effects of anxiety, achievement motivation, and talk importance upon performance on an intelligence test. *J. educ. Psychol.*, 1962, *53*, 150–56.
Measures: American Council on Education Psychological Examination (ACE); the Cooperative English Tests; Taylor MAS; the Test of Insight (a projective test measuring achievement motivation); and the Adaptability Test (which was given under conditions of the set that the test was very important or not important to the subject). Subjects: 234 college freshmen. Results: No sex differences on any of the measures. Anxiety was significantly negatively related to the Adaptability Test under high-importance set but not for low-importance set. This correlation was greater for women than men, but the sex difference disappeared when ACE was partialed out. No other significant sex differences were found in correlations.

Wyer, R. S., and G. Terrell. Social role and academic achievement. *J. Pers. soc. Psychol.*, 1965, *2*, 117–21.
Measures: Grade-point average and aptitude as measured by the Scholastic Aptitude Test were compared to select over- and under-achievers and high-aptitude, high-performance and low-aptitude, low-achievement subjects. Motivation for social and academic success was measured by use of the Goal Preference Inventory. Certainty of vocational choice and two personality traits: self-sufficiency and self-sentiment formation from the Cattell Sixteen Personality Factor Questionnaire were assessed. Subjects: 225 male and 351 female college students. Results: Social group dependence related negatively to academic performance in men but not in women. Self-sufficiency and self-sentiment formation increased significantly with performance in men but not in women.

Wyer, R. S., D. A. Weatherley, and G. Terrell. Social role, aggression, and academic achievement. *J. Pers. soc. Psychol.*, 1965, *1*, 645–49.
Measures: The Siegel Manifest Hostility Scale, divided into subscales of direct aggressive expression, feelings of aggression, and guilt over aggression, was administered. S's academic achievement was assessed as the discrepancy between his grade-point average and his aptitude on the verbal and mathematics subtests on the Scholastic Aptitude Test. Subjects: 45 male and 48 female college students. Results: Males were higher in direct aggressive expression and lower in guilt over aggression than females. There were no sex differences in feelings of aggression. Males high in expression of aggression and low in guilt over aggression were better achievers than those low in aggression and high in guilt. For women, there was a tendency for high guilt, low aggression to be associated with high academic achievement, but this was not significant.

Wylie, Ruth C. Children's estimates of their schoolwork ability, as a function of sex, race, and socioeconomic level. *J. Pers.* 1963, *31*, 203–24.
Measures: SRA Primary Mental Abilities Test was used as a measure of intelligence. S's were tested in classrooms and asked to name another student in the room who was equal to them in ability to do schoolwork. They were also asked to say whether they

were in the upper or lower half of the class in ability, and whether they had the ability and would like to go to college. Subjects: 823 boys and girls in 7th, 8th, and 9th grades, both Negro and white and from a wide range of socioeconomic groups. Results: White girls made more modest estimates of their ability than did white boys. In the upper classes somewhat more white boys than girls wanted to go to college, while there were no differences in the lower classes.

Yarrow, Marian R., and J. D. Campbell. Person perception in children. *Merrill-Palmer Quart.*, 1963, *9*, 57–72.
Measures: Children's descriptions of cabin mates at camp were obtained. The protocols were divided into units and categorized as the data indicated. Subjects: 267 boys and girls, aged 8–13. The children spent 2 weeks at summer camp and described cabin mates at the beginning and end of camp. Results: Children tended to describe each other in terms of social-interactive dimensions. There was little relation between the dimensions used and the actual characteristics of the child. Girls emphasized nurturance in their descriptions, and boys emphasized conformity-nonconformity.

Yedinack, Jeanette G. A study of the linguistic functioning of children with articulation and reading disabilities. *J. genet. Psychol.*, 1949, *74*, 23–59.
Measures: Teachers named children who had reading or articulation disabilities. These children were tested by either Gray's Standardized Oral Reading Paragraphs Test or by an articulation test. Subjects: 2d-grade children. Results: 75% of the sample of 44 children with articulation problems were boys, 67.5% of the 40 children with reading problems were boys, and 77.8% of the 27 children with both problems were boys. All 3 of these proportions were significant.

Yonge, G. D. Sex differences in cognitive functioning as a result of experimentally induced frustration. *J. exp. Educ.*, 1964, *32*, 275–80.
Measures: S's were given the Amer. Council of Education Figure Analogies and Number Series Completion subtests before and after frustration by administration of unsolvable problems presented as an I.Q. test. Subjects: 36 college subjects: 16 were frustrated and 20 were not. Results: Frustration had little to no effect on men. Women attempted more problems and made more errors after frustration.

Young, F. M. An analysis of certain variables in a developmental study of language. *Genet. psychol. Monogr.*, 1941, *23*, 2–141.
Measures: Verbatim recording of 10-minute intervals in nursery school in 4 settings: outdoor play, indoor play, dinner, and picture time. Subjects: 74 nursery school children, age 30–65 months. There were 2 distinct SES groups, one on relief and one primarily from the upper 3 SES categories. Results: Girls were significantly superior to boys in mean number of words per sentence and total number of words spoken. Rank order of excellence was high SES girls, low SES girls, high SES boys, low SES boys.

Zeligs, Rose. Children's attitudes toward annoyances. *J. genet. Psychol.*, 1962, *101*, 255–66.
Measures: Children listed things that they disliked, hated, or feared, and indicated degree of dislike. Subjects: 145 boys and 140 girls in 6th grade. Results: Girls were more often and more extremely annoyed by things.

Zunich, M. Children's reactions to failure. *J. genet. Psychol.*, 1964, *104*, 19–24.
Measures: S's were observed while they worked on a very difficult puzzle problem. Behavior categories scored consisted of attempt to solve alone, destructive behavior, directing the adult to do something, emotional response, facial expression, motor

manifestation, no attempt to solve problem, rationalizing giving up, seeking attention, seeking contact with adult, seeking help from adult, and seeking information. Subjects: 20 three-year-olds and 20 four-year-olds, half male and half female. Results: Significantly more boys than girls showed destructive, emotional response, facial expression, rationalizing, and seeking-help behaviors than girls. Girls expressed more behaviors such as attempting to solve alone, seeking contact, and seeking information.

Classified Summary of Research in Sex Differences

The following section summarizes the findings on sex differences in selected behavior areas. Mean differences from relevant studies are summarized under each behavior variable. Studies involving only correlations or higher-order interactions are listed at the bottom of each subsection under Related Studies. This classified summary also serves as an index to the Annotated Bibliography; under each behavior variable the reader will find a list of the studies which report differences for that variable. The behavior categories are as follows:

Aggression	323	Cognitive Styles	343
Dependency	326	Curiosity and Creativity	344
Social Reinforcement	328	Need Achievement	344
Conformity and Suggestibility	329	Problem-Solving Behavior	346
Nurturance and Affiliation	330	Moral Development	346
Anxiety	332	Sex-Typing and Identification	347
Cognitive Abilities, Verbal	334	Socialization Practices	349
Cognitive Abilities, Other	338	Methodology	351

Study	Age	Differences	Comments
AGGRESSION			
OBSERVATIONAL STUDIES			
Dawe 1934	nursery school	boys	Boys participated in more quarrels
Green 1933	nursery school	boys	Boys had more quarrels
Sears et al. 1953	nursery school	no diff.	Total aggressive responses—boys slightly higher, but not significantly so

Study	Age	Differences	Comments
Sears et al. 1965	nursery school	boys no diff.	In 7 out of 10 types of aggression Verbal disapproval, tattling, and prosocial aggression
Jersild and Markey 1935	2–5	boys no diff.	More physical quarrels Verbal quarreling
Muste and Sharpe 1947	2–5	no diff.	Boys slightly more physical and girls slightly more verbal aggression
McKee and Leader 1955	3–4	no diff.	Pairs of children playing
Siegel 1956	3–5	boys	Like-sex pairs playing
McCandless et al. 1961	3½–5	boys	Initiated more conflicts and resisted attack more frequently
Siegel et al. 1959	5	boys	In type of interaction, aggression was rank order 3 for boys, and 7 for girls, out of 9 possible categories
Walters et al. 1957	2–5	boys	Aggressive contacts with peers
Whiting and Whiting 1962	3–6	boys	Physical aggression in six cultures

RATING STUDIES

Study	Age	Differences	Comments
Hattwick 1937	2–4½	boys	Negativistic behavior
Beller and Neubauer 1963	2–5	boys	Mothers' reports of hyperaggression and hyperactivities in clinic children
Beller and Turner 1962	preschool	boys	Several subscales of aggression
Sears et al. 1957	5	no diff.	Mothers' reports
Beller 1962	5½–6	boys	General aggression
Digman 1963	6–7	boys	Teachers' ratings—more negativistic, aggressive, noisy
Feshbach 1956	5–8	boys	Teachers' ratings
Toigo et al. 1962	8	boys	Nominated by peers as more aggressive
Tuddenham 1952	8 and 10	boys	Considered more quarrelsome by peers
Sanford et al. 1943	5–14	boys	Teachers attributed aggression more to boys

EXPERIMENTAL STUDIES

Study	Age	Differences	Comments
Bandura et al. 1961	nursery school	boys no diff.	Imitative physical aggression Imitative verbal aggression
Bandura et al. 1963	nursery school	boys	Total aggression and nonimitative aggression
Bandura et al. 1963	nursery school	boys	Imitative and nonimitative aggression
Bandura 1965	nursery school	boys	Aggressive acts
Hartup and Himino 1959	nursery school	boys	More doll-play aggression with isolation as a precondition

Study	Age	Differ-ences	Comments
Hicks 1965	nursery school	boys	Imitative aggression
Moore 1964	4–6	boys	Directed aggression with less displacement after frustration
Jegard and Walters 1960	4–6	boys	Hitting a punch toy after frustration
Buss 1963	college	men	Aggressive to a frustrating "victim"

PROJECTIVE TESTS

Sanford et al. 1943	5–14	boys	TAT aggression
Spache 1951	6–13	boys	Outward aggression toward peers on the Rosenzweig P-F Test
		girls	Outward aggression toward adults on the P-F Test
Sarason et al. 1965	college	men	Formed hostile rather than neutral sentences in sentence completion
Lindzey and Goldberg 1953	college	no diff.	TAT protocols
Kagan and Moss 1962	20–29	men	Recognized more tachistoscopic pictures of aggression

SELF-REPORT

Sears 1961	12	boys	Antisocial aggression
		girls	Prosocial aggression
Gill and Spilka 1962	12–18	boys	Manifest hostility (S's were Mexican-Americans)
Lansky et al. 1961	13–18	boys	Aggression toward father, self-rating on aggression
Rothaus and Worchel 1964	college	men	Hostile to an E before and after hostility arousal
Wyer et al. 1965	college	men	Direct expression of aggression
Bennett and Cohen 1959	15–64	men	Overt aggressiveness
		women	Covert hostility

FANTASY AGGRESSION IN DOLL PLAY

Bach 1945	preschool	boys	Hostile, aggressive acts
Sears 1951	preschool	boys	Direct physical aggression
		no diff.	Verbal and indirect aggression
Sears et al. 1965	nursery school	boys	Antisocial and total thematic aggression
Pintler et al. 1946	3–6	boys	Aggressive themes
Moore and Ucko 1961	4–6	boys	Aggressive responses to home problems
Durrett 1959	4–6	boys	Total and physical aggression
		girls	Verbal aggression

Study	Age	Differences	Comments
Gordon and Smith 1965	nursery school and 6 yrs.	boys	Overall aggression

ANXIETY AND GUILT ABOUT AGGRESSION

Sears 1961	12	girls	Self-report, aggression anxiety
Buss and Brock 1963	college	women	Guilty about having been aggressive to a "victim"
Rothaus and Worchel 1964	college	women	TAT aggression anxiety
Wyer et al. 1965	college	women	Guilt over aggression

RELATED STUDIES

Bach 1946
Becker et al. 1962
Cosentino and Heilbrun 1964
Eron 1963
Eron et al. 1963
Hall 1964
Heilbrun 1964
Lefkowitz 1962
Levin and Sears 1956
Maccoby and Wilson 1957
Richardson et al. 1964

DEPENDENCY

OBSERVATIONAL STUDIES

Levy and Tulchin 1925	6–53 mos.	boys	Cling to mother during infant intelligence tests
Heathers 1955	nursery school	no diff.	10 measures of dependence-independence on teachers
Marshall and McCandless 1957	nursery school	no diff.	Observation of dependency bids to teachers
McCandless et al. 1961	nursery school	girls	Girls higher on emotional dependence only
Sears et al. 1953	nursery school	no diff.	
Sears et al. 1965	nursery school	boys	Negative attention seeking, but no other measures
Hartup and Keller 1960	nursery school	no diff.	Active dependency bids and passive moves to be near adults
Zunich 1964	3–4	boys girls	Ask for help on problem solving Seek contact while problem-solving
Stith and Connor 1962	preschool and 5 yrs.	no diff.	7 categories of dependent behavior

Study	Age	Differences	Comments
Whiting and Whiting 1962	3–6	girls	Succorance-sociability higher in 5 of 6 cultures
Siegel et al. 1959	5	girls	Succorance was higher in rank order of frequency
Shirley and Poyntz 1941	2–8	boys	More upset when separated from mother
Kohlberg and Zigler 1966	3–8	no diff.	Verbal dependency responses in a design-making situation

RATING STUDIES

Study	Age	Differences	Comments
Goodenough 1929	1½–2	boys	Negativism and shyness at older ages
Beller and Turner 1962	nursery school	girls	Seeking physical contact and nearness
Beller and Neubauer 1963	nursery school	girls	Overdependence as a psychiatric symptom at a clinic
Tyler et al. 1962	nursery school	no diff.	Ratings of independence needs from interviews
Hattwick 1937	nursery school	boys girls	Ask unnecessary help Stay near the teacher
Sears et al. 1953	nursery school	girls	Dependent on teacher
Crandall and Rabson 1960	3–5	no diff.	Help and approval seeking from adults and peers
Sears et al. 1957	5	no diff.	Mothers' reports of dependency on her
Crandall and Rabson 1960	6–8	girls	Help and approval seeking from adults and peers
Lynn and Sawrey 1959	8–9½	girls	Father-absent girls more dependent on mother in mothers' reports
Sanford et al. 1943	5–14	girls	N. succorance considered feminine by teachers

SELF-REPORT AND PROJECTIVE MEASURES

Study	Age	Differences	Comments
McGuire 1961	12–14	girls	Lower on independence-dominance
Lansky et al. 1961	13–18	girls	Lower on n. independence-autonomy (p = .10)
Kagan and Moss 1962	adult	women	Recognized tachistoscopic presentation of dependency scenes sooner
Brim et al. 1962	adult	women	Less self-sufficient
Spangler and Thomas 1962	adult	women	N. succorance

RELATED STUDIES

Beller 1957
Kagan and Freeman 1963
Ruebush and Waite 1961
Weatherley 1964

Study	Age	Differ- ences	Comments

SOCIAL REINFORCEMENT

SUSCEPTIBILITY TO MALE MODELS

Study	Age	Differ- ences	Comments
Gewirtz et al. 1958	3–6	girls	After deprivation with a strange E
Hill and Stevenson 1964	5–7	boys	Strange E, with or without social depri- vation
Patterson et al. 1964	5–9	girls	Fathers served as E
Hetherington 1965	4–11	girls	Fathers as E
Rowley and Stone 1964	9	no diff.	Strange E
Stevenson and Allen 1964	adult	women	Strange E

SUSCEPTIBILITY TO FEMALE MODELS

Study	Age	Differ- ences	Comments
Stevenson et al. 1963	3–5	girls	Strange E or mother
Gewirtz et al. 1958	3–6	boys	After deprivation, strange E
Gewirtz and Baer 1958	6–7	no diff.	Strange E
Stevenson 1961	6–8	boys	Strange E
Hetherington 1965	4–11	girls	Mothers as E
Patterson et al. 1964	5–9	boys	Mothers as E
Ruebush and Stevenson 1964	7	boys	Mothers or strange E in a marble-drop- ping game
Ruebush and Stevenson 1964	7	girls	Mothers or strange E in an embedded figures game
Rowley and Stone 1964	9	no diff.	Strange E
Meyer et al. 1964	9, 11	no diff.	Strange E
Rosenthal et al. 1964	adult	women	Strange E; males were influenced in the opposite direction
Stevenson and Allen 1964	adult	men	Strange E

EFFECTIVENESS OF MALE VS. FEMALE REINFORCERS
FOR BOTH SEXES

Study	Age	Differ- ences	Comments
Stevenson et al. 1963	adult E's	women	Strange E or mothers with children 3–5
Rosenblith 1959	adult E's	men	Strange E with 5-year-olds
Stevenson 1961	adult E's	women	Strange E, children 3–5
Stevenson 1961	adult E's	no diff.	Strange E, children 9–11
Hetherington 1965	parents	no diff.	Children 4–11
Patterson et al. 1964	parents	no diff.	Children 5–9
Rowley and Stone 1964	adult E's	no diff.	Strange E with 9-year-olds
Cieutat 1964	adult E's	men	Strange E with adults, study I

Study	Age	Differ- ences	Comments
Cieutat 1964	adult E's	women	Strange E with adults, study II
Sarason and Harmatz 1965	adult	men	Strange E with adults, faster serial learning

CONFORMITY AND SUGGESTIBILITY

EXPERIMENTAL GROUP PRESSURE STUDIES

Study	Age	Differ- ences	Comments
Harper et al. 1965	6–7	no diff.	Adult stooges in small groups
Iscoe et al. 1963	7, 9, 12 and 15	Negro boys, white girls	Small peer group
Allen and Crutchfield 1963	adult	women	Same-sex peer group
Crutchfield 1955	adult	women	Peer groups
Nakamura 1958	adult	women	Small peer groups
Steiner and Rogers 1963	adult	no diff.	Yielding to judgments of respected peers

OTHER EXPERIMENTAL STUDIES

Study	Age	Differ- ences	Comments
Hovland and Janis 1959	6	no diff.	Experimental attempts to change opinions
McConnell 1963	6–13	no diff.	Yielding to an authority's judgment
Stukat 1958	8, 10, 12 and 14	no diff.	Direct suggestion such as body sway tests
Barber and Calverley 1963	6–22	no diff.	Barber Suggestibility Scale
Goldstein 1959	14	no diff.	Attempts to change opinion by propaganda
Hovland and Janis 1959	high school	girls	Persuasion by propaganda
Patel and Gordon 1960	high school	girls	Accepting suggestions for answers on test questions offered by another class
Stukat 1958	adult	women	To social influence such as a co-judge situation
Scheidel 1963	adult	women	Propaganda persuasion

PAPER AND PENCIL TESTS

Study	Age	Differ- ences	Comments
Kates 1951	8	no diff.	Submission to authority
Getzels and Walsh 1958	8–13	girls	Expressed more socially acceptable attitudes
Hurlock 1930	average age 13	no diff.	Otis Group Test of Suggestibility for Children (Negro and white S's)
McGuire 1961	12–14	girls	Acceptance of cultural and school standards

Study	Age	Differ-ences	Comments
Gill and Spilka 1962	12–18	girls	Conforming to rules (Mexican-American S's)
Kelman and Barclay 1963	adult	women	California F scale (Negro S's)

RATINGS AND OBSERVATIONS

Gellert 1961	preschool	girls	More submissive in same-sex dyads
Gellert 1961	preschool	boys	Less resistive to dominance in same-sex dyads
Crandall and Orleans 1958	preschool, 6, 7, and 8	no diff.	Observation of social compliance
Douvan 1957	10–18	girls	Break rules less
Tuma and Livson 1960	high school	no diff.	Acceptance of authority, and ratings by teachers, parents, and peers

NURTURANCE AND AFFILIATION

NURTURANCE

Hartup and Keller 1960	3–4	no diff.	Observation in preschool
Whiting and Whiting 1962	3–6	girls	Observation of succorant behavior in 6 cultures
Stith and Connor 1962	3–6	no diff.	Helpful behavior, time-sampling observation
Sanford et al. 1943	5–14	girls	Teachers' ratings of n. nurturance
Yarrow and Campbell 1963	8–13	girls	Emphasized nurturance in describing peers
Barry et al. 1957	children	girls	Nurturance expected of girls (S's from 100 cultures)
Terman and Miles 1936	adolescent and adult	girls	Interest in maternal care and active sympathy
Lindzey and Goldberg 1953	adult	girls	N. nurturance on TAT
Spangler and Thomas 1962	adult	women	N. nurturance on the EPPS
Beier et al. 1957	adult	women	Rated pictures of young children more positively
Schopler and Bateson 1965	adult	men	Yielded to dependent plea when dependency was slight
Schopler and Bateson 1965	adult	women	Yielded to dependent plea when dependency was high

POPULARITY

McCandless et al. 1961	nursery school	no diff.	Observation of child's popularity with peers

Study	Age	Differences	Comments
Marshall and McCandless 1957	nursery school	girls	Higher ratings on sociometric measure
Moore and Updegraff 1964	3–5	no diff.	Sociometric popularity in preschool
Tuddenham 1952	6, 8, and 10	girls	Sociometric ratings of popularity
NEED FOR AFFILIATION			
Whiting and Whiting 1962	3–6	girls	Observed to display more sociability and affection in 6 cultures
Digman 1963	6–7	boys	Gregarious by teachers' ratings
Tuddenham 1952	6, 8, 10	girls	More friendly by sociometric measures
Sanford et al. 1943	5–14	girls	N. affiliation on TAT
Lansky et al. 1961	13–18	girls	French Test, n. affiliation
Bayton et al. 1965	adult	women	Negro judges considered sociability a feminine trait
Bennett and Cohen 1959	adult	women	More social orientation and positive evaluation of social activities
Borgatta and Stimson 1963	adult	men	More social acknowledgments in same-sex discussion groups
Exline 1962	adult	women	In experimental groups women preferred to send personal rather than task-oriented messages
Exline 1963	adult	women	More visual interaction in a group
Exline et al. 1965	adult	women	Maintained eye contact with an interviewer
Lagrone 1963	adult	women	N. affiliation high in daydreams and fantasies
McClelland 1953	adult	women	N. achievement went up with social motivation
Spangler and Thomas 1962	adult	women	N. affiliation on EPPS
DIFFERENTIATION OF SOCIAL PERCEPTION			
Abel and Sahinkaya 1962	4–5	boys	At age 5 preferred own race to Negro
Gollin 1958	10, 13, 16	girls	More attempts to explain behavior
DeJung and Meyer 1963	10–18	no diff.	Guessing how others evaluated self
Kohn and Fiedler 1961	adult	men	Made more distinctions when rating others
INTEREST IN AND POSITIVE FEELINGS FOR OTHERS			
Goodenough 1957	2–4	girls	Drew more persons and talked more about them
Bach 1945	preschool	girls	Themes of affection in doll play

Study	Age	Differ- ences	Comments
Witryol et al. 1964	10	girls	Preference for social rather than material reinforcement
Richardson et al. 1961	10–11	girls	Ranked social handicaps less favorably
Campbell 1939	5–17	girls	Earlier development of interest in boys
Carlson 1965	10–12	no diff.	Social rather than personal orientation
Winker 1949	7–16	girls	Interested in interpersonal relations
Smith 1963	12	girls	Positive ratings of others
Meltzer 1943	9–16	girls	Pleasant and accepting responses when describing parents
Meyer 1959	10–17	girls	After 7th grade, perceived boys as able to satisfy play-mirth needs
Johnson 1932	11–16	girls	Reading interests included social topics
Adams 1964	10–19	girls	Concerned with interpersonal problems
Carlson 1965	16–18	girls	Social rather than personal orientation
Vinacke and Gullickson 1964	7–8, 14–16, adult	girls	Arranged coalitions for mutual satisfaction rather than competition
Wright 1962	adolescent	girls	Valued personal relations in describing ideal self
Douvan 1957	adolescent	girls	Concerned with looks and personality rather than internal controls
Terman and Miles 1936	adolescent and adult	women	Women stress personal adornment and interpersonal interests
McDonald and Gynther 1965	17–18	women	Rated selves as higher on a love dimension (Negro and white S's)
Jourard and Richman 1963	adult	women	Disclosed more personal information to others and knew more about them
Kohn and Fiedler 1961	adult	women	Evaluated others favorably
Steiner and Rogers 1963	adult	women	Less likely to reject a peer whose opinion conflicted with theirs
Witryol and Kaess 1957	adult	women	Remembered names and faces of persons in a memory task

RELATED STUDIES
Douvan 1960
Hammer 1964
Hill 1963
Reese 1962
Tyler et al. 1962
Webb 1963
Wyer and Terrell 1965

ANXIETY

PAPER AND PENCIL TESTS

Rosenblum and Callahan 1958	children	girls no diff.	CMAS (S's mentally retarded) CAP (projective test)

Study	Age	Differ- ences	Comments
Sarason et al. 1960	6–12	girls	General and Test Anxiety Scales for Children
Rie 1963	6–12	no diff.	CMAS
Penney 1965	9–11	girls	CMAS
Castaneda and McCandless 1956	9–11	girls	TMAS
Palermo 1959	9–11	girls	CMAS (S's white and Negro)
Keller and Rowley 1962	9–11	no diff.	CMAS
Knights 1963	10	girls	TASC
Loughlin et al. 1965	9–13	girls	CMAS, TMAS, and GASC
Malpass et al. 1960	11	no diff.	CMAS
L'Abate 1960	9–13	no diff.	CMAS
Phillips 1962	12	girls	Castaneda-McCandless Anxiety Test
Carrier et al. 1962	11–14	no diff.	Girls somewhat higher
Keller and Rowley 1962	12–14	girls	CMAS
Feldhusen and Denny 1965	12–14	girls	CMAS
McGuire 1961	12–14	no diff.	GASC
Goldstein 1959	14	girls	Sentence completion
Goda and Griffith 1962	13–21		CMAS
Bendig 1954	adult	no diff.	TMAS
Sinick 1956	adult	women	Test Anxiety Questionnaire and TMAS
Goodstein and Goldberger 1955	adult	women	TMAS (S's psychiatric patients)
Lazowick 1955	adult	no diff.	TMAS
Taylor 1953	adult	no diff.	TMAS
Bendig 1960	adult	no diff.	Cattell's IPAT Anxiety Scale
Brim et al. 1962	adult	women	TMAS
Wrightsman 1962	adult	no diff.	TMAS

OTHER MEASURES

Baruch and Wilcox 1944	1–5	girls	More reactive to parental tensions
Siegel 1956	3–5	boys	Observation of guilt and anxiety in play after aggression arousal
Weinstein and Geisel 1960	9–15	boys	React with maladjustment to home stress
Sontag 1947	12	girls	Physiological measures of reaction to stress
Berry and Martin 1957	adult	women	GSR reactivity in conditioning to shock

Study	Age	Differences	Comments
Moffitt and Stagner 1956	adult	women	React with more need for closure after stress

RELATED STUDIES

Cosentino and Heilbrun 1964
Crandall 1965
Davidson and Sarason 1961
Fischer 1962
Gray 1957
Harmatz 1962
Iscoe and Carden 1961
Phillips et al. 1960
Reese 1961
Ruebush and Stevenson 1964
Ruebush and Waite 1961
Russell and Sarason 1965
Sarason 1963
Walter et al. 1964
Weatherley 1964
Webb 1963

COGNITIVE ABILITIES—VERBAL

AGE OF FIRST SPEECH

Study	Age	Differences	Comments
Gesell et al. 1940	preschool	girls	18 months for girls
Terman 1925	grade school	girls	Parents were more likely to remember gifted girls as early talkers

ARTICULATION

Study	Age	Differences	Comments
Irwin and Chen 1946	1–30 mos.	girls	After the first year NS*
McCarthy 1930	18–54 mos.	girls	Fewer incomprehensible utterances
Beller and Neubauer 1963	2–5	girls	Boys show more speech disturbances in a clinical population than girls
Wellman et al. 1931	2–6	girls	On consonants only
Templin 1957	3–6	no diff.	Individual tests
Yedinack 1949	7	girls	Fewer articulation problems
Templin 1957	7–8	girls	NS
Davis 1937	5½, 6½, 9½	girls	Spontaneous remarks

* NS = not significant. The policy in these summaries has been to report nonsignificant differences as no differences (frequently with a comment to point out the direction of differences). But because of the large number of studies that show slight but consistent differences in favor of girls in language development at the preschool level, these differences have been indicated with a note to mark those that are nonsignificant.

Study	Age	Differ-ences	Comments
VERBOSITY AND VERBAL FLUENCY			
Jersild and Ritzman 1938	18–71 mos.	girls	NS
Young 1941	30–65 mos.	girls	In nursery school play
Paivio 1963	9–10	boys	Talked longer when telling stories
Labrant 1933	9–17	girls	Girls write longer essays
Gallagher and Aschner 1963	12–14	boys	More fluent in verbal behavior in class
Havighurst and Breese 1947	13	girls	PMA word fluency
Hobson 1947	13, 14	girls	PMA, word fluency
Trumbull 1953	15–17	no diff.	PMA, word fluency
Herzberg and Lepkin 1954	16–18	girls	PMA, word fluency
Lindzey and Goldberg 1953	college	girls	Verbal responsiveness on the TAT
Carment et al. 1964	college	men	Spoke more in 2-person debate
LENGTH OF STATEMENT			
McCarthy 1930	18–54 mos.	girls	Girls were ahead in 6 out of 7 age groups
Smith 1936	18–66 mos.	girls	Girls were ahead at each age level except age 5, but significantly so only at age 2
Jersild and Ritzman 1938	18–71 mos.	girls	Nursery school conversation
Day 1932	2–5	girls	The difference was greatest at 5 years
Young 1941	30–65 mos.	girls	Nursery school conversation
Anastasi and D'Angelo 1952	4½ and 5½	girls boys	Whites Negroes
Davis 1937	5½, 6½, and 9½	girls	In play with an adult
Goda and Griffith 1962	13–21	no diff.	Girls slightly superior (S's mentally retarded)
VOCABULARY			
McCarthy 1930	18–54 mos.	girls	Spontaneous utterances
Jersild and Ritzman 1938	18–71 mos.	girls	NS
Templin 1957	3–6	no diff.	Individual tests
Templin 1957	7–8	boys	NS
Davis 1937	5½, 6½, 9½	girls	In play with an adult
Clark 1959	8	boys	CTMM, verbal concepts
Dunsdon and Fraser-Roberts 1957	5–15	boys	British sample

Study	Age	Differences	Comments
McNemar 1942	7–15	no diff.	Stanford-Binet
Clark 1959	8, 10, 13	no diff.	California Achievement Test
Stroud and Lindquist 1942	8–14	girls	Iowa Achievement Tests
Miele 1958	8–15	boys	WISC vocabulary
Clark 1959	10 and 13	no diff.	CTMM, verbal concepts
McGuire 1961	12–14	no diff. girls	CAT Vocabulary completion
Havighurst and Breese 1947	13	no diff.	PMA verbal
Hobson 1947	13 and 14	no diff.	PMA verbal (boys slightly ahead)
Trumbull 1953	16 and 18	no diff.	PMA verbal
Trumbull 1953	high school	no diff.	PMA verbal
Herzberg and Lepkin 1954	17		PMA verbal
Miele 1958	adult	women	WAIS vocal
Wechsler 1958	adult	women	WAIS vocal

GRAMMAR

Study	Age	Differences	Comments
Smith 1935	2	girls	Fewer grammatical errors
McCarthy 1930	18–54 mos.	girls	Use of simple and complex sentences
Smith 1935	1½, 2½–5½	no diff.	Spontaneous conversation
Menyuk 1963	preschool and 6 yrs.	no diff.	Syntactic complexity
Davis 1937	5½, 6½, 9½	girls	Grammatical correctness
Clark 1959	8, 10	girls	CAT, mechanics
Haggard 1957	8–12	girls	Excel in language arts
Heilman 1933	10	girls	NS language usage
Norman et al. 1962	11	girls	CAT, mechanics (gifted S's)
Stroud and Lindquist 1942	8–14	girls	Iowa Achievement Test, language
McGuire 1961	12–14	girls	Mechanics
Clark 1959	13	no diff.	CAT, mechanics
Wesman 1949	15	girls	Sentences, DAT
Book and Meadows 1928	9–23	girls	Pressey Test

SPELLING

Study	Age	Differences	Comments
Haggard 1957	8–12	girls	School achievement
Heilman 1933	10	girls	Stanford Achievement Test

Study	Age	Differ-ences	Comments
Clark 1959	8, 10, 13	girls	CAT
Norman et al. 1962	11	girls	CAT (gifted children)
McGuire 1961	12–14	girls	CAT
Wesman 1949	15	girls	DAT

REASONING

Lee 1965	3–6	girls	Learning concepts
McNemar 1942	4–17	boys	Stanford-Binet, picture absurdities, and water-jar problems
Klausmeier and Wiersma 1964	10–11	boys	Analogies
Klausmeier and Wiersma 1965	12	boys	Analogies
Bennett et al. 1959	adolescent	no diff.	DAT, verbal reasoning
Raaheim 1963	15–16, adult	women	Problem solving

READING

McNeil 1964	kinder-garten	boys	Programmed instruction
McNeil 1964	first grade	girls	Regular 1st-grade reading
Balow 1963	6	girls	Reading readiness and reading achievement
Crandall et al. 1962	6–8	no diff.	CAT reading
Yedinack 1949	7	girls	Fewer reading problems
Wozencraft 1963	8	girls	SAT
Hughes 1953	8–9	girls	Reading tests
Monmouthshire Ed. Committee	7–8, 10–11	girls	Fewer reading problems
Anderson et al. 1957	grade school	girls	Learn to read sooner
Haggard 1957	8–12	boys	School achievement
Stroud and Lindquist 1942	8–13	girls	Iowa Achievement Tests
Clark 1959	8, 10, 13	no diff.	CAT
Norman et al. 1962	11	girls	CAT (gifted children)
Wozencraft 1963	11	girls	SAT
Sinks and Powell 1965	9–13	no diff.	Overachievement in reading on California Reading Test
Hughes 1953	10–13	no diff.	Reading tests
McGuire 1961	12–14	no diff.	CAT
Stroud and Lindquist 1942	high school	no diff.	Iowa Achievement Test

Study	Age	Differences	Comments
GENERAL VERBAL SKILLS			
Lezine and Brunet 1950	1 mo. to 4 yrs.	girls	French adaptation of Gesell scales
Peisach 1965	6	no diff.	Deciphering mutilated speech
Clark 1959	8	boys	CTMM language mental age
Peisach 1965	11	girls	Deciphering mutilated speech (lower-class S's)
Peisach 1965	10–13	no diff.	CTMM language mental age
Edmonds 1964	16	no diff.	SCAT verbal ability
Bieri et al. 1958	adult	no diff.	SAT verbal aptitude
Wrightsman 1962	adult	no diff.	Cooperative English Tests
Rosenberg and Sutton-Smith 1964	adult	women	ACE Psychological Exam

COGNITIVE ABILITIES—OTHER

Study	Age	Differences	Comments
COUNTING			
McNemar 1942	2–4	girls	Stanford-Binet
Gesell et al. 1940	2–6	girls	Gesell developmental scales
Buckingham and MacLatchy 1930	6, 6½	girls	Counting and number identification
COMPUTATION			
Koch 1954	5–6	no diff.	PMA number
Woody 1931	5–7	no diff.	Boys slightly ahead
Crandall et al. 1962	6–8	no diff.	CAT
Wozencraft 1963	8	girls	SAT
Schiller 1934	8, 9	no diff.	
Clark 1959	8, 10	no diff.	CAT
Stroud and Lindquist 1942	8, 13	no diff.	CAT
Norman et al. 1962	11	no diff.	CAT (gifted S's)
Wozencraft 1963	11	no diff.	SAT
McGuire 1961	12–14	no diff.	CAT
Havighurst and Breese 1947	13	girls	PMA
Clark 1959	13	girls	CAT
Hobson 1947	13 and 14	no diff.	PMA
Book and Meadows 1928	9–23	boys	Pressey Test
Trumbull 1953	high school	no diff.	PMA
Bennett et al. 1959	high school	no diff.	DAT

Study	Age	Differences	Comments
Herzberg and Lepkin 1954	high school	no diff.	PMA

MATHEMATICAL REASONING

Study	Age	Differences	Comments
Clark 1959	8	boys	CTMM
Wozencraft 1963	8	girls	SAT
Schiller 1934	8, 9	boys	Arithmetical reasoning
Gainer 1962	6–12	no diff.	WISC arithmetic
Heilman 1933	10	boys	Stanford Achievement Test
Miele 1958	5–15	no diff.	WISC arithmetic (in favor of boys 7–15)
Clark 1959	8, 10, 13	no diff.	CAT
Wozencraft 1963	11	no diff.	SAT
Clark 1959	10, 13	no diff.	CTMM
Alexander 1962	12	no diff.	SRA Achievement Series
McGuire 1961	12–14	no diff.	CAT
McNemar 1942	11–18	boys	Stanford-Binet, arithmetical reasoning
Stroud and Lindquist 1942	high school	boys no diff.	Geometry / Algebra (girls slightly ahead)
Fisher et al. 1961	16–64	no diff.	WAIS arithmetic (S's mental retardates)
Bieri et al. 1958	college	men	CAT
Miele 1958	adult	men	WAIS arithmetic
Osborne and Sanders 1954	adult	men	Graduate Record Exam
Norman 1953	adult	men	WAIS arithmetic
Rosenberg and Sutton-Smith 1964	adult	men	ACE Psychological Exam
Wechsler 1958	adult	men	WAIS arithmetic

SPATIAL

Study	Age	Differences	Comments
Gesell et al. 1940	18 mos. to 5 yrs.	no diff.	Kuhlman-Terman Form Recognition Test
Koch 1954	5–6	no diff.	PMA space
Mellone 1944	6–7	boys	Mazes, block counting—space factor for boys but not for girls
Schiller 1934	8–9	boys	Army Beta and Otis batteries
Gainer 1962	6–12	no diff.	WISC block design
Porteus 1918	4–15	boys	Mazes
Havighurst and Janke 1944	10	boys	Minnesota form board
Emmett 1949	10–11	boys	Moray House Test (British sample)
Lord 1941	10–13	boys	Orientation in space
Havighurst and Breese 1947	13	boys	PMA space

Study	Age	Differences	Comments
Hobson 1947	13–14	boys	PMA space
Wesman 1949	15	boys	DAT
Janke and Havighurst 1945	16	no diff.	Minnesota form board
Herzberg and Lepkin 1954	16–18	boys	PMA space
Bennett et al. 1959	high school	boys	DAT
Trumbull 1953	high school and college	boys	PMA space
Fisher et al. 1961	16–64	no diff.	WAIS block design—mental retardate
Norman 1953	adult	no diff.	WAIS block design

ABSTRACT REASONING

Havighurst and Breese 1947	13	girls	PMA
Hobson 1947	13 and 14	girls	PMA
Wesman 1949	15	no diff.	DAT (slightly favored boys)
Kostick 1954	15–17	boys	Deduction in home economics and science
Herzberg and Lepkin 1954	16 and 18	no diff.	PMA
Herzberg and Lepkin 1954	17	girls	PMA
Trumbull 1953	high school	no diff.	PMA
Sweeney 1953	adult	men	Wide variety of reasoning problems

BREAKING SET AND RESTRUCTURING

Cunningham 1965	7–12	boys	Overcoming set, and susceptibility to set (the latter NS)
Luchins and Luchins 1959	grade school	boys	Less susceptible to set
Luchins and Luchins 1959	adult	no diff.	Susceptible to set: males somewhat higher
Sweeney 1953	adult	men	Restructuring in problem solving
Guetzkow 1951	adult	no diff. men	Susceptibility to set Overcoming set
Nakamura 1958	adult	men	Restructuring problems

MEMORY

Bryan 1934	5–6	no diff.	Verbal, numerical, and object memory
Gainer 1962	6–12	no diff.	WISC digit span

Study	Age	Differences	Comments
Havighurst and Breese 1947	13	girls	PMA
Duggan 1950	14–16	girls	Object and word memory
		boys	Number memory
Book and Meadows 1928	9–23	girls	Logical memory
		no diff.	Rote memory
Miele 1958	5–64	no diff.	WISC and WAIS digit span
Sommer 1958	adults	men	Quantitative memory
		no diff.	Nonquantitative memory
Witryol and Kaess 1957	adults	women	Memory for names

PERCEPTUAL SPEED

Study	Age	Differences	Comments
Koch 1954	5–6	no diff.	PMA perceptual speed
Gainer 1962	6–12	girls	WISC coding
Minuchin 1963	9	girls	WISC coding
McGuire 1961	12–14	girls	DAT clerical
Schneidler and Patterson 1942	10–18	girls	Minnesota Vocational Test for Clerical Workers
Wesman 1949	15	girls	DAT clerical
Miele 1958	5–64	girls	WISC digit symbol
Fisher et al. 1961	16–64	no diff.	WAIS digit symbol (mental retardates)
Norman 1953	adult	girls	WAIS digit symbol
Wechsler 1958	adult	women	WAIS digit symbol

MANUAL SKILLS

Study	Age	Differences	Comments
Gesell et al. 1940	18 mos.	girls	Drawing a circle
Lezine and Brunet 1950	1 mo. to 4 yrs.	boys	Handling objects (French sample)
Gesell et al. 1940	2–4	girls	Dressing self
Gesell et al. 1940	3–6	boys	Walking a board
Gesell et al. 1940	3½–5	boys	Throwing
McNemar 1942	2–9	girls	Buttoning and folding
Peterson 1930	12	boys	Minnesota Assembly Test
	college	no diff.	Card sorting and block sorting

MECHANICAL

Study	Age	Differences	Comments
Havighurst and Janke 1944	10	no diff.	Separate tests for boys and girls
McGuire 1961	12–14	boys	DAT mechanical
Wesman 1949	15	boys	DAT

SCIENCE

Study	Age	Differences	Comments
Heilman 1933	10	boys	SAT
McGuire 1961	12–14	no diff.	CAT

Study	Age	Differ-ences	Comments
Stroud and Lindquist 1942	high school	boys	Iowa tests, science and physics
Edgerton and Britt 1947	high school	boys	Science Talent Search
Osborne and Sanders 1954	adult	boys	Graduate Record Exam

TOTAL I.Q.

Bayley 1965	1–15 mos.	no diff.	Bayley Scales of Mental and Motor Development
Bayley 1933	1 mo. to 3 yrs.	no diff.	Bayley Developmental Scales
Anastasi and D'Angelo 1952	4–5	girls	Goodenough Draw-a-Person
Koch 1954	5–6	no diff.	Primary Mental Abilities
McNemar 1942	2–15	no diff.	Stanford-Binet
Kennedy and Lindner 1964	6–12	no diff.	Draw-a-Person (Negro S's)
Terman 1925	grade school	boys	More boys than girls in sample of gifted children
Miele 1958	5–15	no diff.	WISC
Havighurst and Janke 1944	10	no diff.	Stanford-Binet
Hughes 1953	8–13	no diff.	PMA
Norman et al. 1962	12	boys	Significantly more boys with I.Q.'s over 130
Book and Meadows 1928	9–16	girls	Pressey Test
Book and Meadows 1928	16–18	boys	Pressey Test
Herzberg and Lepkin 1954	16–18	no diff.	PMA
Janke and Havighurst 1945	16	no diff.	Stanford-Binet
Miele 1958	adult	no diff.	WAIS
Fitt and Rogers 1950	adult	women	Cattell intelligence test

RELATED STUDIES

Bayley and Schaefer 1964
Bing 1963
Honzik 1963
Poffenberger and Norton 1963

Study	Age	Differ-ences	Comments

COGNITIVE STYLES

FIELD INDEPENDENCE

Study	Age	Differences	Comments
Crudden 1941	5–6	no diff.	Finding embedded figures
Ruebush and Stevenson 1964	7	girls	Finding concrete figures in familiar scenes
Witkin et al. 1962	8 to adult	boys	Embedded Figures Test and Rod and Frame Test
Chateau 1959	10 to adult	boys	An embedded figures test
Andrieux 1955	adolescent	boys	EFT
Bieri et al. 1958	adult	men	EFT
Gardner et al. 1959	adult	men	EFT and Rod and Frame Test
Bennett 1956	adult	men	Rod and Frame Test
Newbigging 1954	adult	men	EFT
Vaught 1965	adult	men	Rod and Frame Test
Bauermeister et al. 1963	adult	men	Rod and Frame Test
Witkin 1949	adult	men	EFT
Witkin 1950	adult	men	EFT

CONSERVATISM IN JUDGMENT AND RISK TAKING

Study	Age	Differences	Comments
Kass 1964	preschool, grade school	girls	More conservative in risk taking in a game
Wallach and Caron 1959	11	girls	Narrower categories in two judgment tasks
Crandall 1965	adult	women	Pettigrew's Category Width Test: narrower categories
Pettigrew 1958	adult	women	Category Width Test: narrower categories
Wallach and Kogan 1959	adult	women	More conservative in probability choices

CONSERVATISM IN AFFECTIVE JUDGMENTS

Study	Age	Differences	Comments
Zeligs 1962	11	boys	Life problems arouse less extreme annoyance
Anderson 1962	15–18	no diff.	Rokeach's Dogmatism Scale
Crandall 1965	adult	men	Less extreme values given in judging pleasantness of words
Hammes 1964	adult	men	Less extreme values given to pleasantness in rating faces
Sherriffs and Jarrett 1953	adult	men	Less extreme values in judging traits
Terman and Miles 1936	adult	men	Less extreme expressions of affect, of likes and dislikes

Study	Age	Differences	Comments

Beller 1962
Corah 1965
Iscoe and Carden 1961
Kagan et al. 1960
Spivack et al. 1964

CURIOSITY AND CREATIVITY

DIVERGENT THINKING

Study	Age	Differences	Comments
Torrance 1962	6–8	boys	Ways to improve toys
Torrance 1963 and 1961	9–11 9–11	boys no diff.	Uses for scientific toy (1959 sample) Uses for scientific toy (1960 sample)
Klausmeier and Wiersma 1964	10–11	girls	5 of 10 divergent tasks
Klausmeier and Wiersma 1965	12	girls	3 of 7 divergent tasks, while boys were better at 1 of 7
Feldhusen and Denny 1965	12–14	no diff.	5 divergent tasks
Trembly 1964	children and adults	women	Ideaphoria

CURIOSITY

Study	Age	Differences	Comments
Walker 1963	nursery school	boys	Rated more active and curious by teachers
Mendel 1965	nursery school	boys	Preferred greater novelty in toy choice
Smock and Holt 1962	6	boys	Preferred the more novel stimulus on 3 of 4 tasks
Penney 1965	9–11	no diff.	Paper-and-pencil curiosity test

NEED ACHIEVEMENT

OBSERVATION AND RATINGS

Study	Age	Differences	Comments
Beller and Turner 1962	preschool	no diff.	Observer ratings, autonomous achievement striving
Crandall and Rabson 1960	3–8	no diff.	Observation of achievement behavior
Barry et al. 1957	children	boys	Boys are pressed to achieve more than girls
Wisenthal 1965	7–11	girls	Favorable attitudes toward school

PROJECTIVE TESTS

Study	Age	Differences	Comments
Crandall et al. 1962	6–8	no diff.	TAT, n. achievement
Lindzey and Goldberg 1953	adult	no diff.	TAT, n. achievement

Study	Age	Differ-ences	Comments
McClelland 1953	adult	women	TAT, n. achievement
		men	Greater n. achievement arousal with intellectual motivation
Wrightsman 1962	adult	no diff.	Test of Insight

SELF-REPORT

Study	Age	Differ-ences	Comments
Kagan 1964	7–8	girls	Both sexes, but especially girls, saw school-related objects as feminine
Stanford et al. 1963	8	no diff.	Achievement anxiety
Crandall et al. 1965	8–18	girls	From 11 on, take responsibility for own achievement
Wylie 1963	12–14	boys	Wanted to go to college
Wright 1962	adolescent	boys	Valued achievement in ideal self-description
Adams and Sarason 1963	17 and adult	no diff.	Need for achievement, self-report
Bennett and Cohen 1959	adult	men	Greater need for attainment

SCHOOL GRADES

Study	Age	Differ-ences	Comments
Norman et al. 1962	11	girls	Tend to overachieve in school
Phillips 1962	12	girls	Better grades
Schmuck and Van Egmond 1965	grade and secondary schools	girls	Better classroom achievers
Coleman 1961	high school	girls	Higher grades
Northby 1958	high school	girls	Higher grades

RELATED STUDIES

Beller 1957
Cole et al. 1962
Crandall et al. 1964
Dember et al. 1962
Kagan and Moss 1962
Katowsky et al. 1964
Long 1964
Phillips et al. 1960
Poffenberger and Norton 1963
Sarason 1963
Shaw and White 1965
Walter et al. 1964
Wyer and Terrill 1965
Wyer et al. 1965

Study	Age	Differ-ences	Comments

PROBLEM-SOLVING BEHAVIOR

TASK PERSISTENCE

Study	Age	Differ-ences	Comments
Zunich 1964	3–4	girls	Attempt to solve puzzle problems alone without asking help
Crandall and Rabson 1960	3–5	no diff.	Prefer puzzle not completed earlier
Crandall and Rabson 1960	6–8	boys	Prefer puzzle not completed earlier
Nakamura and Ellis 1964	5, 8	girls	Teachers' ratings: more persistent. More persistent in extinction trials at age 5
McManis 1965	10–11	boys	Persisted at pursuit-rotor after trials were over
Hartshorne et al. 1929	10–13	girls	Persistence on tasks, particularly during distraction
Carey 1955	adult	men	Attitudes toward problem solving more favorable

PROBLEM SOLVING UNDER STRESS

Study	Age	Differ-ences	Comments
Moriarty 1961	preschool	girls	Initial adaptation to I.Q. testing
		boys	Coping when problems become difficult
Moore and Ucko 1961	4, 6	girls	Constructive solutions to home problems presented in stories
Solkoff et al. 1964	5–9	girls	Increased performance after frustration
French 1961	17	girls	Improved math scores with anxiety
Yonge 1964	adult	women	Attempted more problems after frustration and failure
Yonge 1964	adult	men	Made fewer errors after failure

RELATED STUDIES
Russell and Sarason 1965

MORAL DEVELOPMENT

MATURITY OF MORAL CODE (PIAGET)

Study	Age	Differ-ences	Comments
Boehm and Nass 1960	6–11	no diff.	Response to stories of transgression
Grinder 1964	7, 9, 11	no diff.	Moral realism and immanent justice
Whiteman and Kosier 1964	7–12	no diff.	Response to stories of transgression
Porteus and Johnson 1965	14	girls	Less immanent justice, moral realism, efficacy of severe punishment

RESISTANCE TO CHEATING

Study	Age	Differ-ences	Comments
Sears et al. 1965	nursery school	no diff.	Experimental situation

Study	Age	Differ- ences	Comments
Walters and Demkow 1963	5	girls	Resisted breaking a prohibition longer
Grinder 1964	7, 9, 11	no diff.	Experimental situation
Hartshorne and May 1928	8–17	boys	Experimental situation
Rebelsky et al. 1963	12	girls	Experimental situation

CONFESSION AND UPSET AFTER DEVIATION

Sears et al. 1965	preschool	girls	Upset in a test situation
Luria et al. 1963	11–13	no diff.	Story completion confession (Jewish S's)
Luria et al. 1963	11–13	girls	Story completion confession (Gentile American S's)
Rebelsky et al. 1963	12	girls	Story completion confession
Porteus and Johnson 1965	14	girls	Story completion confession, upset

STRENGTH OF MORAL CODE

Sears et al. 1965	preschool	girls	Mother's report
Sears et al. 1957	5	girls	Mother's report
McDonald 1963	8–15	girls	Consider stealing categorically wrong
Lansky et al. 1961	13–18	boys	Self-report
Douvan 1957	adolescent	girls	Interevaluation of societal rules
Terman and Miles 1936	adolescent and adult	men	Abstract moral code
Bennett and Cohen 1959	15–64	women	Social morality and honesty
Rempel and Signoi 1964	adult	women	Consider conscience a determinant of behavior

RELATED STUDIES

Burton et al. 1961
Douvan 1960
Grinder 1962
Hoffman and Salzstein 1960
Maccoby 1961

SEX-TYPING AND IDENTIFICATION

PREFERENCE FOR SEX-APPROPRIATE ACTIVITIES

Borstelmann 1961	3–5	boys	It Scale for Children
Rabban 1950	3–8	boys	Toy choice and parental role choice
DeLucia 1963	5–9	boys	Toy choice
Hetherington 1965	4–11	boys	It Scale for Children sex-typed at a younger age

Study	Age	Differences	Comments
Brown 1957	5–11	boys	It Scale for Children
Sutton-Smith et al. 1963	8–11	boys	Game choices more predominantly masculine
Maccoby et al. 1958	adult	men	Men watched male movie character more

DRAW-A-PERSON TEST

Study	Age	Differences	Comments
McHugh 1963	6–10	girls	Like-sex figure drawn first at 7 and 10, and larger at all ages
Lynn and Sawrey 1962	7	girls	Draw like-sex parent larger, first, and in more detail
Weider and Noller 1950	8–10	girls	Like-sex figure drawn first and larger
Weider and Noller 1953	8–12	girls	Like-sex figure drawn first and larger

EVALUATION OF MALES AND FEMALES

Study	Age	Differences	Comments
Smith 1939	8–15	boys	Both sexes more favorable to boys
McKee and Sherriffs 1957	adult	men	Both sexes rated men as more worthwhile

GENERAL BEHAVIOR

Study	Age	Differences	Comments
Goodenough 1957	2–4	boys	Parents felt boys reject girls' things earlier
Gesell et al. 1940	2–5	boys	Girls slightly more likely to say they are boys
Tuddenham 1952	6, 8, 10	boys	With age increase, boys rated by peers more as "real boys" and girls less as "little ladies"
Hartley and Hardesty 1964	8–11	boys	Aware of sex roles of both sexes rather than just their own
Trumbull 1953	adolescent	boys	MMPI M-F test: girls more masculine than boys feminine

CHOICE OF LIKE-SEX DOLL IN DOLL PLAY

Study	Age	Differences	Comments
Emmerich 1959	3–5	boys	Imitation of male parent doll in doll play
Lynn and Sawrey 1962	7	girls	Chose like-sex parent doll in doll play

PERCEIVED SIMILARITY TO PARENTS

Study	Age	Differences	Comments
Carlson 1963	11	girls	More similar to both parents
Jourard 1957	adult	no diff.	Assumed similarity and closeness to either parent
Gray and Klaus 1956	adult	women	More like mother than men like father

Study	Age	Differ-ences	Comments

RELATED STUDIES

Brim 1958
Brodbeck 1954
Gray 1957
Gray 1959
Hartup and Moore 1963
Heilbrun 1965
Heilbrun 1964
Kagan and Freeman 1963
Koch 1956
Kohlberg and Zigler 1966
Lambert 1960
Lefkowitz 1962
Levin and Sears 1956
Lynn and Sawrey 1959
Mussen and Rutherford 1963
Webb 1963

SOCIALIZATION PRACTICES

DIFFERENTIAL TREATMENT OF THE SEXES BY FATHER

1. Punishment and Control

Study	Age	Differ-ences	Comments
Rothbart and Maccoby 1967	nursery school	boys	Less permissive than mothers of dependency and aggression
Kagan and Lemkin 1960	3–6	girls	Child's perception, punitiveness
Digman 1963	6–7	girls	Teachers' ratings, dominating and overprotective
Emmerich 1962	6–10	boys	Parents' report, power
Tasch 1952	infancy to 17 yrs.	boys	Parents' report, use of corporal punishment
Grinder and Spector 1965	14, 15, 17	boys	Child's report, controller of resources
Bronfenbrenner 1960	15	boys	Child's report, pressure and discipline

2. Nurturance and Affection

Study	Age	Differ-ences	Comments
Kagan and Lemkin 1960	3–6	girls	Child's perception, affection
Digman 1963	6–7	boys	Less rejecting, teachers' ratings
Kohn and Carroll 1960	grade school	boys	Parents' report, supportive of child
Devereux et al. 1963	11	boys	More attention, child's perception
Droppleman and Schaefer 1963	12	girls	Child's report, affection and praise
Bronfenbrenner 1960	15	girls	Child's report, affection and praise

3. Achievement Expectations

Study	Age	Differ-ences	Comments
Aberle and Naegele 1952	children	boys	Expected to go to college and have careers

Study	Age	Differ-ences	Comments
Barry et al. 1957	children	boys	Boys should be self-reliant and achieve (S's from 110 cultures)
Poffenberger and Norton 1963	college	no diff.	Expectations of algebra grades, child's per cent in 1955
Poffenberger and Norton 1963	college	boys	Higher expectation of algebra grades, 1960 report

DIFFERENTIAL TREATMENT OF THE SEXES BY MOTHER

1. Punishment and Restrictiveness

White House Conf. 1936	children	boys	Parents' report, restrictiveness
Gordon and Smith 1965	preschool, 6–7	no diff.	Permissiveness for aggression, strictness, or use of physical punishment
Sears et al. 1957	5	girls	Restricted in expression of aggression
Digman 1963	6–7	girls	Dominating and overprotective, teachers' ratings
Emmerich 1962	6–10	girls	Parents' report, power
Grinder and Spector 1965	14, 15, 17	girls	Controller of resources, child's report
Henry 1957	high school	girls	Child's perception, mother is disciplinarian

2. Nurturance and Affection

Digman 1963	6–7	boys	Teachers' ratings, less rejecting
Devereux et al. 1963	11	girls	More attention
Droppleman and Schaefer 1963	12	girls	Child's report, love and nurturance
Bronfenbrenner 1960	15	girls	Child's report, affection and praise

3. Achievement Expectations

Lynn and Sawrey 1962	7	boys	Mothers stress achievement of positive goals (Norwegian sample)
Barry et al. 1957	children	boys	Boys should be self-reliant and achieve (S's from 110 cultures)
Poffenberger and Norton 1963	college	no diff.	Expectations of algebra grades 1955, child's perception
Poffenberger and Norton 1963	college	men	Expectations of algebra grades 1960

CHILD-REARING DIFFERENCES BETWEEN MOTHERS AND FATHERS

1. Punishment and Control

Emmerich 1959	preschool boys	fathers	Child's report, controlling

Study	Age	Differ- ences	Comments
Emmerich 1959	nursery school, grade school girls	no diff.	Child's report, controlling
Simpson 1935	5–9, boys	fathers	Child's report, spanks
Hess and Torney 1962	7–15, boys	fathers	Child's report, father is boss
Hess and Torney 1962	7–15, girls	no diff.	Child's report, who is boss?

2. Nurturance and Affection

Emmerich 1959	preschool boys	mothers	Child's perception, nurturance
Emmerich 1959	preschool girls	no diff.	Child's perception, nurturance
Landreth 1963	preschool	mothers	Child's choice for care and companionship
Simpson 1935	5–9	fathers	Child's perception, plays with child
Emmerich 1962	6–10	mothers	Parent report, nurturance
Droppleman and Schaefer 1963	12	mothers	Child's perception, nurturance and affection
Heilbrun 1964	adult	mothers	Nurturant

3. Achievement Expectations

Brim et al. 1963	9–11	fathers	Concerned with children's work habits

RELATED STUDIES

Baruch and Wilcox 1944
Bing 1963
Cox 1963
Hoffman and Salzstein 1960

Meltzer 1943
Sears et al. 1953
Schaefer and Bayley 1963

METHODOLOGY

The following articles describe measures of masculinity-femininity and validation studies involving the scales:

Barrows and Zuckerman 1960
Brown 1957
Dahlstrom and Welsh 1960
DeLucia 1963
Franck and Rosen 1949
Gough 1952
Jahoda 1956
Johnson 1963
Krippner 1964
Lansky and McKay 1963

McElroy 1954
Oetzel 1961
Rosenberg and Sutton-Smith 1959
Rosenberg and Sutton-Smith 1964
Shepler 1951
Strong 1943
Terman and Miles 1936
Tuddenham 1951
Walker 1964
Wechsler 1958